International Aid and Urban Change

Pablo de Roulet

International Aid and Urban Change

Humanitarian Presence in Bamako, Abidjan, Nairobi and Juba

PETER LANG
Bern · Berlin · Bruxelles · New York · Oxford

Bibliographic Information published by the Deutsche Nationalbibliothek
The Deutsche Nationalbibliothek lists this publication in the Deutsche Nationalbibliografie; detailed bibliographic data is available online at http://dnb.d-nb.de.

Library of Congress Cataloging-in-Publication Data
A CIP catalog record for this book has been applied for at the Library of Congress

Book published with the support
of the Swiss National Science Foundation.
The printed copies have been published with the support of the Fonds Rappard,
Geneva School of Social Science, University of Geneva.

ISBN 978-3-0343-4412-8 (Print)
E-ISBN 978-3-0343-4562-0 (E-PDF)
E-ISBN 978-3-0343-4563-7 (EPUB)
DOI 10.3726/b20053

Peter Lang Group AG
International Academic Publishers

This publication has been peer reviewed.
www.peterlang.com

Acknowledgements

I thank prof. Hy Dao at the University of Geneva, who supervised the PhD thesis that was the basis of this book, for his guidance, advice and support during my research.

I am thankful to prof. Frédéric Giraut for accepting to presiding the Jury of my dissertation. I extend my thanks to the evaluators, prof. Karen Büscher, prof. Armelle Choplin, and Dr Fiifi Edu-Afful, for their interest in my research and their constructive critique and perspective.

I must thank all those who supported my research during fieldwork and writing. This work would not have been possible without the help and inspiration of a multiplicity of people, including aid workers, civil servants, academics, administrators, friends, colleagues and others. They are too numerous to be listed here, but I wish to express my deepest gratitude to Jennifer Barella, Clara Barrelet, Sandrine Billeau Beuze, Claire Camblain, Nicola Cantoreggi, Bernard Debarbieux, Moussa Doumbia, Blaise Dupuis, Nicole Efrancey Dao, Ian Florin, Zoë Goodman, Mary Honderich, Allison Huetz, Estelle Kabran, Clémence Lehec, Pierre-André Leisi, Thierry Maeder, Laurent Matthey, Pauline Plagnat Cantoreggi, Yannick Rousselot, Oumar Samaké, Salimata Samaké, Sandrine Sciarrino, Anne Sgard, Ola Söderström and Mariane Toukam.

Lastly, I wish to thank my family and stepfamily, for their multi-layered assistance. In particular, I have relied so much on the support of my partner Joséphine Chaix, for her sharp comments, her encouragement and help around every possible aspect of this research. Although he did not participate directly to the research presented here, I feel I must mention the influence of our son, Lazaro, whose presence in the last year of writing this dissertation helped me wake up early and brightened this period of my life with day and night entertainment.

Table of Contents

List of Abbreviations

AfDB	African Development Bank
DRC	Danish Refugee Council
ECOWAS	Economic Community of West African States
ICRC	International Committee of the Red Cross
IFRC	International Federation of Red Cross and Red Crescent Societies
MINUSMA	United Nations Multidimensional Integrated Stabilization Mission in Mali
MISMA	Mission internationale de soutien au Mali sous conduite africaine
MORSS	Minimum Operational Residential Security Standards
MOSS	Minimum Operational Security Standards
MSB	Swedish Civil Contingencies Agency
ONUCI	United Nations Operation in Côte d'Ivoire
Oxfam	Oxford Committee for Famine Relief
SCI	Save the Children
SDC	Swiss Agency for Development and Cooperation
UN	United Nations
UNDP	United Nations Development Programme
UNDSS/DSS	United Nations Department of Safety and Security
UNEP	United Nations Environment Programme
UNHCR	United Nations High Commissioner for Refugees
UNMAS	United Nations Mine Action Service
UNMISS	United Nations Mission in South Sudan
WFP	World Food Programme

Chapter 1 Introduction

This work is the result of research started in 2014, on the processes of urban transformations in Bamako Juba, Nairobi and Abidjan in relation to the presence and security policies of UN missions and international aid. The results of this research highlight an uneven process of territoriality where humanitarian organisations operate.

The focus of this work originates in my work as a cartographer for humanitarian demining in Mali during the year 2013. My arrival at the beginning of the year in Mali was part of a larger trend of aid workers landing after the French military intervention that pushed back the jihadist movements that had taken over the north of the country the previous year. I stayed in the city of Bamako most of the year and left in December. From the time I arrived in Bamako to when I left, the atmosphere had changed spectacularly.

In the wake of the French intervention, French flags were hanging everywhere, along with pictures of then-French President François Hollande. Malians enthusiastically asked me if I was French and looked almost sad and disappointed when I answered by the negative. By the time of my departure, a number of demonstrations against the French and the UN presence had taken place, and the word on the street was no longer as positive as before. Many Malians were accusing the French army and the United Nations of supporting Tuareg separatists in the North.

During the course of this year, I lived and worked, as a number of expatriates, in the affluent neighbourhood of Badalabougou, located south of the Niger River. Like many fellow aid workers, I lived in hotels for months, and at other times along with colleagues in a villa. I was struck by the power of the UN and the aid community in general taking over public and private places. Barriers and sandbags were installed in streets. Hotels and bars were crowded with expatriates. This newcomers' power was not always benevolent and sometimes reflected in diverse forms offensive remarks against Malians. During this year, the streets of Bamako changed a lot, with highly visible United Nations-marked white cars now part of the city scene. Roadblocks completed the picture, along with street checkpoints operated by security companies.

These changes in the Malian capital are not an exception, and many African cities witness similar processes. The presence of international aid in different places produces relatively similar marks of presence. The place of security measures and devices appears ubiquitous wherever international aid settles in. This research is in line with an ambition to observe and understand a socio-spatial process much wider than Bamako and the other case studies presented in this document.

1.1 Research Questions

The intriguing process of urban transformation by an outside social body absorbed me enough to start a doctoral research, based on a number of questions and assumptions centred on security policies and practices in relation to the urban environment. The questions that prompted this research focused on three main aspects: the production and dissemination of security discourses, the materiality of the aid presence and the transformative aspects of this materiality. Humanitarian aid, despite being generated by a number of different organisations, responding to different social or political ambitions, and thematic specialities, form a coherent social body able to influence a variety of social environments. The discourse of fear and security needed to implement models of defensive urbanism are organised under global security structures. How are these discourses produced and disseminated throughout the wide and diverse social body of aid workers? How are these discourses translated into the material environment and social practices? What social and spatial transformations occur in the cities with a large presence of humanitarian aid?

1.2 Case Studies

Four case studies illustrate the spatial aspects of security norms of international aid agencies and their influence on the broader urban environment. The four capital cities of Bamako, Abidjan, Nairobi and Juba constitute four distinct paradigms in the intervention of international aid in contexts of diverse levels of political violence. The presence of a UN mission in Bamako and large-scale humanitarian aid is a recent feature in Mali, although development agencies have been implanted there since a long time. In Juba, the capital of the new state of South Sudan, humanitarian presence has already lasted decades as war and famine have repeatedly ravaged the country. Nairobi hosts major UN offices and has long been a hub for international agencies serving as a central node in the provision of aid, both within Kenyan territory, and to several neighbouring countries. Abidjan presents a rare case of the official end of a UN mission, which terminated in 2017.

The four cities studied for this research constitute a multi-sited research rather than a comparatist approach, for theoretical and practical reasons. The theory underlying this multi-sited approach is to understand these cities not as a number of case studies but as fragments of the same space. The different cities where the research was conducted are relatively peripheral to globalisation while at the centre of the humanitarian and peacekeeping world. From a practical point of view, the research in multiple sites in a domain that has frequent access restrictions, allows the collection of enough data to both nuance and generalise the theoretical conclusions of the research.

1.3 Theory

The theoretical approach to the subject is that the territoriality of international aid presence manifests itself in the creation of a landscape of aid in African cities. Academic literature has highlighted the insularity and segregation of aid presence in a number of African (and other Global South) cities, driven by security discourses and risk evaluations. The complex apparatuses maintaining the isles of aid within cities include norms, architecture, finance, and aesthetics, all of which tend to create separate spaces within a city. The space-time contraction of the late capitalist world economy has produced a particular space of aid where international airports create a catastrophe-hopping class of humanitarian workers, moving from one short-term mission to the other. At the scales of the receiving cities, this means a territorialisation process akin to the creation of a landscape of risk.

The research borrows largely from the three disciplines of Urban Studies, Political Geography and the Anthropology of Development. A tradition of Political Geography permits locating aid within broader trends of the globalisation of capitalism in the scalability of its materiality and ideologies, including recent trends in humanitarian policy and practice. The tradition of anthropology of aid has helped discuss the practices of aid as separate objects of studies from the declared policies of humanitarian and development aid. Urban studies as an assemblage of a multidisciplinary research approach has nourished this project in the theoretical framing of humanitarian use of cities as well as an openness to a multiplicity of research methods to describe and analyse complex urban realities.

I have developed and used a variety of techniques and methods for this research. It involved field visits in all the four cities and the collection of diverse forms of documentation, including policy documents, maps, spatial and non-spatial databases. In complement to the collected documentation, I have produced a variety of data in order to understand and describe the interactions between the aid industry and the urban social and material environment in the four African cities, mostly in the form of interviews, photographs, drawings and maps. This combination of quantitative and qualitative methods, of data produced and collected allows a comprehensive picture of the complex and multiscalar phenomenon of the interaction of the aid industry with local urban settings.

The particular focus of this research on cities that are amid violent political processes influenced greatly the limits of the field research and data collection. The sensitivity of the subject, and the sensitivity involved in gathering data from the field required a careful evaluation and selection in data collection. In two different instances, in Juba 2016 and in Abidjan 2017, armed conflict forced me to interrupt or modify the course of my research. These times of crisis during my research resulted in the unexpected and partly uncontrolled collection of empirical materials and helped me develop some theoretical findings of this book. A short section describes this particular epistemology of non-controlled experiment.

1.4 Chapters

The book is divided in five main chapters highlighting the process of territorialisation of international aid in African cities. The first chapter highlights the state of the art, the theoretical framework and the methodology used for the empirical research. The following four chapters *Aid Industry*, *Panorama*, *Layer*, and *Transformations* present the four interconnected elements in the creation of a landscape of aid. The intermediary short chapter *Landscape of War* describes how violent events have shaped the theories used in this research.

The chapter on the *Aid Industry* presents the social field of aid and its spatial habitus. Using statistics from humanitarian employment websites, it presents the main trends and polarities within the aid industry and the socio-spatial division of labour within aid organisations. This approach furnishes description of aid workers as part of a global, albeit North-dominated, middle-class workforce linked to a spatial habitus. This spatial habitus, learnt social norms in relation to the use of space, stems from general middle-class aspirations as well as a security culture assimilated through institutional trainings. Within the context of cities where electricity and water access standards and personal security are often at risk, these imported spatial norms and habitus pave the way for separated modes of dwelling from the poor majority towards enclaves of high consumption.

The chapter on *Panorama* refers to the context of the four case studies of Bamako, Juba Abidjan and Nairobi, following an understanding of the urban environment through the social lens of the aid industry. It presents a broad overview of the political and social histories of the four countries and cities that constitute the case studies.

The *Panorama* chapter introduces a history of the social and built environment of the four cities. It presents the political history of the cities and a series of common socio-spatial features, and notes the short history of all these cities, their relationship to French and English colonialism and the spectacular growth after their independence. However, the lack of comparable data and documentation on these cities – and the complexity of gathering the existing documentation – witnesses the limited resources of the territories studied in this research about themselves, particularly in relation to urban histories. This scarcity also partly explains the limited vision that aid organisation produce when working in African cities, focused on security and strictly functionalist.

The use of the concept of landscape as a theoretical framework for this dissertation stems from personal experience during this research. Apart from the overall structure and chapter development, this reflexion aims to present the influence of witnessing large-scale combats from within the humanitarian system in orienting the general theoretical framework of this research. The short chapter *Landscape of War* combines recollection of events, perceptions, feelings and ideas that explain in large parts the directions and choices taken during fieldwork and writing phases.

The cities considered as a palimpsest and as the site of complex histories present a relatively similar way used by the aid industry to settle in. The *Layer* chapter describes the process of settlement and segregation initiated by the aid industry over the local environment. It considers that explicit and implicit norms either formed or justified by security concerns structures the settlement process of aid workers. Contractual obligations and constant discourse in relation to risks maintain the bodily discipline of aid workers in remaining in enclaves combining offices, hotels and secured houses, while movement is limited and controlled.

The construction of a separate layer of aid workers from the city is a process that includes some sections of the local population as well as non-humanitarian expatriates, in pre-scripted roles where aid agencies and aid workers use segments of the local population as service providers. The array of actors needed to maintain the enclaves of aid within African cities produces a specific socio-spatial layer with loose connections to the local environment. Multiscale processes of settlement imply different levels of directives and actions over the territory from the scale of the country to the city, the neighbourhood, buildings, and ultimately control over bodies. The body of the aid worker is controlled and disciplined, while the body of local employees is often put in a vulnerable situation by the very structure of the aid industry.

The last chapter, *Transformations*, deals with the transformations induced by the presence of international organisations. The impact of the presence of aid workers in the cities is multiple. Their presence influences African cities at different scales and on seemingly distinct issues. Institutional relationships with the local authorities unveil different strategies from the part of local officials, whether elected personnel or technical specialists. While it is important not to depict local actors as passive servants or victims of the international aid, it should be emphasised that the uneven relationship makes the aid industry a powerful player in the territoriality of the city. The private economy is impacted, and the local population unevenly receives the dividends of the presence of aid. Capital, in all its forms (financial, social and cultural) is crucial to understanding the capacity or not of local actors to benefit from new flows of cash in the urban economy.

The aesthetics of international aid constitute a strong and effective sign of the presence of humanitarian organisations. Security devices multiply and become normalised in cities that might not have been used to it and constitute the most important visible transformation. However, other impacts are difficult to measure and quantify in the context of African cities where data on the urban economy is scarce and rarely distributed. Representations of the impact of aid workers must however be discussed in relation to the important combinations of discourses on the positive and negative impacts felt within the local population. It appears that rent hikes often is the one most talked about regarding impact, and clues of the rationalisation for this impact can be found in the strategies of homeowners, as well as in the complaints of a local middle class directly or indirectly put into competition with an international middle class earning ten or fifty times more than them.

This book presents the territorialisation processes of the aid industry. It addresses unsought and unthought-of aspects in the implementation of specific spatial norms centred on the security lens of humanitarian actors. The vehicular influence of social habitus and security discourses produces a new facet to existing cities. Theoretically, it highlights one aspect of modern capitalism – aid structured as an industry – as an urban actor in the cities of the Global South and analyses the mechanisms of enforcement and justification in the creation or reinforcement of enclaved and fragmented urbanism in Africa.

Chapter 2 Theory and Method

This chapter will present the main theoretical and methodological approaches used for this book. Three sections compose this presentation. The first section presents a state of the art of the research on the presence of aid workers and organisations in sites of humanitarian interventions. The second part will present the theoretical framework used to synthesise the results of this research and propose a theory of the territorialisation of aid organisations. Finally, a methodological discussion on the variety of methods and tools introduces the practical collection of empirical data to support the overall thesis.

2.1 State of the Art

This research aims at identifying the role of international aid as an urban player in the cities where it is implanted. It lies at the crossroads between the study of defensive urbanism in the cities of the developing world and the sociology of aid workers. It aims to present a new perspective on the spatial practices of international aid and discuss how the connections between security and international aid shape material and social urban environments.

The existing literature on the question of the presence and spatial influence of international staff highlights a series of key features of the urbanism of aid. It appears at first heavily spatially segregated, where the line of divide is clearly drawn between the international and the local, coupled with a social divide where the international is largely richer than the local. It is characterised by high levels of consumption in water, power, fuel and space.

Existing research has shown the links between changing political goals of international aid and its increased self-isolation from the local environment. Recent studies in the question of space in international aid have highlighted interesting links between construction of knowledge, power and physical terrain. The literature on defensive architecture in both the North and the South echoes aid housing and allows categorising its main features and foreseeing its presumed outcomes. Literature helps identify the role of international aid as an architect and urban planner, situated at the junction of the questions of security, the lifestyles of expatriates and the management of space.

2.1.1 Aid, Security and Space

The links between security and international aid have been (and are currently being) discussed by aid practitioners and academics at two different, but interlinked levels: politics of development as a tool for political stability and the safety of aid workers and operations. Research in political science discuss how the aid sector policies are closely tied to issues of security at various levels. Underdevelopment understood as a threat to national and international stability has been a strong force justifying the funding of developmental programmes from international bodies and cooperation agencies since the end of the Cold War and through the "War on Terror". Numerous scholars specialising in development have discussed the question of the links between security and development at the international policy level, often dubbed the "development-security nexus". Duffield (2007), D. Chandler (2007), Stepputat (2012), and Stern and Öjendal (2010, 2011) present how the major donors in aid and development[1], have increasingly moved their understanding of aid from investment projects to a tool to provide political stability. A politically and economically liberal agenda dominates development discourses to support security as a strategic goal of Western countries.

During the same period, the development and humanitarian sector has seen an increasing focus on the personal security of aid workers. This concern has been triggered and accompanied by an increase in diverse types of attack on aid workers by state and non-state actors in conflict zones (Stoddard, Harmer, and Haver 2006b; Fast 2014). As discussed by Renouf (2011), it resulted concretely in significant investments in security infrastructures and procedures, a process discussed and debated by most of the main institutions involved in aid (Renouf 2011). The question of security in the context of aid operations has produced a large amount of literature within aid and development circles (Stoddard, Harmer, and Haver 2006b; Combaz 2013; Stoddard et al. 2017). This literature is mainly structured as an evaluation of security from an ethical, practical and political standpoint focussed on enhancing the efficiency of aid delivery. Scholars have largely discussed one of its most contentious aspects: how the use of the private security industry by aid agencies is facilitating the entry of these companies into new markets (Spearin 2008, 2007; Patterson 2009).

1 Such as the European Commission Humanitarian Aid Office (ECHO), United States Agency for International Development (USAID) and Department for International Development (DFID) and other national development agencies.

An increase of attacks on aid workers since the end of the Cold War has been widely attributed to the association of the provision of aid and the promotion of a political agenda of security and stability (Olson 2006). This model culminates in the form of the "integrated missions", where the political and humanitarian arms of the United Nations are under the same command (Donini 2007; Duffield 2010b). This relation of causality supports the claim of an increasing violence against humanitarian. However, the perception of an increase in the threats against aid workers is sometimes questioned, as the data supporting the claim is problematic without precise definitions of security incidents (Fast 2007, 2014). A deconstruction of the quantification of the violence against aid workers show that the sense of increasing threat against aid workers might be caused by an increase in the overall number of aid workers, rather than increased vulnerability of humanitarians (Dandoy and Montclos 2013).

The quantification of attacks against aid worker could be a discursive as much as an epistemological tool. Using a Bourdieusian framework, Dandoy identifies the discourse relating to the increased insecurity of aid workers to a "moral panic", a redefinition of subjectivities within a social field (Dandoy 2014). Extending this critique, Beerli locates the use of statistics on violence against aid workers within aid organisations as a tool of power between programmatic and security wings of humanitarian organisations, where programming becomes increasingly controlled by sieges of organisations and its security apparatus (Beerli 2017, 2018).

The presence of international aid has been shown to be far from neutral in its influence over the social and political environments. It translates by the exertion of a degree of power, often akin to sovereignty. As discussed by Edkins, the sovereign power of aid resides, on the one hand, in the power of giving and on its reliance on its own security infrastructure on the other (Edkins 2003). Conflicts of sovereignty arise, at least at the level of legitimacy, where "good governance" discourses justify attempts by international aid agencies to bypass established governments to propose their own social and political agendas (Mosse 2005). When the state is unable or unwilling to protect personnel working for the aid community, aid institutions consider that they have a mandate to define new types of zones, governed by their own laws – rather than those of the host state – and with the protection of their security infrastructure and associated rules. One aspect of this dynamic is an increasing role for the private security sector (Patterson 2009).

Most of the academic discussions about development and humanitarian aid tend to focus on the effect of programmes. A number of academic and practitioner's publications specialises in on area or another, such as the Journal of Development Studies, International Peacekeeping or the Journal of

Humanitarian Affairs, among many others. However, the study of the presence and impact of aid workers and institutions is comparatively scarce. This topic is being researched within a variety of social sciences – political science, sociology, anthropology, among others – to draw a picture of the relations of power between the international and the local often focussed on the negative aspects of humanitarian presence, either as a policy or in practice (Autesserre 2017). A certain number of places come out in the study on the presence and effects of international aid. A number of research hotspots among the cities and countries that witnessed large aid operations, in Africa, the Americas and Asia have been studied by different scholars, such as Haiti, Liberia, DR Congo, Kosovo, Kabul and Juba, either as single case studies or in multi-sited research (Henry and Higate 2013; Jennings 2014). Studies of humanitarian interventions in the North are less frequent, but not absent with the work of Lisa Smirl on New Orleans (Smirl 2015), for instance.

Literature on aid presence often focusses on the insularity of aid workers such as in the concepts of "peaceland" (Autesserre 2014), "aidland" or the "aid archipelago", while other concepts such as the "peacekeeping economy" allows a focus on the unequal and destabilising nature of international presence to the local environment. As noted by Harrison, many of the publications on the "bubble of aid" tends to focus mainly on the world of expatriates, often from researchers straddling between academia and international aid (Fechter and Hindman 2011; Mosse 2011). The limits to a body of "study up" research on aid workers is that researchers mostly conjecture on the consequences of aid presence for the local populations, rather than listening to their voices (Harrison 2013).

Some academics and aid practitioners more focussed on the impacts of the presence of aid rely on the notion of "peacekeeping economy" to describe the relationships induced by the presence of aid agencies. This concept has inspired Jennings (2014, 2015) and Anning and Edu-Afful (Aning and Edu-Afful 2013; Edu-Afful and Aning 2015) to analyse the gendered aspects of the relationships between peacekeepers and the local populations. Studies on the presence of aid agencies are mostly grounded on qualitative research than quantitative, partly because systematic data collection is scarce, with a few exceptions (Carnahan, Durch, and Gilmore 2006).

The diversity of processes of spatial transformations and governance induced by humanitarian aid has been studied under the umbrella concept of "humanitarian urbanism". Coined by Potvin (2013) to describe the multiple, yet related spatial practices of aid organisations under a neoliberal regime, the term has since been used to describe a multiplicity of phenomena. Although originally designed to the examination of humanitarian aid as a modeller of space in relation to beneficiaries, the notion has been expanded to include the combined effects of the presence of aid workers and aid policies.

The notion of humanitarian urbanism addresses a broad front of actions and transformations of space, where the planning of sites of interventions and unintended effects come as occurrences of an urban regime where donors influence social relations, urban forms and the modes of governance (Büscher, Komujuni, and Ashaba 2018). Jansen uses the term to describe the multiple and unexpected spatialities and mobilities of the social life in a Kenyan refugee camp (Jansen 2018), while, Humphrey and Valverde use it to picture diverging narratives of crisis and development in the city of Medellin (Humphrey and Valverde 2017). The fluidity of the concept permits using it regarding voluntary or unintended effects of both policies and practices of aid.

2.1.2 Aid Workers and the Built Environment

Research on the impact of humanitarian presence on the urban environment often relies on successive fieldworks spread on a large period of time to distinguish specific effects. Works on the city of Goma, in the eastern Democratic Republic of Congo (Büscher and Vlassenroot 2010; Vlassenroot and Büscher 2013, 2009; Büscher 2016; Büscher, Komujuni, and Ashaba 2018) highlight long-term processes in urban changes. It identifies directs and indirect effect on the labour market with opportunities for white and blue collars and on investments in real estate designed for internationals, resulting in stronger spatial inequalities. Lastly, the impact of a regime of shared sovereignty results in separate delivery of public services, with two different standards.

The question of space in aid operations is a relatively new subject, where most of the literature dates from the years 2000 and after. However, a widening body of literature influenced by the wider "spatial turn" of the social sciences, such as work by Smirl (2008, 2009), Higate and Henry (2004) and Henry and Higate (2013), has discussed aid and UN missions as spatial actors, where the understanding of space is defined by security evaluations above all else. Higate and Henry (2004) have outlined the importance of the projection of power on spaces of UN interventions and the practice of military mapmaking as a central tool in the construction of knowledge by international peacekeepers. Real-life effect of the humanitarian mapping cities transforms perceptions and uses (Andersson 2016; Lemay-Hébert 2018).

The work of Lisa Smirl, inspired by Henri Lefebvre and his theories of the social production of space (Lefebvre 1974), analyses emblematic places and objects in humanitarian interventions: hotels, compounds and SUVs. She highlights the centrality of an "auxiliary space" in the practice of humanitarian interventions. The important focus on the creation of lived space from within aid agencies offers a precious typology of types of places used by humanitarians (Smirl 2008, 2015). The limit of this approach is a constrained discussion on how this space is lived from outside, as pointed by a reviewer and aid worker (Says 2016).

2.1.3 Procedures, Design and Security

The body of research on the physical presence of aid workers highlights that the common model for both offices and housing relies heavily on design for the safety of staff and institutions. Reminiscent of the gated communities, and the notion of the "defensible space" of architect Oscar Newman (1972, 1973) where design aims to participate in the prevention of crime, the housing of aid workers is centred on security. The control of urban spaces in which aid workers are located involves defining risk and security zones, as well as enforcing security apparatuses surrounding a living or working compound. These measures are enforced by the security officers of various international organisations, and are centred around the Minimum Operational Security Standards (MOSS) and Minimum Operational Residential Security Standards (MORSS) developed by the United Nations (United Nations 2006; Renouf 2011; Duffield 2010b).

Studies of how humanitarian organisations implement their security standards primarily focus on the impacts on the delivery of aid to affected populations (Fast 2014). As noted by Collinson et al. (2013), the contradictory dialectic of current humanitarianism involves intervention in a variety of dangerous sites coupled with a withdrawal of personnel behind security procedures and design. More specifically in relation to the built environment, as Duffield (2010b; 2012a) and Felix Da Costa (2013) show, the MORSS residential security standards plays a structural role in the culture of "aidland". These authors suggest that fortified compounds are representative of diverse shifts in the structure and goals of aid. The living conditions and social practices of expatriates have been documented from different perspectives, by sociologists, anthropologists and political scientists. Academics have tended to focus more on "cosmopolitan" shared culture and networking practices than management of space, where questions of housing and mobility are largely left apart. This body of literature helps, however, to highlight several key characteristics of aid dwellers. They are young, highly mobile due to the prominence of short-term contracts and typically upper-middle-class working in technical and managerial positions (Lewis and Mosse 2006; Mosse 2011).

Examining the security training of aid workers, Duffield (2010b) presents housing security procedures in the wider context of the disciplining of aid workers. Current procedures are shown to encompass many aspects of their daily life, including mobility, behaviour and body hygiene. These comprehensive disciplinary regimes are phrased in a patchwork of documents highlighting the expected normative conduct of employees: contracts, security procedures and additional codes of conduct.[2] An architecture separating aid from the surrounding environment is the material embodiment of a larger disciplinary training. Felix Da Costa (2013), defines the socio-spatial processes by which aid workers are as disconnected from local life as possible as the normalisation of restrictive security procedures. Road should be strictly limited to functional circulation, where walking is advised against or simply forbidden, as is any contact with the local environment, perceived primarily as a potential threat (Collinson et al. 2013). Urban space becomes segregated between those inside and outside the UN/NGO world, while staff increasingly live in archipelagos with their own standards of consumption and living – an elite existence protected by parallel security regimes. The high standards of consumption, in water, power, fossil energy and commodities in these enclaves, present a striking contrast to the local environment (Smirl 2009). Moreover, these living standards are often higher than those expatriates would be able to afford in their own countries (Rajak and Stirrat 2013). Aid workers residences are especially voracious of space, where villas have become a standard housing choice even for young professionals.

The literature on the presence of aid organisations and their effects on the urban environment presents a number of case studies and discussions of space practises and impacts. Written from a perspective on aid policies, rarely dives into "urban geopolitics" (S. Graham 2007), that is the global creation of new urban spaces, where global policies are translated into a socio-spatial urban reality. Cities experiencing the presence of international aid are somehow the opposite of Global Cities in the sense of Sassen, where the increase of multiple connections creates global hubs for flows of capital and information (Sassen 2013). However, located at the political and economic margins of an interconnected postmodernity, the cities where aid operates constitute a series of policy-connected urbanities where the presence of international aid shape city metabolisms. While no encompassing, theory is yet usable to describe the various ways in which spatial norms related to global policies influence a variety of

2 The chapter "Aid Industry" presents a comparative analysis of the codes of conducts of various organisations.

cities in a multiplicity of ways, a large body of literature on security urbanism supports formulating a skeleton of theory to explain this process.

The works of Sassen, and other theorists of critical urban studies in a materialist perspective, such as Harvey (1989, 2005) and Lefebvre (1978), constitute an important body of work in the critique of the mainstream urban theory that presents liberal governance as natural models. As this materialist critique successfully deconstructs the pretention of liberal models to present themselves as natural aspirations, it generally fails in defining the urban outside Northern paradigms. The limitations in using this critical urban theory as reference to study African cities lay in its understanding of Northern cities as paradigm of the urban, as Schindler reflects when arguing for a "Southern paradigm" in urban studies (Schindler 2017). Cities of the South can not be uniquely, even mainly, depicted as dialectic relation between capital and labour, as many large conurbations grow with no direct relation to capital or industrial development.

Discontinuous social and infrastructure metabolisms of Southern cities place them in a category by themselves with their own contradictions, rather than a subgroup identified by dysfunctionalities in relation to Northern paradigms. As Sheppard et al. (2013) argue, a discussion and analysis of Southern cities require a distancing, or "provincializing", both from mainstream liberal and critical models of the urban.

Numerous research about the growing influence of aid and development in city programmes in the Third World has shown that programmes often bypass local preoccupations, by promoting particular types of urban features and policies (Davis 2006; Myers 2011; P. Jenkins 2013). The power of aid as a land consumer and particular urban player in cities of the developing world is much less known. Its capacity to impose specific urban forms onto an environment that far exceeds residential and office boundaries has been left aside from most studies of Global South cities impacted by the presence of international aid.

While there are only a limited number of studies on the specific impacts of aid presence on the urban environment of the cities where aid is present, studies of the implementation of urban models can provide an overview of its probable effects. First the classic studies of "fortress urbanism", City of Quartz (Davis 1991), Fortress America (Blakely and Snyder 1997), and Cities Under Siege (S. Graham 2010) highlight the relationship between social inequalities and the use of militarised management techniques in city governance. On the question of security, Sorkin (2008) shows that the securitisation of space through urban design is doomed to failure on its goal of a complete securing of space, but highly successful in instilling a culture of fear.

As discussed by Coaffee (2016) in its study of the City of London, the US model of security architecture corresponds to a specific construction in time and space, and cannot be simply generalised to other contexts. The implementation of defensive features follow a process that depends greatly on local concerns and takes different sources. While in the case of London, the primary inspiration was the separation walls put in place in the centre of Belfast, the model of security urbanism for international aid takes its sources from different sites of crises. Cities witnessing armed conflicts, such as Kabul, Baghdad and Mogadishu have seen the presence of security and aid building its own know-how before extending its infrastructure more largely. For instance, the International NGO Safety Organisation (INSO) had been working in Afghanistan for years before providing security advice more largely to aid organisations in other countries. Similarly, the United Nations developed their security doctrine relating to housing in the most dangerous countries and cities (Van Brabant 2010a).

Research on the circulation of culture and ideas show that the circulation of Western cultural models consistently experience a process of adaptation in a new environment (Featherstone 1995). The application of a specific security model can be expected to have different local declinations. As shown by Lemanski (2006), gated communities form a mode of segregation, but also imply some sort of spatial integration to the local urban life. The emergence of gated communities do not represent a mere copy of a foreign model, but rather an adaptation, where imported apparatuses of security merge with local social cultural and economic realities.

2.1.4 Urban Form and Segregation

Following the notion that in modernist architecture, the form of buildings is dependent upon their function (Frampton 1985), the form of buildings follows the goals of aid industry of building autonomous spaces within the capital or main cities of countries in crisis. The question of the form and its interpretation is important at two different scales: (1) the urban morphology and (2) the architectural features of individual buildings. Complementary to this interpretation of form, the notion that "form follows fear" as coined by Ellin (1997) is central to understand aid architecture. Driven by the fear of diverse types of attacks or intrusions from the outside, the use of defensive architecture depends on a reading of existing urban morphology while producing new forms, deemed safer.

The question of form in its two scales needs to be assessed from two perspectives: (1) how is the form being read and comprehended by security officers and (2) how it is being transformed by the aid institutions, as a community of practice. At the level of urban morphology, Weizman (2007) and Gillem (2007) have shown that for the Israeli and United States armies, respectively, specific urban morphologies symbolise order and security while others are associated with potential dangers. Spatial irregularities are deemed suspicious and potentially dangerous and the regularity of urban morphology is understood as the safest.

The transformation of the form goes primarily through the dwelling unit, houses and sometimes apartments, where interventions are direct and relatively simple. The larger transformation of the urban fabric is more the result of distinct choices at the level of the housing unit rather than direct intervention. The question of the form of houses implies the question of land use and land consumption and sprawl. The establishment of aid housing implies both a specific reading of the morphology of the local urban fabric and a specific consumption of land. The question of the land use depends greatly on the type of architecture promoted by the security discourses.

The concept of segregation is central to the understanding of the results of the urbanism of the aid industry. Segregation in urbanism means the construction and maintenance of an inside and outside of a territory, where the inside is richer (Gillem 2007). This character is widespread in all models of urbanism centred on security, from the American model (Low 2004) to its multiple adaptations worldwide (Lemanski 2006). Segregation in architecture materialises the separation of social classes and "races" sharing a territory. The segregation of space does not limit itself to living areas but extends to the different spheres of life of a specific elite community, including work and leisure. Segregation in the dynamics of gated communities is not only the separation from the outside, but also signifies a specific order and discipline inside it where those inside adopt rules and personal discipline.

Segregation do not mean a complete separation from the outside, but rather a tight control of its access points. Points of contacts between the segregated social groups are both very controlled and highly unequal. As discussed by Lemanski (2006) and Manzi and Smith-Bowers (2005) there is frequently some type of spatial interaction between contiguous areas of different types, because poor neighbourhoods provide the workforce necessary to make the gated communities work, such as guards or housemaids.

Case studies on the presence of humanitarian organisations and literature on the type of urban models that are being implemented on sites of interventions allows to conjecture how a number of security discourses are being translated into a variety of urban environments and producing new socio-spatial relations. Unlike in the doctrines of military urbanism (S. Graham 2010), existing security documentation does not specifically produce a discourse on the urban phenomenon and crucially does not present aid agencies as an urban actor. While international aid agencies produce new urban relationships, this urban role remains an unthought-of effect rather than a conscious policy.

To understand how security policies can translate into the making of new urban spaces requires the identification of the main institutional and discursive channels in the implementation of a defensive architecture and behaviour. The central vector of the security discourses and practices relating to international aid is the United Nations, which takes a leading role in the implementation of defensive architecture as the main provider of security for aid personnel is structured on the centrality of the United Nations Department of Safety and Security (UNDSS) within the aid community. As the main reference point for a security strategy, UNDSS produces a discourse on housing that makes defensive architectural apparatuses the cornerstone of aid workers' safety. The political context that led to the creation of the MOSS/MORSS rules and their implementation by the UNDSS is heavily influenced by the multiplication of integrated missions (Muggah 2013), where the humanitarian and political arms of the UN are both under the same command. The centrality of UN security standards in the deployment of aid workers reflects its political and operational centrality translated in the largest presence. The residential standards that accompany these wider security regulations appear then as part of a political discourse.

The centrality of the UN in defining security procedure does not mean unanimous agreement by aid organisations. As Renouf (2011) shows, the wider programmatic goals and cultures of organisations play a large role in defining a nuance in methods of protection by aid organisations. Furthermore, within aid organisations, as Beerli shows (Beerli 2018), internal debates shape largely the dialectic between humanitarian access and risk aversion. These organisational debates result is a wide variety of practices. These practices are, however, largely tending towards greater risk aversion by the humanitarian community as a whole, varying mostly in the degree of the consequent securitisation.

Discourses instilling fear are key vectors to the implementation of "defensive architecture" in housing (Davis 1991; Blakely and Snyder 1997; Sorkin 2008). The aid industry's goal is to use defensive architecture to minimise risk for its employees within areas considered poor and insecure. The particular case of the aid industry where many professionals willingly live and work in areas of high risk, or perceived to be high risk, creates a specific discourse regarding security. The "moral panic" (Dandoy 2014) of the humanitarian community can be related to the self-reinforcing fear effect of gated communities (Low 2001).

A construction of otherness within the aid community itself also shapes the security discourses around housing. Understanding of safety and danger diverge depending on the type of aid workers. Factors of gender and nationality greatly influence risk analysis and security procedures, providing higher security measures for women, and lower for local employees. Visibility of security apparatuses is deemed an additional security for expatriate women but is presented as its exact opposite – additional danger – in the case of local male employees as it points to their foreign affiliations (Wille and Fast 2013).

The adoption of a model of defensive architecture by aid workers and agencies reflects a degree of variation depending on organisational culture and individuals. The translation in social practices and material security apparatuses supposes a gradual and contextual acceptation. The use of security standards in architecture encompasses a large array of material apparatuses such as compound walls and concertina barbed wire as well as human surveillance. The aid-security community favours the techniques and technologies of security if they correspond to a recognisable international standard. International organisations prefer hiring transnational security company rather than "casual watchmen" (Vaux et al. 2002). This preference towards standardisation has the direct effect of favouring the penetration of private security companies into the world of humanitarian aid (Spearin 2008).

The professionals in charge of implementing security within a specific compound, or employed to give advice and protection to aid workers, do not come from an architecture or planning background, but from the field of security (Schouten 2011). The experience of security officers in public or private military establishments shapes their understanding of danger and space, which frames the way they act upon it, relying on specific techniques. This body of professionals will tend to comprehend the urban fabric and conceive safety and security from the perspective of military control (Higate and Henry 2004).

2.1.5 Organisational Discipline and Its Spatial Consequences

It is mandatory for aid workers to have their housing, as well as their workplaces, approved by security officers. The enforcement of security for the aid industry is done through techniques that would not be accepted as such in other contexts. For instance, in most of the industrialised world the use of barbed wire is generally limited or hidden; because of the aggressive imagery it is associated with (Razac 2000). In contrast, in the context of international aid, the body of security officers is strong enough to impose the use of this segregating device onto the homes and workplaces of tens of thousands of employees around the world.

Michel Foucault's works on the notions of control and surveillance have deeply influenced human sciences, including geography. Crampton, for example, positions the pertinence of the notions of heterotopia and biopower to human geography (Crampton 2013). However, as Foucault elaborates on disciplinary institutions, his focus is the disciplining of dominated groups. With respect to their social positions, expatriate aid workers can hardly be seen as a dominated group, as their presence reflect executive positions and elite lifestyles and mentality. For this reason, although the works of Foucault perspire all literature related to control and discipline, this research does not mobilise his works and concepts directly. As the notions of control and discipline (Foucault 1975), biopower (Foucault 2004) or Mbembe's necropolitics (Mbembe 2008) would be relevant to much the study of humanitarian policies in Africa, they do not work so well to explain the internal discipline of expatriate professionals. Instead, this dissertation relies more on the Bourdieusian notions of field and habitus (Bourdieu 1980, 1986, 2004) to reflect the adoption of social norms, in relation to security and other straits of life.

As working hypothesis, I will consider that the concrete implementation of a defensive architecture is mediated through a process of dialogue between security professionals and aid workers. The authority of security professionals lies on both contractual documents and a perception of danger from the surrounding environment. On the other end, aid organisations and aid workers have themselves a specific and sometimes divergent culture of security. The extent to which the defensive architectures will be implemented depends on a process of negotiation between the tactical understanding of terrain by security officers and the symbolic value that aid workers and organisations are willing to present to donors, the local population and to themselves.

The process of translation of security measures within the aid community is still short of explaining how sites of intervention are impacted by humanitarian presence. What effects does humanitarian security standards have on the local urban fabric, as well as on social and economic life in the host country? The process of transforming cities is both a cognitive process, in separating permitted and forbidden space, and a material implementation where the diversity of action to secure the space impacts those living inside and outside.

An important step taken by the UNDSS is the definition of safe and non-safe spaces within a city. Similarly to the evaluations made by the US military (Gillem 2007), the security sector of the aid industry will tend to reject "traditional" local layout in favour of an "international" style of villas and apartments inspired by a Western model of housing. This type of land use results in a much higher space consumption than most of the local urban fabric.

The retreat of aid agencies' buildings and personnel behind security walls has had the effect of creating new forms of cosmopolitanism within expatriate archipelagos, which connect the professional and social life of foreign aid workers (Duffield 2012a). The presence of these aid workers will likely have an effect on the local housing market, and more largely the urban environment (Büscher and Vlassenroot 2010). The predictable consequence is that the aid industry's defensive architecture has the effect of increasing spatial segregation and urban sprawl in the cities where it is implemented, by producing its own spaces of work, residence and leisure separated from most of the local population in symbiosis with local urban elites.

The development of housing for the aid industry depends on the application of power over a territory, often in its most radical fashion, where physical barriers are used to separate social groups (Coaffee 2016). In consequence, one economic impact over the local environment lies in the security sector, including by the employment of security guards. It also results in alliances in forms of contracts with the local elites for the provision of land and real estate as well as specific services to support humanitarian presence. In particular, the aid community relies in the capacity of a section of the local and international sector to provide better standards than the local provision of public services.

The translation of the provision of services to the aid community that are exceptional for local inhabitants leads to a relative detachment from the local urban fabric. Aid compounds are highly autonomous, where tools such as fuel-powered electricity generators reflect the disconnection from the local milieu. The urban form that is promoted by this model is the sprawl and a heavy land consumption implied by a rejection of urban density considered as increased vulnerability (Gillem 2007). In consequence, patterns of mobility follow a strictly privatised model, where SUVs are the norm, rather than the exception.

The creation of a segregated urbanism in cities by institutions of the aid industry will probably have a multiplicative and lasting effect. Defensive architecture to protect aid workers will likely follow dynamics of gated communities: growing in periods of higher danger but not diminishing when threats go down as this model of housing becomes normalised (Low 2001, 2004). Similarly to the example of the recycling of colonial architecture by elites of newly independent states (Amutabi 2005), it can be expected that gated compounds will influence local urban life for longer than the duration of aid operations. This production of a new layer of urban form and practices is adopted and influenced by an array of local players, developing strategies and skills to benefit from the inputs of a new urban dweller.

The widening body of literature on aid and security, aid and space, and more generally defensive urbanism presents a good insight on the presence of aid workers and its effects. It lacks, however, a discussion of the phenomenon across scales (both spatially and institutionally) to understand the spread of the defensive urban models of international aid in different cities. This research will attempt to produce the theoretical and empirical base for explaining the process of city transformation from security norms to its implementation in the urban fabric and subsequent consequences.

Beholden to current research on the presence of humanitarian aid in African cities, this book will attempt to deepen some aspects of the study of the spatiality of aid. It is inscribed in and indebted to literature focussed on the presence rather than humanitarian programmes. The focus, beyond the study-up perspective (Nader 1972) in analysing aid archipelagos, is to discuss both the social interactions that produce a distinct quality of urban space and the possibilities of assessing the impact of humanitarian presence.

A geographic focus on the phenomenon of the bunkerisation of aid and the making of segregated space within African cities will discuss the interactions between institutional levels and geographic scales in a process of territorialisation of aid at a global level. A general theoretical framework of the power of aid will highlight how a global landscape of risk is created. It postulates that the confrontation of institutional powers, spatial habitus, financial and political dominance produces city models marked by increased security design and socio-spatial inequalities, in a play of confrontations and alliances with sections of the local populations.

2.2 Theoretical Framework

The humanitarian presence in capitals of countries in crisis implies a certain use of the local urban space. This use of space differs depending on each context but comprises a certain number of common characteristics. I postulate that the social body that forms humanitarian aid has a spatial effect of the city where it settles. This effect is to a large extent determined by norms that translate directly or indirectly into space. The territorial effect of the international presence may be described as the creation of a landscape in the sense that international aid transforms the perception of the city, as well as its materiality.

The definition of the urban and the city has been a long-disputed debate and always seems to fall short of an universalisable concept to describe it in all contexts. This discussion will not enter the debate on the nature of cities, although it is useful to note a few characteristics that transverse the different sites of research (Bamako, Juba, Nairobi and Abidjan) and present a working definition of the urban before looking into the particular space that is the subject of this research, the urban layer of international aid.

A working definition of the city, or even the capital, does not necessarily fit into the institutional definition that is given in different countries, but rather follows a sociological definition of this type of settlement. First, it is an area with higher population density than the surrounding environments that involves a sense of economic, social and political centrality, as well as relative autonomy in the creation of new social norms (Park and Burgess 2012). As a territory, it is also marked by specific dynamics of density increases and spatial sprawl. Importantly, if understood as a territory, or part of a territory, its materiality is marked by a cumulative (and sometimes subtractive) nature, where the different periods and uses mark the past and will influence its future (Corboz 1983). The relationship between the built environment and its users creates a metabolic and iterative process where the built environment influences the social and vice versa (Burgess 2008).

2.2.1 Landscape: Panorama, Viewers and Viewpoints

Following this definition of the city as a dynamic entity, this book presents the argument that international aid participates in a process of territorialisation, where various social groups compete over a territory. The territorialisation process should not be seen as limited to international aid, but as conducted by all social groups, albeit differing strongly depending on the relative importance of their power and capital (Coaffee 2016). This process of territorialisation is best explained by the concept of landscape. While the notion of landscape contains multiple, and sometimes competing understandings (Mitchell 2001), this work proposes a definition that allows describing the process at work between social groups and the built form while highlighting the central role of social representation. The definition of the landscape used for this research is constituted by the following elements: a frame of reference, or panorama (the city), a viewer (the expatriates), a physical point of view (where the viewer stands) and a subjective point of view (the representations of the viewer).

The concept of landscape helps understanding the power of international aid, as it constructs a social reality in the sense of proposing a representation of a territory, and that it can actually modify it. The frame of reference of the landscape that international aid creates fits largely within the approach proposed by Jackson, focussing more on the processes at play than on aesthetics (J. B. Jackson 1994). This frame of reference, while dynamic and conflictual, constitutes a panorama, as a distinct social and spatial entity from an outside viewer. The notion of landscape allows to understand the process of settling into the city and how a social group can influence a city as a whole.

The landscape lays on a social body that can read and view it, but it also needs a point of view. The point of view is to be understood both in the sense of a physical place and a constructed representation. This approach considers the physical viewpoint not as one fixed point, but rather the "set" of places that are used by a given social group in a given situation (Bronfenbrenner 1977). In the case of the expatriate community, it can be the view from the window of hotel rooms or apartments, but it is also constructed from mobile viewpoints, such as the window of an airplane or a car. The latter constitutes a hodology (Besse 2004), an understanding of the territory by circulating through lines. The structure of the physical viewpoints over the landscape is especially important in a context where some spaces are restricted, because the blanks in the visible landscape need to be filled. In this context the representational viewpoint takes on a major role in forming the perception of surrounding spaces from a variety of sources.

2.2.2 Social and Material Layer

To distinguish the socio-spatial environment of the city, as the frame of reference from the space produced by international aid, this work relies on the idea of the layer. The "layer" combines the socio-spatial elements of international aid forming a coherent (even if sometimes self-contradictory) part of a city at a given time. I will argue later how one specific layer can influence its receiving environment in its interaction with the wider city. The notion of layer, borrowed from cartography, allows to distinguish a specific socio-spatial phenomenon from the city as a whole, while showing how it is still part of and interacts with the city (Söderström 2006). The layer can describe both actual and virtual entities. A building and a road are material entities that can be described in the exact space they occupy, while virtual space can mark the potential events that may occur in a specific area. It will also mark the social representations that are created on it. In short, the layer represents the coherence of the projection of power from one social group (or field, as will be discussed below) over a territory. It also distinguishes the particular segregation process at stake. This layer of international aid is important because it will present one specific iteration in the territorialisation of the city.

The international aid layer is formed by the people who produce and reproduce it. As such international aid is strongly marked by the Bourdieusian "field" and "habitus". That is, it constitutes itself as a social universe with its relative autonomy from the wider social environment, in the "field", where the missions occur, and at the headquarters, such as Nairobi, New York or Geneva (Adly 2013). The notion of field in the case of international aid is particularly relevant, since, similarly to Bourdieu's own concept, the boundaries of the field itself is a matter of debate and struggles within it (Bourdieu, Wacquant, and Ollion 2014). This aspect of the notion of field is especially relevant in the case of humanitarian aid, where its boundaries are often floating. Its relationship with the development field, for example, presents a continuum rather than a clear division of tasks.[3]

The notion of layer could be applied to all social fields within a specific spatial setting, as all social groups and classes construct modes of territoriality. The focus on this book in the particular layer of aid does not deny the existence of the translation into space of social relation of complex environment in cities often heavily fragmented along social and ethnic lines before the arrival of international organisations. However, the use of the notion helps to illustrate the dwelling process of one particular group in relation to the complex web of social interactions and conflicts at stake in a particular location.

The difficulty to mark the boundaries of the field that forms the humanitarian community is not only between humanitarian and development sectors. It also encompasses the large number of tasks and professions that are active in humanitarian settings. The final distribution of goods and services, implies a large infrastructure and a variety of professionals from both the international and local workforce. One key structural division in the organisation of labour in international aid is the division between national and international staff. The latter being specialised technicians, for which it is deemed justified to bring them from abroad and pay higher salaries. The local staff includes skilled technicians, albeit generally regarded as less qualified than the international, as well as all the low-qualifications jobs that are needed in the functioning of the organisation, most typically drivers.

2.2.3 The Aid Industry as a Social Field

The current institutional core of international aid is the United Nations, which takes the lead in both distribution of aid and the definition of security policies that perspires to the overall NGO world. In this regard, what can be easily identified as the core of the social group that makes the international aid is a

3 See for example the debate between David Miliband as head of the IRC when he argued for including the Millennium Development Goals within humanitarian aid, and the cold reception by MSF (Miliband 2014; Whittall 2014).

"technoscape" of aid centred around the UN. As developed by Appadurai (1996), the concept of technoscape allows understanding the moving and constantly self-reshaping the social body of global industries. Like other industries, the process of neoliberal globalisation brings together joint-venture industrial processes in various places of the world, with the combination of technical specialists from all over the world. Similarly, the international aid workers today come from all continents and countries. One big difference between international from North and the South is that the first category generally starts directly as international staff while the latter are often coming from countries in which they were working as national staff, before raising in the hierarchy to international staff status.

This aid technoscape is structured as a job market, with key polarities in major international agencies like UN, Red Cross and major NGOs, such as MSF or ACTED, staff rosters that hire experts to lend them to agencies. Salaries are variable depending on the position and the agency but aligned to the living costs in the North, meaning from a couple of thousand dollars a month to tens of thousands for heads of UN offices. As a social body, the field witnesses variation of status, but largely within the bounds of university-trained professionals.

The territorialisation of the technoscape in a local context builds from a socio-spatial habitus, an acquired sense of place that gives a number of dispositions in "place-making" (J. Hillier and Rooksby 2005). The city habitus of the expatriates is certainly not uniform and is formed by the multiplicity of experiences of its actors, coming from both North and South, and different professional fields and social classes, with an important representation of the university-trained workforce. This middle-class dominated technoscape brings with it a sense of living that is influenced by its place in the social spectrum in a given place and time. But the life as expatriate is also influenced by the time spent living in missions and the particular way of dwelling that is entertained during the stays, transforming a space habitus.

Additionally to the sense of space of the expatriates, the dwelling of the international aid workers is strongly influenced by a more explicitly defined way of using space, that of the security analysis and risk assessment (Doevenspeck 2012). The perception and the definition of pertinent risks are crucial to the territorialisation of international aid in cities. It constitutes a prelude to strong forms of territoriality, which is the implementation of a degree of power over the territory. Aid power concurrences other forms of power in the existing environment, such as the state, municipalities, and a variety of public and private space users. Fitting in the particular way of constructing knowledge and projecting power over space the notion of "riskscape" (Müller-Mahn 2012) captures well the spatiality of risk matrices that shapes the perception of a territory. These

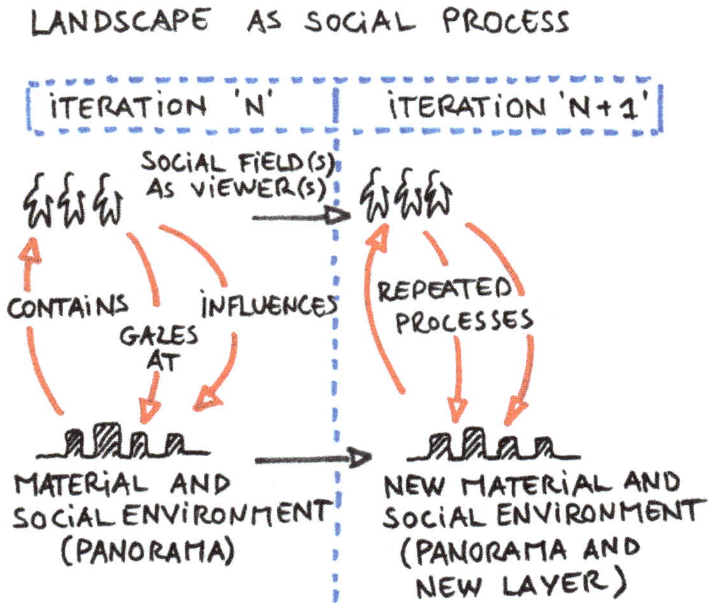

Figure 1: Landscape as an iterative process of social and material transformations

representations fit in the definition of a spatial habitus, in the sense that while individual perceptions are diverse they are strongly structured collectively by a series of social agents within the field of international aid, primarily the security wing of the organisations.

2.2.4 Norms and Transformations

The transformation of the landscape as a perception and in its materiality goes through a normative process using risk analysis as spatial grammar. While it is possible to attach to any social group a form of spatial habitus, humanitarians in conflict environment get to integrate very specific ways of reading and acting over the territory, similar to the "observation/norm interface" developed by Piveteau (1996). The "observation" refers to observation of a given space while the "norm" is the spatial application of a given social grammar. This process allows to enlarge the scope of an understanding of the spatial habitus as not only creating spatial strategies, but also enforcing social norms.

As noted by the psychologist Kurt Lewin (Lewin and Blower 2009) from his experience of WWI, the "landscape of war" presents the characteristics of a radically transformed environment by the changing perception of any individual during changing conditions even though the material frame of reference of the field of vision has not (yet) changed. Called the "apocryphal landscape" by Don Mitchell (2001), the landscape as perception permits to understand both the individual perception and projection over a region and how this vision is organised and constructed through different means, as a collective representation.

Referring to the built and social environments, the dialogue between the individual and collective representations constructs the normative tools to understand the surrounding territory. The learnt abilities to project norms over a specific territory of the missions are mediated by the experiences and training given to expatriates. Both are organised through a structured (and hierarchical) process of dissemination of territorial knowledge.

The dissemination of this spatial knowledge follows generic and specific forms. The generic understanding of the urban environment is typically transmitted through training sessions and documents advising how space should be used and dealt with (Duffield 2012a, 2012b). How one person should behave in a street, in a car, in their house, the difference between night and day, passed as generic instructions are translated in the spatial practice of the aid community. These new norms build the spatial habitus of the aid technoscape in the course of their missions.

On the other hand, specific instructions on how to behave are also transmitted to the aid workers through warnings, instructions and orders, depending on the situation. The advice is then not given on a generic instruction but will instruct on one area of a city that is considered safe or unsafe. Hotels where it is allowed to go and others where it is not. In this sense, the generic learning of the spatial habitus are mobilised to produce a spatial discipline referring to an exact place (Andersson 2016).

The normative injunction that is produced by the security sector aims largely at what Hillier (B. Hillier et al. 1976) dubs as architectural "depth". A topological reading of the spaces that are recommended and used by international aid shows quite clearly that the use of the built form focusses primarily in pushing aid workers in the inside, away from the local environment, whether at work, at home, or during travel. The emphasis is put on the separation from the social environment of the city through built features and security apparatuses.

The physical depth constitutes an important step in the creation of the landscape of international aid since it structures the physical point of view of the aid community. The topological depth formed by SUVs, barriers and walls means that the direct access to the socio-spatial reality of the city beyond the layer of the international aid is limited. Compensating for this lack of direct access, the knowledge of the territory is constructed through descriptions provided by the security personnel (Andersson and Weigand 2015). In terms of landscape, this means that the lack of visibility from the physical points of view has to be replaced by representations provided by the security wing with maps and situation reports focussing on violent events, colloquially referred to as "SitReps". Centred on security incidents, the discourse of fear perspires on the international aid, coupling the physical depth with distance in representation. While not absolutely segregated as a result, the process of creation of this landscape of risk and the international aid layer can be seen an iterative process, mainly directed towards itself.

2.3 Research Methodology: Four Case Studies and Diverse Techniques

2.3.1 Methods, Techniques and Tools

This section will present the general methodology used for the field research and analysis. For the sake of clarity, the general methodology will be presented here as three distinct strata, from the general to the particular. While in the actual practice of research, the distinction between what will be termed as "methods", "techniques" and "tools" might not appear as clearly as discussed below, I will present here the reason to conceptualise these three distinct strata of the research process, mobilised in relation to each other.

Methods are understood as the general research strategies. They are the operational framework that will help answer the research questions, and verify the formulated hypothesis. Techniques, on the other hand, are all that are used to support the practical implementation of the method. They are the mid-level tactical aspects of the practicalities of research. And at the micro level, the tools constitute the material support of the techniques. Conversely, they might also, sometimes, constitute a serious limitation in the use of a given technique.

The form of access to fieldwork prevented a systematic collection of data that would make it directly comparable. The multiplicity of sites of study came together with a multiplicity of techniques for the research. I do not consider whether any of the collected data is strictly comparable or not. In fact, it is inscribed in a continuum of comparability. The weight of the evidence presented in the course of the analysis will be discussed at different levels during the empirical presentation.

Location	Dates	Duration
Bamako	24 Frebuary–25 April 2016	2 months
Juba	14 June–14 July 2016	1 month
Nairobi	14 July–9 September 2016	2 months
Abidjan	13 March–25 May 2017	2.5 months

Figure 2: Fieldwork summary

The diverse nature of the data that was gathered during the research means that I had to proceed by sorting and listing all the materials before being coded and further analysed. The materials were organised in order to use the data either in synergy or in compensation. The classification and organisation of collected data were processed following the return from my last fieldwork, in May 2017.

2.3.2 Methodology: General Strategy and Physical Access to Sites of Research

It seemed to me from the very start that research on the presence of international organisations in African cities would be best built on a comparative, multi-sited methodology. International aid is by definition not limited to one place, and might potentially be involved in all areas that are at some point affected by large-scale humanitarian emergencies. The decision taken for this research was that a multiplication of case studies would allow a deeper understanding of the phenomenon as a global policy implemented in many places. The multi-sited methodology can help distinguish what is generalised across places and what belongs to a particular case or context.

The methodology of research for this PhD takes inspiration from a comparative tradition in Urban Studies, and social sciences more generally. This practice lies on the idea that comparative analysis of cities can show variables, similarities or differences that would not be visible in a single case study (Abu-Lughod 2007). As noted by Robinson, the comparatist approach to cities is partly grounded on the colonial experience, dating to when governors and other colonial administrators went from one place of assignment to the other and came to compare cities from that experience (J. Robinson 2011). There is an obvious link with current humanitarian missions and their frequent turnovers.[4] In contrast

4 The critique of the international aid as a continuator of colonialism has become common in postcolonial critique (Manji and O'Coill 2002; Yala 2006; Hearn 2007; Dogra 2012; Ndlovu-Gatsheni 2013).

with the practice of comparing places of assignment, my approach to comparison is to observe the relations between the missions and the environment in which they operate. In that sense, this research forms a large transect through the worlds and cities of humanitarian presence, in order to gather all possible information in the different instances of a spatial phenomenon. The selection of case studies replaces the line used in transect analysis and all types of data and information -qualitative, quantitative and spatial- are gathered or created (Talen 2002b).

This research methodology borrows from Peck and Theodore (2012) who advocate a "distended" approach, following policy implementations. The research strategy is to jump from places of the implementation of a policy model (or, more accurately, an array of distinct but parent policies). In the case of this research, security procedures and their implementation constitute the moving policy model that I followed across the sites of study, the cities of Bamako, Juba, Nairobi and Abidjan. One case study is not enough to describe and interpret the implementation of security policies, because one case could be the only example where things happen that way.

As noted by Hannerz (2003), the traditional ethnographic study, as presented by E.E. Evans-Pritchard, from his classic ethnography of the Sudanese[5] Nuer (Evans-Pritchard 1940), would usually be focussed on a single site. It might involve the learning of one or more languages and an immersion in the society for a long period of time. As Hannerz and Marcus (Marcus 1995) show, this canonical approach in ethnography strongly limits one's ability to study mobile networks of professionals. In selecting several case studies, one has to abandon the idea of knowing in depth any of the case studies, but use instead a good sample of sites that shows the articulation between mobile networks, on the one hand, and exact places on the other.

This multi-sited research strategy will allow discussing the influence of a global process on a series of cities. In these places, the socio-physical space that is produced represents the local implementation of "global" norms through a process of two localised territorialisation processes. As Burawoy shows in his "extended method" and his description of the "manufacture of the global", global policies emanate from local settings, where specific organisations follow their own processes (Burawoy 1998). The uneven space of social disparities and contradictions, which is produced in a particular site, is the interaction of two levels of localness, where the international-local (Persky and Wiewel 1994; Snyder and Wenger

5 In today's South Sudan.

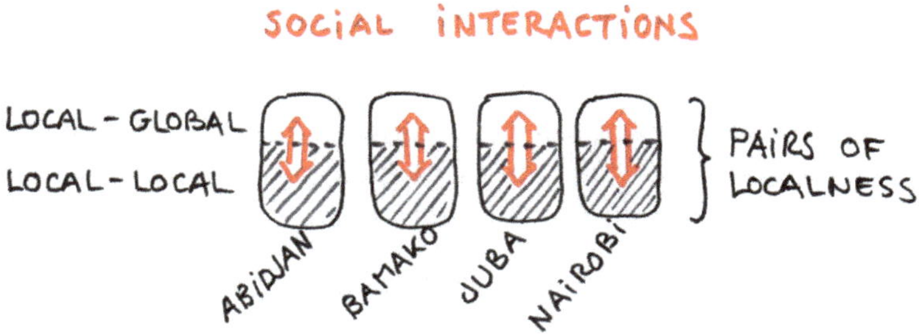

Figure 3: The Local-Global and Local-Local pairs of localness in the four cities

2010) (international aid's personnel on sites of intervention) is in dialogue or conflict with the local-local (states, municipalities, city dwellers).

This means that for each site of study, two local social entities interact with each other. People and cities vary largely from one place to the other. However, international organisations may also vary significantly from one field office to the other. To detect the "agreement and differences" of these territorialities, I focus first at the highest level of the global policy, but will need to go down to the level of local, or localised policies (Abu-Lughod 1997). At the level of the sites of research, four pairs of localness interact, collaborate and conflict with each other. Importantly, the localities are not of similar levels and structures, depending on the constitution of both the local organisation of international aid, and the urban policies of the four capital cities. At some point, this research will highlight a number of differences and similarities of the four sets of half-pairs, which is between all the cities and between all the instances of international aid in their respective cities.

The selection of the sites of research has been a weighing between selecting paradigmatic cases and the practicalities of access to these places. The number of sites of studies for this research is unusual even by the standards of comparative geography, which generally compares between two cities (J. Robinson 2016). As explained below, the four case studies partly owed to opportunities of travel. However, the approach was initially to analyse three paradigms of cities with an important presence of international aid, and a fourth paradigmatic case (Abidjan) was included later as a site of research.

This research of distinct case studies follows the idea of comparing cities one to each other, only to a certain extent. The research do not aim to compare cities to highlight policies and spatial dynamics, but rather to observe the creation by the presence of international aid of a single space across these cities. The aim of the analysis of the four cities is the observation of four instances of the territorialisation of international aid in African capitals. It is thus not a comparative study, since comparisons between these cities are contextual to the observation of the networks and spaces that they host. This approach makes the analysis more focussed on intra-city disparities between the local and the international than inter-city differences and similarities.

I made two distinct choices limiting the geographical scope of this research. One was to limit the zone of interest to the African continent. The choice of four African cities was conscious and responded to my early impression from within the aid community that there was some specific way to dealing with safety and security in Africa, even though on other aspects, the contexts might be completely different, depending on the political situation in the country. The two key features of the visibility of the white expatriates and the health hazards, reputed more dangerous than elsewhere, have been from the beginning forming part of my interest in focussing the research only in Africa. The other choice was to stay on two African sub-regions, East and West Africa. This choice of regions stemmed partly to the practicalities of access, and the possibility to travel from one country to the other.

The physical access to the sites of research has been different in every instance and, as discussed below, influenced the type of data that I collected. The specificity of contexts of conflicts had an effect on the access to the cities and to the institutions that are the subject of this book. In particular, access was contingent to authorisations and ensuring relative safety.

The starting point of this study has been my experience and knowledge of the city of Bamako, which in many ways remained my point of reference when studying the other cities. My access to documentation, informants from all directions and the duration of all my stays meant that my knowledge of this particular city has helped me form most of my theories and test my methods of research. Having known the city after working there as a cartographer for the United Nations in the course of the year 2013, I had made friends and colleagues, on whom I could rely to grant me some level of access to relevant places and people for my study. Some were interviewed for this research, other facilitated access to one or the other of the sites of research. This experience of Bamako also allowed understanding change in time in the city, and gave a benchmark to comprehend and compare the other sites of study.

The access to the city of Juba, which appeared more difficult from the start, was facilitated by a push of luck, when I was offered to cover a position of GIS officer (cartographer) for the UN, in May 2016, just coming back from my first fieldwork in Bamako. The period of three months spanned just during the summer break, which allowed me to officially leave the University of Geneva, during the calm period of the summer to work there as a consultant, hoping to make observations of the city and making useful contacts to interview or to be reactivated later, when back to Geneva.

The research in the city of Nairobi was granted by the coincidence of my presence in Juba during the very serious combats in the city that prompted the UN to evacuate all "non-essential staff" from Juba to Nairobi (or Kampala in some special cases). In my particular case, it meant that the cartographic work would be done remotely for routine tasks and on demand. The period of two months which I spent in Nairobi allowed me to conduct some data gathering on the UN offices in Nairobi, and on the city more generally.

The last phase of the study, the city of Abidjan was added late in the research process to address both practical and an epistemological issue. My experiences in Juba and Nairobi had been as difficult as they were interesting. The possibility of coming back to Juba as a simple researcher with no support from an international organisation was clearly impossible (if it ever had been possible). In contrast, the city of Abidjan appeared as an interesting site to study, because the country was witnessing the rare event that is the end of a UN mission. The research in this city was thus focussed on the effects of the (partial) departure of international aid on the urban environment.

2.3.3 Techniques: Practical and Analytical Articulations

The various techniques which I have used have the final purpose of creating data relating to sites of research that will respond to the hypothesis and, hopefully, help make emerge new themes and questions. During the steps of data collection, and during the analysis, the ideal setting is the use of all different types of data in synergy. And when not possible, to use the variation of data (and the multiplicity of sites) as a compensation.

The development of this dissertation will illustrate that this articulation of techniques constitutes the most conceptually challenging as well as the most interesting aspect of the research. The density of data/site/theme is at his highest when the combined techniques described below can be mobilised, but the multiple techniques also constitute a form of clearinghouse to maintain the robustness of the overall argument. If some information is missing for a place, or a type of data, other data types or similar data on a different place can be used to help solve the problem, or part of it.

This section examines the different techniques that were mobilised during the research, starting with "ethical" questions. I decided here to treat it as a technical element, integral to participant observation. The field research included both observation and participant observation as a starting point and as an attempt to understand the socio-spatial logics of the aid community.

The transversal theme of this description of techniques is the reliance on the body of literature on sensitive/dangerous fieldworks. All techniques presented had to be dealt with in accordance to the sensitivity of the research and the risks of suspicion of being from the other camp, a terrorist, or a spy. As Sluka notes relating to research in dangerous environments:

> *"People act on the basis of what they believe to be true, rather than on the basis of what may in fact be true, and this is precisely my point. It is not enough to be innocent, one must be seen to be so, and it is not enough to dismiss such beliefs or suspicions simply because they are not true."(Sluka 1990)*

The techniques of research need to not only answer the question of research but also protect both the research and the informants in their reputation and physical integrity. As Jenkins puts it, the collection of data from a sensitive field is a selective process. Some of the data can be written down, while some will have to stay only in memory (R. Jenkins 1984). In practice, this means that I wrote some of my notes only after returning from fieldwork.

Deontology: Ethics as a Technical Element

Setting aside the terms of "research ethics", which borrows from philosophy and morals, I will refer to the notion of deontology in the sense that it emphasises working properly and respectfully towards individuals and communities. In this regard, deontology can be seen as one specific aspect of the technicity of research. Deontology in this particular research is two-fold: security of individuals and responsibility towards organisational secrets.

The Hippocratic "Do no harm!" perspective, widely referred to in research (Hugman, Pittaway, and Bartolomei 2011), is interestingly also commonly used by international organisations to state their aims to provide assistance being aware that their presence is not neutral to individuals and communities that depend on them (M. B. Anderson 1999). The stated goal aims to embed in the activities a special caution on the possible side effects that may occur due to my presence and research work. I have constantly kept in sight that there is a potential harm to individuals in my research and the publication of results.

As my responsibility towards individuals and their security constitute a major aspect of my deontological obligations, this book will not present information that was gathered without the consent of the informants. This responds to the need to protect reputations. The physical security of the informants is, however, the most important issue in the presentation of my results. The very focus on security for this research means that I had to work collecting information that may present a risk if disclosed publicly. An academic critique of risk perceptions and policies cannot replace the judgement of people over their own safety.

For the security of individuals, as much as their own perception, the text will ensure that no data presented in the text might be used against them. The specificity of working in sensitive environment needs the application of a "localised ethics", as Kovats coins it, where the will and wishes of informants take precedence to the interpretations of the researcher (Kovats-Bernat 2002). The information that was gathered, when of sensitive nature will be blurred to a level that prevents the identification of exact places and individuals. The blurring of the data mostly means hiding some names and places to obfuscate the possibilities of identification.

Organisational Secrets

During the period of participant observation, I have worked under contract from humanitarian organisations. Contractual requirements as an employee of these organisations include levels of secrecy related to sensitive data. Researching on security makes very sensitive most of the information to which I had access. Nevertheless, all information that I accessed have been used in a way or another. This information helped me shape my understanding of my problematic. I have also been able to work on some of the information within the organisation. The limit to what can be disclosed publicly is defined by the internal organisational rules. Documents from within these organisations that are not both designed for public access and already published (mostly on the internet) as treated with enough obfuscation to prevent the identification of places, names and any sensitive information.

2.3.4 Observation and Collection of Data

The observation and participant observation is the starting point of all techniques I have used. It is the inductive methods that allow the wide collection of thoughts and memories that permits the construction of the theories tested in the course of the research process. Observations are consigned in different formats presented below.

The first important distinction with the research material is between collected and created data. The first are pre-existing documents in various forms, but

Collected				Created					
Texts	Maps	GIS	Statistics	Notes	Interviews	Drawings	Chorèmes	Maps	Photographs

Figure 4: Main data types

mainly written (either on paper or electronic support), while the second type is data created by the researcher in the course of the research, using the techniques described below.

Collected Data: Written Documents and Maps

This research has been built upon an increasing number of written papers on the issue of humanitarian aid and security. A diversity of this kind of material will be discussed in the chapters. They include policy papers, field manuals. For reasons of confidentiality, emails and contractual documents are used at different stages, but never presented in full, to prevent possibilities of identification. The field visits as well as research documentation on the Web provided many written documents relating to housing and security policy for international missions. Those can be of generic scope or localised in specific contexts (the cities and countries where international aid operates).

I have used the support of quantitative lexical software in contents of written documentation to identify major trends in texts. The combined reading with the computer allows identifying and charting important associations and dissociations in the texts. Reinert's Descending Hierarchical Classification (DHC) (Guerin-Pace 1998; Hamman, Anquetin, and Monicolle 2017) was well suited and allowed the systematic exploration and comparisons of a number of documents. It also helped distinguish the main thematic relationships within the documents and their spatial components.

As well as written documents, maps provide information relating to a specific place. Maps constitute a practical tool as a measured representation of the world (or a part of it). They constitute an object and a projection of power through knowledge using a language that is distinct from the power of written documents. Let us just note two of the distinct aspects of the maps. They constitute a specific projection of power through knowledge and representation (Harley 2006). The importance of maps as instruments of power should be a starting point rather than the end of an analysis in the context of international aid. In addition, maps should also be understood as powerful vector for the imagination (Besse 2006). The social use of maps mobilises imagination partly freed from the cartographer's intentions.

The location-specific nature of maps can tell more about the ideas behind their creation. The elements represented and the ways this information is represented in the map belong to a wider visual culture that informs of how the categories of elements represented on a map are perceived and apprehended by the creators of the map (Bertin 1973). The signs and symbols that are mobilised to represent the outer world, as well as the elements represented, respond themselves to a particular reading of space and the social world.

I have also collected some primary data to process with statistical and mapping software. These include data distributed publicly by various organisations, such as urban data and violent events relating to the case studies. Institutional and open-source urban GIS data was also collected. This array of data and its use will be described in the course of the book.

Created Data

Data is produced at different stages of the research process, during and after fieldwork. Created data are of different types and purpose. The various challenges in the production of new data might be practical or epistemological. The main types of self-produced data, interviews, notes and visual documents, are presented below.

Interviews

Formal and informal interviews were conducted on all fieldworks. These were usually conducted taking exclusively written notes. The goal was to understand the vision of different types of actors involved in the local management of the aid industry. It involved among other actors, aid professionals, urbanists, hotel managers and employees. Although the interviews include aid workers, the focus of the interviews had been a diversity of actors within the local population.

My ambition was to conduct the interviews in the form of the "Grand Tour" as coined by Spradley (2016) to ask interviewees to describe their work as a means for understanding language and professional culture. This was not always possible, as time and location did not always permit full-length in-depth interviews. Interviews were also used as a pad for further interviews and contacts, with attempt to "snowball" each interview to reach new actors using the interviewees' formal and informal social and professional connections (Atkinson and Flint 2001; Noy 2008).

The names of representatives of public and private institutions interviewed during the research are preserved. In other cases, only the first names are used to report statements and comments of interviewees. The obfuscation of the full names responds in some cases to the confidential nature of the remarks. In most cases, the full names are not necessary to follow the words and opinions of private individuals.

Visual Methods: Drawings, Maps, Chorèmes

I have extensively used a range of visual methods for this research. The use of hand drawings includes as much as plans, cross-sections and observation drawing that aim to describe as well as analyse space. Hand drawings serve multiple purposes. It sharpens the observation by forcing a certain way of looking at architecture and landscape (Unwin 2007). The observation drawings will be presented in the discussion of the aesthetics of international aid, and how this aesthetics is part of a problematic, but also problematised, practice of making spatial segregation visible from the inside and the outside of the layer of aid industry.

The process of drawing during research questions and make visible the places and people studied as subjects and in relation to the researcher. The position of the body and the time available to sketch, among other constraints, fully participate to the understanding of a specific situation. Although drawing rarely carry the value of proof, often associated with photography, it stimulates "the imaginative logic of discovery" (Taussig 2011). Its use in research completes written notes as much as it may uncover specific social settings through the simultaneous acts of visually describing a subject of the drawing (human or material) and inferring adequate time and position to draw it.

Another set of technical instruments has been used to circumscribe, problematise and partially solve the issues of this research. The combination of a series of tools that can be linked to what William Bunge would call "mathematical geography" (Bunge 1979). I prefer this expression to the over-used and under-understood term of "quantitative" geography, since it not only refers to the use of statistics, but also to mapping of qualitative data and schematisation methods that borrows from mathematics, especially from topology, but also from separate fields, first of all, semiology.

The use of mathematical-graphical techniques in maps, schemas (chorèmes) and statistics do not pretend to a higher degree of scientificity than the qualitative methods used in conjunction. They should not be fetishised, but neither rejected. They offer the possibility to problematise different objects and bring rich and complex answers. Data visualisation permits to see connections that could not be seen if they were not transcribed graphically. But this must be first set by ordering where to look, in the sense of finding the data as much as preordering it logically and thematically (Bertin 1977).

Numbers, in that regard, will be presented in the course of this text at different chapters to bring different answers to a number of separate questions. The statistics used for this work connect to relatively simple questions, but for which the only sure way of finding answers seemed to be the use of quantitative data produced by a variety of institutions, including UN and NGOs. The strong potential of quantitative analysis starts with the critical examination of the taxonomies proposed by the institutions that produce and publish them. Furthermore, the statistical examination of the data constitutes an important bridge to discuss organisations' taxonomies, by testing their internal consistencies.

Maps are used as a practical instrument to represent spatial relations. The two-dimensional structure should not be seen as a limit to its potential for explaining spatial relations, but as a strong potential through simplification that allows modelling. The maps and plans are used to model socio-spatial relations in the real sites of studies at large and small scale. They are not only descriptive in this regard but also constitute analytical tools.

Complementary to these maps, the higher abstractive modelling tool which is the "chorème" was used as a complement. The chorèmes and other spatial schematisations permit to go to a high level of abstraction and generalisation that follows the aim of this work to present not only case studies but also a series of paradigms in the territoriality of the aid industry. The use of schematisations to describe territorial dynamics borrows from the elementary grammar used and theorised by Brunet, to support the description of spatial dynamics (Brunet 1986). This visual technique was essential to circumscribe the spatiality of international aid. The conceptual framework of this research owes much to this technique in this regard.

Most visual documents presented in this book, such as maps, drawings and charts are original creations, unless presented as collected in the figure legend.

2.3.5 Tools

The discussion about tools presented below do not intend to give a detailed account of brands or even the exact type of all the instruments used to conduct the research, but present their main characteristics and how they were able to support the research. The tools used consisted of three main instruments the combination of a smartphone, a computer and pen, pencil and notebook.

The use of a smartphone was critical in the ability to gather different types of data with the same instrument. Modern smartphone quality allows among others to record geographic locations, sounds and take photographs, in combination if needed. It allows the compactness of a tool that facilitates the travel in its practicalities. It constitutes a practical easy to use and easy to carry instrument, while also allowing a degree of discretion that professional tools of the sort would not have provided.

The corollary to this compactness is that the tools as gathered in a standard phone are not of excellent quality. This was not, however, felt to be a serious shortfall, except for sound recordings where the output quality needed serious post processing, since the desired quality and precision were largely met for the purpose of the research. Geographic coordinates and photographs are certainly not as aesthetic and precise as the state of the art, but good enough to locate the places and keep visual records of places visited. The need to later blur the collected data also meant that top precision would likely not be necessary.

The key question in the use of a smartphone for data collection is the dialectic of the standardisation of data collection versus the manoeuvrability and adaptability to encompass the scope of possible places and situations in the imparted time. In relation to the techniques referred above, this meant that the data collection process was adjusted and modified over time to adapt better to the practical challenges of the research as much as the relevance of the information that was collected.

The computer is extensively used in analysis of data and writing. I will simply note here the different analytical processes that were supported by my computer. Statistical analysis was used to describe the object of international aid. Statistics were also used in a heuristic procedure to analyse text, including security manuals. Inspired by the methods of Moretti (2005), the quantitative analysis of texts aimed to provide a wider overview than the sole linear reading of text, by allowing incorporating larger numbers of texts, and sometimes to highlight clues and bring hard evidence of patterns that might not have been possible otherwise.

The greatest risk in the quantitative analysis is to lose the tracks of the calculations made by the computer. This case increases with the complexity of the statistical operations, where the background calculation of the computer are most important. To keep track and control of this specific variable, statistics have been organised by simple steps following other and always keeping track of the exact calculation.

Most manoeuvrable, but also most difficult to use sequentially, are the pen and notebook. It constitutes the support in the recording of all qualitative observations and drawings. I constantly attempted to keep at least one notebook for drawing and one for writing all the time, to keep things in good order. Still, most of the time, the notebooks served both purposes. The only exception was Juba, where for reasons of discretion, I never draw any sketches during the stay not to attract suspicion of spying and making sure the drawings would not endanger anyone.

The notebook was used as the only way of documenting the content of interviews. It requires special effort and concentration to follow the discussions but also provides valuable advantages. It does not have the intimidating effect of the sound recording to the interviewee. It requires a serious attention to the discussion all the duration of the interview. This can be challenging during long interviews lasting more than an hour, but also shows the interest in the discussion to the other person, encouraging to speak broadly and openly.

The limit of manual notes is that some elements might be missed in the process. To mitigate this risk, all interviews were immediately transcribed from the rough notes taken. The method offers the resulting interview as a compact document, without hesitations and clears surrounding noises of the interview. This compact interview data forms the base of the interviews. To facilitate repeated reading and computerised reading during the analysis, all observations made on the notebooks have also been transcribed in digital format after the fieldworks.

2.3.6 The Body as a Technical Ensemble: Interface between Methods, Techniques and Tools

The interface between the two abstract notions of the methods and the techniques and the more concrete tools is the very concrete and sensitive entity of the body. The body is where the supporting theory is built. It is the same body that investigates and look for empirical evidence. In the course of the research, the body can be understood as a technical ensemble in the sense of Simondon, the place where the techniques are coordinated and structured through specific management of information (Simondon 2012).

The body is the tool that will interpret space before transcribing it on paper or in digital in a written, drawn, photographic or any other form. But the body also harbours the possibility of kinaesthetic epistemology (Volvey 2016). That is the capacity to develop an understanding of the social and spatial environment through body sensations. These sensations can be pleasure and pain, fear and joy. As developed by Kovats, these sensations form part of the collected data:

> "Feelings and responses to violence and terror be included in the data set when such information might shed light on the circumstances under which that information was acquired and how those circumstances modified the social relations amid which it was obtained."(Kovats-Bernat 2002)

The quintessentially subjective element to the kinaesthetic understanding of the environment, the feeling and sensations of the city becomes data itself. It becomes one of the most serious techniques to order and organise the collection of data.

During the research, the body is likely confronted to its own vulnerabilities. This bodily fragility shapes in many ways the limits of the practicalities of the research. However, in the context of sensitive environments, it also constitutes a measure and an indication of the geographies of risk. As Anderson shows, research on security and perception of danger implies a mirror game when the researcher enters the site of research. While being critical of a vision of security, the researcher is also entangled with its own feelings of security/insecurity and builds his own security practises and procedures (Andersson 2016). The critique of a policy does not mean that the researcher is outside of it, and he might very well rely on this same policy for its own safety, albeit to a different degree, but from a distinct perspective.

During this research, two main types of fragilities have both affected my capacity to work and allowed me to learn more about my own subject: health and violence. I have contracted a series of illnesses that included malaria, diarrhoea and flu. These have limited my capacities as a researcher in preventing me during several days to carry my research. These experiences can be related almost literally to "visceral methodologies" (Sexton et al. 2017), as they also participated in giving me a direct understanding of body fragility.

The bodily fear also affected more largely my understanding of the environment, during times of crisis, as during the war in Juba and to a much lesser extent, during the military rebellion in Abidjan. These experiences helped me understand and use the notion of the landscape of war, borrowed from psychologist Kurt Lewin (Lewin and Blower 2009). Fear of the environment can also be present in the case of normal (as not during war) conditions, depending on the place and time. In particular, the feeling in Juba, was never comfortable, even during the few normal weeks that I spent in Juba. Also to a lesser extent in Nairobi, where the experience of mugging by colleagues added to the general reputation of the city did not encourage me to break the security rules and walk at night. Except for a visit in the informal settlement of Mathare, which was organised through people in whom I had confidence.

In yet another mirror game between my critique of the aid industry and my own practice, the colour of my skin (white) surely affected the way I was able to research during fieldwork. Within the general problems of research, my skin colour meant different possibilities in field observations. Practically, white skin means that it is instantly clear, at any of the sites of research, that the researcher is not a local, and attracts the curiosity of passers-by. This visibility has different implications in the way the researcher is welcomed in the sites. Nevertheless, it is difficult to evaluate without discussions of comparable experiences for this research. I will mention, however, that it has been impossible to be discreet during the research. In fact, the rare places where I felt unnoticed were in areas and venues where there is a larger community of white expatriates.

My skin colour might have helped socially to gain access to both the local institutions and in the spaces of the aid industry. Several of my friends and informants pointed to me that it might help to be white to get access to local institutions: "They will think you bring funding with you!" This is plausible, but impossible to verify. When trying to see if my access to institutions was different to that of African colleagues (geographers and other social scientists), it did not seem that either delays for appointment, or the nature of information shared was much different from what was granted to local colleagues.

This chapter presented the epistemological and practical stakes of this research. It is based on a growing literature on the presence of humanitarian aid in sites of interventions. It presented how the concept of landscape supports the description and analysis of urban transformations in the context of aid presence. Finally, the methodological considerations introduced the outline of empirical data for the next chapters. After this presentation of the theory and methodology, the following chapter on the aid industry will present the social field of humanitarian aid in historical perspective and in the main outlines of its political, social and spatial structures.

Chapter 3 The Aid Industry: Social Field and Spatial Habitus

3.1 International Aid and the History of Capitalism

International aid has built itself as a form of industry. The degree of specialisation and professionalisation, as well as the dominance of a number of big players over the whole field makes it akin to many multinational industrial programmes. Within the framework of the particularities of the nonprofit sector, the aid industry borrows from capitalism many of its doctrines and modes of management.

Within the reconfiguration of capitalism in the era of neoliberal globalisation following the Cold War, industries tend to bring together an increasingly complex and cosmopolitan configuration of the worlds of material and informational cultures and techniques. This phenomenon can be observed using the notion of technoscape borrowed from Appadurai. The technoscape describes the occurrence in the current state of capitalist globalisation of the process bringing together personnel, funding and specific industrial or infrastructure project coming from different origins to one location (Appadurai 1996). International organisations constitute one element of a limited number of private and public actors to operate in settings of otherwise impervious boundaries. The sense of international organisations operating at the extremity of the reach of globalised connectedness places them as a focal point of globalisation in many areas of the Global South.

The field of international aid widely perceives itself as an industry. Its practitioners in fact often advocate what may appear as a critique of the humanitarian sector. Recognising the status of an industry with its particular economy (IRIN 2016), also allows claiming professionalism and efficiency presented through transparency mechanisms and quantifiable outputs. OCHA's Financial Tracking Services (OCHA 2017) include for example the liberal ethos of "transparency".

The specific processes at stake in this particular industry does not make it directly comparable to "standard" industries of services at the age of globalisation. The nonprofit sector does not aim at returns on investments and profits for shareholders. Indeed, following the definition of capitalism as the quest for profit, "nonprofit" organisations seem completely separate from the market economy. However, charities develop their activities in parallel to the practice and ideology of contemporary capitalism, largely influenced by it (Maier, Meyer, and Steinbereithner 2016). Market-like strategies for funding and the perception of other NGOs as concurrent has been familiar to the nonprofit sector for decades (Liebschutz 1992).

It should not be a surprise that humanitarian aid reflects its epoch and its social practices. The dominant social model of an epoch seems always to have this dual aspect of contradictions and mutual influences with humanitarianism. This goes back in history as far as the eighteenth century at least. As discussed by Haskell (1985a, b) and Ashworth (1987) the British anti-slavery movement born in the Eighteenth Century Bourgeoisie formed an important part in building the ideology and practice of early capitalism. The relationship between capitalism, slavery and anti-slavery is crossed with contradictions if capitalism is understood only in the strict perspective of financial profits. Nevertheless, bringing the spirit of Weberian rationalisation and the legitimacy of wage labour might have been worth trading immediate profits against a change of perception (Haskell 1985a).

The Red Cross movement was born in the particular context of nineteenth century Europe. The nineteenth century humanitarianism as thought and developed by Dunant and Nightingale appears as a moral response to the increasing firepower of modern weaponry. In turn, the later organising of the Red Cross movement by Moynier brought management techniques of the day to the development of a transnational organisation (Ryfman 2016).

The current state of international aid follows neoliberal globalisation. Neoliberalism influences international aid at the different levels of practice and ideology. This section will present the major trends that relate the aid industry and capitalism. The list of elements that allows relating epochs and their products are endless; I will, however, highlight what seems to be the most characteristic trends in this relation.

The aid industry responds to the production of crises that are the product of its epoch, commonly described as the post-Cold War world of the globalisation of capitalism (Knudsen 1996; Weiss 2018). An explanation to the rise in the humanitarian technoscapes is precisely the increase in humanitarian catastrophes due to the disengagement of the State and its regulatory functions to the benefit of the private sector. In this perspective, the increase in inequalities and the disengagement of the State from social affairs constitutes the condition of the constant development of activities by humanitarian organisations. As early as 1976, critiques started to point the social nature of natural disasters, coining the "classquake", where the poor are located in the most vulnerable places, under the most fragile structures. In short, "Disasters are historically and spatially the specific outcome of the process of contemporary capitalism" (Blaikie et al. 2014).

Conversely, the increase of humanitarian disasters and armed conflicts justifies the rise and increase of humanitarian organisations and their activities. In that regard, the growth of the humanitarian sector appears as self-nourishing in the context of a growing number of crises. Since the number and the extent of humanitarian crises are going to expand, there will be need for humanitarian organisations to fill the void.

3.1.1 Neoliberal Ideology

The response to the crises goes through the same dominant system of neoliberal globalisation. In terms of programming, neoliberal ideology affects the design and management of programmes, and seem to rephrase older paternalistic views of local beneficiaries. The most overused cliché of the goals of development aid, " Give a man a fish, and you feed him for a day; show him how to catch fish, and you feed him for a lifetime", sometimes attributed to "China" and other times to "Africa", is being rephrased in standardised corporate language (Ferguson 2015). In development circles, the World Bank has worked in imposing its own language and vision of development. The "bankspeak" coined by Moretti and Pestre to describe the evolution of the World Bank discourses since the 1990s into the vaguest detemporalised and decontextualised terminology can be found in many programmatic reports of the aid industry (Moretti and Pestre 2015).

As noted decades ago by Bourdieu and Boltanski, the dominance of an ideology is marked by its capacity to present its programme as a non-political solution. The technical purity of the solutions proposed are always between two "extreme" alternatives (Bourdieu and Boltanski 1976). This technical approach is reflected in the language of the common sense used by aid organisation. Among this common sense, trends and "new" ideas to "show how to fish" seems to work in justifying, rather than providing actual new ideas. "Cash transfers, for example, turn out to be used wisely by recipients, and spur entrepreneurialism rather than trapping people in dependency," as stated by David Miliband, current director of the IRC, in 2015 (Miliband and Gurumurthy 2015). This language by the former British Foreign minister reflects a discourse where the purpose of development and humanitarian aid seems to spread liberal values as much as saving lives.

For Townsend et al., adherence to liberal programming stems partly in the NGOs intentions to "sustain and increase their funding streams, and provide employment for their real beneficiaries, the middle classes" (Townsend, Porter, and Mawdsley 2004). In the wide field of humanitarian aid, the influence of neoliberal policies is variable, from the strict implementation of market rules to the aim to limit the influence of the market. Organisations critical to neoliberal agendas also find their ways in the large array of organisations (Edwards 1999). Nevertheless, among major players of aid, even organisations most critical of neoliberal globalisation criticise the "selective basis" of free trade, rather than the free market mechanisms themselves (Berry and Gabay 2009).

Internal to aid organisations, humanitarian planning and work increasingly relies on neoliberal solutions. In particular the "New public management" methods that were adopted by states and other public actors. The NPM model applied to aid and nonprofit was proposed from the early 1990s at least (Alexander 2000). NPM relies on a series of key concepts, which have been implemented in different fashions by states and other organisations from the 1980s. The core concepts are largely being used within aid organisations. In particular, NPM aims to use formal standards and measures of performances and successes, replacing an earlier more qualitative and implicit set of norms and standards of achievements. The corollary to the implementation of new modes of measuring performance is a higher emphasis on the control of outputs and outcomes using new quantitative instruments of control of results (Hood 1995).

The language of the humanitarian community varies depending on their own "corporate culture". Most, however, float in the management keywords of the day. Three key notions of neoliberal management are being deployed in the settings of crises correlate well with the short-term and moving nature of humanitarian work: management by project, flexibility and the belief in the comparative efficiency of the private sector. These key notions are used by the humanitarian community at different stages, levels and scales of intervention.

3.1.2 Project Management

The management by project adopted decades ago and now structuring the private industry (Boltanski and Chiapello 2011), has become the reference in humanitarian settings. Project management fits like a glove to an industry that aims to act on a temporary basis and the temporalities of crises. As pointed by Krause, management by project also reflect in the building of humanitarian "products", with specific modes of commodification and marketing for the organisation as well as the beneficiaries (Krause 2014). This culture of management involves a multiplicity of projects with a beginning and an end. When a project end, another one follows and replaces the last one. Employees may be working on one or several of these project, structuring the relationships between a network of fluctuating relationships within the organisation (Boltanski and Chiapello 2011).

The project structures the positions of employees in diverse specialities through the "logframes" that aim to rationalise humanitarian actions in the language of goals, inputs and outcomes.

The responses to specific crisis seems moulded for humanitarian sector. "Sudden onsets", "protracted crisis", the language of humanitarian aid structures the temporalities of programmes and project. The funding practices and structures adapt perfectly for this type of management (Duffield 1994; Hendrickson 1998). In its concrete application, management by project by humanitarian aid is reflected by the presence of an array of organisations, UN and NGOs, managing a multiplicity of specific projects in response to the multifaceted aspect of a crisis that may be affecting, for example nutrition, health and livelihoods. Apart from their function, budget organisations submit specific frameworks of actions to donors and regularly report their outcomes through statistics, maps and pictures.

At the programmatic level, the management by project sets the landscape of the international response. As noted by Lombart et al., these types of management focussed on short-term outcomes from multiple agencies damages the quality of their integration between themselves and to a higher administrative level (Lombart, Pierrat, and Redon 2014). In the context of humanitarian aid, the industry has shown its awareness of the issue, and brought its own coordination mechanism to facilitate the integration and geographical repartition of humanitarian aid in the form of the "Clusters" since 2005, to coordinate priority areas in humanitarian interventions. The response of the aid industry to the shortcoming of project management is the coordination mechanisms of these projects.

Human resource management of humanitarian organisations also borrow heavily from the neoliberal trends. In particular, staff flexibility shapes the industry's workforce through frequent relocations following one crisis after another in different countries and continents. The organisational, spatial and thematic discontinuities of the management by project as well as the mobile nature of emergency work are reflected in the short-term contracts of employees. This flexibility does not affect the whole body of employees of international organisations, as the upper ladders, in particular within the UN system are rewarded long-term positions (Yi-Chong and Weller 2008), but mostly field contracts. The fragility of the work contract of aid professionals tends to worry part of NGO management and research since a high turnover may limit the capacity and skills within an organisation (Korff 2012; Korff et al. 2015).

3.2 Reliance on the Private Sector for Goals and Models

Liberal ideology and methods inspired by the private sector also perspire in the practice of humanitarian organisations of hiring private contractors for a number of specific professionalised tasks. Emblematic of this vision of the private sector efficiency are success stories of private companies able to bring their products to the remotest areas. One of the most popular stories involves the emblematic product of modern capitalism: Coca-Cola. Popularised by then UN Secretary-General Kofi Annan, this story relies on the myths of the efficiency of the private versus the indigence of the public sectors:

> *Almost any village you go into anywhere in the world you will see a Coca-Cola bottle. They manage to get it there. And yet when it comes to vaccination [...] we can't get it there. How can we do it that we get the vaccines to all the villages that need them? That is the kind of area where we really learn from the private sector.(As cited in Wadham and Warren 2013)*

Success stories of the sort tend to leave a number of problematic blind spots of capitalist efficiency. Unsurprisingly, Kofi Annan did not mention the Kalashnikov as another industrial product and global brand capable of reaching the remotest areas as a business model. The idea of using the networks, as well as the funding of private companies, while still discussed as an opportunity or a danger, is being increasingly proposed as the latest solution for providing support to humanitarian programmes.

The presence of private actors of many types has in fact become a feature of the humanitarian industry. For diverse reasons, either side did not always see the collaboration between private and nonprofit positively (Haksöz, Seshadri, and Iyer 2011). In fact, the private sector still struggles for its legitimacy in the humanitarian field (Simplr.co.za 2018). Its management language and practices have, however, already been part of the functioning for a while (IRIN 2013). The last area where private companies remain controversial is the security sector. Part of the humanitarian sector tends to identify and associate private security companies operating in conflict to mercenaries (Spearin 2008, 2007).

The outlook on the relation between humanitarian aid and capitalism depicts their growing ideological and organisational affinities. These interconnections result in specific spatial and social structures as aid develops as a global industry. The following section will present an analysis of primary data, highlighting the main contours of the geographies of aid in their social and spatial dimensions.

3.3 Statistics of Funding, Personnel and Sites of Operations

The humanitarian community and the UN in particular produces an increasing number of documents and statistics on their internal organisation, following a wider trend of open data philosophy (Palen et al. 2015). The distribution of humanitarian data has started to be used to produce studies of the humanitarian communities, by academics, but also specialised reviews, magazines and more generally humanitarian research centres. This distribution policy provides a large amount of data to put in relations to the economic geographies of aid. However, internal consistency of information, impractical distribution methods and formats and gaps in the data brings some limitations. An important critique of the actual implementation of transparency policies by international aid stems from the lack of efficient and practical data distribution tools (Custer et al. 2017). The notion of "data graveyard" has been used to describe the distribution of data in formats, typically PDF, which complicates access, and the possibility to work directly on the statistics.

The economic geography of international aid shows an uneven repartition in the provenance of funds and personnel and the concentration of the recipients of aid in the poorer regions of the world. This situation gives the uncomfortable impression that the South provides sites of intervention, while the North provides funding and administrators. The provenance of the money follows political priorities of donors. In particular, the funding of humanitarian aid increasingly follows the rationale of a development aid focussed on security and preventing flows of population from South to North (Duffield 2010a; Agier 2013).

3.4 Funding for Interventions

A number of research has discussed humanitarian funding in its political and practical implication. Complex mechanisms of pooled funds and redistribution among UN and NGOs structure the coordination of humanitarian responses between donors and agencies. Using the data distributed by OECD and OCHA's Financial Tracking Service, IRIN highlights the ever-increasing funding for humanitarian assistance that structures the "humanitarian economy" (IRIN 2016). Since the beginning of the 2000s, the funding for humanitarian interventions has multiplied more than tenfold, from 2 to 22 billion US dollars. Concentration of the donors shows a strong predominance in funding states by Northern countries. Gulf countries are starting to weigh in, but the USA, European Commission and European states are by far the largest funders of aid with three quarters of the contributions. Private donors funding is marginal concerning standard funding processes, with few exceptions. Since the beginning of the 2000s, it is only the 2004 Asian tsunami and the 2010 Haiti earthquake that has brought the private donations to humanitarian intervention out of the margins of funding. Major sources of financing come from states.

The concentration of humanitarian donors is reflected in the concentration of funding for humanitarian agencies. WFP, the leading food emergency and logistics agency takes one third of the funding by itself. Other major UN agencies, Red Cross and major NGOs take most of the rest of the pie, while local NGOs collect a much smaller share of the resources. Critics of this model point that concentration of resources in the hands of few limits the efficiency of operations (Edwards 1999). The question of consistency of programming may also be affected when the theme is deemed controversial, such as reproductive health (Tanabe et al. 2015).

3.5 Peacekeeping and Humanitarian Presence

The scope of this study is thematically larger than the sole UN presence since it aims to discuss the social field of humanitarian interventions. Peacekeeping is a distinct political process as humanitarian assistance, although the use of the term "humanitarian intervention" in the sense of preventing human right violations by force since the 1970s has entertained an important linguistic and political confusion (Guillot 1994; Cottey 2008). This meaning has been opportunistically used well beyond peacekeeping operations by Western powers to wage war and overthrow governments in number of occasions adding only more to the confusion of the term (Weizman 2011). In this regard, this research only focusses on two interlinked types of intervention: peacekeeping as materialisation of the UN political and military presence and humanitarian assistance in the provision of a variety of civilian emergency services.

The study of the combined presence of peacekeepers and humanitarian assistance is justified by a web of relations between the two activities. The presence of peacekeeping is related to armed conflicts of diverse forms, which produces vulnerabilities and humanitarian emergencies to which UN and NGO humanitarian organisation aim to respond (Natsios 1995). The difficulty to provide assistance in violent contexts, to which natural catastrophes and social conditions render aid provision more critical and limited access to populations needing assistance more complex has set mechanisms of cooperation between political-military and humanitarian wings of international interventions (Keen 2008). The "complex emergencies" have justified mechanisms of so-called integrated missions in which the political and humanitarian aspects of UN interventions are placed under the same command (Combaz 2013). The mechanism is controversial within humanitarian circle as it places humanitarian in an explicitly political position and might endanger aid workers and limit aid provision (Harmer 2008).

Institutional structures of interventions are distinct and reflect the missions assigned. Although humanitarian organisations do not follow the instructions of political bodies, their presence is related to the political and military conflicts as well as the UN presence and missions. Large UN missions tend to be large humanitarian missions because of the amplitude of humanitarian needs, although scales of interventions are highly dependent on political situations. Moreover, the funding of NGOs and other humanitarian organisations being covered by the same countries supporting UN missions, the capacity of these organisations to deploy on the field comes from the same origins (Wallace 2004; AbouAssi 2013).

The relationship between humanitarian organisations and peacekeeping is problematic. This, however, is mostly a one-side controversy, where humanitarians are often incomfortable with peacekeeping. Humanitarian organisations have a complicated approach to the collaboration with military units as it puts into question their neutrality and might subsequently affect their missions (Harmer 2008). This controversial relationship is constantly being redefined and sorted on a case-by-case basis, pondering between the risks posed in the different countries following evolving situations (Karlsrud 2015).

Their structures, practices and their separate missions divide peacekeeping and humanitarians. As social fields, humanitarian and peacekeeping spheres present distinct structures. Peacekeeping military units come from the armies of different countries involved in operations. Within peacekeeping, these units keep the same structures as in the country of origin (Bellamy and Williams 2013).

The humanitarian workforce is a civilian field. In most cases, humanitarian workers are recruited as individuals to work in autonomous structures. Differences between the peacekeeping and humanitarian fields are political and practical, as they operate on different goals and organisational systems. This distinction in work structures places expatriate humanitarian workers in individualised roles and social positions, as the examination of their recruitment illustrates.

3.6 Workforce Data: Job Websites and UN Board

The following section purports to visualise and discuss some of the statistics on the aid workforce distributed by the UN, or made available for this research by humanitarian job advertisement websites. The available data does not necessarily

	Period covered					
Data Source	**Start**	**End**	**Number of files**	**Number of Records**	**Number of People**	**Number of Agencies**
ReliefWeb	19.12.2016	06.04.2018	1	50000	~50000	1778
UN Jobs	01.01.2017	05.04.2018	1	10971	~10971	433
UN Board Data	01.01.2016	31.12.2016	2	2718/4769	82812/ 83102	35

Figure 5: Comparisons of data sources

comprise the industry as a whole. A series of shortcomings prevents a complete overview of the relationship between funding, sites and personnel in the whole industry.

Times of reporting constitute a difficulty, since the different organisations do not necessarily follow the same schedules and reporting cycles. Discrepancy on the reporting forces to choose not one year of reference, but either the most internally consistent/complete data per source, which may likely be the latest reporting or distribution. Data tables are not necessarily synchronic, as their time of reporting and purposes are different. Nevertheless, most of the data concerns the years 2016–2017, which should ensure some level of consistency.

The data illustrates some general tendencies. I have selected three main sources of raw data relevant to the question of sites of interventions and the humanitarian workforce. The three sources, listed below, comprise limitations and potential for this study (Figure 5). ReliefWeb and UN Jobs data are extracts from humanitarian job advertisement websites, and constitute a snapshot of the state of the humanitarian aid workforce needs. Working with this data required the extraction of tens of thousands of rows of tabular data using APIs. On the other hand, the "UN Board" data is a global reporting for the UN system based on internal HR data and is prepared into two key files on the duty station and the nationality of staff. There is a small discrepancy in their numbers, which accounts for less than a percent of the total eighty thousand plus UN staff worldwide.

The raw data sources described have strength and weaknesses for a description of the humanitarian workforce. UN data allows the finest level of analysis in relation to humanitarian social structure. This is largely due to the possibility of accessing this data freely, which is not necessarily the case with other humanitarian organisations. While data from the UN cannot be generalised to the rest of the aid community, its examination gives a good overview of the relations between sites of interventions, and between international and local employees.

Country	Number of positions
South Sudan	31
Iraq	4
Globally	2
Libya	2
Somalia	2
Denmark	1
Ethiopia	1
Kenya	1
Total	44

Figure 6: CTG Global recruitment in April 2018

The data provided by the job advertisement websites UN Jobs and ReliefWeb do enlarge the scope of the data. It is limited in the available information given, but the possibility of using APIs gave the opportunity to work with significant extracts of job advertisements for humanitarian work in a variety of sites, agencies and positions. These two data sources are very likely to overlap, since they are designed for similar audiences. UN Jobs despite its name is not only, not even primarily, focussed on UN job advertisements. It also includes non-humanitarian, diplomatic or development positions. The main common characteristic being they are expatriate work. ReliefWeb works on a similar basis, with a broader number of organisations using their website to advertise.

These overlaps forbid merging the database for analysis. They will be used separately to indicate how the hotspots of the humanitarian workforce can be visualised. This includes the major sites for duty stations, in the North and in the South, the types of jobs and the organisations that operate on the field and HQs.

One should be careful with the publicly available data in representing this workforce. Data provided by the UN does not include, for example contractors of CTG global (GTC Global 2018), an interim agency for the United Nations, or in-kinds, that are lent by other institutions to humanitarian agencies. A sequence of time in the emergency contracting of CTG might show that the urgency to hire personnel might change depending on emergencies, but at any point in time, the recruitment will be directed towards the South in general, and African countries in particular. Consider for example this snapshot of their website in April 2018, where 37 out of 44 positions were for African missions, with 31 positions for South Sudan only (Figure 6).

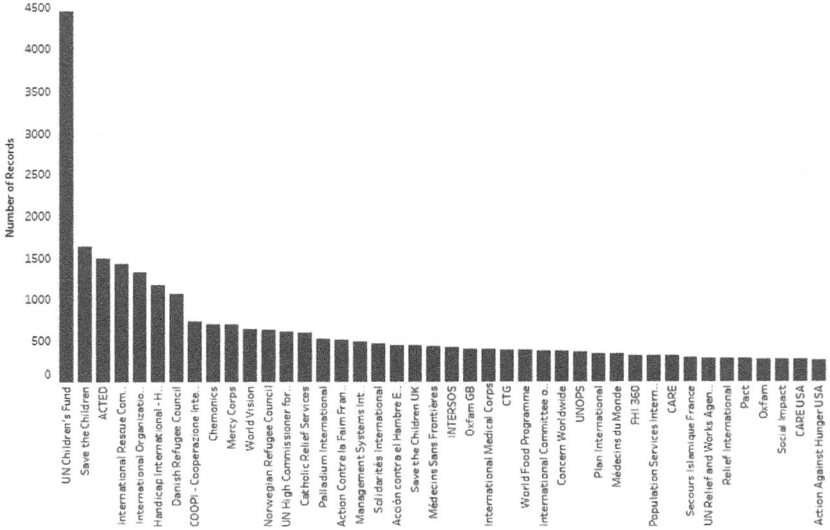

Figure 7: Organisations that have posted 250 or more job advertisement in 2017. Source ReliefWeb

Similar snapshot of the larger humanitarian job advertisement websites, some of which proposes different types of positions for both National and International staff, across many international organisations will allow a more accurate overview of the geographies of aid. The tens of thousands of job postings extracted from ReliefWeb and UN Jobs website indicate some of the major tendencies in the expatriate presence in the field of aid.

These websites represent a relatively global vision of the main players of aid. It is, however, not a perfect picture. Most telling is the relative absence of most of the job advertisement for any of the Red Cross movement branches, either the IFRC and ICRC, or by country. It is however clear that among the first postings are several UN agencies and major iNGOs, while hundreds of organisations offer much smaller number of positions, reflecting the concentration of the humanitarian workforce in relatively few organisations (Figure 7).

The fifty thousand job advertisements posted on ReliefWeb reflect the spatial distribution of these positions thanks to the indication of the "duty station" of staff. Duty stations are cities, towns or villages where staff have their offices when they work on the field. The highest number of job posting for the year 2017 reflects four major clusters in the geographies of aid: Northern countries,

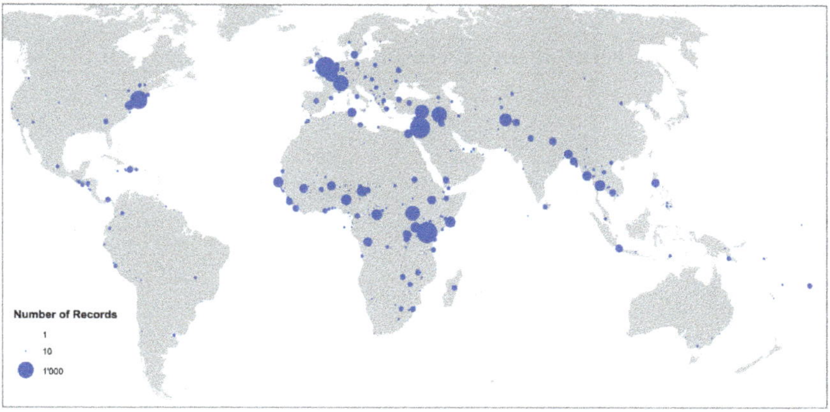

Figure 8: Map of the ReliefWeb duty stations for job advertisements in 2017. Concentric circles indicate the relative importance of each city

where the HQ of most major organisations are located, the South-East Asia, the Middle East and Africa. The mapping of the sites of intervention is relatively close in highlighting which duty stations are the most important across the three datasets (Figure 8). The multiplicity of sites of intervention per aid agencies partially follows internal logics. As Krause notes, the project management methods of the aid industry requires organisations to spread their activities on a number of locations to secure overall funding. Dividing their activities helps aid agencies to guarantee their own financial stability in case an intervention is stopped (Krause 2014).

It is in the North that the relative importance of a number of cities varies the most between NGOs and United Nations, as the comparison of the ranks between the main sites for jobs show. Ten most important duty stations have a relative importance that favours UN HQs in the UN data. The inclusion of NGOs in the calculation (as the UN Jobs and ReliefWeb website do) shows the increasing importance of three major political capitals of the North: Washington, London and Paris, which have a strong NGO history (Figure 9). This presence of major NGOs in Northern capitals is also likely to be linked to the advocacy aims of NGOs structured as transnational networks and their ambitions to be included in the "global governance" formal and informal structures (Hudson 2001).

UN ;Jobs		UN Staff data	
Duty Station	**Number of job advertisements**	**Duty Station**	**Number of UN Staff**
Washington	1916	Geneva	9570
New York	534	New York	8906
London	334	Vienna	3701
Geneva	303	Rome	2963
Paris	274	Nairobi	2593
Nairobi	226	Addis Ababa	1528
San Francisco	215	Bangkok	1439
Kampala	207	Paris	1234
Amman	206	Juba	1194
Abuja	187	Kinshasa	1099

Figure 9: Comparison of the ten most important duty stations between UN Board data (2016) and UN Jobs website (January 2017–April 2018)

3.6.1 UN Board Data: The Classes of Humanitarian Workers

As part of a policy of transparency of data, the "UN Board" distributes lists of its staff disaggregated by duty station, nationality and professional categories. The description given by the UN to the personnel lists that it provides publicly is defined as being part of the UN pension system or long-term employees. As stated on the UN Board website:

> *Staff are defined as (1) all persons participating in the UN Joint Staff Pension Fund (UNJSPF) in accordance with article 21 of the Pension Fund Regulations (i.e. six-month contract or employment) and (2) all "staff members" according to common system definitions (i.e. persons with a contract or employment of one year or more), whether or not they are Pension Fund participants.(UN Board 2017b)*

This means that the personnel listed is the most stable in terms of its contracts. It excludes different types of employees present on field positions, including all short-term contracts. Those constitute an important workforce resource in the case of international aid, as shown on job advertisement platforms, where many jobs are for three to six months. The practice of hiring consultants for eleven-month renewable is also regular practice in UN agencies, as was reported to me by numerous UN employees during research[6]. By the terms and definition

6 Observation Notebook, 20 July 2016.

provided on the website, none of these cases would be integrated in the data analysed here.

The data also excludes in-kind and personnel hired through contractors and other third parties: "[…] those persons who are employed under special contractual arrangements" (UN Board 2017a). This was for example my case when I was working for the UN in Juba during 2016, as well as personnel hired through temporary agencies, such as CTG. It also clearly states that contracting companies hired by the UN are not included in the lists. This particular aspect is not limited to the UN and any company contracted by a humanitarian agency would also be excluded from humanitarian numbers.

UN staff data is disaggregated between Ps and Gs, which represent the two main classes of workers at the UN. As defined by the UN, the "P" categories are "professional and higher categories [which,] entail work that are analytical, evaluative and conceptual duties, and typically require an advanced university degree (Master's degree or equivalent) and relevant work experience." The Ps represent the upper section of the UN social ladder, with higher salaries. They are executives, or "white collars" of the industry. On the other part, the "Gs" are supporting positions, for "procedural, operational or technical" tasks, supporting, "the execution of programmes". The requirement does not include University education, but secondary school (UN Board 2017b).

Data on the personnel is listed either by duty station or by nationality, but not both in the same tables. One sheet shows the number of staff, disaggregated between Gs and Ps, and their nationalities, while the other sheet shows the disaggregation between Gs and Ps in relation to a duty station. This level of aggregation limits the possibility of exploring the relations between the international workforce and the national. It will nevertheless help locate some key trends in the UN workforce. For the clarity of the discussion, I choose to use the official UN regions (UN DGACM 2017) to describe the North-South relationships in the UN workforce. The grouping by UN region allows a description of the key trends in the division of humanitarian labour at the global scale.

3.6.2 Sites and Staff

The first observation is that in the thousands of records, 184 countries have staff working at the UN. The share of the different countries is, however, very variable. Looking at the world share of UN staff shows that the four biggest sites for UN employment are all located in the North, with Switzerland (9726) and the US (9484) having by far the largest numbers, followed by Austria (3903) and Italy

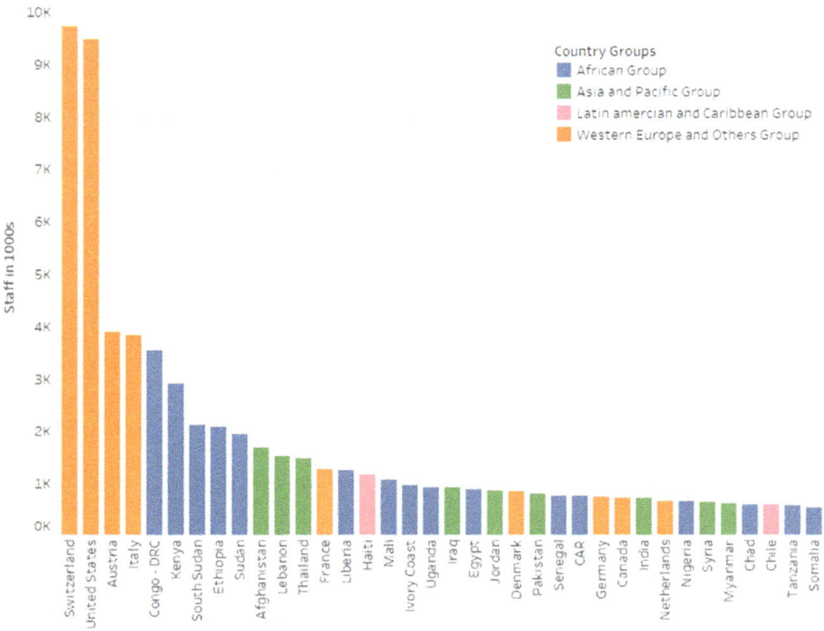

Figure 10: Countries with more than 500 UN staff in 2016. Western countries are represented in orange and African countries in blue

(3846). These countries host headquarters of major UN organisations, which explains the large presence of employees (Figure 10).

The importance of Africa follows immediately in the numbers of employees, as shown by the next five countries, all from the African group. These countries are sites of intervention for humanitarians. Kenya (2913) and Ethiopia (2078) also constitute regional bases for the activities of UN agencies, with many Somalia operations directed from Kenya.

Sites of intervention have a large proportion of "G" status for humanitarian personnel. Duty stations in Africa have a much larger number of Gs than professionals. The fact that African countries require a number of personnel to implement the programmes explains this proportion. Headquarters have a much larger proportion of executives, while sites concentrate personnel to implement (Figure 11).

In the major headquarters of international aid, such as Geneva and New York have, the G/P ratio shows much higher number of executives. This ratio is the

Country Groups	Staff	Gs	Prof
African Group	28320	21305	7015
Western European and Others Group	25960	9724	16236
Asia-Pacific Group	17597	11655	5942
Latin American and Caribbean Group	6544	4110	2434
Eastern European Group	4296	2152	2144
Other	385	229	156

Figure 11: Number of UN employees per country group and status in 2016

inverse in the case of sites of interventions, where the "G"s are more numerous. This reflects the importance of having staff to implement on the field and the prominence of analysts and programming at the global level. This relation shows eloquently that the North-South divide has the organisation HQs directing from the North the types of response to bring in the South, and especially Africa.

Nairobi duty station is the only major UN HQ that has a predominance of the Gs (1490 G/1103 P). This is due to the specific place of Kenya in the UN system, which is both a major HQ and a site of intervention. It is the Global HQ for UNEP and UN-Habitat, for example, and the East African Regional HQ for many UN agencies, including Unicef and WFP. Major refugee camps for the Somalian and South Sudanese conflict are located in Kenyan territory. The UN also operates within Kenya, particularly in poverty reduction, education and other programmes (Kemoni and Ngulube 2008).

The data on the nationalities of the Gs and Ps are also a valuable look at the relation of work between white and blue collars at the global level. A tabular join between nationalities and duty stations permits a scatterplot of the G-workers (Figure 6). Linking Duty station and Nationality tables show the close correspondence between the number of African G workers and the total number of G staff at duty stations. Not all Gs positions are from the local workforce in the different duty stations. As shown eloquently in the example of Switzerland, most G positions in the country are not covered by Swiss citizens. In the case of Africa, however, the relationship between the nationality and the country of the duty station of G staff is almost perfectly linear. This witnesses that most Gs working in African countries come from the country where the aid programmes are implemented. The same chart shows that the picture is quite different for all other groups (Figure 12).

As for the P staff, the picture does not compare. At the continental group level, the dominance of executive positions within the UN system by the "Western

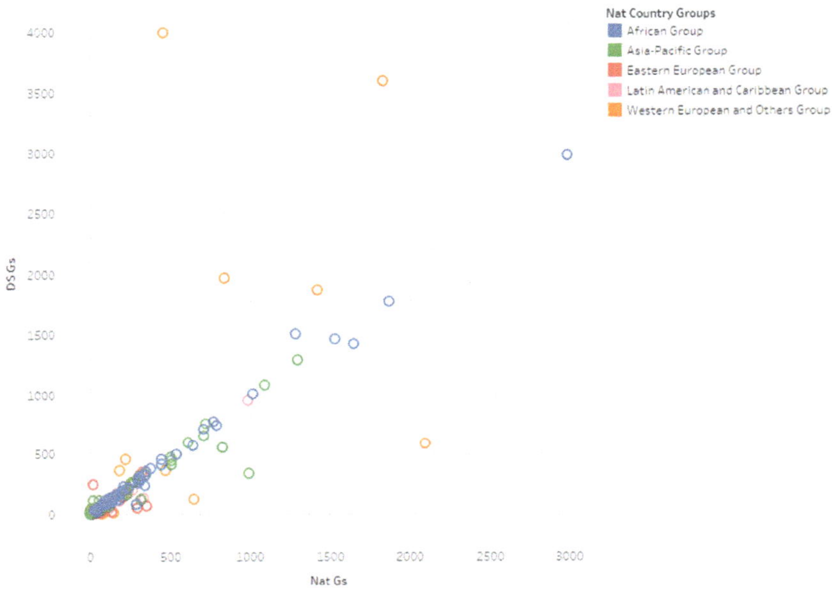

Figure 12: Countries of duty stations (Y axis) and staff nationalities (X axis), in 2016. Linking Duty station and Nationality tables show the close correspondence between the number of African G workers and the total number of G staff at duty stations

European and others" is the most evident. The UN Board data shows the ratio between Gs and Ps, as levels of qualification in both duty station and as the provenance of the staff. The data is very eloquent in showing the domination of the North in the field of international aid. The vast majority of decision-making and analytical position are for the North, and the implementation is mostly for the South.

In this light, the international aid industry reproduces to some level ancient colonial relationship, although this picture should be taken with a degree of nuance, since Africans constitute the second contingent of executive professionals in the UN system. Switching from the domination of the different colonial powers on their colonies, the workforce data indicates in this case a relationship where the major trend is domination from the North, "Western Europe and Others" over the African group. The importance of the three other groups are relatively small, in absolute numbers, but also more ambiguous in the proportion between the decision and execution positions (Figure 13).

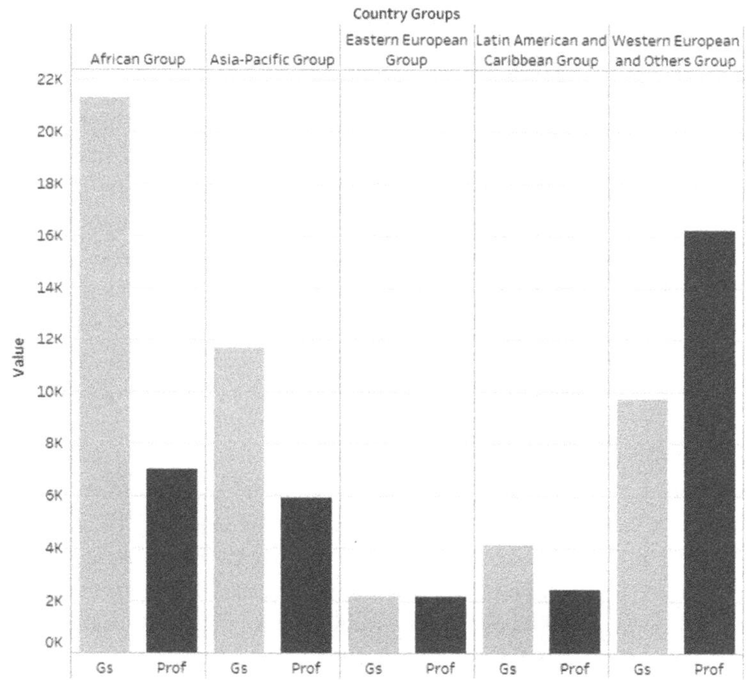

Figure 13: Country groups and the number of G and P staff in 2016

Considering its continuous Northern domination, is the aid industry a renewed and rebranded form of colonialism? It is striking both in the relation of the workforce and the sites where the aid industry operates that the power relations are largely inherited from the colonial domination of Africa. However, this perspective does not account for a critique of aid in its own rights and wrongs. It is arguable that many of the policies implemented by the aid industry reflect in a Northern political, economic, and cultural domination, which originated in colonialism. Nevertheless, current power relations that international aid induces, both in terms of programming and in the structure of its workforce belong to the contemporary World. The critique of the aid industry as reproducing colonialism is partly valid, but insufficient.

To nuance this critique of humanitarian aid, this I will propose a picture of the workforce that follows current trends in the structure of the industry. The international workforce of the aid industry is not homogenous. Although Northern countries dominate largely executive positions, some level of inclusion of the

South is present. Structural and historical reasons help to explain the importance of Northern countries in the field of humanitarian aid, as large modern humanitarian organisations are born in the North (Ryfman 2016). International aid is structured by job markets characterised by domination by Northern upper and middle class. However, the social structure of the humanitarian field witnesses an increasing importance of Southern executives, and Africans in particular, in the humanitarian workforce. Aside the stable career contracts, the aid technoscape relies largely on short-term contracts and the flexibility of this workforce, where it regularly moves from place to place. In that sense, it constructs a transnational field that crosses national borders. Finally, let us note that a wide local workforce supports the implementation of aid programmes. The local workforce is subordinated to the international aid workers in the hierarchy and under much lower salaries.

Websites of job offers illustrate how much the international staff comes at executive positions. Out of the fifty thousand averts retrieved from ReliefWeb, more than six thousand mention the position as "manager" in the job description, more than 10 % of the total. Another three thousand are designed for "directors" and two thousand more for "chiefs" or "leaders". Positions for local staff, national officers, interns or assistants combine fewer than a thousand entries of the total. The share of executive positions in job advertisements demonstrates how much the aid industry relies on expatriates with high cultural capital and connections, and how much this type of positions structures the control of international aid distribution under expatriates.

The reproduction of the Northern humanitarian workforce can be related to job descriptions fitted to the North and largely to men (Hyndman 2000). As part of hiring policies, aid organisations have introduced measures to balance the North-South equilibrium in international organisations, such as the "affirmative action" in recruitment processes. As is standard in all UN recruitment platforms, UN Jobs lists this reminder in all job postings:

> *Qualified female applicants and qualified nationals of non-and under-represented member countries are encouraged to apply.*
>
> *Persons with disabilities are equally encouraged to apply.(UN Jobs 2018)*

At the macro level, these measures have more the effect of limiting an unbalanced process of socio-spatial reproduction rather than changing the structural causes. Their effects are limited.

The implementation of international aid programmes in countries of the Global South relies on the local workforce for two separate types of tasks. Clerical jobs, from university trained personnel and manual work, or less skilled work.

Typically pertaining to this category are drivers, but also the cleaners and other types of low qualification jobs. The time duration of the mission will bring these two categories of local workers in two different directions. Clerical jobs have the potential to be raised to international (Hyndman 2000). Local employees are paid according to salary grids of the country of intervention. Often well paid by the local standards, they are also quite low compared to the salaries of the international employees, whose salaries are indexed to the North.

The lower part of the local workforce will not have a chance to raise to international. While dependent on the international aid for their current job, they have an impact on the local economy, but are not part of the aid technoscape in the sense of constituting part of the transnational workforce as with the more skilled and clerical categories of employees. The possibility of working for the international aid industry is dependent on the duration of the mission for the blue collars.

From the part of the national clerical employees, there is, however, the prospect of building an international career in the long term. Many international employees coming from the South started working for the aid industry under a national contract before starting missions in other countries, under international contracts. This does not appear in the data tables, although it is the most often heard story from the non-Nothern aid workers. Indeed, the relative precariat of many workers in the aid sector tends to discourage employees from the North. However, in the case of aid workers from the South, the conditions are often considered better than local private or public contracts (Korff et al. 2015).

This high turnover of the lower part of the executive white collars represents one of the crucial aspects of the relation between the aid workforce and the environment in which they work. Aid workers cross this environment formed of clusters of duty stations in which the aid industry directs funds and personnel in short time rotations. These networks of places and employees are the primary elements of the field of humanitarian aid. From this structure of the technoscape of aid, social relations to the local environment are held from the dominant position and the gaze of the executive professional.

3.6.3 Highlight on Capital Cities

The geographies of aid are differentiated and follow specific spatial logic at the scale of the countries of intervention. The African continent constitutes one of the major sites of international humanitarian intervention, with a number of armed conflicts driving in the presence of aid. At the scale of the countries, location of aid workers overwhelmingly concentrates in capital cities. The examination of

Country	Number of duty stations	Percentage of positions in the capital
Ivory Coast	4	85.4
Kenya	139	64
Mali	26	57
South Sudan	118	55.7

Figure 14: Number of duty stations per country in 2017. Percentage of positions in the capital. Many positions also include some postings in the capital. Source ReliefWeb

staff data in Kenya, South Sudan, Mali and Ivory Coast illustrates quite well the structure of aid presence in the four countries visited for this research.

Humanitarian missions in the cities of Nairobi, Juba, Bamako and Abidjan have variable importance in size of staff. Using the UN Board data and ReliefWeb job advertisements it is apparent that the relative importance of each city in terms of international presence is congruent. Within the general numbers of aid presence, the most important postings are Kenya/Nairobi and South Sudan/Juba, which concentrates most humanitarian staff among the four case studies.

One major difference in the relative importance of each city between the two datasets is the place of Ivory Coast/Abidjan, which is relatively more significant in terms of UN staff presence than overall humanitarian jobs. This difference is likely explained by the fact that the humanitarian response in the country is decreasing and few new positions are offered. The data reflects the overwhelming presence of the staff (national and international) in the capital cities. In all cases, the number of staff based in the capital exceeds all other postings in the country. With regards to the presence of humanitarian workers in a country, HQ duty stations are likely to be the places where their influence is the greatest.

ReliefWeb data illustrates patterns of spatial repartition within each country. The case of Kenya shows that apart of Nairobi, which hosts most expatriate workers, all other postings are in the refugee camps spread in the country. The numbers of duty stations within each country indicate a degree of staff repartition, which is unequal depending on the country and crisis (Figure 14).

The number of duty stations is misleading to assess the degree of repartition of staff within the country. The concentration of staff in each of the capitals exceeds largely the total of all other duty stations in the country. The table also includes positions that are partly in the capital and partly in the field. Humanitarian workers are thereby even more present in the capitals than the percentage of staff suggests. The case of Kenya and South Sudan show that out of more than

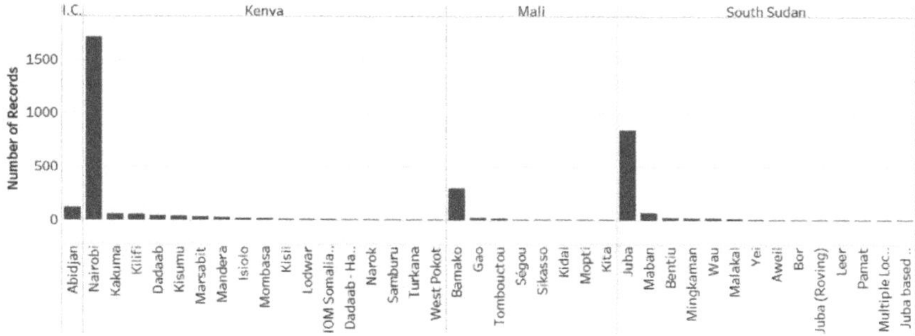

Figure 15: ReliefWeb job postings in 2017. Duty stations with fewer than five positions have been removed to keep the chart within the page

hundred duty stations in a country, the capital still concentrates a large majority of international staff by itself. Charts make apparent the dominant positions of the capitals in absolute numbers, as well as in the fact that no other duty station in any given country of the group has even a tenth of the number of staff in the country HQ. This predominance of the capital in the country-scale geography of aid illustrates the spatial distribution of international agencies policies centred on capitals (Figure 15).

Unlike cities, staff repartition in a country does not follow a rank-size law of Zipf (Soo 2005). As observations of the relation between the rank and size of cities in terms of population show that, despite variations between countries, settlements' population sizes worldwide tend to evolve logarithmically from smallest to largest. Instead, humanitarian staff repartition follows a Pareto distribution, where capitals concentrate most employees. The fact that the population in cities or regions are not related to the geography of aid, apart from the capital reflects well that humanitarian organisations have specific spatial practices. The mission of international organisations to respond to crises (and not population numbers) only explains part of this spatial repartition. Humanitarian policies and practices play the largest role in the geography of aid presence.

The institutional and programmatic structure of aid organisations organises the presence of humanitarian staff as overwhelmingly concentrated in the capitals and much smaller contingents in the rest of the country. A number of factors explain this concentration, although it seems difficult to decide which are the most influential. Among other factors, security policies push organisations to keep staff grouped as humanitarian access is restricted by risks for staff safety (Stoddard and Jillani 2016; Stoddard et al. 2017). Humanitarian policies and

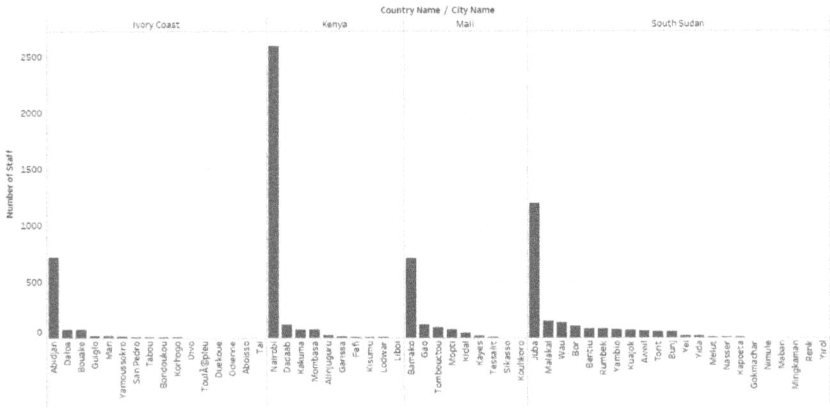

Figure 16: UN Board data on UN staff in the different countries, in 2016

practice also favours staff concentration in relation to logistics and administration. In particular, they require access to transport and communication networks (S. Gupta, Sahay, and Charan 2016). Humanitarian agencies have a large administrative, and more generally clerical, component in missions whose work does not justify posting on the field. An increase in a number of desk tasks and creation of new types of positions, such as monitoring and evaluation (M&E) in humanitarian and development policies and practice has marked an evolution of the field for two decades (Mosse and Lewis 2005; Duffield 2014). Although, other factors also partly explain the staff repartition, it is notable that security policies largely participate to the spatial distribution of humanitarian organisations at the country level.

UN staff is more concentrated than the humanitarian community as a whole, as the former holds permanent staff only on a limited number of locations (Figure 16). The UN Board dataset tends to confirm the analysis of geographic spread linked with risk policies, logistics, and administrative positions. As the UN data allows a breakdown by professional categories between expatriates and local staff, it illustrates how the proportion of local G staff increases in cities where overall staff reduces. The example of South Sudan – similar to other countries[7] – illustrates that both the absolute numbers and the proportions of expatriates among staff are the highest in the capital (Figure 17).

7 There are some exceptions to this rule. For instance, the Democratic Republic of Congo has two main bases for international staff. As a result, the city of Goma, in the east of

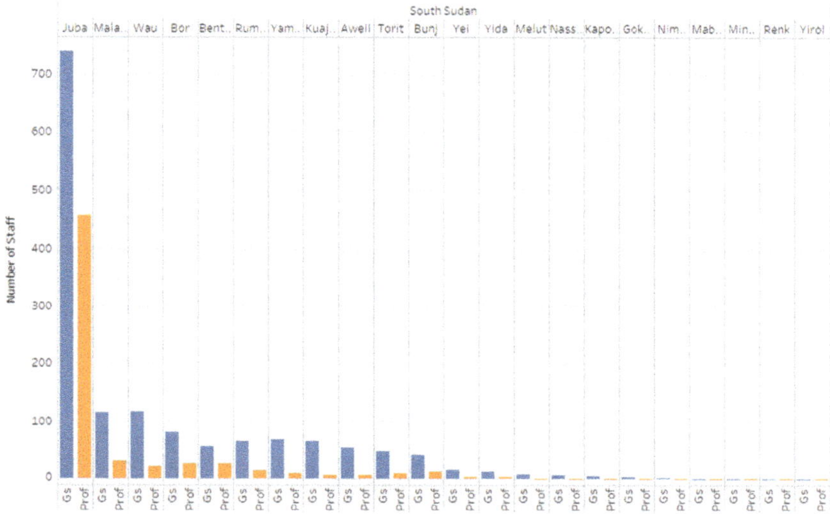

Figure 17: G staff categories proportion increase in duty stations with less overall staff. This example (only showing South Sudan for space and clarity) is similar to other countries (2016)

This overview of the staff data repartition between the cities of Bamako, Juba, Nairobi and Abidjan is useful to understand the geographies of aid in two perspectives. In the comparison between the case studies, it illustrates that the four capital cities hold different numbers of staff reflecting either the importance of the mission or at least of a particular stage of the humanitarian presence. The numbers inside of each country, in turn, demonstrate the overwhelming importance of capital cities in hosting humanitarian staff.

3.7 Security Gaze

Does the international aid have a vision for the use of space? This section examines different types of written and other preparatory documents that aim to prepare and guide aid employees and employers in their missions. In this section, I have taken advantage of the propensity of organisations to distribute reports and other types of data through their website to constitute a corpus of texts reflecting

the country, has comparable humanitarian presence to the political capital Kinshasa. Apart of rare cases of dual HQ, the staff statistics follows a similar Pareto distribution.

some level of representativeness of the aid community, including UN, Red Cross and iNGOs. The key documents selected in the corpus are produced by major international aid organisations, such as OCHA, and major INGOs, similarly to the Stay and Deliver report, which is often presented as the analytical authority for security in the humanitarian field (Baas 2017). Other documents are more practical and have a direct effect because they involve contractual obligations of either organisations or employees. The following sections will discuss security manuals coming from diverse organisation. These documents present a relatively homogenous documentation, with diverse emphasis on one or the other understanding of security. Finally, the Codes of Conduct also have a contractual liability and present ethical guildelines for the aid industry.

3.7.1 Strategic Papers, Research and Policy Documents

Strategic papers on security in humanitarian operations all seem to recognise a contradiction in the aim of providing humanitarian aid in conflict environment and the security of its staff. These documents constitute the product as much as the synthesis of the struggles within organisations between the security and humanitarian wings of humanitarian organisations (Beerli 2018). The struggles to play security against access can be understood as disputes between programmatic and security wings, but also partly between HQ and field workers. The fields of aid and security have witnessed changes of philosophy in recent decades balancing the power of humanitarian programming and security. According to Stay and Deliver report, the "bunkerisation" phase of the aid industry, which subordinated all humanitarian operation to the needs of security is over:

> *One of the most important conceptual shifts in humanitarian operational security thinking in recent years, particularly affecting the UN agencies, is the enabling approach. This approach inverts the previous model—that identified risks and limited activities accordingly—and instead focusses on programme goals—aiming to identify all possible measures to allow for secure delivery against those goals. The approach requires a significant change in mindset for some security managers and officers who must begin to think in terms of 'how to stay' as opposed to 'when to leave'.* (Egeland, Harmer, and Stoddard 2011)

Security policies may diverge, but the base of their rationale relies on the understanding of risk management as a response to an increase in violence against aid workers since the 1990s (Duffield 2012b). The exact response to violence may diverge in time and depending on organisations, but they commonly take their legitimacy in the belief of unprecedented levels of violence against aid workers.

As noted by Dandoy and Pérouse (Dandoy and Montclos 2013) and Beerli (Beerli 2017), the use of statistics on violence is largely used as arguments by either security or programmatic side of the organisations. The quantified claims of an increasing violence against aid workers have led to a greater power of security over operations. In the same movement, verticality in the hierarchical relations within organisation increased, with HQs increasing their control over field operations. Whereas a greater autonomy was granted at the field level in the past, humanitarians notice a tighter remote control of their operations by the sieges.

The perspective of security management has been adopted by the whole industry, following distinct but parent practises. According to Patrick Brugger, an ICRC security delegate, most humanitarian organisations share a common set of principles for security. All humanitarian organisation hold their specificity in their action on the field, such as the principle of "Acceptance" for the ICRC, but more importantly have a common ground for security, that are "adopted by most organisations or multinational corporations to protect their staff" (Brugger 2009). While the author aims to distinguish the specific emphasis of the ICRC, he notes that organisations understand broadly security from the same perspective: protecting staff while allowing programme to pursue. This security perspective offers an equally diverse but broadly similar vision of the spaces in which they intervene.

Commissioned by OCHA in 2011, the Stay and deliver (Egeland, Harmer, and Stoddard 2011) report aims to "offer an analysis of the broader challenges to securing humanitarian action and recommends areas for improvement." The broad scope of these documents puts it apart from a security manual, in different ways. It aims not only to give a day-to-day response to security threats, but more largely to design a security strategy in line with the humanitarian objectives of the aid community. The discussion on the "good practices" was reassessed five years later by the publication of another document also commissioned by OCHA, noting progress and proposing recommendations for the future deployments (A. Jackson and Zyck 2017).

Research and policy documents constitute a class of documents in themselves, its authority stemming from diverse sources of legitimacy. This legitimacy may come from fitting with the general goal of an organisation, or the methods used to produce the presented knowledge. Quantitative analysis constitutes most often the prime argument to gain scientific aura. Based on research these documents build their authority on the force of numbers in presenting an overview of the security situation in quantitative data. They also aim to include the perception of aid workers through the construction and analysis of questionnaires.

The arguments of these documents follow the logic of the "moral panic" described by Dandoy. These documents reflect the impression of an unprecedented assault against humanitarian workers that stems from the chaos following the Cold War (Dandoy 2014). However, they also claim to put a distance in relation to "bunkerisation". Bunkerisation aims to describe and characterise the tendency of the aid industry to rely on security apparatuses and procedures that separate the humanitarians from the local environment. The presence of this critique in policy documents of international aid might be analysed in different ways.

Policy papers and reports represent the stated ambition of the aid community, rather than the actual practice. This discrepancy builds the legitimacy of the industry, in stating its awareness of a specific issue (bunkerisation), while leaving the actual practice to the operational side. A radical understanding in the discrepancy between policy and operation by Mosse, states that policy documents are in fact voluntarily kept as separated as possible from the operations of an organisation. Policy documents in that regard has the goal and effect of working only internally as a legitimation device: "development policy ideas are important less for what they say than for whom they bring together; what alliances, coalitions and consensuses they allow, both within and between organisations" (Mosse 2005). It states internally its understanding of issues raised by operations, but does not involve modification in policy implementation. A more nuanced vision of the relation between policy/research documents and actual practice can be that the production of documents critical to the functioning of the organisation can give a general guideline not to go too far in one direction. It does not aim at actually changing the practice. But it presents a referential of possible course of action to frame the practice between acceptable possibilities.

The recognition of bunkerisation through internal critique thus has the paradoxical effect of legitimising it as a non-ideal, but possible implementation when deemed necessary. The critical outlook towards "bunkerisation" does not mean the abandonment of security devices:

> *A protection approach uses protective devices and procedures to reduce vulnerability to a threat, but does not affect the threat itself. In security terms this is called 'hardening the target'. Although UN agencies rely on protection measures more heavily than NGOs do, some forms of additional protective measures will be required by most international entities in insecure settings (if only to prevent opportunistic crime).(A. Jackson and Zyck 2017)*

Stay and Deliver proposes different approaches of relative discretion, remote programming and other acceptance strategies. The alternative to "bunkerisation" in a "protection" approach is mainly in limiting the visibility of the security devices and procedure to both humanitarians and the local population. One option is to bring "discreet security measures", while the other relies on "international enclaves with restricted traffic access" (A. Jackson and Zyck 2017).

Generic policy documents produced on security present a first level of the management of space. They offer general recommendations and orientations, overarching the second level of security manuals, which not only presents the general policy of an organisation, but also offer a first procedural step towards the actual implementation.

3.7.2 Security Manuals

Humanitarian organisations have produced a variety of security manuals since the 1990s. This trend follows the widely held belief that humanitarian agencies have come under increasing threats when operating on the field. While the risks that aid workers take are certainly true, the perception of humanitarians under unprecedented threats has been criticised from the inside and the outside of the aid industry, in particular in their reliance on poorly defined statistics (Dandoy 2014; Fast 2014). This perception was strong enough to stimulate the production of specialised manuals and encouraging the professionalisation of security within humanitarian organisations. The generic security manual produced by ECHO, the European Union humanitarian body, grounded its legitimacy on "a widespread perception of escalating threats to aid workers and their programmes", by humanitarian organisations (ECHO 2006, p. 11).

This production of a security literature for humanitarians claims different levels of authority over the security and humanitarian personnel. The ECHO guide states clearly that not only should professionals use its manual in conjunction with other security framework documents but also that its authority is limited: "The advice it offers may be inappropriate in some circumstances and in some cases could even place people at risk of death or injury. Its contents should be modified and adapted as appropriate, to suit the needs of particular organisations and situations." (ECHO 2006, p. 1). Ultimately, the authority on security pertains to the organisation. Other documents present a much more authoritative tone than this generic synthesis by the EU humanitarian funding body.

In fact, organisation security manuals state clearly that the security instructions are not optional. As one major NGO directed in the late 1990s: "World Vision's senior management [...] expect full compliance with these policies by all World Vision personnel." (Rogers and Sytsma 1999, p. xi). This categorical instruction aims to make the risk management policy of the organisation accepted in its application of two ways. First, security manuals present the diversity of techniques to sustain the security of humanitarian employees from a risk management perspective as efficient, justified and mandatory. Second, manuals commit humanitarian employees, to integrate and actively apply security recommendations, as being part of the overall safety net.

Security manuals aim not only to submit employees to security rules, but to integrate them, and their behaviour, as part of the security infrastructure, as World Vision states: "Even with the protection provided through a carefully created security profile, field workers are vulnerable. This is especially true of international staff. For this reason, each World Vision staff member must view security as an individual responsibility." (Rogers and Sytsma 1999, p. 13). The statement of World Vision shows a shift in the perception of danger relative to the provenance of staff. It is now widely considered that in fact national employees are the vast majority of casualties, death and injuries in humanitarian operations (Stoddard, Abby; Harmer, Adele; Haver 2011). Nevertheless, the overall spirit of this statement remains two decades later the motto of aid industry security: security is the concern of all employees.

Security manuals of the different organisations embrace a relatively close understanding of the notion of risk. The IFRC manual, for example states that security goes through: "determining the risks facing the operation [and] developing effective security plans that will mitigate these risks" (IFRC 2011). Risk management as used by aid organisations follow the equation that "risk" is the relation a between the "likelihood" of an event and its "impact", the severity of the damage it may cause. The risk matrix ranks all types of risks from "low" to "extreme" and the place of said risk informs the course of action to take.

The security manuals present the safety and security strategies following a triptych of "acceptance, protection and deterrence" (ARC International 2004, p. 9–10). Acceptance refers to the reduction of the threats by the acceptance from the local communities. The strategy of acceptance goes through different levels of communication with the local communities, to explain the scopes of the programmes. It also aims to give the impression to local communities that aid organisations are well integrated. As the ICRC puts it: "The image of the organisation is potentially damaged by clearly identifiable vehicles being parked outside a five-star hotel when local beneficiaries are suffering […]" (IFRC 2011, p. 17).

Acceptance may go against some of the other recommendations of "protection" which aims at making harder potential threats to reach the aid workers. Protection aims to separate from the threat, but may also separate from the local environment, typically with the use of barbed wire and sandbags.

The last pillar of security, "deterrence" aims at posing a counter threat. It is widely recognised that its implementation in humanitarian settings is often problematic and can send mixed messages. The NGO ARC recognises for example that the presence of armed guards is the most controversial aspects: "Use of armed guards may send conflicting messages about ARC's humanitarian mandate. It may also put ARC's neutrality into question, thus jeopardising its being accepted by the community it is trying to reach." (ARC International 2004, p. 11).

The first level of territoriality reflected in security manuals is the institutional relation between the state and international organisations. The legitimacy of the authority of the state is explicitly recognised and states are considered the responsible for public order and the safety of aid workers. This relation is nevertheless questioned on an efficiency ground when states are not considered entirely able to protect aid organisations (United Nations 2006, p. 19).

At the level of the organisation on a duty station, the hierarchy of security transfers the highest responsibility for security to expatriates:

> *Field Security Officer is usually an international staff ("expat") designated by [Country Director] to serve as the field focal point for all safety and security-related matters impacting on a specific country program, activity, or operation. A local staff may function as [Field Security Officer] and [Local Security Officer].(ARC International 2004, p. 3)*

Beyond institutional questions of security, security manual points specifically to types of spatial relations in movement and immobility. Travels outside or inside a city constitute the essential issues concerning movement. The car is considered safest transport in most manuals. Walking is rarely advised: "never walking alone, driving rather than walking, or walking with body guards, are all measures to reduce the risk" (Brabant and Institute 2010). In some cases, a more holistic approach to safety in movement is advised. Walking may "help increase exposure to the community and build acceptance, dispelling the image of the privileged aid worker taking a vehicle everywhere" (Macpherson and Pafford 1999). Most of the time, however, the car is not just recommended, but mandatory.

3.7.3 UN Field Security Handbook

The *UN Field Security Handbook* presents the requirements and recommendations for UN field security and staff worldwide. As a general, mostly decontextualised document, the *Handbook* presents a "System-wide Arrangements for the Protection of United Nations Personnel and Property in the Field". That is, from the most generic perspective an overview of the political aspect of guaranteeing security of the field as well as its practical aspects of securing the personnel in countries.

The handbook reviews the many aspects of safety and security from the macro perspective. It relates to different generic themes, that may be explicitly spatial or not, material or procedural. Procedures define the hierarchies and the chains of decision that affect the management of security in times of crisis separately than normal times. Large parts of the handbook are also dedicated to describing the effects of specific security situations on contracts. Lastly, the standard equipment comprises communication devices as well as the means of travel and protective equipment, for buildings and for personal.

Nowhere does the relation between space and the discipline of aid workers in security is stronger than the UN Field Security Handbook. In addition, nowhere is the discipline of aid workers emphasised as much as in the case of the MORSS residential standards, whose outlines are defined in the Handbook. The residential standards for UN workers stipulate the necessity for the UN to have a defined set of standards that must be accepted by all employees. Interestingly, the Handbooks reflect the worry that newcomers may not be ready to have the Department of Security overlook fully their housing:

> *Newly assigned staff members to the duty station should routinely be advised that security is one of the most important criteria in the selection of a place to live and they should be encouraged to seek accommodation which offers the necessary guarantees of safety and accessibility in case of emergency.(United Nations 2006, p. 19)*

The residential standard implies that employees be given financial support for renting their house. The handbook makes it also clear towards finance officers

> *Staff members responsible for certifying the "reasonableness" of accommodation for the purpose of the rental subsidy scheme should consider this [MORSS compliance] a most important factor. The importance of adequate communications (telephone) and residential protection should be emphasised.*

The UN understanding of the residential standards presents the two main reasons for breaching the recommendations as being either the naïvety of youth or the avarice of finance officers. If the importance of compliance to residential standards is not clear enough, the hierarchy should step in:

> *Failure to comply with advice given should be brought to the immediate attention of the agency Headquarters.*

The MORSS may be very different depending on the duty station. While the MORSS compliance and discipline are everywhere the same, the specificity of its application varies between duty stations and the security phases, ranked 1 to 5 from lowest to highest risk. Within the bounds of the security levels system, the Security Management Team (SMT) has the responsibility to "conduct of a threat and risk assessment for the duty station, to include all locations where staff members are deployed and resident", and security equipment should follow (United Nations 2006, p. 19).

As for offices, the protection measures must be hard. “Perimeter integrity is a function of the threat which in the case of Terrorism requires, in some cases, extreme counter measures”, states the UN handbook. As a result, the recommended equipment to ensure “perimeter integrity” include sandbags, razor wires and other fencing. The guards and the supervision of the DSS ensure the integrity of the overall security apparatus (United Nations 2006, p. 23).

3.7.4 Codes of Conduct and the Non-Spatial Ethics of International Aid

The “codes of conduct” present an ethic of international aid, and may vary in its sense depending on international organisations. The umbrella name of “code of conduct” may refer to a variety of documents that have a very different scope and aim. They can, however, be grouped together in the sense that they represent the attempt to write a formalised ethic of humanitarian interventions (P. Walker 2005)[8].

This formalisation of the ethics of humanitarian intervention started in the 1990s with the development of the Red Cross’ *Code of Conduct*. This document presented in broad terms, discusses ten aspects of the commitment of the Red Cross movement (IFRC 1994). This document was in its inception a document designed for organisations, the IFRC-ICRC and the national societies of Red Cross and Crescents. The *Code of Conduct* is a guideline for the organisation. It presents a humanitarian policy, rather than the orientation these codes take ten years later, as moral guidelines for employees.

Other documents listed under the “code of conduct” are typically used by UN agencies, and refer to the way an agency should deal with their suppliers. These documents aim to ensure that contractors with the UN respect certain standards in human rights – in particular in the case of various ILO labour rights conventions- and protection of the environment (UNDP 2013).

In recent years, the code of conduct has started being used to refer to the individual behaviour, rather than organisation policy. The Red Cross movement has started issuing a specific Staff codes, aiming at bringing the responsibilities of

8 Among those « Code of Conduct » the 2017 attempt by the Italian state to standardise rescue operations in the Mediterranean under its own political priorities divided the NGO participating in sea rescue operations. However, this specific document does not belong to the same type as those discussed here, since it is imposed from a state and its purpose is to subordinate humanitarian aid to the priorities of Italian state (Euronews 2017).

employees towards beneficiaries, and the local population in general. This individualisation of the codes of conduct aims to direct the employees' behaviour on missions within the bounds of an ethical framework that reflects positively on the organisation and purports to align moral standards of the humanitarian discourse. Scandals of diverse forms of abuse of the local population have triggered this policy trend, with mixed concrete results (Allais 2011).

I have selected twelve documents titled code of conducts by different organisations, pertaining to the galaxy of international aid: UN, NGO, Red Cross, government organisations. All the documents below have been made public by the organisations on their website (Figure 18).

What appears clearly in the grouping of documents, using lexicometric tools and Reinert classification method (Reinert 1990), is that, even within the group of personal ethical documents, organisations' concerns are different and may change in time. The key themes standing out of the documents and shared across organisations are harassment and sexual abuse, respect of the beneficiaries and the rejection of criminal activities (Figure 19). While all stress the reputational risks for the organisation along the goals of humanitarian aid, some organisations are very explicit on the potential sanctions in the breach of the code. Serious breaches with the code might mean, at least in theory, termination of contract.

Among codes for staff, broad common themes emerge from the corpus of documents. The Reinert descending classification (Figure 19) shows five main themes emerging in three groups: The first is the prohibition of sexual abuse, in particular relating to beneficiaries and children. Another group aims at presenting rules against criminal activities, with a focus on corruption. Lastly, the codes insist on the programmatic aspects of humanitarian ethics. This last category fit to the definition of the first Red Cross code. These recommendations are diversely used in staff codes of conduct, and organisations tend to separate the personal and organisational ethics in their most recent documents, similarly to the Red Cross and UN's practice.

Grouped together, many of the codes of conduct for staff resemble strongly each other, seemingly almost copy-pasted from one to another. Consider for example, how the following organisations prohibit in similar manner and language sexual activities with children:

Year of Publication	Organisation	Title
1994	International Federation of the Red Cross and Red Crescent Societies (IFRC)	Code of Conduct in Disaster Relief
2004	United Nations High Commissioner for Refugees (UNHCR)	Code of Conduct
2007	Danish Refugee Council (DRC)	Danish Refugee Council Code of Conduct
2007	International Federation of the Red Cross and Red Crescent Societies (IFRC)	Staff Code of Conduct
2008	Swiss Development Cooperation (SDC)	Code of Conduct for SDC Employees and Partners
2010	International Rescue Comitee (IRC)	The IRC Way: Standards for Professional Conduct
2011	Save the Children (SCI)	Code of Ethics and Business Conduct
2012	Oxfam	Oxfam's Joint Code of Conduct Code of Conduct: Standards and Values
2012	United Nations Ethics Office	Putting Ethics To Work A Guide for UN Staff
2013	United Nations Development Programme (UNDP)	UN Supplier Code of Conduct
2017	Oxfam	Oxfam's Joint Code of Conduct Code of Conduct: Standards and Values
2017	Oxfam	Oxfam Non-Staff Code of Conduct
2017	Swedish Civil Contingencies Agency (MSB)	Code of Conduct – International operations

Figure 18: List of organisations and Codes of Conduct for international operations

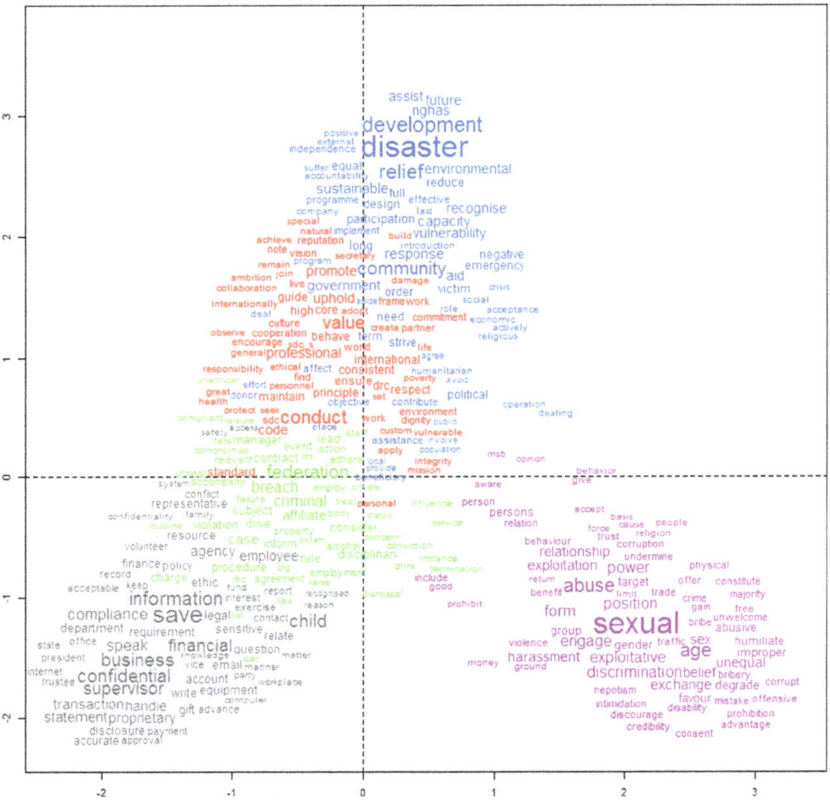

Figure 19: Staff Codes of Conducts and the five main themes using Reinert's descending classification

CRS *Sexual activity with children (persons under the age of 18) is prohibited regardless of the age of majority or age of consent locally. Mistaken belief in the age of a child is not a defense*

DRC *I will not engage in sexual activity with children under the age of 18. Mistaken belief in the age of the child does not constitute a defence.*

IFRC *[I will] Not engage in any sexual activity with persons (adult or child) that look to or benefit from the Federation's protection or assistance, or with any persons under the age of 18 years, regardless of the age of majority or consent locally (mistaken belief in the age of a child is not a defence).*

SCI *Sexual activity with children (persons under the age of 18) is prohibited regardless of the local age of majority or age of consent. Mistaken belief in the age of a child is not a defense.*

This similarity, and many other in the phrasing of ethics suggests that the aid industry, whether NGO, GO, UN works in theory from standardised morals, at the very least considering a series of aspects. The first thing to appear in the staff code of conducts is the prominence of directives relating to sexual abuses, in different ways. Children abuse as seen above is strictly forbidden in what seems to be a specificity of humanitarian aid as an employer. Indeed, employers do not normally ask their employees to refrain from sexual abuse. The insistence of humanitarian organisations in pointing to the prohibition of child abuse reflects important problems relating to humanitarian aid.

The relation of power of the aid workers working in countries in crisis is sufficiently strong that it may allow events that would normally be entirely in the hands of the state, if said state is able and willing to ensure the safety from abuse to vulnerable populations. In this sense, this eloquently shows a difference in the relative powers at stake. More specifically, codes of conducts point that along with harassment, exchanging humanitarian support for foods or goods are prohibited. All these warnings, which again would seem strange in most industries, stem from past and present history of abuses.

The mainstream of the aid industry also forbids the solicitation of services from sex workers. Nevertheless, the discrepancy between the contents of the codes of conducts and the actual policies implemented on the field often comes in the form of public scandals. The cover-up within Oxfam of the predatory behaviour of its head of mission in Haiti (Reporters 2018) is only one recent and resounding example of the variable tolerance by the different staff and organisations towards abusive behaviour. While the stated ethics of organisations direct towards similar direction, albeit with different emphases, the practice of enforcing these rules diverges between organisations, with some stricter than others.

The use of drugs and abuse of alcohol is also rejected widely across all codes of conducts, both because of the criminal liability and the reputational risks. Substance abuse, and alcohol abuse in particular, is widely considered to be a common issue in the humanitarian field, due to the high level of stress supported by aid workers (Britt and Adler 1999). In a complement to the contractual obligations against substance abuse international organisations have started to provide employees with psychosocial support to manage stress (Ehrenreich and Elliott 2004). The ethics of aid rarely names space, but present a clear discourse on the body promoting sports and yoga against alcohol cigarettes and drugs. It is not clear if these types of anti-substance abuse policies lead to a higher use of fitness instead of bars, but it is taking an increasing place in the aid industry (Aebischer Perone et al. 2009).

Space is largely absent from the ethics of international organisation, at least explicitly. Rarely, such as MSB's 2017 code, some type of places are explicitly forbidden: "visits to pornography, striptease or similar clubs are not allowed since this can entail support to criminal activities such as sex trade"[9]. However, even this example of naming a particular category of places, "clubs", constitutes an exception among codes of conduct. Most codes do not mention types of places. The forbidden spaces must be implicitly recognised, deducting which places are forbidden consequently to the prohibition of practices. The aid industry's ethical norms are only implicitly spatial. They are, however, specific enough to imply uses of space and places.

The first level of implicit spatial norms is the relation to the legislation to which employee must abide. It is very clear from all codes of conduct that in any matter, the stricter viewpoint on any matter takes prevalence in assessing the behaviour of international aid employees. The documents stress that employees are bound to the legislation of the home country of their organisation, the local laws and the specific regulation of the organisation that may go beyond the law, in the restriction of certain patterns of behaviour. As the Swiss cooperation states, "The Code of Conduct outlines the behaviour and the manner in which the SDC expects its employees and partners to act it does not reiterate the norms and regulations already laid down in Swiss legislation or those in force in the countries in which the SDC is active"[10]. Employees are asked to "pay attention to

9 MSB, Code of Conduct, 2017.
10 SDC, Code of Conduct, 2008.

local norms and conventions". Some codes, such as for MSB and the Red Cross, may include explicit demands to respect what they seem to worry might most easily be transgressed by employees, traffic and drinking laws. Codes of conduct present a flattened version of the ethics of the aid industry, where the category of "forbidden" seems to bring together the crime and the delict, the banal and the exceptional.

Codes of conduct do not present the relation to the local environment spatially, but through the notions of respect to the laws and customs of the place. This adaptation with the local norms is coupled with a suspicion towards the local environment, where lax rules and corruption may present temptations to aid workers in breaking the humanitarian ethics. The social norms promoted by the codes have a spatial implicit that affects the gaze of aid workers to the cities. The codes of conduct present a curious contrast with security documents, as the former do not contain any ethical rules in the use of space. This might have been the case in the housing policies of organisations or in relation to the domestic workers and labour rules. The ethics of international aid largely leaves apart the question of the effects on socio-spatial relations induced by the presence of their employees.

3.7.5 Training and Storytelling

As part of the humanitarian industry and its attempts to standardise and professionalise the practices of humanitarian aid, international organisations put up training sessions aimed to add up to the earlier training. Some of the courses provided by international organisations might even have the level of a Master, but most of the trainings are short term modules, either as person-to-person, but also largely as online continuous trainings. These trainings follow the managerial and marketing technique of storytelling "to make sense of events, introduce change, and gain political advantage" (Boje 1991). Narrative technique complement the contractual requirement that bounds employees to specific security discourses and norms by bringing order and control (Boje 2008).

Experience of these trainings may diverge depending on the path taken, where organisation have variable emphasis on security trainings. In my personal case, an affiliation with two international rosters led me to attend the "induction courses" of the MSB and DRC, which combined the attendance of on-site training in Sweden and Denmark and online components. I also attended a variety of other sites and online trainings in the course of this research and earlier moments. I will present here some of the contents of these trainings that, if it does not mean that aid workers completely adapt and integrate its contents, it surely says something about the intended message that is transmitted to workers.

As James Scott discusses the Gramscian concept of hegemony (J. C. Scott 1990), he notes that the discourses of domination produce both public and hidden transcripts. The notion of hidden transcripts permits to understand the role and place of these trainings in forming the internal organisation discipline of the aid industry. The content of these training should not be understood as accepted at face value by aid workers, neither as completely coherent within the discourses of international organisations. They constitute a multiplicity of discourses that fit in the general strategies of these organisations. They support building its professional character, including an ethic of work, social relations and security. While aid workers may react to these trainings with the public transcript, the security reflexes expected from them, they might very well keep for themselves a hidden transcript in which they do not submit entirely to the organisation's discipline and open the possibility of transgressing security rules and policy.

The trainings do not constitute a spatial habitus per se, in the sense that they are only a course and not the learnt dispositions of a social class or field. However, they do add up to the social and spatial abilities of the humanitarian employees, as a specific capacity of reading space through the lens of security. In doing so, it presents not only the expected behaviour of the employees but also the representations and positions in the social ladders, as part not so much as specialised workforce in terms of cultural capital, but as a dominant class, with property to protect. Its managerial responsibilities extend to the workplace and at home. The characters depicted are in charge of drivers and subordinates at work. At home, they are taught how they must deal with their guards and domestic workers.

3.7.6 Training the Good Soldiers of Humanitarianism

When working for the UN, I had the opportunity to complete a mandatory "non-harassment certificate". The online training I did consists in a series of stories told by two female and male colleagues, in an office environment explaining how harassment can poison a working environment. Strangely enough, this training aiming to depict, describe and neutralise potential harassment situation never focusses on the victim and the damage done by harassment towards them, but only as a liability to work productivity and corporate reputation:

> *Studies show that harassment and abuse of authority can decrease productivity and morale, while increasing absenteeism and employee turnover.*
>
> *In many cases, overall job effectiveness is diminished and performance is impaired.*

As a result, productivity drops and results decrease.[11]

This mandatory training does not mean that within the hierarchy of UN agencies, the only worry is towards productivity and image. Nevertheless, the fact that this training material is used says something about the overall functioning of the UN system and its sense of priorities in relation to its employees and their mission. Commissioned by the UNDP, this training mobilises the techniques of storytelling that have affected all types of organisation, from the private to some military (Salmon 2013). Discourses on the effect of harassment in the workplace are being told as stories to level and harmonise the behaviour and practices of a diverse workforce, in terms of social and geographical backgrounds.

The development of storytelling in humanitarian context is reflected in the multiplication of online training platforms, on a variety of themes, specific or not to the aid industry. In this regard, security seems to have been a major driver in bringing these types of narrative techniques into the humanitarian field.

3.7.7 Storytelling and Role Play

The use of stories and scenarios to present security is apparent in the numerous online trainings provided by organisations, including the Basic Security Training in the Field (BSITF) and Advanced Security Training in the Field (ASITF), and other trainings available on the UNDSS website. These UNDSS trainings are often used as reference for other organisations operating in conflict environments, and the certificates are condition of engagement and deployment with many NGOs. In recent years, other security trainings have been added to this UNDSS online trainings, in relation to cyber security and "active shooter" incidents, likely prompted by the famous Westgate terrorist attack in Nairobi (Pflanz 2013).

Following the fashion of storytelling that emerged as a specific branch of marketing, the mandatory trainings aim to bring a conscience of risk, and adherence to security policies to humanitarian workers using the power of narration. Narration can mobilise a variety of aspirations and fears to instil a multi-faced sense of risk that may affect the reputation, wellbeing, physical or psychical integrity of oneself and others.

The BSITF and ASITF contain warnings and instructions on how to behave safely relating to a series of risks, ranging from illnesses, including HIV, food

11 HLT – UN Programme on the Prevention of Harassment, Sexual Harassment & Abuse of Authority – SHAP [EN], 01.09.2016.

poisoning and malaria, to terrorist attacks, kidnapping and burglaries.[12] The Basic level, a thirty questions quiz requiring an 80 % of correct answers, is often seen by humanitarians as ridiculous because it contains some most obvious precautions of security. Regarding watchmen, for example, one question asks: "If you notice that your watchman is constantly sleeping, you should provide him with a portable bed and blanket?" But the questions are very telling in picturing the understanding of humanitarian organisations of the settings in which they work and their position on the social ladder: "Should you give your domestic staff keys to your residence?" presents in the most natural way the position of the humanitarian as having domestic workers.

The assumptions of the online lessons and tests on the effect of space on safety and security are reminiscent of Newman's theory of defensible space (Newman 1972). Before instructions on the fencing and grilling of houses, which are largely present in the questionnaires, the subtext in relation to security, is that the demarcation and separation, even if only symbolic, is the first step to safety. "Any perimeter barrier, even if it is only a hedge, serves as a deterrent to crime," states the questionnaire. Lightning on the streets is equally seen as the first level of preventing crime.

The vision of mobility is similar. The only assumed safe transport is the car, and said car must have doors locked and windows closed up. This insistence in separating from the local environment, noted by Duffield about an earlier version of the BSITF questionnaire, included strictly avoiding "local food" (Duffield 2012a). This warning, which seems not to be included anymore in the most recent of the training – maybe in reaction to critiques – seems to take its force from the mixture of common sense propositions and more specific instructions to produce new bodily and spatial reflexes as well as differentiated use of the environment than in "normal" life. The basic of residential rules, for example, explains quite clearly that the first step when choosing a home is advising security. The other options are this time assumed for a normal situation, and the message is that the normal spatial habitus does not apply here: neither the personal preferences for the price or the choice of location are priorities in the context of a mission.

Security trainings change over time, but the use of storytelling has remained the norm for a number of years, and seem to be promised some future in the multiplication of online trainings on the UNDSS platform. In the latest version of ASITF, the storytelling is mandatory, in the sense that it is not possible just to

12 If not specified otherwise, the following citations are taken from the BSITF and ASITF training as of April 2018.

pass the test, but have to go through all the examples and short stories presented as potential types of events. The scope and understanding of risks goes from personal attack to volcanoes and sexual harassment and aims to discuss all types of procedures, including VHF radios, CPR first aid and emergency evacuation. While the basic training presents elementary behaviour precautions, the Advance course aims to give a more complete picture of the types of security risks and the possible responses. The ASITF presents a gradation in the gravity of situations, where potential harm ranges from stress and alcohol addiction to severe body injuries and death. But the situations also very variable in their nature, threats potentially coming from bad communication and misunderstandings in the office to terror attacks and car accidents.

These stories are made in collaboration between UNDSS and a specialised marketing company, Christie Communication, that purports to bring their clients "From Dream to Mainstream" (Christie & Co 2018). They may use cartoons, photo-stories or sound as well as written stories to present a situation. The images used in the training aim to pick a diverse population, where both genders and many nationalities and cultures are represented. The positions of the characters are rarely presented in detail can generally assumed to be programme officers or managers. The realism of the situations and depictions is deemed serious enough that the UNDSS feel the need to warn that "programmes like this occasionally cause psychological disturbances, such as flashbacks or intrusive memories". One might also wonder whether the warning itself is not also a way of stamping the online training with a guarantee of authenticity.

Presenting its understanding of security to UN employees, the training takes the task to deconstruct "security myths". Those security myths are "It will not happen to me" and "it will not happen here". The purpose is to show different assumptions deemed as naïve, and the morale is "You are not safe", in a situation where you might believe you are. Interestingly, the last security myth, is that the security apparatus of humanitarian are enough to ensure the safety of employees. The UNDSS is very keen in pointing that the safety reflexes should be integrated and used by all: "If even one person is complacent about security, you, your colleagues, or your family can be exposed to risk." The "safety for your family" argument is quite usual in the security warnings, and it often seems to be the ultimate argument in the disciplining the minds of humanitarians. The "active shooter" training, for example advises practising the exercises of escape in public places with the family.

The stories prescribe safe spatial behaviour. The scenery may occur in daily life as in extreme situations: "Because of the mined path, you and [your colleague] Paul had to take a detour, which meant that you were unable to reach the main road before dark. You will have to stay overnight again". The story told at the second person involves a catastrophic scenario, where two UN employees are forced to escape a situation where their car was met by gunfire and their driver killed. The themes of the night, and the standard possibilities of circulating are recurrent in the UN trainings, and survival depends on earlier preparation, as well as the constant maintenance of means of communication with the security.

Catastrophic scenarios may also happen in the daily life of a clerical worker. The threat of terrorism is one of the main themes of these catastrophic scenarios, where highjacking, active shooters and bombs should be envisioned as a realistic probability:

> *In the first seconds after the explosion, you realise that you are alive, unhurt, and still in your office. The building is filling with smoke and you can hear people screaming downstairs. It is clear to you that a bomb as exploded. What actions would you take in this situation? Select the answers in the next screen.*

So neither travels nor office work can be considered safe from catastrophic events. Nevertheless, the training also shows the risks of more standard personal office stress. Burnout, sexual harassment, alcohol and drug addiction and other types of situations affecting the wellbeing of employees are considered amplified in humanitarian work. The sensitivity of the environment increases the risk of losing control of events.

Security discourse is keen to point that catastrophic threats are only an addition to other dangers of the outside environment. The behaviour of employees and the respect or not that they show to the local population is considered a strong factor in the possibility of a "security event" occurring. The clothes that the characters of the story, Maria and Paul, wear when visiting a market should be adapted to the local customs. Their clothes should not send the "unwanted messages [of] irreverence and sexual availability", presenting an undetermined African fish market and the local passers-by.

The control of the clothes is one part of the general control of the body, which includes personal hygiene and an understanding of gender norms. The story of Maria and her movements in a dark street illustrates both the spatial assumption of the UNDSS on street lighting and how gender is seen as changing the perspective of risks. Leaving an office party and walking in the dark side of a street towards her car, Maria is heading towards a group of men standing. Concerned by the presence of the men, she moves to the opposite sidewalks that have street lights, before going to her car when no man or "potential threat" is in sight. Next she moves quickly and opens her car, then "enters car, locks door, and drives off safely".

The example of Maria illustrates the standard "security awareness" expected from humanitarian workers. In the words of security management, she "identified a threat", then "analysed her vulnerabilities", before taking "measures to reduce risk". Her model behaviour was congruent with the understanding of risk as the relation between likelihood of an event and its impact by taking prevention measures.

The stereotypical story of Maria was able to build a relation between a common sense and security management understanding by the UN. It presents dark streets and groups of men as potential dangers in the street, while light and the possibility of sheltering in a car improves safety. The fact that the threat is not presented explicitly allows the imagination of the reader to identify to diverse types of unpleasant situations that may involve violence, theft or sexual aggression, makes an easy and strong identification. And showing that common sense behaviour is close to security management gives it a legitimacy that can be relied on in other cases.

Role Play

Role play is part of the Safe and Secure Approaches in Field Environments (SSAFE) trainings provided on site to employees by the UNDSS, to replicate difficult situations where the employees are being exposed to stress and danger. The exact content of the training may vary, but the general idea is that a group travels a territory with a number of hazardous situations.

The level of realism is dependent on the place and organisation that provides the training. It is calibrated proportionally to the perceived typical threat that might occur to humanitarian workers. In a continuum of realism of the scenery and aggressiveness of the trainers, some training may occur in a classroom where a security officer asks how attendees would react to a specific situation. At the other end, the Hostile Environment Awareness Training (HEAT) trainings might include mock kidnapping, the use of blank ammunition and the physical constraints of the trainees.

The SSAFE training I attended in Mali for example, included the crossing a checkpoint with aggressive "rebel forces", walking in a path contaminated with mock UXO, a kidnapping and the aftermath of a large explosion in a crowded area. I was always struck by the level of actual stress that these exercises put myself and other participants in, considering that despite the realism of the scenes, trainees are perfectly aware that it is only an exercise. The situation that is constructed is not only extreme for each individual event, but also because it happened in the space of a very short time. This SSAFE training in Mali (and others) typically have this succession of events in less than two hours.

The sensation of the role play is still present, and I remember enjoying the fun thrill of these trainings, like most participants. To make sure that the moral of the stories in the role play are well understood, each dramatic event is followed by a debriefing of the situation, where the participants are being instructed about the good and bad reflexes they had, and how their decision could have made the situation better or worse. The morals of the stories are rather direct: when in movement in a car, it is important to stay in, and have the doors and windows closed.

To prove that point, checkpoint exercises commonly start with an armed man trying to open the car. At that point, the correct action was to have the door closed beforehand. One should not resist, and open the car when asked. Radio communication should be regular to indicate one's position to the security. The very direct instruction given by the security instructors are not necessarily always categorical. The question of paying some "fee" at a checkpoint is normally not accepted, but instructors point that it might be better not to refuse in order to simplify the situation.

To my knowledge, unlike the online trainings, these security exercises do not normally include situations at home or in the office. The exercises focus on movement, moving in a car. A technical part includes the use of radio communication equipment and procedures to allow the monitoring of the position by the security. The morals of the stories in mobility are that unless ordered or forced to, one should not stop, not leave the vehicle, and keep the car as closed as possible. One should not attempt to resist armed men, but slowing their access to your body, with soft closings. In short, the humanitarian should be wary of the environment, and only focus in circulating from one point to another.

These trainings and the use of scenarios have an ambiguous role in forming the space habitus of humanitarian workers. Their mandatory character gives them a power of authority, although the instructions and the morals of the stories told are not necessarily orders. However, the integration of "advices" from the stories of the security system might also be more efficient than formal interdictions in some ways. The informal stories about breaches of security might actually work better than hierarchical instructions in facilitating the integration of the behavioural recommendations (Rader, Wash, and Brooks 2012). In that sense the storytelling n has the potential to form part of the spatial habitus of humanitarian workers. While strict instructions might provoke greater resistance to the security procedures, stories smoothen the message and facilitate a compliance with consent.

This chapter presented the social field supporting the aid industry, and its spatial habitus. It illustrates the spatial and social structure of humanitarian aid as an instance of North-South relations. The next chapter on the Panorama will present a picture of the specificities of the sites of study as scenes of political conflicts and social contradictions.

Chapter 4 Panorama

This chapter will introduce the urban and political history of the sites of study, the cities of Bamako Juba, Nairobi and Abidjan. Both the history of the cities and the history of political violence constitute a "panorama" in which aid agencies operate. They constitute a point of reference to which humanitarian organisations set their analysis and understanding of risk. This posture of presenting the socio-spatial local environment as a panorama aims to reflect a position of a viewer with analytical instruments to assess the city. The particularity of these analytical instruments is their almost unique perspective in gazing at the local environment through dangers and risk. This chapter, however, will not attempt to highlight the rights and wrongs of the security analysis, which could reasonably be criticised, from a problem-solving perspective focussing on flaws in the analysis or from a critical view of risk analysis itself. Although I do think there is ground for both critiques, this will not be the focus on this chapter.

The panorama to which I refer here is what constitutes the context of the case studies of this research, the cities of Bamako, Juba, Nairobi and Abidjan. This presentation will highlight some of the particularities of the socio-spatial entities and processes in which international aid operates. On the other hand, it will also describe the contexts of violence in the cities and countries, which have led to the implementation of humanitarian assistance. As hinted above, this presentation does not pretend to present a situation as a better analysis than humanitarian organisations, but present the referential setting from which international aid territorialises itself in African cities.

The notion of the panorama, as used in this chapter, is the materiality to which aid agencies will apply their security gaze and later transform socially and materially. I will note an important issue with this presentation in the fact that the referential (the cities and the political contexts) are not immutable elements. In fact, they constitute ever-changing situations, which the presence of the aid industry greatly influences. The panorama itself is constantly changing, sometimes marginally, and other times more thoroughly.

In this discussion of the four cities, here is the place to present these case studies as different paradigmatic cases of the urban geopolitics of aid. The history of peacekeeping and humanitarian interventions and peacekeeping are two distinct political moments. However, they often come together and although separate, they both constitute a reflection of a political will from dominant diplomatic and political powers. In the cities concerned by this research, only

Nairobi is not the site of an intervention itself. The presence of international organisations is the basis for this grouping of Bamako, Juba Nairobi and Abidjan, and their presentations as context.

4.1 Contexts of Political Violence

The four cities studied for this research constitute different paradigmatic cases of political importance, as well as levels and type of risks. The danger of violence is the main worry of risk management within organisations. The political implications of violent incidents are the most damaging, compared to accidents or illnesses. Indeed the most emphasis on security and safety training and manuals relate to violence. The particular reasons of the moral panic affecting international aid, discussed elsewhere include internal shifts of power, and the linking of security to development programmes. Nevertheless, all cases studied here are cities that have witnessed important degrees of violence.

Interlinks and co-dependency between cities and rural areas in peacetime shapes times of war. Conflicts in rural areas affect cities in different ways. Network and logistical centrality of cities and capitals often makes urban areas important havens for refugees fleeing conflicts (Mwaruvie and Kirui 2012). Whether refugees settle within cities or on organised camps on the outskirts all four capitals have been affected by an afflux of internal or external refugees.

Capital cities are most often affected by conflicts in the country, either directly or indirectly. Their political and economic centrality typically makes them vulnerable from shockwaves of a conflict, even when the stakes primarily concern rural issues. In Ivory Coast, the final hours of the armed conflict happened in Abidjan, in battles involving the Ivorian army, rebels, the UN peacekeepers and the French army. In South Sudan, while most of the civil war affects rural areas, the city of Juba was twice, in 2013 and 2016, the theatre of the main turns in the civil war. In both Mali and Kenya, the political centrality and visibility of the capitals incited jihadist groups to stage major terrorist attacks against expatriate-frequented amenities.

This section will present contextual information on the political developments and levels of violence. These cities and their hinterland did all witness different levels and nature of violence that constituted the reference points of the risk management in international organisations. The political developments summarised in the section below present the political and military developments that have prompted the implementation of UN missions and the broader humanitarian intervention.

The political/humanitarian interventions have not been focussed on the cities for themselves, but rather as a bridgehead to a wider territory. The presence of the main UN and humanitarian bases in capital cities uses them as an intermediary point between the sites of intervention in a country and a wider network of supplies. The humanitarian HQ city is a means to a wider end of intervention in crisis with larger geographic base.

4.1.1 The Conflict in Mali

Since the fall of General Moussa Traoré in 1991, elected civilian governments have ruled the country. The opening of trade and the dependency on cotton makes the country fragile economically. Increasing inequalities linked with structural adjustment programmes and forms of social compromise, such as community support and cronyism, balance an increasing liberalisation of the economy (Adekanye 1995; Bouju 2000). Most of Mali's territory remained unaffected by the conflict with the Tuareg in the North of the country until the fall of Muammar Gaddafi in 2011. A relatively small guerrilla force in Northern Mali has been challenging the Malian state since the late 2000s with limited effects on the rest of the country, which hosts most of the population and economic resources (Krings 1995).

The chaos ensuing the fall of Mr Gaddafi brought fighters and weapons to the country. The pillage of weapons storage in the chaos of the Lybian revolution gave numerous armed groups firepower able to change the equilibrium of the political dispute in the North of Mali. The Malian army, under-equipped and mostly constituted from soldiers from the South found themselves beaten severely by the coalition of Islamists and separatist Tuaregs in the beginning of 2012 (Saraceno 2015). The advances of the rebels were blamed by sections of the Malian army on the political class and the president Amadou Toumani Touré, himself a former general, and resulted in an open revolt and a coup d'état by paratrooper Captain Amadou Sanogo in April 2012.

The military coup backfired quickly and Tuareg nationalists used the disorganisation of the Malian state to conquer more territory, including the cities of Kidal, Gao and Timbuktu, and declare the independence of North Mali, as the "Republic of Azawad" (Zounmenou 2013). Paradoxically, the coup, which was supported by the hardliner nationalist sections of the Malian political scene against a "balkanisation" of the country, enabled its effective partition. The coup not only disorganised the state internally, but it also prevented it from seeking external aid from the regional body of West African states, ECOWAS (Bøås and Torheim 2013). The jihadist groups then attacked their former Tuareg allies and took most of the North under their control and administration. At the end of the year, jihadist groups then brought the fight again against the Malian army and started marching south towards the regions of Segou and Mopti.

The advance of jihadist groups a few hundred kilometres from Bamako brought a French military intervention, along with the African-led International Support Mission to Mali (AFISMA) comprising West African states and Tchad against the jihadists. The power of the combined military mission quickly routed the jihadist groups from the whole country. Tuareg nationalists used the defeat of the jihadists to present themselves as a major actor in the North and gained some level of political and military control, mainly in the Kidal region.

Military victory against the jihadist brought a new political equilibrium in the country. The coup leader Amadou Sanogo was eventually jailed for extrajudicial killings and referred to the ICC before the end of 2013. Between these events, the UN Security Council gave a mandate to the MINUSMA to support stabilising the country. The mandate to support the reconciliation process in Mali has brought the MINUSMA at odds against the nationalist sectors of the Malian political scene, as it sought to integrate Tuareg nationalists in the north towards a reconciliation process with Mali. The participation of the Malian state in this political process was followed with an election cycle and subsequent political recognition of the new government (Karlsrud 2015). It brought the civilian and veteran politician Ibrahim Boubacar Keita, nicknamed IBK, to the presidency. The Malian state and the Tuareg nationalists have since entered phases of open hostility and a reconciliation process, still under way.

The mandate of the MINUSMA to support a political stabilisation process includes the nationalist Tuareg movement in the North. Malian authorities have been reluctant to some aspects of the mission, which the criticise as empowerment and protection of the Tuaregs, although their hands are tied militarily since the defeat of the army (Boutellis 2015). The Malian government has nevertheless agreed to a peace agreement with promises of decentralisation, excluding jihadist groups from the political process. The complex political situation reflects in the difficulty in humanitarian assistance, which, despite a large organisational presence, has difficulties reaching beyond the south of the country (A. Chandler and Zogg 2017).

The French-Malian-West African military victories on the open field against jihadist groups and the MINUSMA have turned to a war of attrition. The dispersion of the jihadists resulted in regular use of improvised explosive devices against Malian and foreign troops in the country. These tactics continue to this day and have placed Mali as the deadliest current UN mission, with more than 150 dead in five years (Guterres 2019). In response to these events, the

UN has increased its counter-terrorism capacities, pushing the strategy of the MINUSMA increasingly in the role of a counterinsurgency force aside of its goals of political stabilisation. While the MINUSMA had increasing tactical success in the north, it was unable to contain threats of terror attacks in cities of the south, including the capital Bamako (Karlsrud 2015). Jihadist groups have started attacking public places frequented by foreigners in the capital since 2015. These attacks have caused dozens of deaths in Bamako, most famously at the Radisson Blu hotel (Dembelé 2015). Although the number and lethality of attacks is much higher in the North, the capacity of jihadist cells to struck expatriates in Bamako grants much more publicity and demonstrate the fragility of the political and military situations. The reluctance of some Western countries to maintain armed support to the MINUSMA further weakens UN-driven political stabilisation (Berthiaume 2019).

The latest developments in Mali suggest an intensification of the conflict. Recent fighting between armed groups, the army, and attacks on civilians further south to the earlier conflict zones also suggests risks of a geographic expansion of the conflict to the whole country (Magassa 2019). The dynamics of the conflict in Mali have stretched from a localised conflict in the little-populated North towards an increasingly complex and geographically extended situation.

The dynamics of the war in Mali also illustrates the volatility of a conflict and its transition from a mostly rural phenomenon in remote areas to new dimensions of urban conflicts (Saraceno 2015). The first signs of urban transition of the conflict are probably the attacks against Tuaregs installed in Bamako by nationalist hardliners. Beating up Tuaregs or torching their houses have been the first violent expression of deep frustrations in the state's incapacity to control its territory (Zounmenou 2013). The hardliners' demonstration of force in Bamako culminated during the coup d'état of 2012, although it also signalled their fast decline as a political force.

These events of urban violence in the capital and later jihadi attacks against foreigners in Bamako illustrate the vulnerability of Malian cities to political violence. Beyond political conflicts, arrivals of refugees in the city have increased the proportion of urban dwellers in dire conditions and lack of basic services (Kamusoko 2017). As a result new forms of tensions emerge in the city, where the presence of refugees from the North – often seen with suspicion by southern Malians – produces renewed tensions between ethnic groups in Bamako, inciting many to seek refugee status in neighbouring countries (Bardelli 2019).

The increase in violent events expresses a miniature of the national tensions. The intensity of conflicts in Bamako rarely compares to the countryside infighting in the north and centre of the country. However, as with the cases of jihadist attacks and civilian-military tensions, their consequences affect the political equilibriums more strongly.

4.1.2 South Sudan and the Never-Ending Wars

South Sudan have repeatedly experienced war since the first movements for autonomy or independence from Sudan in the 1960s. The SPLA movement originally used regional rivalries to gain the support of Ethiopia, attacking sensitive targets, including Sudanese army garrisons and foreign companies operating in the country. Rivalries among South Sudanese political movements, broadly affiliated to the main ethnic groups have sometimes been bloody. Geopolitical allies in the SPLA's struggle for independence shifted from one patron to the other gaining at times support from socialist countries and later from the USA and more broadly from the West who acted as a sponsor for the secession from Sudan under humanitarian grounds (Autesserre 2002). The majority Dinka factions, under John Garang and the Nuer under Riek Machar have been reconciled at the beginning of the 2000s, when Western support put pressure on Sudan to accept a political solution that may end with secession. African diplomatic circles, on the other hand, had been wary on South Sudanese independence, since the African Union had until now always refused to recognise secessionists movements that would break away from the borders of colonial times. The fear of starting a precedent, which could potentially trigger a wave of secessions in other countries, had until the independence of South Sudan refrained the African Union to recognise any fragmenting of its member states (Christopher 2011).

After the death in a helicopter crash of the movement's leader John Garang in 2005, the leadership of SPLA rested in the hands of Salva Kiir, now allied with the leader Riek Machar, who unified their political movement in the build-up of political independence. The presence of oil fields attracted interest of major international powers interested in extraction. With the support of China and the West and the willingness of Sudanese President Omar al Bachir to accept the results of an independence referendum – except the disputed North Kordofan and Abei regions – the country declared its independence in July 2011.

The important resources in petrol, at a time of historically high price of oil, led to the widespread idea, in the country and beyond, that a newly independent South Sudan with a regular flow of crude exports would sustain a prosperous development once peace was achieved with Sudan. Enthusiasm in the North by diplomatic, political and media circles was rarely questioned except by a small number of sceptics. The belief in the new opportunities offered by the newly independent country extended to a diversity of investors, including Chinese and US companies (Shankleman 2011). Early expectations soon proved overly optimistic.

Since the independence of South Sudan, the civil war has marred the country. The repeated episodes of violence marks how the capital and the country hinterland have been touched differently. In the countryside and towns of South Sudan, attacks and ambushes between armed factions have cost more lives by repetition, but did not witness the intensity in Juba. The capital, on the other hand, has been touched by the war twice in extreme outburst claiming thousands of lives. These episodes have each lasted only a couple of days, although regular acts of violence by the security forces, mainly as a racket, have regularly claimed victims among Juba population.

In December 2013, claiming that vice-president Riek Machar was attempted a coup; president Salva Kiir ordered his army to move against his vice-president in Juba. The SPLA army failed to capture or kill Machar but conducted a massacre of thousands of Nuer citizens in the capital Juba. Nuer factions of the SPLA left Juba and started putting themselves in military opposition to the government, forming the SPLA-IO. The following years have seen the defection, and sometimes reintegration, of many generals and their troops in the SPLA side. The reintegration with promotion of defecting high-ranking officers might have acted as a perverse incentive to defect and participated in the atomisation of the SPLA into a myriad of armed factions (Mamdani 2016).

The civil war in the independent South Sudan disappointed the many Western sponsors of the independence of South Sudan. Western government's original support for independence and the SPLA movement have moved towards an increasingly critical stance against the South Sudanese government. NGO reports have blamed the government and warring factions' chiefs for war crimes as well as graft and war profiteering (Adeba 2019).

The economy of South Sudan is based on oil for almost all exports and state budget. Oil revenues plunged with the civil war, which severely limited extractions. The South Sudanese Pound (SSP), worth a third of a dollar when the first notes were emitted fell dramatically. With the slowdown of the economy, criminality rose in cities and roads, facilitated by the widespread circulation of firearms, and the documented involvement of security forces. Theft and murders on the roads only worsened the already ailing economic situation.

In 2016, Machar came back to Juba under a peace agreement that will reinstate him as vice-president and allow 1500 of his soldiers to camp in the capital. Only a few months after the return of Machar in Juba, infighting between SPLA and SPLA-IO in the capital broke the peace agreement again in July 2016. The superior military capacity of the SPLA, using heavy weapons, tanks and helicopter gunships, crushed the IO in Juba and forced Machar and the remainder of its army to flee.

Since the combats in Juba, the civil war continued and the country tops the Fragile State Index (Fragile States Index | The Fund for Peace 2019). The survival of Riek Machar and the pressure from foreign governments, in particular within the East African regional bodies has pushed for a renewal of peace talks. The provisional result to these renewed negotiations is the signing of a peace agreement in Addis Ababa in September 2018. Past peace agreements by the warring South Sudanese factions cast a doubt on the sustainability of the most recent. As some critiques pointed, the tribal structure of the state, set in place to guarantee a balance between the main ethnicities, will reinforce the major military factions, instead of a more democratic political representation (Mamdani 2018).

4.1.3 The Regional Hub and the War on Terror in Kenya

The independence process of Kenya was one of the bloodiest in the British colonies, where the repression of the MauMau rebellion from 1952 to 1960 cost tens of thousands of lives (Elkins 2005). However, the leadership of the independent Kenya maintained strong links with its former colony, structuring its stability with political repression of opponents and military alliances (Cullen 2016). Jomo Kenyatta placed himself as a reformist alternative to gain a British support for his de facto one-party state. Successive heads of state Daniel Moi, Mwai Kibaki and currently Uhurru Kenyatta (son of Jomo Kenyatta) supervised the development of an economy controlled by landowners, foreign and national capital. Economic growth ensured some level of acceptance of the one-party state for decades among middle classes (Barkan 1993). However, growing unpopularity of the ruling elite has become more apparent and the regularity of elections has been constantly questioned in the street and in the courts since the 2000s (Mueller 2008).

The relative political and economic stability in post-independence Kenya – as a one-party state allied with the West in the Cold War – has made the country an important player in the East African Region. The Port of Mombasa is used across the region for transport of goods, and wildlife tourism has brought important resources for the economy. The relative economic and political power of Kenya allowed Uhurru Kenyatta to place Nairobi as an equally important regional hub for transports, economy and diplomacy, with a city of millions and important HQ for the United Nations.

Surprisingly little documentation exists regarding the establishment of the United Nations in the city of Nairobi. The project of leasing or giving land to the international organisation in the early 1970s. As Ivanova (2007) argues, the strategic location of Nairobi as a key site for the United Nations starts with the creation of the United Nations Environment Programme (UNEP) at the 1972 Stockholm Conference. The institution of a new UN agency created the opportunity for Southern countries to lobby their interests in hosting one site of a UN programme in an attempt to re-equilibrate the locations of UN agencies. However, political ecology academics argue that what allowed the location of this UN agency in Africa is precisely the lack of importance of environmental issues among powerful countries.. Following this analysis, it is UNEP that was placed at the margins international diplomacy, rather than Nairobi being recognised as a potential diplomatic platform (Von Moltke 1996). However, this choice has created the embryo to which other specialised agencies started locating in the Gigiri area of Nairobi.

The process, started in the early 1970s, of placing Nairobi as a credible site for international organisations has stemmed from its political stability, and facilitated by its proximity to Western powers. In this regard, the city geopolitics of Nairobi witnesses the paradoxical situation in which the city is "rewarded" with hosting the UN while the authoritarian policies of one-party state are later criticised by official human rights reports from these institutions and countries (Adar 2000; Adar and Munyae 2001; Brown 2001).

This political importance of Nairobi also puts it in an important landmark event in the history of political terrorism. The 1997 bombings, which destroyed the US embassies of Nairobi and Dar es Salaam (Tanzania), led to a global redesigning of US embassies around the world and had lasting influence on urban security policies and design (Loeffler 2005). Inside Kenya, the embassy attacks have marked the construction of the "counterterror state" within Kenya. War on terror tactics in Kenya often took the aspect of collective punishment, especially directed against the Somali refugee community, as in the expulsion and home demolitions of 2014 (Glück 2017).

Kenya has been strongly affected by conflicts in neighbouring countries, first of all, Somalia. Since the beginning of the civil war in the 1990s, Kenya has hosted a large Somalian community, many of them in some of the world's largest refugee camps. The control of the Somali camps has often led to violent fighting between the Kenyan security forces and armed groups, as well as a tightening control of the refugee population. Since 2011, the Kenyan army occupies part of the south of Somalia to prevent military incursions of the Shabaab group.

The Kenyan state has regularly blamed Somali involvement for a number of terrorist attacks against nationals and foreigners, since the beginning of the 2010s. The most publicised of these attacks has been the WestGate massacre, when a commando of Shabaabs entered one of the largest malls in Nairobi in September 2013. Gunmen left 67 dead behind when the attack was terminated by the Kenyan security forces. Two years later, the Shabaab conducted an even more murderous attack against a school on the coast, leaving more than 150 dead (D. M. Anderson and McKnight 2015; Lind, Mutahi, and Oosterom 2015).

Political violence within Kenya is equally part of the relation between state and citizens. The contested election of Uhurru Kenyatta was marred with street fighting that provoked the death of thousand people in 2007 (Brown and Sriram 2012). Street political violence reflect the poverty and inequalities in the country. While the revenues of the economy profit a minority of the population, pockets of extreme poverty mark the country and the capital. Criminality is high and mugging for money is only one of the everyday types of violence experienced in the city. Violence and banditry in Nairobi might also reflect a deeper sense of maintaining political and economic power by Kenyan elites. The absence of state services and presence have left space to a violent criminality controlled by gangs. Gunpoint theft of cars and cash since the 1990s has become common fear of the Kenyan middle and upper classes, pushing for a siege mentality which translated in design and behaviour change for personal safety (Katumanga 2005). It also encourages vigilantism and extreme police violence targeted at the poorest Kenyan (The Economist 2018).

4.1.4 War and Politics in Ivory Coast

The long reign of President Felix Houphouët-Boigny from the independence until his death in 1993 marked the history of Ivory Coast and marked the political conflicts of the years to come. With a tight control of the press and all political activities, Houphouët-Boigny ensured his political control was not endangered by a military coup by keeping the Ivorian military relatively small. An alliance with France the former colonial power ensured the presence of the French Army in military bases. The artisan of the "Ivorian miracle", economic growth driven by coffee and cocoa exports had been keen to maintain and encourage rivalries among any potential rivals, including Henri Konan Bedié and Alassane Ouattara who would later engage in bitter conflict after the death of Houphouët-Boigny, in 1993. At the time, the historian and trade union leader Laurent Gbagbo organised his political movement partly from exile and jail.

The political and personal rivalries developed between Prime Minister Ouattara and president of the National assembly Bédié under Houphouët-Boigny prefigured their bitter conflict to reach the highest office in the 1990s. Bedié used the restrained nationality definition to keep apart Ouattara, partly of Burkinabe origin. This concept of "Ivoirité" was used again in 1999 to prevent Ouattara from running, which paved the way to Laurent Gbagbo to be elected. Institutional xenophobia in Ivory Coast has opportunistically targeted politicians to keep them from running or discredit them. However, in its most regular occurrence, it is mainly directed at the millions of foreign workers, including many born in Ivory Coast, often in the form of threats and violence (Gaulme 2001; Loada 2006).

Laurent Gbagbo's election in 2000 was followed by a long period of political violence marked by an armed rebellion, a French intervention and a UN mission. The complexity and polemical nature of what amounted to a Western intervention – branded as neo-colonial by supporters of Gbagbo – ended with the military defeat of Gbagbo's party, in a joint operation of French troops, the rebels and the assistance of the UN mission (Hofnung 2011). While the exact nature of the intervention and is legitimacy belongs to a broader debate on the nature of Western "pro-democracy" or "humanitarian interventions", it must be noted that in this context the role of the UN is largely on one of the conflicting sides (Plett 2011).

A striking aspect of the political power in Abidjan during these years had been the activities of open-air "parliaments", spaces of debates in the different neighbourhoods of the capital (Toh and Banégas 2006). These spaces considered pro-Gbagbo and criticised by Ouattara and its allies had been closed since the change of political power. As the Gbagbo camp appeared beaten with the arrest of its leader and its trial at the ICC, recent events seem to draw a possible return in the country, or at least a greater integration of the party in current Ivorian politics. The release pending appeal of Laurent Gbagbo suggests a new configuration of Ivorian politics (ICC Press Release 2019).

As part of the political arrangements after the fall of Laurent Gbagbo, former rebels were included in the Ivorian army. While the ONUCI considered its mission over and prepared to leave in July 2017, sections of the former rebels demanded to the Ivorian state sums of cash that had been promised by Ouattara to his troops before coming to power. As the large sums were not handed to the former rebels, they started a rebellion in January 2017 and another in May (Hervieu 2017). The rebellion blocked parts of the main cities for a couple of days, until obtaining the money, leaving the president in a politically sensitive position.

The departure of ONUCI in June 2017, whose mandate started in 2004, and was repeatedly extended, was not affected by the most recent political developments and armed insurgencies. The DPKO mission had been already largely reduced in the preceding years, as well as the humanitarian presence in the country (United Nations 2017b).

4.2 Violence and Numbers

The linking of the cities of Abidjan, Bamako, Nairobi and Juba in this study requires the use of some primary statistical data to present a comparison of the different situations. As an ad hoc grouping for this research, the four case studies are not presented together in existing comparisons. Mali, Ivory Coast, Kenya and South Sudan suffer different levels of violence. This section will use generic numbers from open access databases on violent events and records on attacks against aid workers to present a broad comparative picture of the contexts of violence.

It is beyond the scope of this work to fully use the available disaggregated data. This section will only observe the broad outlook at the statistics of levels of violence. Leaving aside issues such as criminal violence two important sources can help situate both the intensity of the conflicts and how it affects humanitarian workers. The Armed Conflict Location and Event Data (ACLED) tracks violent incidents implicating state and non-state actors all over Africa (Raleigh et al. 2010). The database attempts an exhaustive statistical collection of violent political events, ranging from riots to wars and attacks on civilians on the whole African continent.[13] On the other hand, the Aid Workers Security Database (AWSD) focusses on attacks on aid workers and is the product of Humanitarian Outcomes, a reference think-tank in the humanitarian field (Hoelscher, Miklian, and Nygård 2017). This worldwide database includes political events as well as criminal incidents.

As much of the data is provided to both databases through information release of the political and humanitarian actors, it is fair to consider that they somewhat represent with certain level of accuracy the perception of risk by aid agencies. The ambition to present exhaustive database of violent events have been criticised for their methodologies as well as their taxonomies. In particular the definition of aid worker itself may be subject to controversy or debate (Fast 2014). The practical conditions for collecting the information from the ground is also complex in locations with little access and communications.

13 Other database projects have produced and disseminated lists of violent events in relation to social conflicts, in Africa and elsewhere (PRIO 2019; CCAPS 2019; UCDP 2019). These databases have not been included in the discussion, as they are comparable in thematic, scope and quality.

The very reliance of both databases on humanitarian agencies, as specified in the methodology of both ACLED and AWSD, places the production of these sources in a context of disputes within aid agencies over the quantification of humanitarian insecurity. The field of humanitarian aid is subject to an internal power struggle between programmatic and security wings over the safety of aid workers. Quantification of these attacks are subject to epistemological and strategical debates within aid agencies (Beerli 2017). Discrepancies in the result of controversial data collection processes likely reflects reported information, as much as lack of precision or data holes. As all other sources of information (e.g. governments and local media) are potentially under the same methodological and practical stress and bias, it is not possible to consider the data strictly consistent.

General numbers of fatalities are provided by the ACLED database show that South Sudan and Mali are among the top ten African countries for fatalities in relation to violent events (Figure 20). Kenya numbers 460 events and Ivory Coast 24 in the same period. The limits of the accuracy of the database is first apparent in the understating of the number of victims in South Sudan, with higher estimates circulating among media and specialists (Specia 2018). The civil war in South Sudan is incomparably more lethal than the three other cases put together. Mali and Kenya suffer relatively close numbers of victims during this period, although in very different circumstances. Only Ivory Coast shows a significantly lower number of victims of political violence, although this is explained mostly by the fact that the civil war is now over (Nossiter 2011).

Attacks on aid workers as recorded by the AWSD database for the period 2013–2017 illustrates the differences in intensity depending on the country (Figure 21). The killing, wounding and kidnapping constitute the three categories of recorded incidents. It illustrates that in recent years a number of diverse types of physical attacks or kidnappings did result in serious harm against humanitarians. As is visible in the database, most casualties among humanitarians occurred against local aid workers rather than expatriates (Abu Sa'Da and Crombé 2015; Stoddard, Abby; Harmer, Adele; Haver 2011). This level of aggregation illustrates the large difference between the countries. Most of any of the types of attacks occurred in South Sudan, which seems to correlate with the generally high level of political violence in the country, as recorded in the ACLED database.

Reading some of the descriptions of individual events also illustrates that attacks on aid workers might come in relation to their work, or from completely distinct reasons. "One security guard was killed when a group of men armed with blades forced entry to the office of an NGO, which they then robbed," one 2013 entry for Kenya notes. On the same year and country, we also learn that "two UN

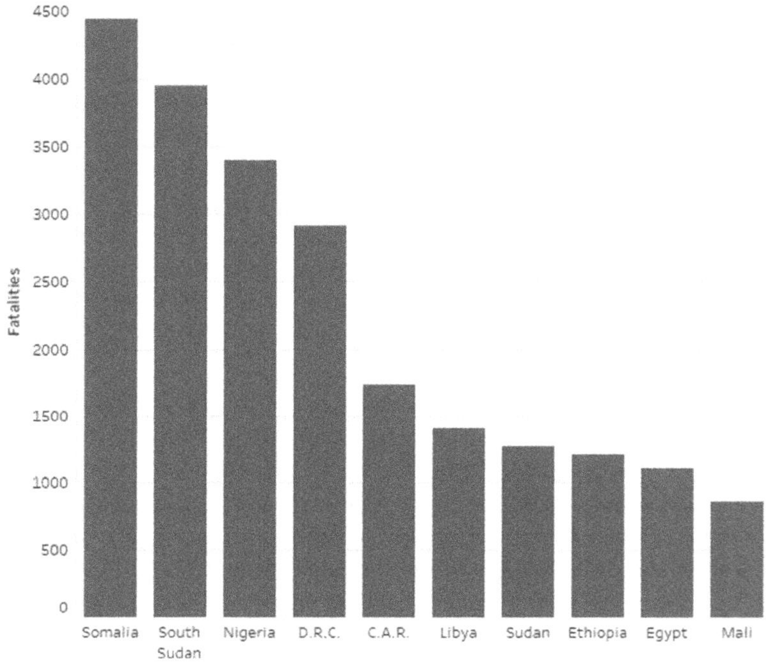

Figure 20: The ten highest numbers of fatalities due to armed conflicts in Africa during the period 2013–2017. South Sudan ranks second and Mali tenth. Kenya with 462 and Ivory Coast with 24 fall out of the chart. ACLED database 2018

personnel and a UN contractor were reported injured during a complex attack by al-Shabaab at the Westgate Shopping Mall in Nairobi".[14] While much of the focus on aid workers attacks is their work, and in relation to the political situation, there are many reasons that might place humanitarians at risk. Moreover, many do not stem from the crisis they aim to respond to, or not directly.

The absence of attacks on peacekeepers in Mali is notable. As DPKO personnel is not included as aid workers in the database, the picture created corresponds to perceptions of risk that does not include the international intervention as a whole. The specific considerations of the UN should be added to the understanding of risk by humanitarian organisations. This absence illustrates the complexity in picturing security issue according to the risks affected by certain

14 AWSD database, entries for Kenya 2013.

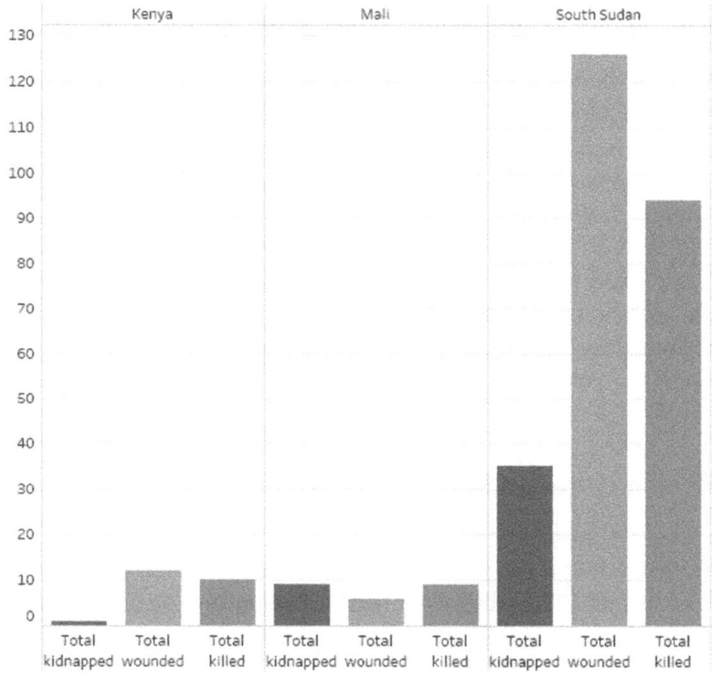

Figure 21: A number of aid workers killed wounded and kidnapped during the period 2013–2017. No incident affected aid workers in Ivory Coast, although AWSD records casualties for earlier periods. AWSD database 2018

groups. This very complexity in turn might explain in part why aid and security professionals tend to rely on standardised and flattening understandings of risk. Consequently, the response to risks passes through a limited number of methods largely depending on internal procedures and material security.

With all their limits, these datasets shows that the case studies witness real and important levels of violence. A disaggregated analysis per place, nationality or gender, as produced by Humanitarian Outcomes (Humanitarian Outcomes 2019), might present a more precise picture. However, this analysis would go beyond the comparison of picturing levels of violence in the four countries, and more detailed discussion of their particularities are provided elsewhere in this chapter, in relation to the political situation or the urban dynamics of violence.

Statistical data on violent events and attacks on aid workers illustrates different levels of violence in the four countries. This data does not represent an exact picture of the violence in the different countries. However, they illustrate well the differences between the panoramas in terms of violence. They also illustrate a relation between violent contexts and attacks on humanitarians. While the overall numbers of humanitarians on the field largely influences the number of aid workers victims of violence (Dandoy and Montclos 2013), the correlation between general violence and attacks on aid workers is all apparent. In short, and almost tautologically, violent contexts are dangerous for aid workers.

A brief outlook of the political situation in Mali, South Sudan, Kenya and Ivory Coast underscores different levels of complexity and violence. The simplified presentation aimed to provide context for humanitarian presence as well as international aid's perception of the situations. The second part of this presentation of the panoramas will concentrate on presenting a picture of urban metabolisms in the four capitals.

4.3 African Cities and Four Case Studies

In their diversity, the cities of Abidjan, Bamako, Nairobi and Juba share a number of similarities. All four are African cities and share common issues of the cities of the Global South. Typically, fast growth, urban poverty, social inequalities and the limited resources of state authorities mark the metabolism of all types of urban services. As a result, disruption of infrastructure of urban services appears as the norm rather than the exception in Global South cities (Silver 2015).

The "heterogeneity" of the cities of the Global South has been a focus of the decolonising Southern urban studies, or provincialising global urbanism (Sheppard, Leitner, and Maringanti 2013). The necessity to consider distinct analytical paradigms from a global urbanism modelled from the North limits the analytical look of cities in the South (Lawhon et al. 2018). The coexistence of modernist infrastructure policies and networks with informal and ad hoc self-provision of services produces "incremental infrastructure" (Silver 2014), where informality complements the official networks.

The dialectic between the formal and the informal in Southern cities is not an opposition between the wealthy and the poor. Rather, they are fractal, spread across the complete social spectrum where informal and illegal practices are integral part of the making of the city at all scales. Class power relations determine whether the informal is accepted rather than the sole rule of law (Roy 2011).

The practical making of the Global South city through informality, however, is built upon the attempts to formalise modernist understandings of planning, both as form and as institutional structure. As the developmental state attempts to rationalise its functions, it aims at expanding its authority through standardisation (J. C. Scott 1998). At the scale of the city, this ambition of the state results in the planning of infrastructure through regular urban grids to simplify its administrative and commercial management. However, social practice and the voluntary and involuntary weaknesses of the state results in widespread bypassing of official rules and existing services to accommodate material and social realities (Anand 2015).

Class contradictions and weak resources produce the Global South city. However, urban social and economic policies and practices vary within this framework. The resources of regional economic and transport hubs such as Abidjan and Nairobi cannot compare to the capacity of Bamako, whose economic importance is much more limited and located within the borders of Mali. The case of Juba is even more striking, as the small city has only recently taken political and economic importance within a context of civil war.

The following attempt to situate and describe the cities relies on different methods. Scientific literature and newspapers. As with all specific comparative description in this research, it has been necessary to work with primary sources. The following descriptions combine field visits observations with statistical and geographical data.

The field observation of the cities has been an integral part of this research. While the main focus has been the observation of the processes of territorialisation between international aid and the cities, it has been necessary to observe urban processes more largely to understand the much larger city metabolisms. A number of visits to city urbanists, when possible, permitted interviewing various professionals, as this was combined with a much larger informal inquiry, discussing with numerous people from different social classes to understand their place in relation to the city, as a place of work, culture, transit and housing. Not all these discussions can be restored here, but they have nourished the reflections below.

I have largely used the hand drawing in this aspect of the research, although I also used photography in some cases. Schematic sketches or direct observation has had practical and epistemological advantages. As a practical tool, it is less invasive than the use of photographs, and in that regard more respectful in the preservation of anonymity of people present on the scene. Sketches can be made and remade after the direct observations, which ensured discretion in the context of studying the city and the security of aid. Epistemologically, the advantage of sketches is the conscious focus on the objects at stake, which forces an analysis of the urban form starting on the field.

Few statistical datasets allow for comparable statistics in the cities of the South. The World Bank[15] and UN-Habitat[16] produce or compile in line with their missions social and economic data aggregated at the scale of cities. The combined use of these sources are used to present broad comparisons of the four cities.

Another important part of this chapter is the observation of the physical form of the cities with the use of geographic data. Although the use of satellite imagery to reconstruct general structure of the urban form was originally envisioned, it appeared that the heterogeneous nature of the building materials (e.g. concrete, soil, plastic, corrugated iron), combined with often dry soil made it complex to treat the data in series. Cement is the predominant material used to build modern African cities, ubiquitous as a travelling material that sets in motion global networks for production, commerce and construction (Choplin 2018). However, the historical fronts of urbanisation in African cities reflect a much more diverse use of materials in the construction of the built form. Access to concrete as building material depends on the capacities of countries to produce or import sufficient quantities of cement to support the urban expansion. Difficulties of access or prices of this primary component of the built form of African explain the large heterogeneity of building materials, especially in the poorest areas of the cities.

The construction of the structure of a house or its roof can include cement, clay, straw, corrugated iron and plastics, among others. The complexity to use the signals of satellite imagery to locate urbanisation fronts, often driven by the migration of poor dwellers, in the cities reflects the heterogeneity of the materials, which can be local or imported, new or recuperated. In Juba, much of the new areas supporting poor new dwellers on the outskirts of the city depend on the cheap and easily accessible materials used to build the traditional houses, the tukuls (Figure 22).

Urbanisation fronts and neighbourhoods not only change depending on the variety of materials. The combination and maintenance of building in the poorest areas of a city produce a highly heterogeneous built form. The area of Mathare, in Nairobi, built informally since the era of the independence of Kenya, presents a current panorama of houses combining mainly clay, wood and corrugated iron (Figure 23), although plastics often complete parts of the building as repairs.

15 https://data.worldbank.org/

16 http://urbandata.unhabitat.org/

Figure 22: A Tukul near Jebel Kujur in Juba. It combines adobe for the circular wall and roofing in wood and straw

Figure 23: House in Mathare, Nairobi. All external walls and roof are covered with corrugated iron

The fragility of the cheap building materials changes the aspect of buildings and neighbourhoods in sometimes a very short time. Corrugated iron can rust or fall (Figure 23). Plastic degrades fast under the sun or heavy rains. Degraded part of a building might in turn fast be covered with a different material. African cities, and their fronts of urbanisation in particular, fit incredibly well to the notion of a palimpsest, even on an extremely short period, and at the scales of neighbourhoods and individual buildings.

Few sources of GIS data are comparable in the context of African cities. The sources used for the spatial descriptions are heterogenous and comprise crowdsourcing, with the retrieving of OSM data, or institutional such as Soviet military mapping, which cover all areas. In some cases, the French IGN and IGM paper maps of Bamako and in Nairobi the Japanese International Cooperation

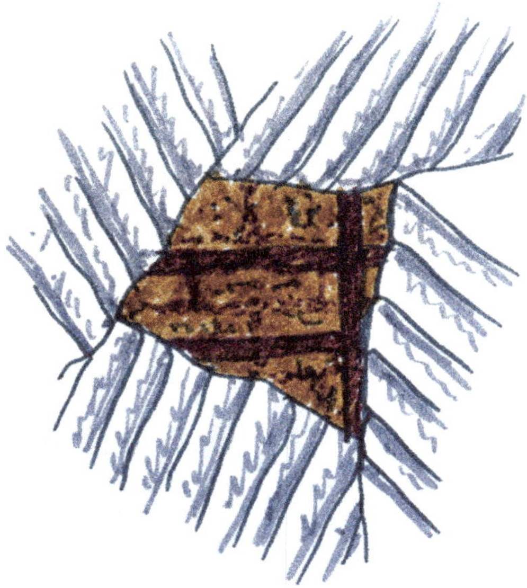

Figure 24: Detail of a house in Mathare. A piece of corrugated iron fallen from a house exposes the structure of the house, made of clay bricks, reinforced with wood sticks

Agency (JICA) digital land use map can complete the verification of data accuracy and precision. GIS software supported the processes of georeferencing, data extraction and treatment as well as map design. The table (Figure 25) summarises the main GIS data sources, their type and the treatment used.

4.3.1 Population Growth and Spatial Expansion in Bamako Juba Abidjan and Nairobi

The four cities studied for this research represent different historical path and distinct political importance. They also have a distinct demographic importance compared to each other, although they all witnessed a spectacular growth in recent history, from villages at the colonial times to major population centres in a few decades. The absorption by the major African cities of an increasing part of the country's population – and often from other African countries in South-South migration phenomenon – represents for most of the new urban dwellers only limited opportunities in the form of low-pay work, most often below the poverty line (Davis 2006).

Source	Location	Type of data	Data provenance	Data status	Type of Analysis/ Treatment
OpenStreetMap	*All*	*Vector*	*Crowdsourcing*	*Open access*	*Extraction/ Selections/ Geoprocessing*
Russian military mapping	*All*	*Raster*	*Institutional*	*Open access*	*Georeferencing/ Digitisation*
IGN France	*Bamako*	*Paper*	*Institutional*	---	*Georeferencing/ Digitisation*
IGM Mali	*Bamako*	*Paper*	*Institutional*	---	*Georeferencing/ Digitisation*
JICA	*Nairobi*	*Vector*	*Institutional*	*Open access*	*Selections/ Geoprocessing*

Figure 25: Principal sources of geographic data

The growth of the urban population in all African cities has been spectacular since the 1960s, when most African countries gained their independence. Ivory Coast and Mali became independent in 1960, and Kenya two years later. These three countries have followed a path of spectacular increase of the urban population, from between 10 and 20 % to more than 50 % in Ivory Coast, and around 40 % for Mali and 25 % for Kenya, according to the numbers of the World Bank. Definitions of urban areas may differ depending on the country, typically on variable administrative and demographic criteria. Consequently, these numbers must be considered as the indication of a trend, rather than exact values (Figure 26).

The case of South Sudan is here an exception, which is also following a different path of urbanisation. Urbanisation of the South Sudan started later than the other countries, in the 1980s, largely due to the renewed period of war following 1983 (Mills 1985; Ati et al. 2011). Population movement linked to the war provoked both inward and outwards migration from cities: "During some intervals, rural households moved to urban areas for greater physical security and access to scarce food supplies and services, while at other times when urban areas were under attack, urban households migrated to neighbouring countries and to the North." (World Bank 2011). The major recipient of South Sudanese refugees was the Sudanese capital Khartoum, rather than any of the South Sudanese towns, including Juba (Ibrahim 1991; Lavergne 1997).

All the four countries have witnessed spectacular increase in the population of the capital in five decades. The absolute numbers of dwellers in the four capitals illustrates the relative demographic importance of each city. The population

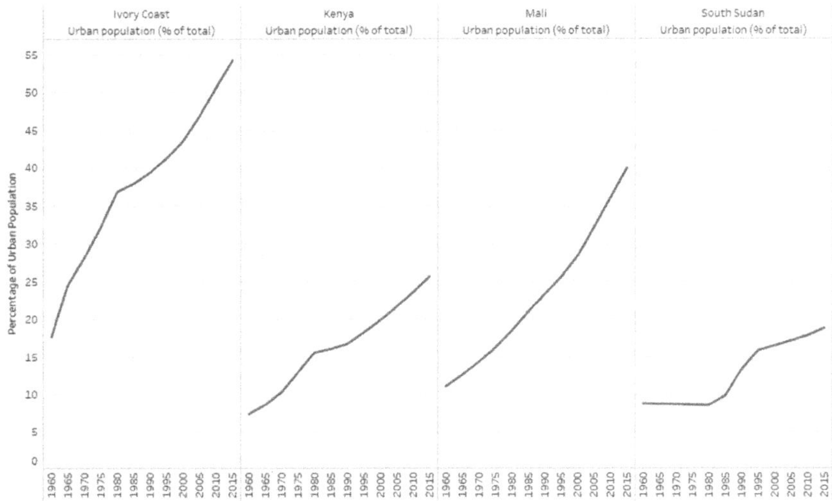

Figure 26: Percentage of urban population from 1960 to 2015

trajectories of the cities follow a remarkably similar pattern of exponential growth after the independences, visible despite different sizes (Figure 27). Numerous research on African urbanisation in light of rural-urban migration association urban population growth to distinct but related phenomena (Groth 2017). High fertility rates, declining mortality and limited resources in agriculture have placed the cities as key recipients of a population in search of subsistence and economic opportunities.

The place of Juba is particular within the group of four cities, for its much smaller population. Reflecting the relatively low level of urbanisation, the city is the smallest of the four with between 300 and 600 thousand depending on the source (Ati et al. 2011). The other three cities are estimated between 3 and 5 million by the World Bank, although these numbers only include municipal boundaries and not metropolitan areas.

The distinct population sizes and paces of expansion helps understand the difficulties of the state at its different scales to both manage the provision of services and to impose its presence and regulations. The scarce resources available to cities in "underdeveloped" economies only increases the difficulties of the state. The result of this is a fragmented urban environment, where much of the provision of services is let to the private users themselves. The private resources depending on the wealth of individuals, the urban quality varies in all aspects;

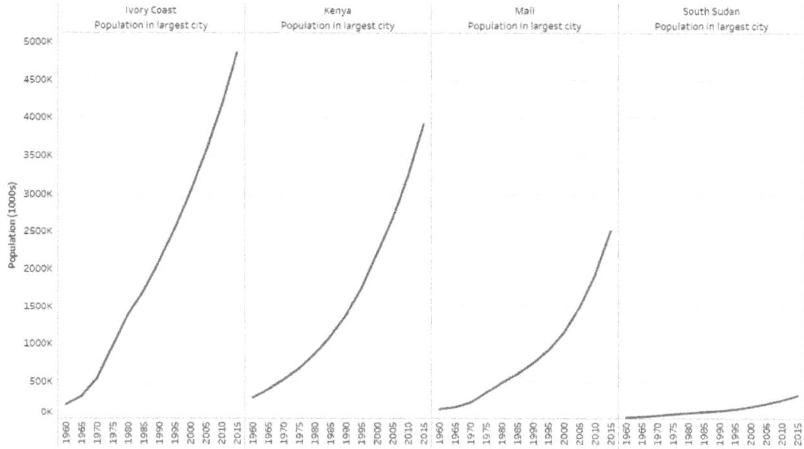

Figure 27: Population in the four capitals from 1960 to 2015

education, health, sanitation and infrastructure splinters in two standards where the private assumes the highest quality and the public sector tends to represent lower quality of service (S. Graham and Marvin 2001; Zwi, Brugha, and Smith 2001; Smit 2018).

Reflecting the intense population growth of the four cities, their built environment has expanded spectacularly since the independences. The lack of comparable data available limits the comparisons. The following comparative map aims, however, to present an overview of the extensive spatial spread of the decades after independence (Figure 28). Created using a combination of archives including Russian military mapping, and the French Institut Géographique National maps for an archive of the development of the city in the past decades and OpenStreetMap data.

These comparisons present a number of limitations. They are not based on standardised documentation. Although OSM data represent the cities in real time (and have proved to be reliable in numerous instances) they depend on the goodwill of contributors and their evolution and updates has different paces. Russian military maps are not scaled for city maps, but at larger scales between 1:500'000 and 1:50'000, which only permits examining the rough outlook of the city and main arteries. Mapping from other agencies and local institutions are often better suited for monographic history of the city, although they might not include the whole city for political reasons, in particular unwillingness to include informal settlements (Roy 2005; Subbaraman et al. 2012). As they are not

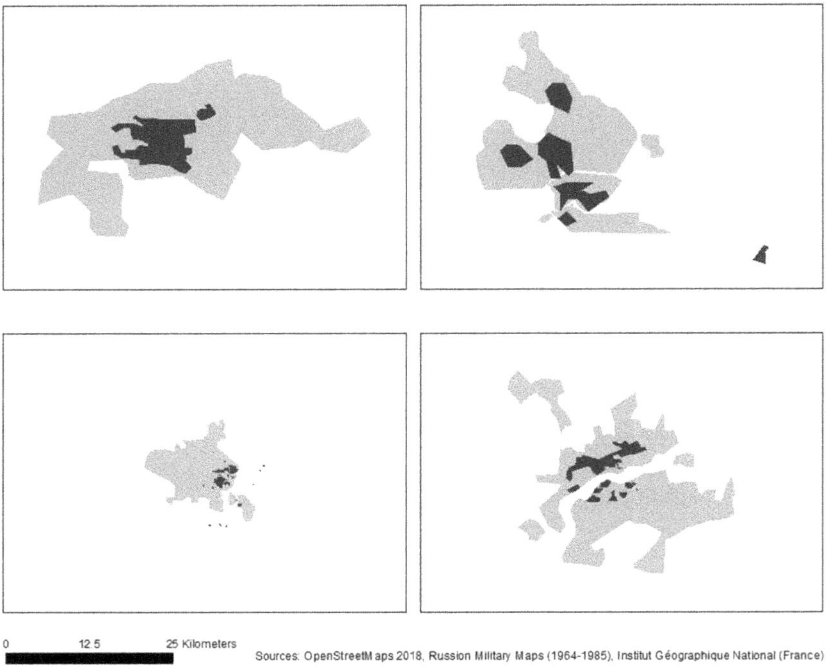

Figure 28: Comparing the sizes and expansion of the four cities studied for this work. From left to right first row, Nairobi 1964–2018, Abidjan 1983–2018. Second row, Juba 1985–2018 and Bamako 1979–2018

built following the same standards, they make comparisons difficult. However, the main limit to working with maps produced by local institutions is accessing them, which requires thorough research in the different institutions that might produce these maps and the willingness – or not – to share them with researchers.

The result of these intra-city comparisons between one roughly defined period, and the contemporary cities can, however, illustrate two things. First, they show that the cities of this panorama are different in dimensions. Second, they clearly show that despite these strong differences in their dimensions and populations, they are witnessing similar degrees of expansion to harbour the new city dwellers in a few decades. A third element clearly visible from at least three of the cities, Juba, Bamako and Abidjan, is how they grew out of multiple cores, which at the time of the colonisation marked the difference between the

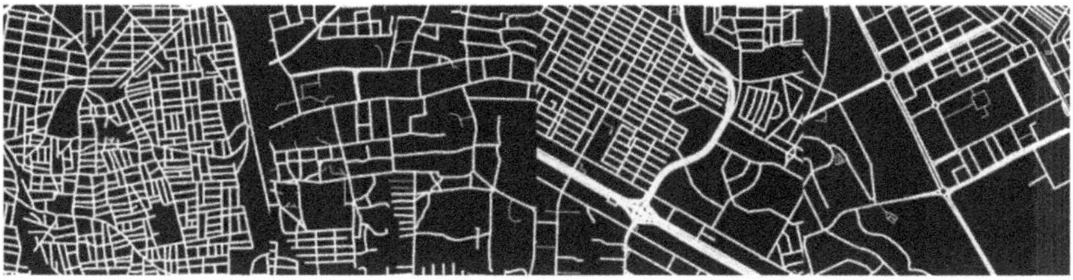

Figure 29: Square mile road extract form (left to right) Bamako, Juba, Abidjan and Nairobi, OSM data 2018

colonial city and the African urban areas and nearby villages which have been incorporated in the city expansion and a continuous built environment.

At the level of urban governance, the four cities have a different history and form. As can be seen in the juxtaposition below of road grids from the four cities (Bamako, Juba, Nairobi and Abidjan) follow distinct forms between each other, but also different types of urban forms within each city. The image below (Figure 29) is four one square mile extracts of current OSM roads, retrieved thanks to a Python library specifically developed to study urban patterns and their relative complexity (Boeing 2017, 2018).

These extracts are selected relatively randomly in each of the cities. Located at central places they illustrate the shared use of space following regular grids and seemingly more random patterns. In the case of Nairobi and Abidjan, they also show an emphasis on heavy infrastructure road projects which are found with effective regularity on the urban street grid as a measure to canalise the heavy traffic of important commuter charges. The use of identical scales facilitates comparisons in visualising their complexity and present the variety of distinct possible usages (Jacobs 1993). Their distinctiveness intra-city calls for an outlook at the distinct regimes of road planning within each city.

The first two squares, representing Juba and Bamako are also representative of two cities that juxtapose regular and irregular road planning. The influence and adaptation to informal settlements are characteristic not just of limited areas where poor dweller settle, but of large parts of the cities, where the state tolerates informal presence. Later state intervention may partly re-square the road network, although it tends to keep most informal layouts.

The four cities have in common a taste for the planning in orthogonal grids of roads. The networks of streets and roads that can be retrieved from OSM data present a precise comparable set of urban data. The streets and roads are traced forming rectangular or square blocks. This regularity reflects the firm belief in the positive impacts of regular grids for movement and safety; still the regular geometry street grids do not define the quality of urban infrastructure. The comparatively similar squareness of the street blocks present very different levels of street paving, 59 and 24 % in Nairobi and Bamako in 2012, for instance (UN-Habitat 2019).

This geometric regularity of grids is interrupted by more heterodox shapes, which seem to follow other logics, in some areas. This aspect, most visible in Nairobi and Bamako reflects almost invariably the presence of informal urban dwelling or slums. Those may follow watersheds rather than the planning of a topographer. Upgraded slums also appears quite clearly on the outline, presenting the irregular outline of streets, crossed with the new ways in it.

The regularity of the street grid itself might not necessarily be reflected in the regularity of the constructions. At the level of the building, the current OSM data does not allow a complete comparison, since it is not consistent in its level of detail in all cities. But where the data is complete, like in Juba, it shows that the buildings, if away from the roads, do not follow clearly plots of land within the blocks. The same can be seen in other places. The city blocks in Bamako are built over time, following needs and financial resources of families (Vauthrin 1989). As mentioned during a talk with the Director of Technical Services in the commune of Cocody, some houses of Abidjan, in turn, might not be even built on the right allotment, when an owner does not check with a solicitor and a topographer.[17]

Outlying from the blocks are typically informal constructions of small businesses like bars and restaurants that might not be limited to working-class areas of a city. The cities of Bamako and Abidjan have a long tradition in tolerating these types of shop on the broad streets of the public way. The demolition of such houses might be carried out in a row, following new policy directions. The area of Badalabougou was cleared in the end of 2016 to make place for a main sewage collector, in a move that many residents saw as the cruel and unjust showcase sanitation projects in sight of the Francophonie summit to be held in Bamako some months later.

The stricter respect of planning regulation is nevertheless visible in richer areas. It also includes the management of water, sewage and electricity that might come either from a private initiative, or because the area was planned as such, generally for upper-middle-class dwellers, as with the ACI in Bamako, or

17 Interview with Mr Ajavon, 2 May 2017.

in some social housing projects, like ATTbougou[18] in Faladié and the numerous SICOGI in Abidjan. Overall the rectangle grid planning is not the bottom line for the rich and middle class, but the upper line for the poor. Upper end areas must be constructed in orthogonal streets. The use in some upper-class areas of coupling with circular roads is one exception to orthogonality, although this design still follows a geometric outline, rather than natural features of the terrain. Regular girds are one feature of wealthy areas, although they extends to all formal neighbourhoods.

The cost ratio between price of land and construction is one of the drivers of a city expanding horizontally rather than vertically. Only the city centres of these cities, dedicated to business and administrations see more than one or two storeys. The city expansion on one-storey buildings is made possible by the low cost of land, especially, when it is not provided with network services, except for the tracing of the road grid. All cities tend to resemble large suburbs, and the effect on transportation is invariably traffic jams.

The streets' outlines designate where major roads and infrastructure projects cross the city. In that regard, Abidjan and Nairobi are more equipped in great urban arteries and interchanges, reflecting their policy of infrastructure in managing traffic with the multiplication of inner city expressways. Some of the wealthiest in Nairobi can afford to take the air road, making the sight and sound of helicopters a regular feature of the Nairobi sky and soundscape. The city of Bamako with a high traffic density also follows that road, but with fewer resources, depending on gifts, as two of the three bridges bear the name of their Saudi and Chinese benefactors, the "Pont du Roi Fahd" and "Pont de l'Amitié Sino-Malienne". Local urbanists point the limits of the management of traffic through enlargement of roads, and some seem to favour relocating commercial activities to spread them in the city to limit displacement.[19]

4.3.2 Visibility of Infrastructure

The notion of "heterogeneous infrastructure configurations" aims to describe the characteristics of the cities in the South as the provision of urban services split between an official infrastructure incapable (and sometimes unwilling) to accommodate all citizens and the informal processes of self-provision of services

18 Named with the contraction the initials of former Malian president Amadou Toumani Touré, "ATT" and the suffix "bougou", meaning "village" or "neighbourhood" in Bamabara.

19 Interview with Gouro Landouré, 9 March 2016.

(Jaglin 2004; Lawhon et al. 2018). The configuration of the service infrastructure out of access to the poorest inhabitants leaves self-help to complete the official grid. While in the North, the social and physical invisibility of networked services provision configures the modernist city (Kaika and Swyngedouw 2000), another mark of the provision of services in the South, across official and informal settings alike, is in fact the visibility of infrastructure. When I arrived in Grand-Bassam in the periphery of Abidjan, the address of my guesthouse directed me to walk to the "Rue du Chateau" from the main coastal road. In this old colonial capital of the Ivory Coast, I expected to find some ancient fortress. The street name was in fact referring to another type of castle as I noticed walking on the street. The raw concrete water tower of the neighbourhood was in fact a common feature of African cities and infrastructure, where network services are visible from the ground to the skyline.

As political ecologists postulate the invisibility of infrastructure as a form of fetishising and commodification of water (Larkin 2013), among other essential services, the characteristics of the city of the South might in fact lay in the visibility of the infrastructure. Water provision populates the skyline of Abidjan as while in the North water tower tend indeed to be made invisible by burying them, in cities of the South the presence of infrastructure is in fact marked by its visibility. The modernist showcase represented by the pride taken in new and large infrastructure projects like airports and interchanges is resolutely voluntarist. On the other hand, the visibility of basic needs provision – when present – signals the presence of the state in the everyday life of city dwellers.

This visibility is not limited to fixed infrastructures, and in fact increases when people organise services away from official channels (Anand 2017). The lack of public services translates sometimes in a form of mobile infrastructures. The trucks and bicycles which bring and sell water to the rich and poor are visible circulating in Juba traffic (Barbarani 2017b; Morbe 2018). While the poor fill their individual canisters, those who can afford larger quantities to have running water have their own water tanks at their disposal inside their compounds. The few existing water piping systems are part of disconnected projects supported by foreign cooperation agencies in localised projects (Miettaux 2019).

Water evacuation has similar levels of visibility. Open sewage is the norm – when there is any – for its relative simplicity to build and manage. The "V"-shaped sewage looks similar in the four cities. A ditch on the sides of the road allows evacuation of wastewater and drain to a greater water collector. Sewage systems constitute a good indicator of the intra-city inequalities. In most informal areas, the water collection is simply inexistent and the flowing of wastewater either takes the shortest way on the slope or stagnates.

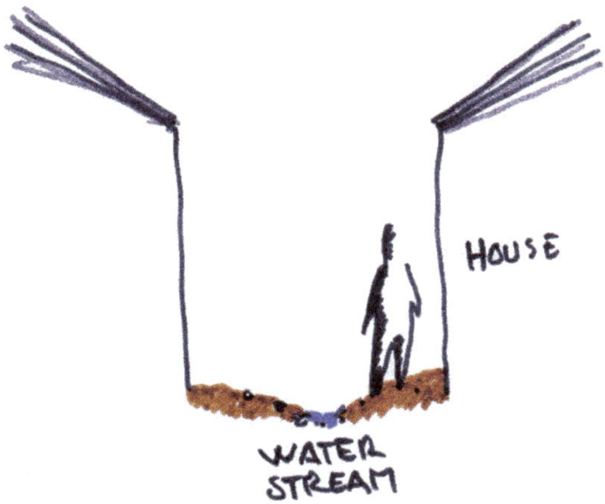

Figure 30: Mathare, Nairobi. Houses are built on natural elevations and water drips down the hill

The lanes that separate buildings in the Mathare slum area in Nairobi, for example, are oriented parallel to the slope and let the small streams flow down to the river forming creek beds in their centre. These creek beds have pushed the installation of the houses on small ridges to avoid flooding in the houses (Figure 30). In this case, it is the absence of planning for the spontaneous constructions, which permitted using the natural terrain to limit the effect of the flooding hazards, rather than locating the houses following rectangular street grid.

Avoiding the small stream running towards Mathare River have formed the main arteries of the informal neighbourhood. The ad hoc practice of building houses in the area has created the small pedestrian streets pointing towards the river in Mathare Valley (Figure 31). The practice is contrary to the official building of urban grids, based on geometric shapes rather than natural terrain. Subsequent "slum upgrading" programmes have involved the construction of a number of larger straight streets in some sections of the settlement.

The spontaneous practice of avoiding natural obstacles and other forms of vernacular architecture form part of the making of cities from their social margins. The resulting spontaneous infrastructure create a material environment of heterogeneous configurations. In neighbourhoods with minimal planning of sewage, ditches on one or both sides of the roads permits evacuation of waste and rainwater, although the water often stagnates when the terrain is

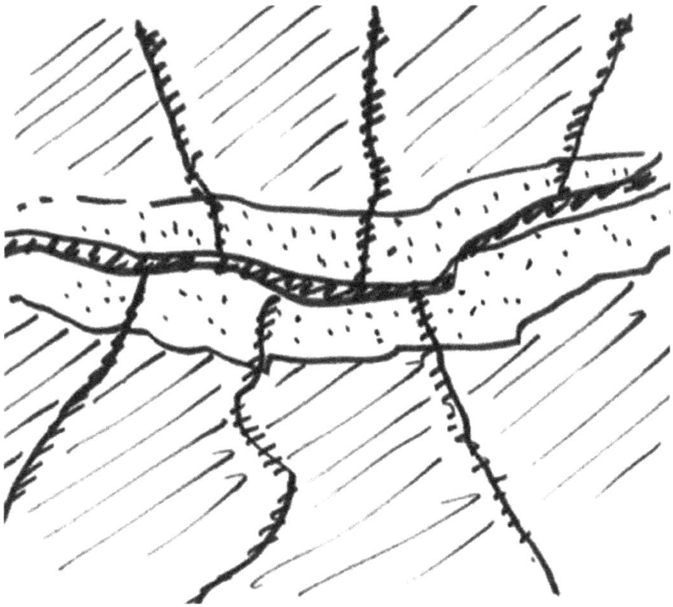

Figure 31: Streams running towards Mathare River from the main pedestrian arteries of the neighbourhood

flat. Coupled with scarce garbage collection and street cleaning, solid waste clogs even more the sewage until the next irregular cleaning. Stagnant open sewage waters host a variety of pests, including rats and mosquitoes are most common in the poor areas of the cities, but also often middle-class areas.

The ditches are sometimes reinforced with concrete plates assembled in V or square shapes to prevent them crumbling on themselves (Figure 32). A concrete topping can also be added to prevent more waste falling inside and sometimes pedestrian walking (Figure 33). This marks important collectors and well-off areas.

The visibility of sewage is a common feature within the cities. The state of sewers, from very well maintained in rich suburbs and the CBDs of Nairobi and Abidjan to non-existent or clogged in other areas show different degrees of state intervention in basic infrastructure. They constitute a visible marker of the lines of poverty and wealth within cities. It illustrates as well the reliance on infrastructure adaptable to most areas, although significant differences in implementation

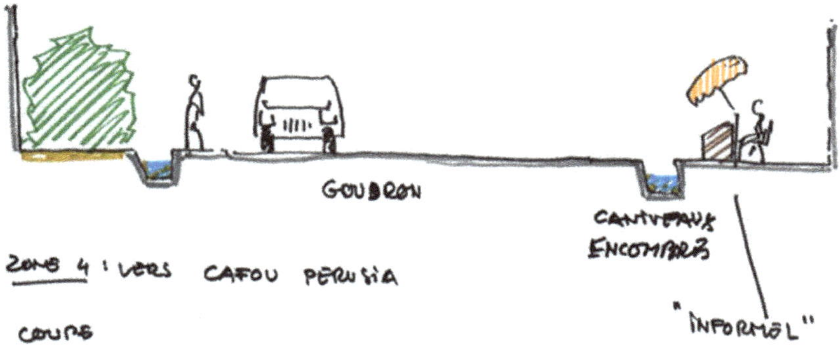

Figure 32: Wastewater collectors in Abidjan

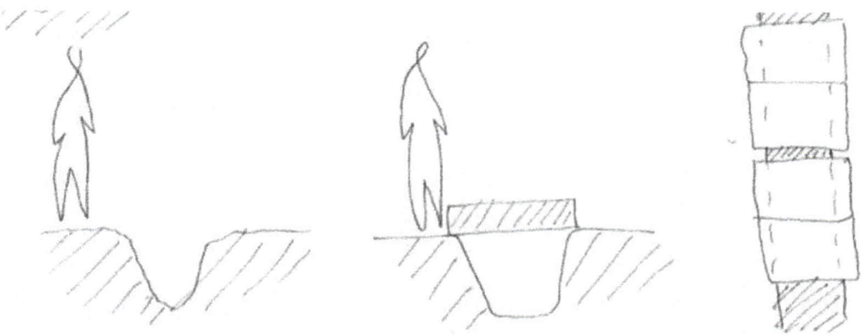

Figure 33: Wastewater collectors in Bamako. Left: V-shaped ditch. Middle: the ditch is covered with concrete blocks. Right: the concrete toppings seen from above. The interstices between blocks are left to permit water dripping. Concrete toppings are much more frequent in wealthier areas of the city

can mark the quality of visual and olfactory panorama (Henshaw 2013), as a marker of spatial class disparities (Inglis 2016).

The class nature of sewage is also apparent in relation to safety. While some sewers are covered with concrete tops, it is exceptional to see barriers, or any other protection, around even around the largest and deepest collectors. The safety issue that this represents is one of many aspects in which the planning and engineering of roads are almost exclusively devoted to motorised transport, where only limited protections are offered to pedestrians.

Urban infrastructure are heterogenous, as the combination of formal and informal metabolisms adapt to population growth and high levels of poverty.

They reflect the scarce resources of municipal authorities as much as the social inequalities within cities. Yet, city developments also depend on a connection with their surroundings and further economic and political networks. The following section will underline the nature and state of transport infrastructure supporting the capitals.

4.3.3 Moorings

The cities are supported by a series of infrastructures liking them to their hinterland, to major national roads connecting them the rest of the country. Internationally, they are connected to the global network of transportation with major roads, ports or airports. At the periphery of globalisation, the state of the infrastructure permits limited connectivity within wider transport flows. Intra-city infrastructure places the four capitals as major hubs within their countries, and as the periphery of globalisation internationally. National and regional communication roads are different between the countries. Without giving a detailed account of all the cases, it is possible to note that the convergence of the infrastructure towards the capitals places the latter as an indispensable hub for most transports of goods and people.

In the periphery of globalisation, infrastructure does not guarantee a fair and free flow of exchanges. The presence of the port of Abidjan proved deadly to seventeen Ivorian citizens in 2006, when a cargo ship offloaded tons of toxic waste, later dumped across the city (Denoiseux 2010). From the ports connecting to the global trade of goods and materials to the African cities, roads of variable quality support city metabolism, from comestibles to building materials. In the context of slow and sometimes dangerous travel by road, prices of materials are often more expensive in African cities than in more connected networks (Calderón and Servén 2010).

Condition of the roads leading to the four cities are different, and marks the relative spatial and economic integration of the cities in trade networks. The Mombassa-Nairobi highway supports truck traffic for large shipments of goods to much of East Africa. Roads leading to Juba are mostly not asphalted and often impracticable during the rainy season, which leads to the use of ship transport on the Nile River for trade. Other dangers, such as highway criminality increases the difficulties of road transports, endemic since the start of the civil war in South Sudan. Attacks against passenger and commercial transports can also be a common occurrence in countries where the state of the roads is recent and relatively well maintained, such as Ivory Coast, with armed "coupeurs de routes" regularly stealing from travellers (AIP 2019).

The presence of former colonial powers in African countries and their control on various types of infrastructure faded considerably in the last decades, with increasing presence of the Upper-Middle Income countries, such as Russia, Brazil, Turkey, and especially China. The large markets of consumers for cheap goods and materials partly opened the way for Chinese investments in infrastructure, which have become an essential part of the engineering project in much of the continent (Wang 2007). As Chinese state companies have become essential investors and builders of African infrastructure, other Chinese companies sell all types of commodities, crossing through new roads and bridges. As infrastructure links African cities to global markets, it allows imports and exports of a diversity of goods, although still on highly unequal terms.

Airports constitute a central element in connecting the cities to the global networks of moorings bending space and time at the time of globalisation (Hannam, Sheller, and Urry 2006). Within countries with limited land connections infrastructure, airports constitute an important bypass, in its capacity to propose faster connections to global moorings, such as major economic and transport hubs. Following a standardised international network of air traffic, airports in the four capitals nevertheless constitute the lower ladder of global interconnectivity. Even as Abidjan and Nairobi airports constitute relatively important transport hubs, they still have a relatively low number of flights and companies, compared to cities of similar sizes in other continents.

African airports trail far after the standardised designs and procedures in place within the air transport industry. Juba airport was voted in 2017 the world's worst airport by air travel website Sleeping in Airports (2017) who noted in its review, "At Juba Airport, travellers don't bother to complain about things like the lack of Wi-Fi and charging points – they're more concerned about the lack of electricity in 40 degree Celsius heat! […] horrific smells and filth, high heat, rain leaking into the tent, corruption and a lot of security walking around with guns." As the traveller websites summarises, "South Sudan is a war-torn state that perhaps has more pressing concerns." (Sleeping in Airports 2017). The description given by this traveller website is far from the airport as a laboratory for socio-technical innovations (Parker 2002), which even African regional aviation hubs find hard to follow. Jomo Kenyatta International Airport in Nairobi airport completely burnt down in 2013, in conditions still unclear today (FlightGlobal 2013). Despite limited resources, the place of airports in the construction of globalisation pushes for investment and constant attempts to reclaim the position within the network of air travel, adapting to new standards and norms. Renewing airports and installing biometric equipment and body scanners aims to integrate the global flows and pace of globalisation in the form of security equipment upgrades (Andersson 2016).

Cities depend on the broader context of their position within short middle and long-distance travels of goods and passengers. As dynamic evolving entities served and serving their hinterland while connecting to global moorings, the infrastructure of connections to the exterior largely shapes their built form as well as economic and social structures.

4.3.4 Bamako

The city of Bamako evolved from a large village in the precolonial times to become a three million people capital. From a town of much less important than many of those that are part of today's Mali. Most famous, since the mediaeval times, the city of Timbuktu is now only a provincial capital. In the agricultural South, precolonial fortress town like Sikasso in the South, or Kayes to the West of the country had a greater importance than Bamako before the French colonisation. The Gallieni military observation mission of 1880–1881, led by French colonial officer Joseph Gallieni, produced a map of Bamako as a small town a few hundred metres from the Niger River (Figure 34). The ancient village surrounded by mud walls is completely erased under the city centre since colonial times (Piétri 1881).

The increasing importance of Bamako owed first to its use of the local topography by the French colonisation. With hills surrounding it, the governorate could be located, in higher ground where the colonist could both easily monitor the city and the surrounding area and crush any revolt from above. The colonial times saw the central part of current Bamako being organised through the railway and a number of state offices, such as post offices and court of law in "Neo Sudanese" style, the use of concrete to mimic the aesthetic of the traditional mud houses of Mali.

The city centre layout owes much to the governor of Bamako, Henri Terrasson de Fougères, who marked the first orthogonal layout in the 1920s and the planting of trees, which still mark the city centre (ENS Mali 1993). Family properties have since evolved with the construction adding new constructions to the family plots to make space for the growth of families.

The areas surrounding the centre of the city, marked by the orthogonal street grid, become from the colonial era the model for urban planning. The orthogonality of the urban grid has become, in Bamako as in many African cities, the start and end points of the planning of any new urban area. In the urge to accommodate the arrival of new dwellers in the capital, from the independence

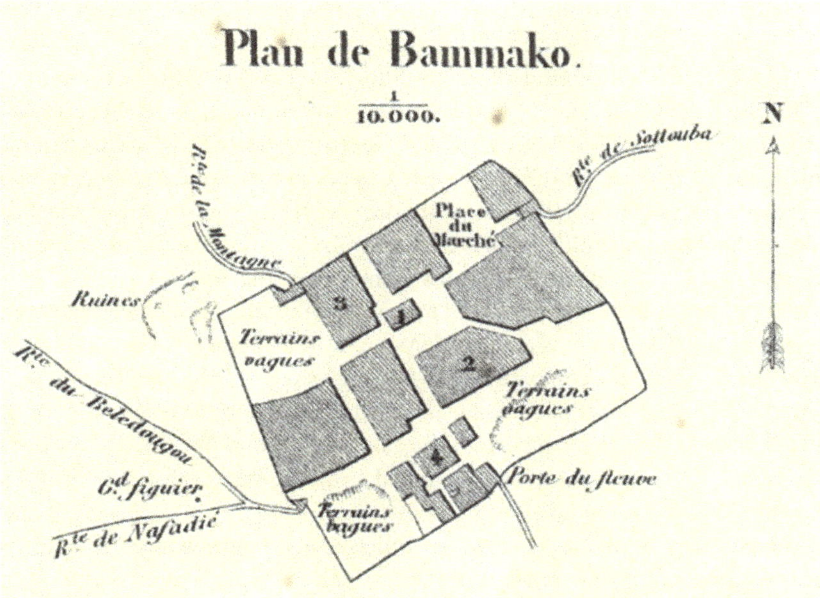

Figure 34: Bamako in 1880, according to the Gallieni colonial mission. Nothing remains today of the precolonial town. Map consulted at the Bibliothèque de Genève, Département des cartes et plans

onwards, the planning did not necessarily include more than creating the roads. Servicing, sewage, water and electricity often fall in the hands of the private, up to this day.

This approach to planning is so strong that maps of Bamako that witness the history of the informal urban expansion allows recognising instantly the areas that were not planned from the outset. The outline of streets is then irregular. The pattern of street networks follows the contingencies of self-building: natural obstacles, and limits in space. The servicing process that might follow the spontaneous settlement consists rarely in more than the creation of new roads, and the installation of basic services, such as schools.

From the 1960s onwards, Bamako, like most African capitals absorbed a large part of the vast increase in population that were witnessed all over Africa. The natural environment, forming a basin with hills surrounding the urban core fixed the limits of the urban area. Within the hull of the built-up area, only limited parts developed in the planned orthogonal fashion, mostly in areas designed to shelter the new class of civil servants. The rest of the city mainly developed informally.

Maps of Bamako from the 1970s until now shows what were the main limits to informal urbanisation: physical barriers and military areas (Figure 35). Within the city hull of the 1970s, the few places that remained uninhabited had only been left by formal or informal dwellers because of difficult topography or the presence military installations. After the end of the Moussa Traoré dictatorship, in the 1990s, the military airfield that lay in the middle of the capital would become ACI 2000, structured around a main avenue that used to be the airstrip. ACI 2000, meant to be a middle- and upper-class dwelling area as well as a commercial area that landmarks the new democratic and liberal era. The old military airport now has airline companies, hotels, congress centres and malls witnessing both the aeronautic past of the area, and the liberal economic orientation of the 1990s onwards. In the same period, the small island that has since become the very high end "Cité du Niger" was planned as a villa area, with a new bridge to allow the crossing on foot and by car.

The built environment is the result of the social compromise, which allowed the settlement of the new dwellers in the city with the limited intervention of the state. Informal settlements can be seen as the incapacity of the state. It can also be understood as part of urban management by the state (Roy 2005; Baumgart and Kreibich 2011). It allows housing of the poor without the requirement from the state to deliver urban services, since dwelling in the area is illegal.

At the scale of the quartier, Bamako mostly shows some levels of spatial integration between the poor and the rich areas of the city. The quartier of Badalabougou shows that the residential zoning is quite diverse in a relatively small area (Figure 36). This relatively wealthy area will be mentioned again in the next chapters, as it has an important expatriate presence. The area harbours six distinct zones within a few square kilometres. Most of the area is strictly formal as it was first developed for the housing of civil servants in the SEMA projects. In this zone, the buildings have a characteristic long shape parallel to the road, hosting several adjacent apartments designed to host a number of civil servants and their families. A working-class area of courtyard habitat grew on the side of the SEMA, following formal planning patterns. In this type of area, however, the task of building their own houses has been left to the owners of the land. The result is apparent on the map of the built environment, as the placement of buildings within properties is relatively random.

In its current shape, Badalabougou is dominated by two areas of luxurious villas, along most of the river shore. This area hosts the Malian elite along with foreigners, embassies and foreign institutes. These specific zones will be described in more

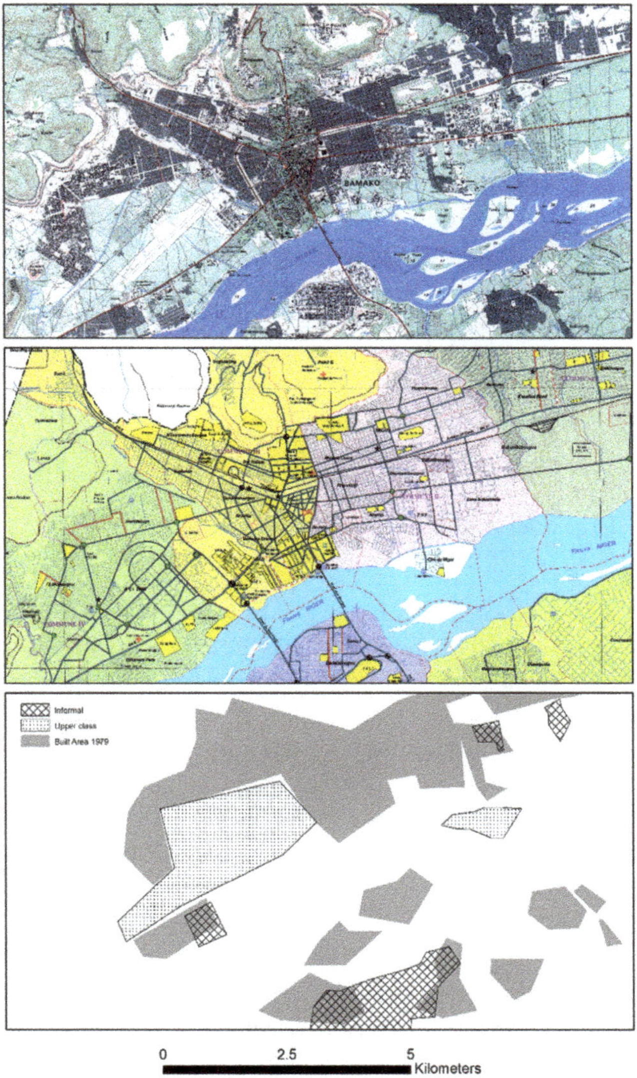

Figure 35: Bamako city centre. From left to right, Bamako in 1979 in 2014 and the evolution of the built environment during this period. All areas within the city hull have been built formally or informally

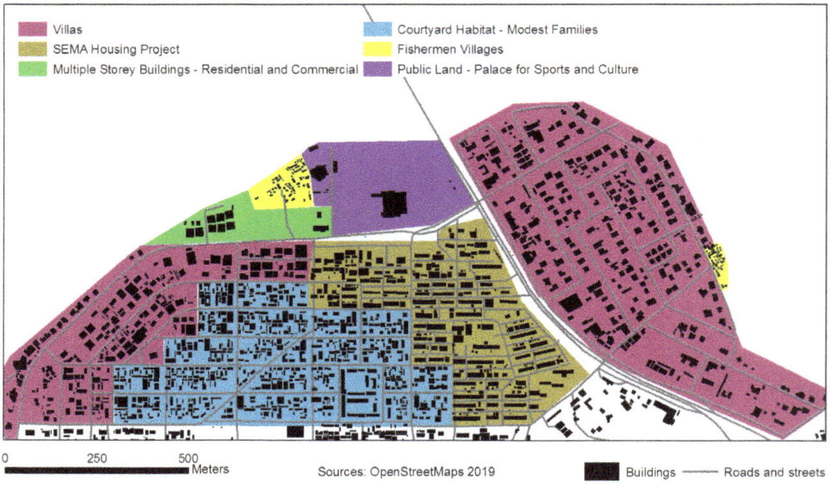

Figure 36: The quartier of Badalabougou

detail later, as they are extensively being used by aid workers since 2013. The contrast in density of the built environment marks the difference in the social position of the different inhabitants of the quartier. Villas have large footprint and are located inside large gardens.

At the very social opposite of the villas, the adjacent fisher neighbourhood are the remnants of an old settlement of families depending on fishing and the cultivation of the areas to the shores of the Niger. Buildings are small in relation to all types of housing within the quartier. Customary rights have allowed these families to remain in the areas, although the shape and concentration of these villages reflect the conflictual relation to their wealthy neighbours. These ancient dwelling areas contradict the ambition of a prestigious microcosm of the wealthy, on the Southern bank of the river.

Note that the presence of the Palace for Culture and sports in Badalabougou is also representative of an ambition by the Malian state to retain a level of control over the development of the riverbanks. While the north bank hosts the administrative ministerial city, the Palace of culture guarantees a level of public ownership on the Southern shore.

The city of Bamako has a distinct institutional status. As the capital city, it is under the supervision of a Mayor of a separate district, which does not belong to any of the administrative regions of the country. The six communes that constitute the district have separate town hall and political responsibilities. The suburbs of the capital outreach the administrative limits of the district struggling to keep the pace of urban planning and expansion to house the constant flow of newly settled inhabitants.

The district of Bamako almost perfectly fits inside the depression of steep natural hills. With the exception of the Koulouba palace and the Point G hospital areas, both purposely located on hilltops, the city has rarely expanded on the slopes. The demographic pressure now pushes more towards the circling ridges. The higher complexity in bringing urban services limited the expansion on the higher ground does not forbid the zoning and parcellation of the land and private construction.

Within the city hull, planning and urban transformations push towards higher density with more emphasis on verticality and the regularisation of the urban grid and buildings. The expulsions, or "déguerpissements" and relocations "recasements", up to a limit of residents of the informal areas are a major preoccupation of the urban authorities. As Gouro Landouré, the Chief Urbanist of a Bamako Commune explained, residents affected by expulsions are sometimes relocated, but not always. Most expulsions aim to reduce the population density of the area and demolish some houses to build access roads, and basic public services, such as schools and local health centres.[20]

The need to house modest families results in most urban services reduced to the local minimum standard. It includes the road network to allow services to drive through the neighbourhood. This is, however, often all the authorities can offer for the price of the land. In consequence, water, electricity and sewage networks are not included in most urban planning. Later initiative between the municipality and the inhabitants of a neighbourhood might upgrade the services if residents are ready to pay and participate. The Commune 4 of Bamako did such projects in several neighbourhoods for street pavement as well as regular garbage collection.[21] Most often individuals pay for bringing the services to their streets.

The relation between the formal and the informal construction in the city marks the spontaneous neighbourhoods, with municipal authorities constantly trying to catch up with the needs and presence of the poor. The relation to urban rules is, however, also chaotic in most formal areas. As Gouro Landouré explained, the relatively high-rise office buildings often do not respond to the construction permits and the planning rules. "No one respects the rules, even in the planned neighbourhoods. If they have the authorisation for two storeys,

20 Interview with Gouro Landouré, 9 March 2016.
21 Interview with Aboubacar Bougoudogo, 16 March 2016.

they will build four, even though the soil is not safe with risks of subsidence and collapse. This happened recently even in an official allotment. A seven storey crumbled. They had the authorisation for five storeys."[22] As the same developer had two of his buildings crumbling on their own weight in a period of two years, the catastrophic failure of buildings illustrates how informality and illegality are persistent as an expression of class power which permits major transgressions by the wealthiest citizens with little consequences (Roy 2011).

4.3.5 Abidjan

Since the presidency of Felix Houphouët-Boigny, Abidjan is not the official capital of Ivory Coast, even though it has the seat of government, ministries and parliament and its port is the heart of the national economy. This authorises to colloquially refer to Abidjan as the capital, leaving Yamoussoukro to its gigantic cathedral. The port of Abidjan trades more than the export of the main agriculture products of Ivory Coast, cocoa, coffee and rubber. It is also one of the key hubs for merchant fleets to West Africa. As such, its importance in the urban economy and the country's economy as a whole is of prime importance.

The site of Abidjan is constituted around a lagoon, and some of the communes that constitute the city are inland and others on islands. The history of Abidjan is short. French colonial authorities made Bassam and later Bingerville successively the regional capital, each time to flee mosquitoes and malaria, before developing the area around the Abidjan lagoon (Chenal 2009).

The structure of the built environment in Abidjan is marked by the continuous presence of the French architects, long after the independence in 1960. The French population always stayed important in Abidjan after the independence, remaining as a professional elite (Bazin 1997; Verquin 2000). This influence is so strong that following the independence almost all bureaus of architecture and urbanism that marked the city of Abidjan were foreigners, and most of all French. A look at the special issue of Urbanisme, sponsored to display the development of Abidjan in 1969 (Urbanisme : revue française 1969), shows that a few companies shared the whole of official building market. One company would specialise in social housing, the other in monumental architecture, and yet another in building the high-end areas of the city. The only major non-French developer of the 1960s, the Mafit Trust under Romanian-Israeli architect Moshe Mayer developed the landmark 30-storey Hotel Ivoire and the town planning for the high-end Riviera neighbourhoods.

---

22 Interview with Gouro Landouré, 9 March 2016.

The 1960s urban planning largely defined the years to come until now. Most of the neighbourhoods built in the decade would later expand around a series of localised centres. As *Urbanisme* noted, "similar to many West African cities, urbanisation has been inordinately horizontal with low density. [...] What could seem a waste of land now appears as an advantage, as the land reserve allows densification and mutation of activities with taller buildings replacing colonial houses on the original site of the city." This observation remains largely true even 50 years later; where most of the expansion is still within the city hull from Port-Bouët to Yopougon and Adjamé.

The development of Abidjan after the independence reflects a strong belief in the functionalist city. As noted by Steck, this feature inherited by the French colonialism presented a carbon copy of the ideas of the Athens charter, even before it was redacted (Steck 2005). This philosophy of the urban was largely followed after the independence, where the faith in ordering the functions of the city, giving great power of influence of the office of infrastructure (Direction Centrale des Grands Travaux – DCGTX), directly under the president's responsibility. As such, the city also plays an important role as a showcase of a certain understanding of modernity. Monumental and landmark architecture plays a role in Ivory Coast (including Yamoussoukro) where verticality and size claim to witness the dynamism of the economy. As noted cynically by Haeringer, the Cocoa or coffee farmer might feel bitter that the added value of his work goes to a luxury hotel, but at least he can take pride in it (Haeringer 1985).

Nowadays, a densified planning surrounds the landmark project of the 1960 hull. The city of the Houphouët-Boigny period was built with very low density and the gaps are filled with other projects, responding more or less strictly on the urbanism planning. Communes of hundreds of thousands of people built their identities in high-end or lower-end purposes. At a smaller scale, the projects of the Houphouët-Boigny years remain reference points for directions in the city "220 logements", or "Liberté", from the name of a cinema that ceased to exist long ago, remain landmarks as nodes in public transports network.

The densification of the city followed a path of spatial inequalities. The state organises the direction of urban planning, while keeping a relatively minor role in housing, leaving most construction to the owners. The role of the state in housing mainly consists in allocating the land to buyers and let them construct their houses in it. The application of the respect of planning regulations concentrates in the upper-class areas following the "unity of the neighbourhood" ideas. At the same time, the combination of promotion of social housing in specific areas, on the one hand, and regular destruction of informal neighbourhoods marked the differentiation of social areas in Abidjan (Parenteau and Charbonneau 1992;

Bouquet and Kassi-Djodjo 2014). Companies of social housing SICOGI and SOGEFIHA have marked the skeleton of the working-class areas of the capital, with the construction of small courtyards-centred housing units (Tratnjek 2010) and some buildings with several storeys.

The difficulties of mobility reflect in large traffic jams in the city. The development infrastructure with new bridges is regularly clogged not long after construction. A public transport system combines private- and public-owned transport companies, operating busses and minibuses. Boats of large and small sizes also operate crossing the lagoon or smaller canals within Abidjan. The naval transports remain at relatively small-scale dues to worries on safety by Abidjanese (Kabran and Eguavoen 2019).

4.3.6 Juba

The city of Juba is relatively small. Its political importance has the peculiarity of being closely linked to the policy of humanitarian aid during the independence war against Sudan. In particular, the location within road networks close to Kenyan and Ugandan borders and the presence of an airport positioned the city ideally to establish a political and humanitarian logistics centre (Duffield 2010b). Its status as the capital of South Sudan came against two main concurrent. The town of Rumbek more to the North and the centre of the country might well have been chosen as a temporary capital, were it not for the choice of the UN to make it its main base of operations.

As a permanent capital, the South Sudanese authorities originally preferred the Town of Ramciel, also more central to the country. In the early days of independence, South Sudan commissioned international planning companies to lay the design of what should become the political and administrative centre of the country. The South Korean company, which won the contest, never had a chance to implement it, as the civil war started soon after independence (Mednick 2018).

The relatively small importance of the city of Juba is one of the reasons the documentation on the history of the city is fragmented. Few sources on the history of Juba are currently available. Past and current conflict in South Sudan made the preservation and valorisation of city history a difficult task. The story of the South Sudan national archive told by a variety of news outlets (Methiaux 2018; Morgan 2018) tell of the complexity of keeping historical material in the context of war where the will and commitment to keep a look at the past drove a small underequipped and underfinanced small team of archivists maintain historical documents. It is rare enough to see the press and media writing stories about archivists, generally perceived as quintessentially boring and monotonous.

Using the few sources available on the history of Juba a number of initiatives have successfully managed to make available to the public the urban history of Juba through the "Juba in the Making" website (Juba in the Making 2019). This resource links to various secondary material written and assembled by researchers to highlight different aspects of the history of the diversity of neighbourhoods of the South Sudanese capital.

The city heritage sometimes remains in the names of neighbourhoods, like Hai Cinema, although the cinema closed long ago. The edifice, built by a Greek merchant in the 1960s, has long since become a church. It had been in full activity during the decade of peace between the 1970s and the 1980s, in which the city renewed its role as a provincial centre for trade. Not far from the area, the mausoleum dedicated to John Garang witnesses an ambition to mark the symbols of the newly created state. The provincial town changes into a status of national importance.

Aid and development agencies optimism for the new country since the Naivasha peace agreement of 2005, through independence, and until the outbreak of civil war also marked their projection for the new capital. The very poverty and lack of infrastructure could appear and be presented as an opportunity for future planning of an inclusive and sustainable city. Plans to include a planned development of cycling lanes and traditional tukul huts witness the project for a green path to urban development (Creative Associates International 2005). However, this type of projection by an aid agency does not necessarily fall within a realistic view of power relations and the aspirations of the local elites, much less of the practices of most aid agencies.

One of the striking aspects of the post-independence planning of Juba as a capital city is that the function of Juba as capital of the state was in fact never clear. Utopian projects by Riek Machar, then Minister of Housing, Public Land and Public Utility, as well as vice-president meant to produce a clean-slate modernist city in an island on the northern vicinity of Juba. Other projects, such as Ramciel, were located more to the north with the similar idea to start a new capital from scratch (Badiey and Doll 2018). It is not clear whether one or the other of these projects will finally come out. It is, however, telling on the vision of Juba by the South Sudanese elite. Projects for a new capital witnesses the elite's awareness of the difficulty to manage the fast expansion of the population in Juba. It signals a mindset where poverty and scarcity of infrastructure are seen as damaging to the country image, internally and externally. As a result, this projection of an outside capital might also explain the difficulty to find a clear strategy and practice of planning for the city.

The conflicts over the tenure of urban land in and around Juba did not stop with the projects of a new capital. Land tenure constitutes the major subject of frictions between those actors involved in the construction of the state and the various strata of the local population (Kindersley 2019). Under the central Sudanese rule at the end of the Anglo-Egyptian condominium in 1956, the new land law determined that most customary land was property of the state. The South Sudanese independence involving the strategic importance of Juba has resulted in the conflicts between the local communities, government and war of independence SPLA veterans. The communities want to keep their traditional control of the land. The South Sudanese government wants to control the use of strategically located land. SPLA veterans who consider the share of land through allotment of housing plots the just retribution for their participation to the armed struggle for independence. Struggles and power relations between these actors have so far shown a number of compromises (Badiey 2013). This ongoing process has started to both reflect and shape power relations in the city of Juba. The set of actors involved in the negotiation constantly define and redefine their relations to each other in mutual recognition of their social power (Lund 2011).

As for the private investment in the city, large profits from land have brought real-estate entrepreneurs to invest in the city. However, the volatility of the urban markets reflects in the attitude of some of the important investors in the top hierarchy of the state, and the army in particular (Roach and Hudson 2018). As the Enough NGO revealed and denounced in 2017, large-scale corruption of the ruling elite, including the president, vice-president and top-level military generals, resulted in the depletion of important reserve to personal profits. Most of the graft made its way into the urban environment. However, the preference for the investment/laundering of tens of millions of dollars ended up mostly in luxury mansions in Uganda and Kenya (Adeba 2019).

The built environment reflects the social contradictions of a city, which has concentrated much of both the wealth and misery of the decades-long civil war (Figure 37). The built environment reflects investments, as the (temporary or permanent) political and economic centrality triggered both private and public investments after the peace agreement with Sudan. Considering its history and strategic location on the Nile and at the crossroads of major trade routes to neighbouring countries, Juba will most likely remain a major economic and population centre, even if the political capital is eventually moved to another location.

The position of Juba also directed many South Sudanese to take refuge in the city. The Large UN camps at the outskirts of Juba host thousands of citizens. In the city itself, the distinction between formal and informal settlement is apparent

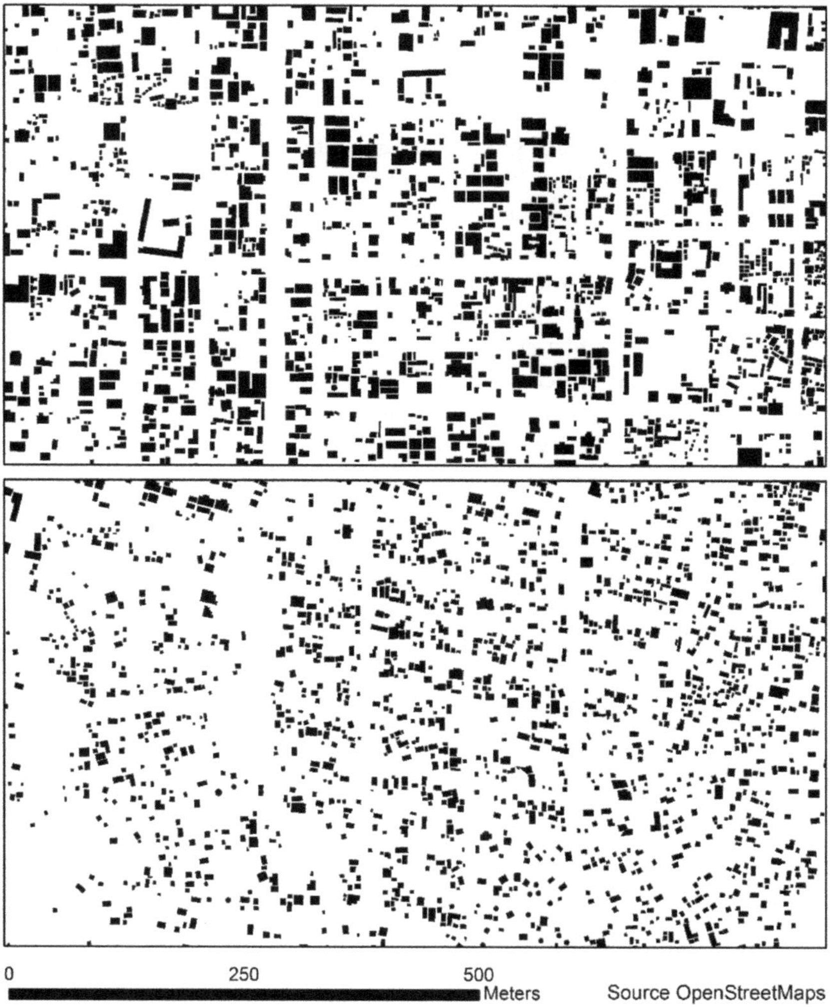

Figure 37: An upper-class area in Hai Munuki (top) and an informal settlement in Hai Gudele, below Jebel Kujur (bottom). Some traditional adobe houses, the tukuls, can be recognised form their round footprint

and reflect the level of access to land and housing for the different social groups. Informal settlements are typically allowed outwards to the city in the most insalubrious and dangerous areas. The Hai Gudele foothills of Jebel Kujur neighbourhood is located in an area, which was long contaminated with mines for its vicinity to a strategic high ground, although it is claimed to be cleared today (McMichael and Massleberg 2010). Footprints of the buildings reflect the spontaneous history of the area showing a layout of small houses including circle-shaped traditional mud houses (Figure 37).

Juba informality reflects the prominence of non-state local authorities. Without formal division of the land into plots, other types of authorities manifest themselves in land conflict and negotiations between neighbours (McMichael 2016). As the poverty structures the inhabitants in an informal area, rules and regulation come from other types of moral authorities. Affiliation with the military constitute the primary claim to legitimacy along with ethnic and family relations within a settlement (Kindersley 2019).

Hai Munuki, on the other hand, has been planned with wide road access. Wealth is again visible from above, where the footprints of buildings are significantly larger than in most of the town (Figure 37). Within land plots, some space is most often left for gardens. The contrast between formal and informal area is in fact not in the built environment per square metre, but in the built space used per person. Many more people live in the small mud or cement and corrugated iron houses of the poor neighbourhoods than in the planned areas.

4.3.7 Nairobi

Few cities have come to brand themselves as a symbol of African modernity as much as Nairobi. The image of giraffes or other wild mammals with skyscrapers on the background has become a most common branding for tourist guides (Pennington-Gray et al. 2005). The Kenyan capital cultivates the crossover of two major geographic clichés: skyscrapers as a symbol of urban modernity and wildlife as a symbol for Africa since the colonial times (Garland 2008). The look at the short history of the city also brands its colonial heritage to build its contemporary image, among others through the conservation of Karen Blixen's house, made famous in the 1985 film Out of Africa (Bendix 2002).

This carefully constructed image is the result of a colonial history, which placed the city of Nairobi as colonial capital on the railroad from the coast to the Kenyan highlands. The current place of Nairobi as a model of an African urban modernity and a major transport and economic hub for the East African region is coupled with high levels of poverty and inequalities. The millions of inhabitants of the metropolitan area share a highly heterogeneous space where modernist planning serves the country's integration within the regional and global economy while being questioned by the informal urban metabolisms organised in the poorest areas.

The modern history section of the Nairobi National Museum of Kenya shows a small model of what is, or should be, a city in Kenya (Figure 38). The model of an ideal town where administrative, commercial, industrial, residential, and religious activities are orderly not only as the most efficient urban model, but as the only alternative to slums developed spontaneously by internal migration. While the model seems to represent the caricature of an ideal small provincial town, the city of Nairobi reproduces the model at the scale of a large metropolis. However, the model does not anticipate and represents the presence and persistence of the informal settlement, the overcrowding of services and infrastructure and social violence and poverty attached to urban and economic growth. The functionalist city might not be so much the antithesis of informality, but rather one in the two sides of a same urban metabolism.

Services and business concentrate in the "Central Business District", as dwelling areas surround the commercial and administrative centre. Meant as a model for any town in Kenya, this model is applied quite closely by the Kenyan planners of the capital. The large CBD area, a commercial hub for the region that irradiates far beyond Kenya, is surrounded by the residential areas. The simplified map of the Nairobi Landuse illustrates the radial model of Nairobi, where the CBD central area is reserved for commercial activities, including shops and office buildings (Figure 39). The building footprints of the city centre are typically large and – invisible to the map – comprise at least several storeys. The width of the footprints is only wider in the industrial area to the South of the CBD.

Very visible even at the scale of the city as a whole, the density of residential areas is much lower. The voracity of land by housing is most eloquent. It only extends to the formal residential sector. Informal settlements, or slums, form a condensate aggregation of small buildings into a relatively small area. This unequal consumption of space is already visible at the city scale is even more eloquent when focussing on the disparities at closer range. These areas of informal settlements also illustrate how the official planning policy is not able to include all city dwellers within its projections.

Levels of inequalities are high in Nairobi, and reflect on the neighbourhoods. Large areas of villas and gated communities lay next to the poorest areas of the capital. The large slums of Kibera and Mathare come to symbolise the fragmentation of the city between the rich and the poor. The high levels of inequality reflect in the access to land and living space showing extremely high levels of

Figure 38: National Museum of Kenya. The functionalist city model presented as the healthy opposite to informal settlements. The legend of the model reads: "After Independence, rural-urban migration increased due to landlessness caused by colonialism. The growth of small towns was inevitable. This led to the displacement of occupants into slum dwellers. This is a model of planned urban settlement with a Central business district, an industrial area, residential areas and other amenities necessary in urban settlements." The museum was contacted for permission to use the picture

inequalities. A comparison between the rich and the poorest neighbourhood is most eloquent (Figure 40).

The spectacular contrasts in the standards of living in Nairobi is in fact so notorious that specialised tourist agencies consider the visits to the slum areas as a resource (Frenzel 2012; Chege and Mwisukha 2013). Slum tourism is controversial, as inhabitants often complain being associated with wildlife tourism, the major touristic attraction in Kenya. The small revenue to local guides, generally themselves inhabitants of said slums, maintains the activity. Without entering this debate, it is important to note that the striking inequalities visible inside the city justify the curiosity of tourists and the interests by tour operators to collect revenue from it.

The modernist-functionalist planning of Nairobi results in a metropolis that competes as a regional hub with businesses in the centre and reserve for housing and investments in most of the city. It also drags all the contradictions of this model and its social and environmental ills. The illusion of wealth of the city

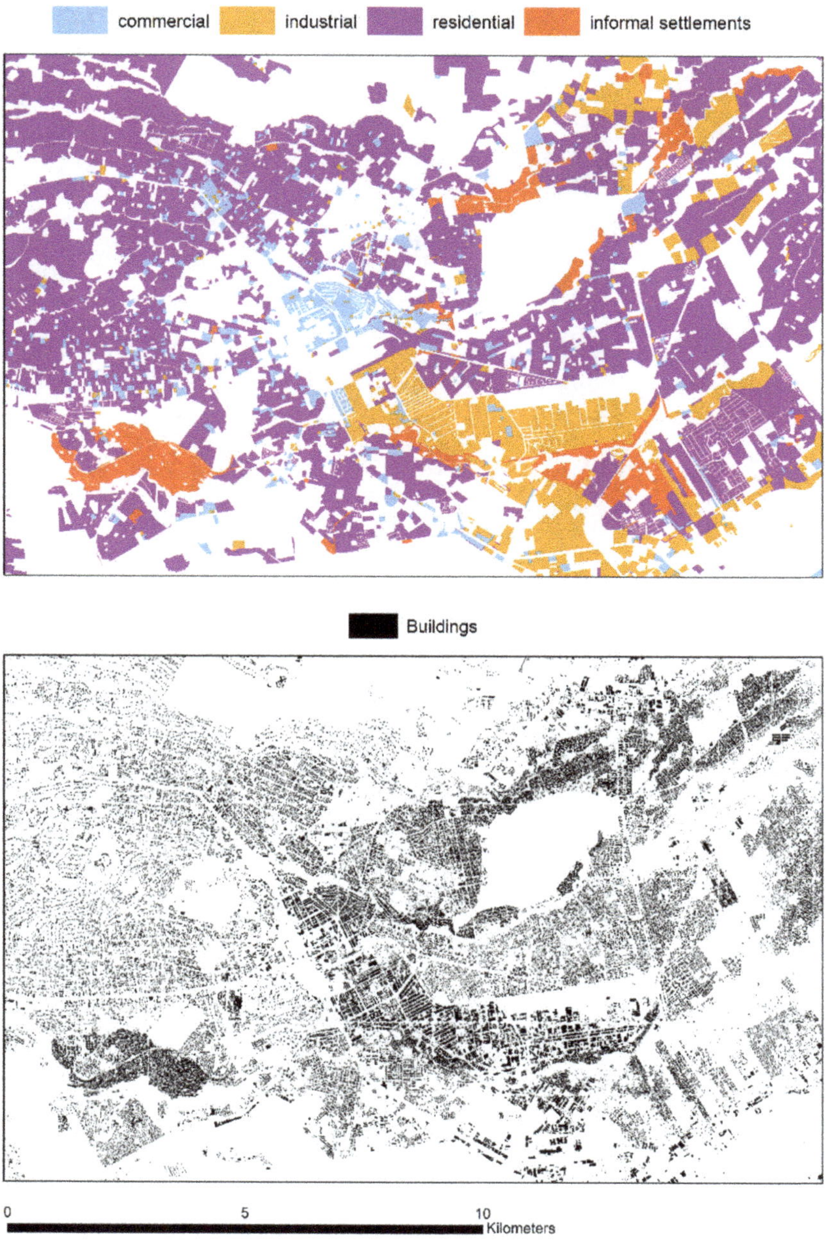

Figure 39: Landuse and buildings in Nairobi. Source: JICA 2010

Figure 40: On the top, the Mathare slum area. The distance between each building is so small that each road lane and passage is visible evidence of "slum upgrading" initiatives are visible with some standardised buildings and larger streets. On the bottom image,

the New Runda neighbourhood is so space-consuming with large gardens that the road outline can barely be guessed

is unable to hide that the city does not support a social balance in the right to the city for the poorest inhabitants. The large city infrastructure is clogged with traffic. The city is built for motorised traffic although most residents do not own one. Public transport policies are shy and result in minibuses and busses to be equally blocked in transports. Sidewalks are inexistent in most of the city (Khayesi, Monheim, and Nebe 2010).

4.4 The Local Population and the Right to the City

This chapter aimed at describing the panorama of the four cities that constitute the case studies for this research. Note that all sites of study are sites of conflicts and social fragmentation albeit at different degrees. The conflicts relate to political, social and ethnic rivalries, which precedes the arrival of humanitarian aid, and form part of the reason for the humanitarian and political interventions. This observation, as this chapter concludes, is important to consider. An analysis of the arrival of a new social body in a territory could present the local environment as a unified and coherent assemblage, only troubled by external factors.

Social and spatial inequalities, in fact, generate conflicting and complex metabolism in the making of the city. The "local population" in this regard does not exist. The local population has a strong class structure although it supports different levels of inequalities in the different cities. The relative social cohesion of Bamako supports an environment seemingly appeased where criminality and political violence remain low. Major commercial and political hubs like Abidjan and Nairobi in contrast concentrate spectacular levels of wealth along with terrible poverty. The local populations and the local urban fabric are an historical palimpsest and the site of territorial rivalries for the right to the city.

These remarks aim to anticipate a risk in the following chapters in pointing the fragmentation created by international aid. As discussed above, socio-spatial inequalities are present in African cities since their creation as colonial bases. The creation of these cities in the colonial times was the most structurally unequal endeavour, as they were built as bases to plunder local resources and exert the arbitrary power of colonial conquest. Urban politics – as part of the policies of the post-colonial period – have reflected different attitudes and relations of power between social classes, the new elites and the former colonial powers. The social fragmentation of the cities has resulted in different outcomes at the time of the massive international interventions and presence in the twenty-first century.

The discussion on the contradictions within the panorama of aid interventions resolutely focussed on the socio-spatial inequalities. This focus on the differences in economic capital has its limits. The very presence of international interventions are due to existing violent conflicts of impact and complexity, which are not considered manageable locally. Political and social tensions are equally important within the capital. Indeed these tensions often tend to form a miniature of the difficulties within the country. To name a few other important contextual tensions within the city itself, the relations of power may include national and local specificities. A myriad of other socio-political groups and organisation influences city metabolism, involving sometimes ethnicity and religion, for example. In both Juba and Abidjan, the presence of war veterans and their claims as payment or recognition of their sacrifices might directly or indirectly affect the relation to land policies. The South Sudanese and Ivorian example shows direct claims for urban land in Juba and Abidjan respectively seen as back payment for political loyalties. In short, the present chapter does not pretend to present an unachievable exhaustive depiction of the social tensions within a city, which would go far beyond the scope of this chapter and constitute a subject in itself. The more modest goal of this chapter is to highlight the relation of one mode of social and political tensions with the built environment.

Finally, this presentation of the panorama of intervention permits to locate the four countries in relation to each other as paradigmatic cases. Neither the nature of the interventions nor the nature of the cities justifies grouping these four cities together. However, the discussion above permits to identify them into paradigmatic cases. It sets the base for further studying the presence of humanitarian aid and subsequent adaptation of a spatialisation of security systems of the aid industry in relation to these paradigms. The new presence of foreign workers do not create the existing inequalities. It will instead interpret, analyse the current places and make a series of informed choices with intended and unintended effects on the cities' metabolisms.

Chapter 5 Landscape of War

In mid-May 2017, I was getting ready to conduct my last interviews of this research in the city of Abidjan, when a rebellion within the Ivorian army limited my capacity to reach my interviewees. These violent events blocked the capital and other major Ivorian cities and left several dead (Reuters 2017). It marked the end of my field research. I spent the last week of my stay in Abidjan in Marcory, where gunfire and explosion could be heard at a distance. The area was not directly affected by the rebellion, unlike most of the city (Figure 41).

I packed some reserves of food, water and withdrew cash in prevision if I ended up blocked in my apartment and contacted my embassy. Instead of interviews, I walked in the calm neighbourhood and inquired my friends in Abidjan on their safety and listening to news and street rumours. I draw some sketches of the fighting to monitor and compile the news I was receiving. The rebellion was over by the time I left Ivory Coast, ending the last fieldwork of this research, on 26 May 2017, after the government accepted the demands of the rebels (Hervieu 2017).

Other violent events occurred in the cities where this research took place. A series of violent armed attacks targeting expatriates against nightclubs, hotels, and the EU military mission took place in Bamako between 2015 and 2018, and they might repeat in the future (Pozo Marín 2017; Jeune Afrique – AFP 2018). The occurrence of violent events during research on situations of conflicts is likely. Although this research has been focussed on the normal functioning of security policies by international organisations, I was also witnessing it during particular crises.

From 7 to 11 July 2016 in Juba, fighting between the government and the opposition took place when I was working for the UN in South Sudan. It constituted the most serious and dangerous event I witnessed during this research. Battles in the city involved artillery, tanks, and helicopter gunships, resulting in hundreds of deaths. Among the dead were soldiers from the warring sides and South Sudanese and foreign civilians as well as two peacekeepers (United Nations 2016).

I had arrived in South Sudan on 14 June 2016, to cover for a three-month position of at the WFP national HQ. I hoped this position would help me familiarise with the city of Juba and make contacts for later interviews and research. Less than a month after my arrival in South Sudan the conflict erupted between the South Sudanese Army (SPLA) and the main armed opposition (SPLA-IO).

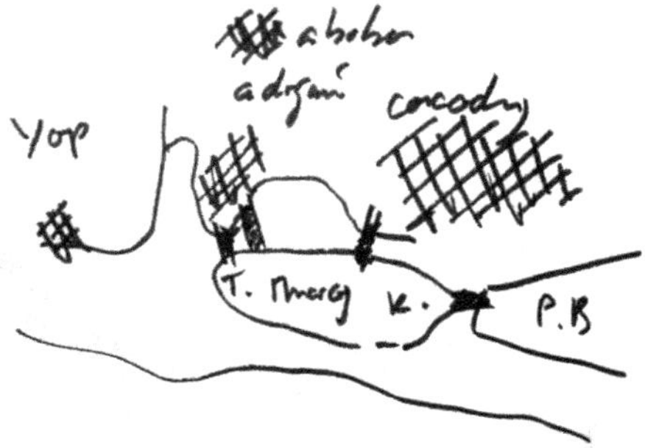

Figure 41: Sketch of the rebellion in Abidjan. Most of the rebellion was located on the Northern parts of Abidjan

When the army effectively destroyed and pushed out the 1500 troops of the SPLA-IO stationed in Juba, the week that followed constituted an exceptional outlook at the reaction of the UN system to a major crisis.

The response of the security system of the UN during the clashes in Juba has been widely criticised for a number of failures in protecting South Sudanese civilians, including inside some UN premises, and humanitarian workers. The critique brought by the Centre for Civilians in Conflicts (CIVIC 2016), presents the most comprehensive description of the sequence of events in Juba. Representative of the critique of the UN response by the humanitarian crisis, the report highlights security failures in preventing number of attacks against civilians within UN premises and attributes it to a large level to incompetence and unwillingness to intervene by peacekeepers and other UN security. The report notes different responses in some locations and commends the behaviour of a number of peacekeeping units.

This critique of humanitarian security is quite separate from the analysis presented in this research, which is focussed on understanding the structural logic and spatial effects of security, rather than highlighting dysfunctions of the system. The attack of the Terrain hotel, a luxurious hotel in the outskirts of the city, by SPLA soldiers resulted in the murder of a South Sudanese journalist and the gang rape of several aid workers. In later months, the South Sudanese government tried and jailed some of the soldiers involved in the attack (Anonymous 2016). Reports on the events have focussed on the response time by UN security once they were informed of the incidents taking place. The discussion regarding the prevention of incidents included whether a stronger barrier and a wall could have prevented the attack. While it concludes that it would probably not be enough to prevent the raid, the report stresses that reinforcing walls should have been done anyways (CIVIC 2016, p. 58).

Violent events cast a shadow over the cities where aid is present. Although the all-out war is an exceptional event in the capital, the scenario and the possibility of occurring informs security planning in normal times. In this regard, my presence in Juba had been an extremely interesting point of observation of the UN system, not in normal times, but in a period of crisis, which informed both my position as a researcher and the general spatial theories developed in this book.

While working in the UN system, I did not prepare for an event of this type and magnitude. While afraid by the situation, I did not set any research method in case such an occurrence. I kept a notebook and wrote my impressions without any specific focus. As a result, a lot of what I saw and heard has disappeared or has probably been transformed in my misty memory. I also consciously limited myself in taking pictures at the time, thinking it might be dangerous. This frightening and fascinating moment to witness in real time how the UN system reacted as events unfolded have marked my thinking and my way of looking at the humanitarian security structure. Although being critical of the general policies of retreat and fencing behind gated, I had not been excessively naïve about the actual risks involved in humanitarian missions. This critique is not rejecting altogether any protection for humanitarians, but including a more general reflection on consequences of space closure. What did the events in Juba change to my perspective on security then?

From the perspective of the critical discussion of security policies, the events in Juba forced me to conduct a reflection of positionality regarding security procedures. Walls and other security measures had been a welcome protection against stray bullets and possibly raids similar to the Terrain hotel. The safety that walls and guards provided (in particular regarding their good relation with the SPLA) ensured my safety along the dozens of guests and employees of my hotel. However, the structural effects of security do not mean they are less segregated. On the contrary, the bounding of the relatively safer places is being reinforced. During the fighting in Juba, I had been among the most privileged in the safety, and even comfort, that was possible to enjoy anywhere in the city. My hotel had enough reserves of food and water (we could even shower daily, unlike most hotels during these days) and fuel ensured the electric generator was running. Phone networks and the internet were functioning well, which allowed me to communicate with friends and family to inform them of my safety.

The conditions were different for different segments of the populations. Large UN compounds had some reserves as well. They were also equipped with "bunkers" made of containers protected by sandbags to absorb stray bullets and explosions. The picture was very different on the outside. Many were trapped in the middle of the fighting without water. Looting by soldiers took place in shops and houses and many residents had to gather to local churches for protection (Burke 2016). Exceptional violent events structure the understanding of risks and its analysis helps understand the structure of security measures in normal times.

These events and subsequent reflection on the events had also been the occasion to conduct a more general reflection on the landscape of war and peace. I stayed in the hotel during all the period of fighting in Juba, and was evacuated to Nairobi by an UN airplane three days after the ceasefire that allowed the remainder of the opposition to flee the city. After landing in Nairobi, aid agencies distributed their staff a list of post-traumatic syndromes, which may occur after violent situations, in order to recognise them, and treat them if needed.[23] "Guilt," reflected my feeling mixed with relief as fear faded away in the airplane.

This sentiment probably reflects, of course, the discomfort of benefitting from a level of protection unavailable to most. Is it possible to present my own critical perspective over a security system on which myself and other humanitarian workers depend for their safety? This question brings in fact two answers. The short answer is that the critique of security urbanism for humanitarians does not necessarily reject physical protection, especially not in all cases. The second and more general argument is that the question is not whether protective walls and other devices are efficient to protect aid workers. It is clear that walls offer protection against bullets, and locked doors against home invaders. Rather, a critical perspective allows the analysis of the production of an unthought-of segregated urbanism by international aid.

Violent fighting in Juba took place in several locations. As the hotel where I was staying lies next to one of the main arteries, and close to a commissariat some severe fighting took place in the area. This extreme event marked a place and time in which social relations had been organised exclusively in relation to the event. Searching for physical protection, gathering information on the events through news websites and information from colleagues and reassuring family on the outside had become the main activity of most. Personal discipline, through physical exercise, or indiscipline, smoking cigarettes and drinking alcohol had marked the routine of the days. Organisational discipline with the

23 « Counselling support for Staff Arriving to Nairobi from Juba », letter, 14 July 2016.

employers imposed a twice-daily radio call through VHF radios, and security reports sent by email.[24]

This week waiting in a hotel for the fighting to stop gives a good idea of what Kurt Lewis called the landscape of war (Krieglandschaft in the German original) a hundred years ago, in relation to his experience during WWI (Lewin and Blower 2009). The meaning of the landscape completely changes for the eyes of whoever witnesses war from close eyes. Lewin's understanding of the landscape is informed by training as a psychologist and presents a phenomenology of the soldier towards the specific war environment. While the landscape of peace might seem to extend to the infinity, Lewin notes that the landscape of war is bounded. Frontlines represent the end of a particular landscape, zones of safety and objects in the landscape are immediately recognised as protection.

The large number of bombs and bullets used during the conflict ended up in all places and directions. The garden of the hotel collected the stray bullets from the war away that finally fell close to us. Broken windows or other impacts on the ground, walls and roofs witnessed the intensity of the fighting. One Scottish UN contractor, and former military, asked me whether I had been afraid during one of the closest fighting (where a bomb fell in a building about thirty metres away). As I answered "yes", his reply noted, "good, anyone who wasn't afraid here must have a mental problem!" However, fear produces different reactions and behaviour, where age, experience, gender, among other factors influence behaviour and reactions to events. Men seem to feel that they have to restrain showing their fear.

The excitement of events might combine fear with exhilarating feelings of excitement. A member of the management of the hotel had been excited to tweet how she enjoyed watching Wimbledon grand slam in the middle of the fighting. The South Sudanese head of security guards of the hotel – and SPLA supporter – enjoyed singing Bob Marley's "Buffalo soldier" at the bar of the hotel when the night fell and shooting noise dissipated and showing the war footage he sometimes filmed just outside the hotel. Those present do not uniformly perceive danger. The experience of a person stranded in a major conflict strongly

24 Retrospectively, the absence of some news seems the most remarkable and bizarre. The news of the attack on the Terrain hotel -where a local journalist was killed and several foreigners were tortured and raped- in particular was never communicated through security emails. I have not been able to find out whether this information was not transmitted to avoid panic among expatriates or other reason. Nevertheless, the missing information felt bizarre when learning of the events through news bulletins afterwards.

influences their vision and perception of both danger and the means they can use for physical protection. With the exception of a few characters excited by the event who tried to see as much as possible of the clashes by climbing on top of houses, everybody looked for protection from the visible danger and the imagined risks.

The notion of depth in architecture, developed by Hillier, can help understand how the built environment was envisioned as protection (Bill Hillier 1996). Hillier presents the organisation of rooms within a building as topological depth. The further number of doors needed to cross the building to arrive at a particular point of a building corresponds to a level of architectural depth. The logic of protecting oneself, behind one or several walls, from the conflict outside can be understood as looking for depth.

The people present in the compound identified two main dangers in our situation. Stray bullets and bombs might hurt or kill someone. Being isolated from the rest of the city and any medical facility only increased fear of it occurring. On the other hand, the possibility of becoming a target of one of the armed factions, in a planned or unplanned attack, as occurred in another hotel in Juba remained possible despite the presence of armed guards.

The immediate fear was being hit by a stray bullet or a bomb, from the intense fighting in the city. To avoid this risk, and depending on the intensity and proximity of the fighting, sheltered in brick-wall bungalows or houses. Blind rooms, such as storerooms when the fighting was the closest offered an extra layer of brick, or another level of depth for physical protection. War changes the purpose and hierarchical order of the building architecture.

Another perceived danger was the possibility of a raid by one of the warring factions in the city. The event did not happen, but its possibility led to another use of architectural depth. This time, the protective purpose of the building is not to prevent accidental fire, but the intentional invasion. Building depth in this regard consists in making the passage from outside to the inside the most difficult. The architectural depth in this regard is focussed in the number of rooms needed to cross the building, as much as the strength of doors and crossing to prevent a home invasion.

Most guests of the hotel were relocated from their rooms close to the road towards furnished houses whose normal tenants were abroad, at the centre of the compound. My colleagues and I were taking shelter in one of the villas at the centre of the hotel compound during the heaviest fighting when explosions were rocking close. Staying inside when bombs and bullets were falling close involves considering which rooms would offer best protection and stay inside to control

Figure 42: One of the few pictures I took in Juba. The "bunker" Ukrainian workers were using. On one corner, piled tables and a deckchair are meant to offer extra protection against stray bullets. 11 July 2016

fear. However, reactions from some of the guests of the hotel where different, and looking for depth took different forms using a variety of physical features.

Three Ukrainians airplane engineers at the hotels were confident that the swimming pool was the most secured place in the compound and waited in the water – sipping vodka. The three men called the swimming pool their "bunker" claiming the place was safer than their rooms, whose windows had been pierced by bullets (Figure 42). The image of Eastern Europeans drinking and swimming in the pool in the middle of a war seems almost like a cliché taken from a B-series film. However, these engineers followed the rationale that the density of water was better protection than walls of hotel rooms.

These men were also aware that this swimming pool would not protect them from the occurrence of an armed raid inside the compound. "If they see us swimming in this luxury when they come from the war outside, they will not like it. And this can be very dangerous." At the time of this discussion, the invasion of a similar compound at the other side of the city had not occurred. The possibility of such an event was, however, present in people's minds. However, the decision to use a pool in such conditions reflected another aspect of the perception of risk: the need to control one's own fear. Most people tried to balance their nervousness one way or another, doing exercises, smoking, playing games or watching TV. Major sports events, the 2016 Euro Cup and Wimbledon, occurring at the same time, were a welcome distraction from the strange mix of fear and boredom induced in the situation.

Locked in relative safety, very few events of the actual combat were visible from the position of the hotel (apart of columns of smoke and helicopters overhead), even though combats often came very close and bombs falling only a couple dozen metres away from the hotel. On the other hand, the attention towards what is happening in the city was probably never greater for anyone in Juba at that time. As anyone that did not have to be outside at that time, most people in any hotel or UN compound, and in fact everyone in the city, was trying to stay as far as possible from the vision of the streets, except for fast outlooks at events occurring. This means that the knowledge of the territory went in major part through non-visual means.

As an example from my own experience, my recollection of what I had seen with my own eyes of the conflict during the week of fighting was helicopter gunships flying over our heads, smoke from large fires in areas of Juba, and rounds of ammunition that had fallen in the hotel. The head of security of the hotel also passed us some pictures and videos that he took outside showing battle events in the road directly in front of Acacias Village. In the long talks that I had with colleagues in the months after the events, I sensed that experience of the landscape had been quite similar to most.

So excluding the visual, people used different means to sense what was happening in the city. Moreover, our spatial inquiry seemed to focus on questioning whether fighting was getting close, whether it was increasing or declining. To attempt to describe the non-visual vision of the conflict, I have tried numerous drawings of the fighting to illustrate the sound and its proximity (Figure 43).

The proximity of warfare has consistently seen people using the sense of hearing to try to understand what is happening. The focus on sound has been consistent in various experiences of conflicts over time (Daughtry 2015; Hartford 2017). Attempts to "see" the sounds of war in the course of events aims to understand what is happening as a political process (is the war still on?), and as an immediate spatial process for personal safety. More specifically the question is whether the fighting is getting closer to one's position. Sounds of gunfire, explosions, and helicopters punctuated the days of crisis in Juba, and all the present had been trying to understand from the noise where the combats were taking place, and whether taking shelter was necessary at that point. Soundscape constitutes the main element of the landscape of war.

I have tried to picture afterwards the mental maps of sound during the fighting. One tries to identify if machine-gun sound is light or heavy weapon, or

Figure 43: A vision of sound from the compound. Loud explosions and machine gunfire in immediate proximity behind the walls of the compound pressed to find shelter

if the explosion comes from a tank firing or a rocket. Listening the sound of the helicopter blades tells if it is getting closer or moving away. One tries to understand if the gunship had already fired its missiles. Noise indicates the distance of fighting as well as its intensity and direction. Listening to the fighting helps locate the direction of the fighting and judging whether danger is far or close to decide whether hiding behind the depth of buildings is necessary. The direction of the noise in turn indicates behind which wall to hide, and the proximity of which window to avoid. The mental map does not indicate exactly what happened, as actual events are invisible in the distance (Figure 44). Instead, it informs how to move and place oneself in relation to the built environment.

Seeing war as an occurrence of a landscape means taking into account a specific temporality for the perception of the environment. The war as landscape gives signs of its presence in specific times that are marked by the attacks and counter-attacks of warring soldiers. A part of sporadic shooting the night were calm and the fighting restarted in the morning.

This section has mixed recollections, analysis, and discussion on positionality aimed to describe the process through which the process of landscape was apprehended. The reflection on the landscape has come from an uncontrolled self-analysis of particular events. Although the urban landscape of humanitarian organisations is a landscape of normal times, a series of very specific violent events have marked the perspective at which organisations perceive and understand the landscape. The events of 2016 in Juba had been the second time in only a few years in which these levels of violence had occurred. The earlier fighting and massacre of Nuer citizens in Juba in 2013 had been present in memories by

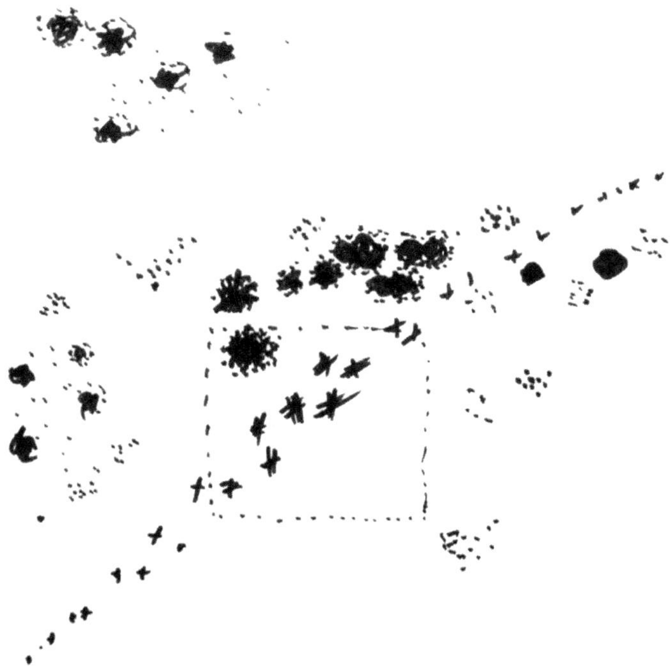

Figure 44: A sketch of the soundscape of the events in Juba. The square in the middle represents the compound. Large marks represent explosions. Dots are automatic rifle bullets. The long trail crossing from the lower left to the upper aims to represent the sound of helicopter blades

local residents and internationals alike, although renewed fighting was unexpected by most expatriates.

Even as the time of war is short, events remains for a long time after as a memory and marks of the war seem to be present to remind everyone that even if passed, it is still there. The rare occurrence of an extreme event marks all time in which the events do not occur. Kurt Lewin considered the panorama of past battlefields as a landscape of peace, since the characteristics of the landscape of war had dissipated. The space is not bounded any more. However, the urban landscape of humanitarian interventions is somehow distinct. Extreme events are past, but their occurrence still marks the perception of the city.

I have tried in this chapter to describe a thinking process, which influences both the actors and subject of this research and myself in trying to propose an analysis of a socio-spatial phenomenon. The immediate proximity of violent events has marked my reflection process on the overall subject, placing the notion of the landscape at the centre of the understanding of the geography of aid agencies. They also reflect how much visual thinking, with the use of sketches to describe the landscape of war, has greatly influenced the general theoretical framework of this book.

Chapter 6 The Layer

The intervention of international aid over a local panorama – the existing local material and social environment – is multiscale. Humanitarians think and implement their presence at a global scale, with the political/humanitarian decision to intervene in a number of countries. Down one scale at the country level, humanitarian agencies decide to intervene in specific regions and places, following criteria such as calculated levels of emergency and funding possibilities (Zhang, Zhou, and Nunamaker Jr 2002; Darcy and Hofmann 2003). Within cities, humanitarian agencies and aid workers decide to locate in specific areas and places influenced by social and security norms.

The use of the concept of layer does not mean that the only contradiction in the socio-physical space of Juba, Bamako, Nairobi and Abidjan is between previously homogenous cities versus international organisations and their staff. As palimpsests, cities are crossed by the territorialisation of a number of social forces (Raffestin 1983). The notion of a separate layer aims to locate this difference as one important marker of current evolution. It marks the internal social and cultural coherence of a social body in its projection over a territory.

Sociology and anthropology of international aid have defined "peaceland" (Autesserre 2014), "aidland" (Mosse 2011) or the "aid archipelago" (Duffield 2012a) using explicitly spatial references of borders or physical features to describe the social or socio-spatial insularity of humanitarian presence. The process of territorialisation of international aid and often its ultimate segregation is more than a spatial metaphor, as it can be actually located, both theoretically and practically in the territory. It constitutes a layer, a coherent set of spaces, material and virtual, separated from, but in interaction with the historical palimpsest of the city (Crang 1996).

Using Brunet's theory of the chorèmes, the layer of aid can be described as a relatively standard application of norms and draw a model of the segregation of aid in the sites of intervention. This attempt to model the implantation of the aid industry at the scale of the city permits the use of visual thinking to generalise expected perceptions and ultimate use of local spaces by international organisations.

The chorème of the layer allows the identification of major places and spaces of aid archipelagos and their structure. The use of Brunet's theory of graphic models to describe the installation of international aid in cities allows the description and modelling of the different cities that constituted as many case studies for this research (Brunet 1986). The built environment and virtual spaces constitute the two main components of the modelling of a layer:

> *The concept of an urban layer is used here to denote a variety of spatial practice rather than a space in itself. It includes two major components: built environment and virtual spaces. The part of the layer constituted by the built environment comprises buildings of various orders (housing, work, entertainment) that are used by staff of international organisations. The other part is virtual and represents instructions from the security departments of international organisations regarding where they are allowed to settle, work and more generally go, thus separating the built environment in two, through the invisible line of security evaluation.(Hwang and De Roulet 2017)*

The chorème allows presenting and design a model of the key elements of the territoriality of international aid. The layer of aid is first a reading of the socio-spatial environment, and the definition of zones according to perceived danger by international organisations. Second, the layer is the material spaces where social interactions occur between expatriates, and with limited segments of the local population (Figure 45).

This chapter presents the layer of aid as a multiscale phenomenon starting from the country to the city, the neighbourhood and dwelling units. Below the scale of individual buildings, social power determines social interactions and body discipline, which frames the relation between the aid layer and the local panorama. The discussion on the layer begins with observations of the general repartition of aid workers in cities, with the examples of Juba, Bamako and Abidjan. Maps produced from security and other sources illustrate the contextual nature of the settlement of aid agencies as well as the generic spatial logic, which infer dwelling patterns.

These observations on the dwelling of aid workers following generic spatial logic adapted to specific settings are followed by a discussion on the virtual spaces of aid and the use of the built environment. The layer of aid is composed by its material surroundings and social representations of the urban environment. The virtual spaces of the city are representations of risks transmitted through specific discursive channels, which will be investigated through aid agencies' use security messages and a variety of discursive channels. The built environment, as material setting for the implantation of aid presence will be described and analysed in function of its use by the aid industry. The combination of formal descriptions of categories of places, such as offices, housing, hotels and shops, with a discussion on its social uses prefigures the social and material transformations to the local panorama.

The concept of the layer of aid presented here could itself be separated into several separate layers comprising the varieties and types of international aid,

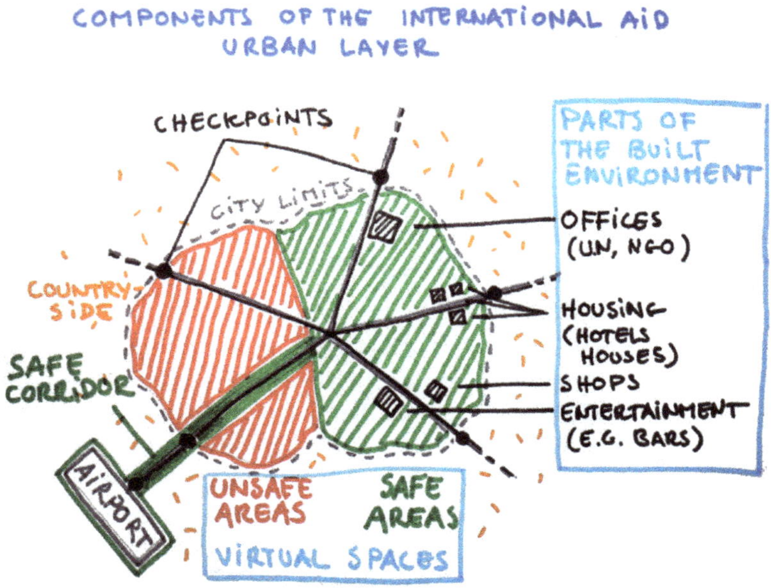

Figure 45: Model of the international aid layer in urban environments. It includes the built environment and virtual spaces of risk and safety as well as topological elements, such as checkpoints and temporary "safe corridors" within "unsafe areas", where temporary crossing may be permitted

including peacekeeping and development workers, along humanitarians. Indeed, the military component of peacekeeping operations make these type of mission relying on a social field distinct from humanitarians – soldiers and officers – and a distinct set of spaces – camps rather than houses and hotels. As a result, the layer presented in this general theory of the landscape mainly represents the civilian component of large international interventions.

Hierarchies within the layer of aid also nuance the division of the city by international aid. Social hierarchies within organisations place high-ranking officials in accommodations of highest standing. This part of the layer of aid also hosts some military officers who do not stay at the peacekeepers' encampments. Different organisations' approaches reveals a continuum of association and dissociation between the layer of aid and standards of the local environment. Large NGOs mostly settle in high-end places, while smaller organisations with fewer resources and an ambition to live within local communities do not dwell in the expatriate areas of the city.

These two lines of tension within the layer of aid, between types of organisations, and internal hierarchies, define the layer as a plurality of social spheres. These different spheres cross each other in some spaces of socialisation. In this regard, the layer could be sliced into sublayers to account for the specificities of these connections and disconnections.

6.1 City Scale: Available Space, Social Fragmentation and Airports

The spatial dynamics of international aid in cities operate at different scales. The result of this territorialisation is a partly segregated social space defined for international aid over the local environment. The layer of aid is superimposed to an already existing social and material environment, and interacts with it at a limited number of spaces and in a limited number of social encounters.

At the scale of the city, the spatial organisation of the aid industry is contingent at first to its need for space and the organisation of its office and housing policies. This will depend in particular on the size of workforce that intervenes in the country. This means that different spatial logics of the aid industry spatialises the UN and NGOs differently across the city. The UN and NGOs have different mandates and the size and the nature of their workforce is diverse. As a result, their territoriality is equally distinct albeit related. In particular, peacekeeping forces as military units are based in barracks, while civilian UN and NGO personnel settle inside the cities (Rolandsen 2015). The variety of organisations and organisational cultures result in a variety of modes of settling in urban environments.

The territoriality of aid is contingent to the organisation of the city where the aid industry settles, and its facilities. The selection of sites by the international aid community primarily follows security reasons. In his review of good security practice, Van Brabant advises to ask a number of questions relating to the urban and political geography before selecting a site for housing:

> *What local authority and rescue services are there in the area? Where is the nearest fire station? Where are the police posts? Where do the influential local leaders live? Find out if there is a police patrol and which are the more regularly patrolled areas.(Van Brabant 2010b)*

This selection of neighbourhoods directs to the well-off areas within the local community. One important polarity, however, that can be verified in most cases, is seeking the proximity to the airport. As a communication line to the outside of the country, the airport represents the most likely evacuation route in case of emergency. Airports attract expatriates in their use of urban environments as much as it allows their movements in and out of the country.

This search for the proximity to the airport is clearly visible at the level of the whole humanitarian community. It is, however, dispatched differently depending on the cities, which have different infrastructure. The availability of housing is one independent variable that may also influence this distribution. I will present below the visible intentions to settle in proximity to the airport in Juba, Bamako and Abidjan.[25]

6.1.1 Juba

Airports structure the geography of international aid in South Sudan since the 1990s. The presence of airstrips in towns and cities defined where the main bases for international aid would be installed in the country (Duffield 2010b). The political importance of the capital Juba itself has been defined by the presence of the airport and international aid's use of the city as country HQ. As the airstrips have largely defined the zones of intervention at the scale of the country, the airport has an important role in the spatial concentration of aid agencies at the urban scale of the capital.

The proximity of NGOs to the airport is most visible in Juba, where maps show the repartition of NGOs through the city. Practising a cartographic history of the city of Juba, different sources can be compiled to present the spatial dynamics of aid in relation to the urban facilities and history of cities. Old Soviet military maps covering the globe constitute an invaluable archive of urban history of remote and little-known places such as Juba used to be. Thanks to these Russian maps, it is possible to identify old city centres preceding urban population boom of the 1990s and 2000s in Juba. A 1979 map was used to identify the old core of the city (Soviet Army General Staff 1979). This information is compared to present days with the use of OSM data which contains the whole of the built environment, thanks to humanitarian involvement in the collaborative mapping project (Westrope, Banick, and Levine 2014). Finally, aid organisations

25 The proximity to the international airport in Nairobi is not an issue, considering the type of threats in Nairobi, above all crime and terrorism, and unrest during election periods. In fact, there is not even a mention of the airports in the "security pack" of the Nairobi UN office. Residential choices are organised differently at the macro level, left to the discretion of the employees. The major regulator for the dwelling of employees is the limit put to the permission to live and move in certain areas.

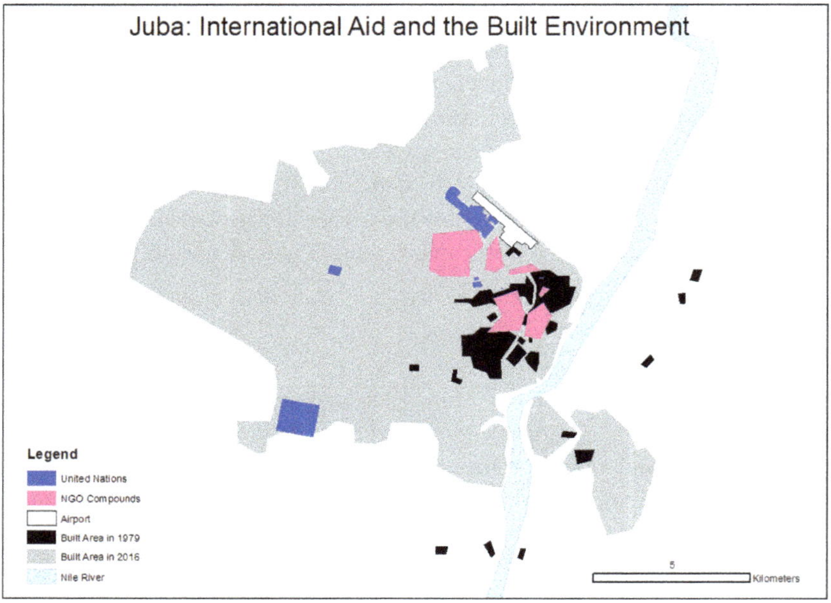

Figure 46: Map of international organisations in Juba

can be located using a WFP map published just after the June 2016 combats in Juba (Logistics Cluster 2016). The NGOs clearly show two separate clusters, which cover a surface of approximately one to two square kilometre each. One of the cluster is located within the bounds of the old city centre, an area already built in the 1970s, which currently hosts part of the South Sudanese administration, and the other on a more recently built area (Figure 46).

I did not have enough time in Juba to inquire directly how the NGOs choose the places and the other micro-processes that organised it. From the comments of expatriates living in, or familiar to, the area, it is apparent that the area was relatively calm and safe compared to other parts of Juba. According to long-time expatriates, from the mid-2000s, when the peace agreement with Sudan was signed, until the start of the civil war in 2013 and the subsequent economic crisis and rise in criminality, it was possible to walk on the central streets until dawn.[26]

Polarities and contradictory logics in the spatial patterns of international aid in Juba highlight the distinct processes that guides the use of space. The main

26 Observation Notebook, 3 July 2016.

base of the UN at Tomping area is the closest to the airport, where it is easier to load and unload personnel and material. Other offices and compounds are located in the periphery based where large open land is available. The WFP and the UN House stand more than five and ten kilometres away from the airport, on both flanks of the main Juba hill, Jebel Kujur. This spatial configuration is the result of important space requirements to host a large number of offices and equipment at the WFP. In the case of UN House, the use of land serves to host internally displaced civilians in encampments. As a result, the individual residential strategies of most employees of these organisations often seek proximity to their offices rather than the proximity to the airport.

The territoriality of international organisations in Juba illustrates the distinct use of space by humanitarian and peacekeeping components of aid presence. The largest patches of land in the city correspond to peacekeeping camps, as they host military encampments and logistics bases, rather than offices. The two single largest uses of land are the peacekeeping mission HQ near the airport and the UN House, which hosts internal refugees in the outskirts of Juba.

Humanitarian aid settles in a multiplicity of smaller units of land, in offices and compounds within the city. The two separate spaces of peacekeeping and humanitarian presence are separate but interwoven. Humanitarian aid workers also operate in peacekeeping spaces, to provide supplies to refugees for instance. Peacekeepers and humanitarians also share common amenities, such as overall UN administrative centres located within peacekeeping encampments, but also shops or medical facilities. Beyond the geographic intersection of common spaces, the overall humanitarian community often relies on the protection of peacekeepers in times of crisis, regardless of location.

The compared use of land in Juba constitutes an eloquent example of the internal spatial differences within international interventions. The layer of international implantation reflects a multiplicity of uses by different actors whose territoriality is both shared and distinct in terms of processes, shapes, sizes and purposes.

6.1.2 Bamako

Seeking proximity to the airport in Bamako materialises in the attempts to locate on the south side of the Niger River. While the headquarters of the UN mission remained for four years after 2013 on the north bank, in one of the main hotels of the city, the Hotel Amitié, many expatriates preferred staying south of the river, which is closer to the airport and does not require crossing bridges. Nowadays, the UN mission uses a new compound for the mission, nearby Bamako-Sénou Airport since 2016.

Mali had enjoyed a relative peace for decades before the current crisis. The Tuareg rebellion was for a long time limited to small stretches of the territory far remote in the deserts of the north of the country. The short war that the country fought against Burkina Faso in the 1980s was also located far away from the capital and most of the country did not suffer directly from war (Reporters 1986; Roger 2015). The location of agencies compounds, which were present for decades in the country, have thus not been located in relation to an evacuation. However, when the political situation worsened the proximity to the airport has become a real question for expatriates.

In the case of Bamako, the fact that the threat of events of a military coup, jihadist conquest or other military and paramilitary infighting seemed to diminish, replaced by increasing fear of terrorist attacks, the residential choices seemed in many ways to adapt. The luxury Radisson Hotel on the north side of the Niger suffered a terror attack in 2015, which left 22 dead (Dembelé 2015). The hotel did not recover its former level of frequentation after the attack. Nevertheless, as most luxurious hotels are located on the north side, they are still frequented by high-level political and humanitarian internationals.

The proximity and easy connection to the airport for residence visibly inform residential choices. Expatriates seem less interested to live in neighbourhoods north of the river, as I could observe during field visits. Although, this is a singular experience, I rarely visited houses of expatriates in the Northern areas, such as Cité du Niger or ACI 2000 in any of my visits there. Mafa Fall, a broker specialised in accommodating internationals with his small company, confirms this impression: "There was always this preferred area: Badalabougou."[27] Other signs of an important international presence in the same neighbourhood reflect spatial choices of expatriates. The hotel industry in the area was shaken by the conflict in Mali, although it found a new prosperity thanks to international presence and the vicinity of several important aid agencies.

The map of Bamako illustrates the main neighbourhoods were international aid workers have settled since 2013 (Figure 47). It is created using UN maps of recommended areas (presented in more detail below in this chapter), OSM data and IGN map from 1979 (IGN France 1980). The South Bank and areas in the North Bank at proximity to the bridges crossing the Niger River are more prized, for their faster connections to the airport. Most international aid

27 Interview Mafa Fall, 22 April 2016.

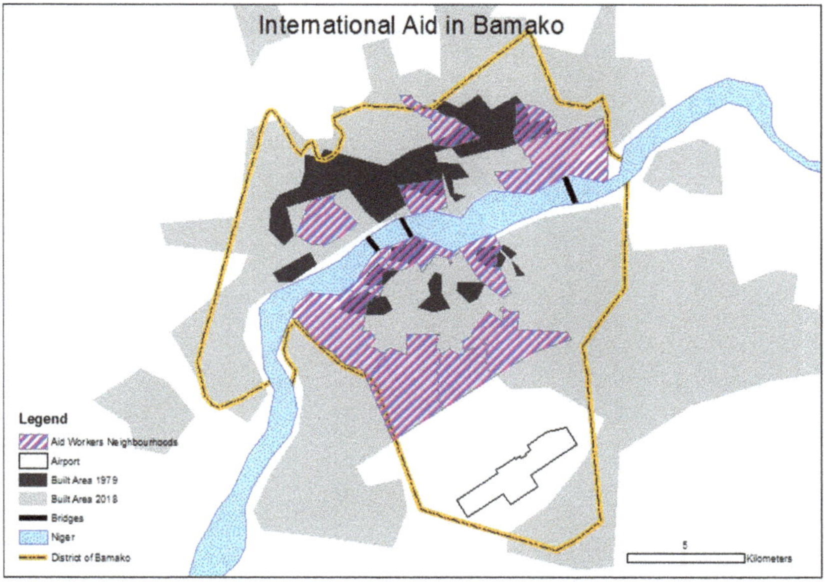

Figure 47: Areas used by aid expatriates in Bamako

neighbourhoods are in recently built areas on both sides of the Niger, although in close vicinity to the old city cores.

6.1.3 Abidjan

The spatial distribution of international agencies and personnel in Abidjan is also notable. Located partly on the mainland and partly on islands, the city of Abidjan presents a particular topography, to which international aid responded in the installation of its agencies in upper end areas on the city's mainland part, where most embassies are located. Aid agencies, UN and NGOs, are located mainly in Cocody and few others in the Plateau, the commercial and administrative centre, both in the north of the lagoon. These two areas are central to the city, on the side of the lagoon opposite to the airport, but closer to it than the working-class communes of Adjamé, Yopougon, and Abobo, which would be excluded for dwelling because of their population density, their poverty and a remaining strong support for the former president Laurent Gbagbo.

The dwelling of employees concentrates the most in the commune of Marcory, located in an island shared with the less affluent communes of Treichville and

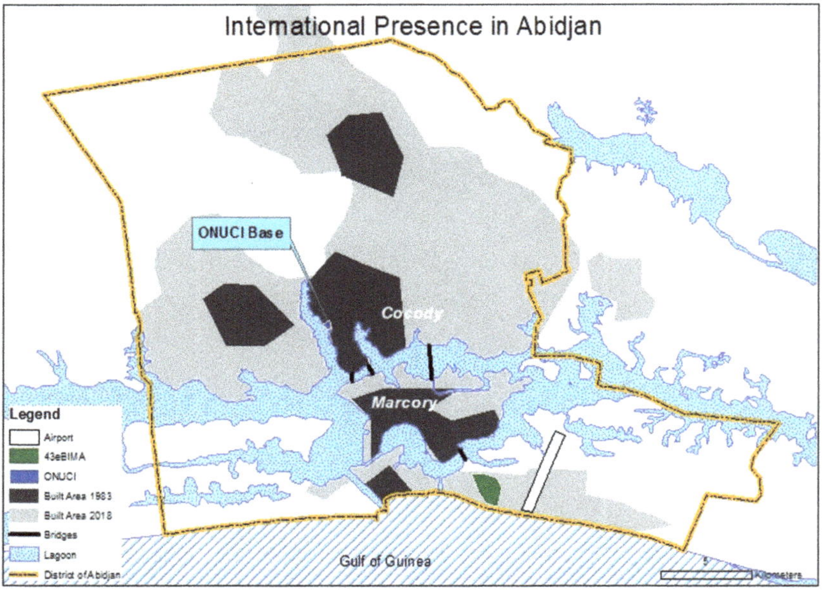

Figure 48: The spatiality of aid in Abidjan follows proximity and road access to the airport. The HKB Bridge connecting Cocody to Marcory opened in 2014

Koumassi. The commune of Marcory, and especially its wealthy Zone 4 are located close enough to the airport. It is only one bridge apart and also has the proximity of a French army base. The map of Abidjan created with OSM data and combined with collections of testimonies and observations on the field illustrate the search for proximity and road connectivity to the international airport and the French army base (Figure 48).

The population of Abidjan recognises this residential choice by internationals seeking fast connection to the airport. As the owner of a bar-carwash-hair salon told me jokingly when I was living in the outskirts of Cocody: "The others will escape by the airport if there is trouble. But not you! We'll catch you!"[28] Abidjanese are fully aware that civilian expatriates are not meant to stay in case of troubles. The joke emphasises the disconnections between local dweller and expatriates in the exposure to danger and in who can benefit from protections and evacuations.

28 Observation Notebook, 21 March 2017.

While the civil war itself is largely considered ended in the country, its aftermath is not yet settled. A number of military rebellions over pay and bonuses occurred since the beginning of 2017, including during my fieldwork there. During these days of standoff and fighting, it seemed completely obvious to everyone I spoke to, Europeans, Ivoirians, or from other African countries, such as Burkina Faso, Mali or Benin, that in case of trouble all "white" foreigners would be evacuated. "They'll come to pick you with a helicopter to get you to the airport," the French middle manager of a supermarket told me.[29] The severity of the rebellion in Abidjan never went so far as to provoke the evacuation of foreign citizens, which makes this assertion impossible to verify. It reflects, however, how much the local dwellers that would not have the chance of an organised evacuation in case of trouble may feel towards the presence of expatriates, privileged, and likely always separated from the local social environment.

Residential choices seeking proximity to the airport appears as a major influence on the spatiality of aid workers at the scale of the city as a whole. The examples of Juba, Bamako and Nairobi show that its structuration is both conscious from the part of the aid community, and recognised as such by the local inhabitants. It also constitutes the link of this local spatial pattern to a higher scale in the territoriality of aid. The aid presence is constituted on a network of moorings, international airports, that supports the global presence of the local UN offices (Hannam, Sheller, and Urry 2006). Linked with the mobility of the borders of international aid workers and the capacity of agencies to organise the flow of their employees, this relation to the airport(s) allows the creation of a transnational urban space.

At the scale of the neighbourhood, the implantation of international aid is spread across the wealthy areas of the city. Despite warnings of aid agencies not to settle in overly luxurious areas and houses (Smirl 2015), housing that meets the expected standards already pertain to the wealthiest parts of the society in the four sites of study. At the scale of the city, this coincides with areas planned orthogonally and with the sanitation equipment and infrastructure. The coupling of the sanitation and the orthogonality of the street grid is a good combination for the security officers who evaluate safety and security. Straight roads and regular construction allow the easy crossing of cars in case aid workers have to be evacuated from the area.

The regularity of the street grid does not necessarily mean that the area is wealthy. Irregular road grids correspond to informal areas, where the

29 Observation Notebook, 15 May 2018.

spontaneous installation of city dwellers did not follow the standards rectangular street pattern. In this regard, street regularity is a first precondition for international organisations, albeit far from enough in respect to the urban form. Planned areas include many poor dwellers and the regularity of the streets do not necessarily translate in the block or building architecture.

Wealth and regularity of buildings are correlated at the scale of building blocks and houses. The construction processes are different in wealthier areas, where owners can invest larger sums to build a house all at once. In less affluent areas, the houses and buildings tend to be evolutional, where the core of a house is constructed, and annexes are added in function of needs for space and available financial resources (Vauthrin 1989). These pictures of different construction processes are very visible in the city of Bamako for instance, were similar street outlines reveal completely different built forms (Figure 49). Only the regular model of neatly isolated building in regular footprints fits to expatriate security standards.

Following a security logic the regularity of the built form ensures maximum safety. It is easier to defend when elements of architecture and fencing, sometimes in relation to vegetation are clearly separated and leave cleared space in between. It is not rare to hear security officers talking about cutting trees in a garden because they would allow a possible passage for a burglar over the fence.[30] The lesson is that there must be an empty space between elements of the built environment (or the verticality in general). This requires space and modes of planning, design and construction that are reserved for a small minority, on the one hand, and takes a disproportionate amount of the city land on the other.

The inequality of wealth brings another factor in the constitution of the built environment as this space must to be protected against outside threats. The smallest scale of security interventions are material devices appended to individual buildings. Added to the walls, a variety of protective equipment is appended to the buildings to close it. Concertina barbed wire is often recommended on top of fences to prevent entrance. The aesthetic of the barbed wire is sometimes debated within the humanitarian community, from the perspective of its symbolic message and unintended risks associated with it (Stoddard, Harmer, and Haver 2006a; Van Brabant 2010b).

One critic of this type of defence is the message that is being transmitted to the local community. Luisa* a UN staffer in Mali, responsible for her establishing working relationships with local communities, recollected that when she settled

30 Observation Notebook, 25 August 2016.

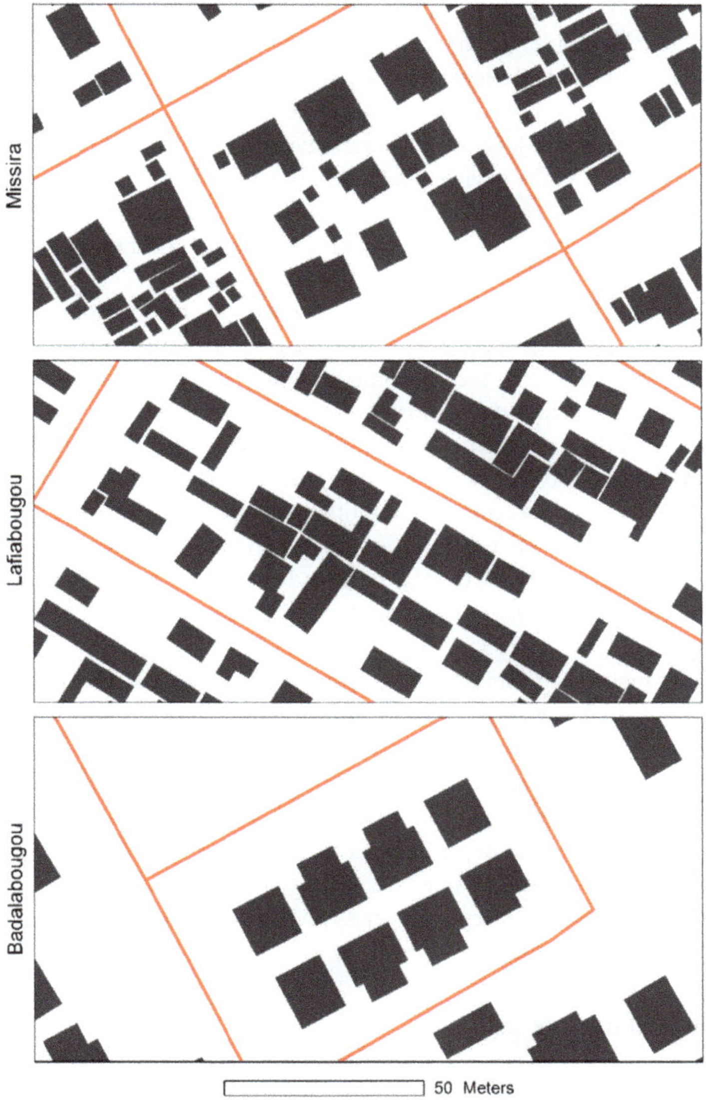

Figure 49: Comparison of the built form at the same scale in Bamako between the working class neighbourhoods of Missira (top) and Lafiabougou (centre) and the affluent area of Badalabougou (bottom). Street grids are similarly rectangular, but the built areas are distinct. In Missira and Lafiabougou, buildings are built over time around the courtyard. In Badalabougou the house is constructed in the middle of a garden. Walls separate the properties. Source: OpenStreetMap

in Bamako, the UN Security refused to validate the house she rented. The demand was that she set up barbed wire on top of the walls. She refused and had to negotiate with the UN Security for a derogation. "I am here to link and establish relations with the community", Luisa* recollected explaining. "If the first thing I do when I arrive is set up a separation with them, I will not be able to gain their confidence." As the device would have broader effect and seriously impair her work, Luisa* had complicated negotiations. The concertina was finally not installed in a balance of interest between her mission and residential security standards in Mali.

The other critique is more functional and relates to the potential unintended effect the concertina may have increasing risks. The presence of barbed wire might suggest the idea that there is something special to defend inside the premises. This could increase the curiosity of a variety of threats bearers, burglars, criminals and others and incite to get inside the compound. A similar argument is being discussed around the "safe room" that may be installed inside a house. A safe room consists of a reinforced door that may serve as a bunker in case of an intrusion. The difficulty to open the door may help the people inside to gain time until help arrives or even discourage the intruders to try opening it. However, the presence of reinforced room might also suggest that there be something valuable inside.

From a functional perspective, the dilemma seems that reinforcing the material apparatus makes it more difficult to penetrate space, but also more visible and seemingly interesting. This dilemma discussed by aid workers and security officers in the humanitarian community, with varying conclusions. In the private sector, hotel owners and managers have similar doubts and respond differently to visible security devices depending on their clientele and budgets. As will be discussed below in the case of hotels as well as individual houses, the implementation of security features largely depends on the perspective about their effects and expected adverse effect.

6.2 Virtual Spaces

This section on the virtual part of international aid layer will focus on two practices in the representation of space that precedes its use: the zoning of areas of a city according to security analysis and the dissemination of security discourse about the local environment. Cities are made of material as much as virtual elements constructing the city. These virtual elements might by memories of past events, or even urban legends, and more generally representations (M. Graham 2013). In countries in crisis, the projection of risk over a territory, or "riskscape" constitute the essential virtual layer which will largely determine use of the built environment (Müller-Mahn 2012). Representation of risk over a territory conveys both administratively enforced and individually integrated disciplines.

Virtual space embeds cognitive and administrative mechanisms and instruments of governance in the construction of the layer of international aid. The projection of risk appears as a major instrument in the territoriality of aid to guide the spatial habitus of aid workers. Humanitarian organisations analyse a territory from the perspective of its risks and disseminate this analysis down to aid workers, influencing their perceptions and behaviour.

The chapter above on the aid industry described how humanitarian organisations use security manuals and training to build the spatial habitus of aid workers in a generic understanding of risk in cities. On the field, the theory of security in cities is applied depending on the situation. Security analysis varies depending on the organisation norms, on the analysis by one or another security officer, and on the place. By contrast, the dissemination of the analysis by the security officers to the aid workers relies on a limited number of discursive tools.

States and administrations develop a variety of instruments of governance – financial, regulatory, analytical, informative and incentive – that materialise and operationalise programmes of action (Lascoumes 2011). International organisations use instruments with both imperative and incentive perspective to direct or orient territorialisation in cities. Among the variety of instruments used by the security wing of international organisations to shape the use of space, two tools are ubiquitous to disseminate spatial discipline: maps and security reports. The scales of the application of security maps and reports diverge and intersect at times.

Maps constitute the major vector to indicate risks and spatial instructions at the scales of a country and a city. They often explicitly forbid or limit the presence of aid workers in an area or a place. On the other hand, security reports tend to describe situations at every scale. They are instrumental in conveying a sense of danger to aid workers through repetition and participate to build a space habitus of weariness towards the environment. Both types of documents may be imperative and incentive in relation to aid workers and their use of space.

6.2.1 Zoning: Forbidden Areas

The prohibition of certain areas of a city for dwelling is strongly linked to the practice of mapmaking, as a language as much as a process. Maps constitute a key mediator in the formalisation of the macro-territoriality of international

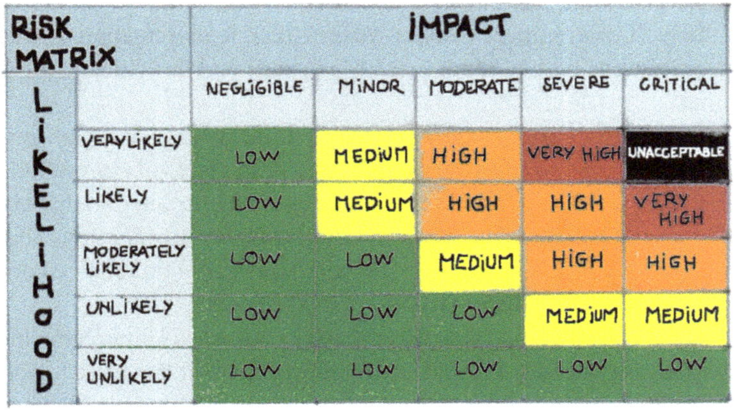

Figure 50: Risk Matrix. Values and colours are mapped in areas following levels of risks in security manuals (UNDSS 2017, p. 4)

aid. The zoning of areas in accordance to security starts at a higher geographical level of the country, dividing the country according to levels of risk. Standard matrices are widely distributed in attachment to UN security manuals. These evaluations affect the procedures for travel within a country, where UN personnel typically needs "security clearances" to leave their duty stations. The level of risk is constructed as the combination of the likelihood of an event occurring against its impact (UNDSS 2017). The risk matrix is similar to most risk models, such as natural hazards (Cox 2008). The institutional response to the two axes of the matrix is to take institutional rules and procedures to reduce likelihood and impact.

At the country scale, the zoning follows the recognised administrative levels in most mappings. However, the mapping methods are subject to controversies as administrative areas may include large areas unaffected by conflict (Dandoy 2013). To address this shortcoming, the mapping generalisations are sometimes presented in a slightly finer manner using cluster mapping, using the density of points of past events to reflect current risk areas. However this practice is generally limited to very specific types of risks, such as landmines, for which the quality, accuracy and precision of geospatial data is robust enough for this type of cartographic work (Dobson et al. 2010; GICHD and Institute 2018). Most mappings use internationally recognised administrative units.

Zoning and mapping of risk mean that contractual obligations and benefits for employees may be very different depending on their duty station, the official

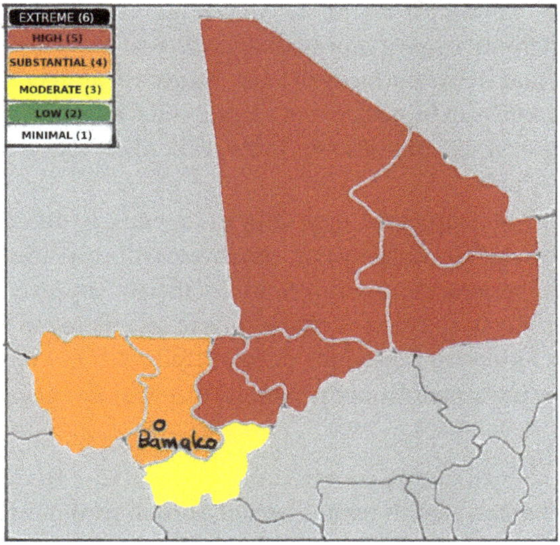

Figure 51: Mali according to UN security levels in 2013

location of their offices. The possibility to work in a place accompanied with the family is generally calculated at the scale of the country. In addition, for the UN and most NGOs, the estimated level of danger in a place affects income, with a "danger pay" added to regular salary and days of rests, through a calculated system of rest and recreation (RnR) (United Nations 2017a).

The mapping by administrative areas has the advantage of simplifying by generalisation and facilitating later recommendation of behavioural adaptation. It relies on a generalisation of risk evaluation per administrative unit. At the level of the programme, the importance of the security evaluation is the balancing between an acceptable risk and the importance of humanitarian presence for the implementation of programmes:

> *The decision as to who remains is based on the "Acceptable Risk Model" [...] and associated mechanisms for determining Programme Criticality and personnel requirements for priority programmes. Personnel who are unable to carry out their assigned tasks effectively due to the security situation and level of residual risk should also be relocated/evacuated. (UNDSS 2017)*

At the scale of the city, the multiple types of risk are most often collapsed into the single indication of "go/no-go". The zoning presents a first level of territoriality, where it is permitted or forbidden to live or travel. The imperative character of the map is blind to particularities of the precise places that lay in any of the two areas. The generalisation using official designations in maps results in inclusion of smaller areas that would normally fit in its category at a larger scale map. Small area looking "unsafe" can be included in a larger "safe" area, and vice versa. If this occurrence happens, security officers would most likely refuse to give the final authorisation to dwell.

The behaviour of employees regarding the zoning is different concerning dwelling and passing. It is unlikely that employees will cross the line of dwelling in an unsafe area, because the dwelling must be officially approved after a security check. However, the trespassing of regulations in circulating in the city is more likely. Going to forbidden nightclubs or marketplaces is frequent, including, if not especially, by the same security personnel that warned against going there.

Colour Symbolism

The colouring of urban areas is reminiscent of a brutal symbolic practice of map-making in military operations. In particular, the US occupation of Iraq led to the securing of the government and administrative quarters of the city behind urban walls and other security devices. Named the Green Zone, this area of Baghdad became to be known as a symbol of blindness of the country's occupiers, and the colonial-like structure of the new US power in Iraq (Chandrasekaran 2010). The case of Iraq is an extreme example of the superposition of the symbolic violence of safety designations over the actual extreme violence happening beyond the walls of the Baghdad Centre. The infamous reputation of the Green Zone may explain why humanitarians have diversified the ranges of colour they use to name the zones where they live and work. This includes in particular the blue colour used in Nairobi as will be developed below.

The colouring of urban zones by the aid community appears to be diverse, although it appears to follow a limited number of standard red-yellow-green colour ramps in most missions (Lemay-Hébert 2018). The greening of safe zones is a classic of the semiology where the green can alternatively or conjointly mean safety, permission, passage, and more generally positive qualities. Opposite of green, red is the complementary colour as well as the strongest colour of the spectrum, carrying heavy symbolic meaning. Red is opposed to green as a symbol of danger most typically, but also to signal interdictions (A. C. Robinson, Roth, and MacEachren 2011; Kostelnick et al. 2013). The symbolic violence of the determination of go and no-go zones in colours on the map is likely understood by most within the aid community. This partly explains the relative discretion in the distribution of risk maps to aid workers, as local citizens rarely appreciate being placed in unsafe areas (Lemay-Hébert 2018). The examples of zoning presented below concern the cities of Nairobi, Bamako and Abidjan, where the influence of the security zoning of the cities is manifest.

Nairobi Blue

As is the case in all duty stations, security briefings expect the UN personnel arriving in Nairobi. Large sections of UN employees in Nairobi, as a major UN HQ, are executive positions. The city of Nairobi is also a "family duty station", which means that UN employees may be accompanied by spouses and children.

This particular status of Nairobi makes the emphasis on presentations of the question of security in Nairobi quite particular. Security briefings in Nairobi are set not as the relation between office, house and field, as in sites of international interventions and emergencies, but as a place to live and raise a family. The documentation is also less subject to change than in countries of interventions, where the security situation and risk analysis is more contingent to political development. Safety understandings of the situation in Kenya are affected by major terror attacks, and to the crises related to the political situation in Kenya, where expatriates are warned to beware of riots and other politically related violence. However those warning remain scaled to an understanding of the country situation as relatively stable.

When the UN started installing offices in Nairobi in the late 1970s, Kenya was, and had already been for a while, relying on tourism for part of its income. This has made Nairobi and its surrounding making an important base for tourism to national parks, and to beach tourism on the coast. The UN offices at Nairobi made an important use of the tourism image of the country to brand the "African-ness" of the place, among others. The "karibUNi" letters at the entrances of the main UN offices use the Swahili for welcome, equally promoted by tourism operators on East Africa. The UN's use of the touristic and exotic image of Kenya in relation with its employees is reflected in the effort on recreation possibilities in Nairobi and beyond. The reference document distributed to employees arriving in Nairobi is titled "Amazing Kenya". The accompanying picture presents a smiling young Kenyan dressed in what are presumably traditional dress and jewellery (Rodriguez Harvey 2016).

The UN have used their own colour to designate the areas for UN personnel as the "Blue Zone", as a less charged term than a "Green Zone". This ostensibly designates the areas around the UN compounds. However, the blue zone extends to areas authorised or advised for expatriates beyond the vicinity of the UN. It is in fact discontinued and extends to all the upper end areas of the city.

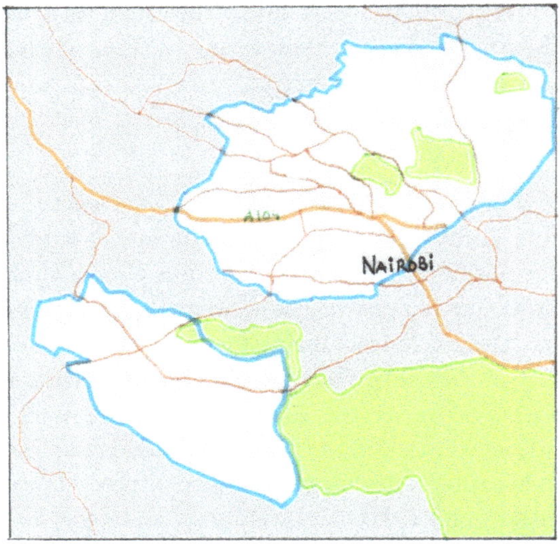

Figure 52: Nairobi "Blue Zone" as delineated and distributed in the UNON security documentation. UN Security uses Google Maps as background of a simple cartographic discourse. Similar blue line maps support most official UN security documents in Nairobi

The term "Blue Zone" in Nairobi has become a colloquial word in the world of real estate marketing beyond the UN system. One company dealing in high-end house renting branded itself as "Blue Zone Property" (Blue Zone Properties 2018), for example. Land developers are aware that there is a housing market for expatriates and indeed specifically target it. It also suggests the importance of the UN in influencing both the use of space and its security grammar externally.

Maps represent the "Blue Zone", indicating areas considered safe to the UN personnel and their families. The zoning directs expatriates in expected patterns of behaviour when they are in or out of these areas. The presentation of the Blue Zone by the UN Security has the effect of flattening the risk by reducing spatial understanding of hazards in their most generalised possible fashion. Every type of hazard is flattened and merged when considered spatially. This follows a well-established practice of hazard mapping for the general public where users should not be confused with complex technical descriptions (Monmonier 1995). Instead, users are provided with an excessively simple cartographic document that only designs an inside and an outside.

The definition of the Blue Zone is presented in simple terms by the UN Security in its 2013 Security Advisory document: "The Blue Zone has been chosen because of the relatively secure environment and the fact that police and other emergency services have good response times to the area." (Department of Safety and Security 2013). Other UN document also point to security as the primary reason to locate in the Blue Zone, independently of personal taste (Rodriguez Harvey 2016). Mapping has a major influence on the spatial practices of international organisations and their employees as a base for important contractual obligations with disciplinary and financial consequences. The expected uses of this division of space are described in texts of recommendation or strict instructions. The power of the mapping of the Blue Zone should not be underestimated, as the residential standards instructions make clear to UN employees that the financial conditions supporting the installation of employees might not be available if outside the Blue Zone (Department of Safety and Security 2016).

Bamako in Red and Green

The zoning produced by the UN for the city of Bamako in 2013 when many expatriates arrived in the city simply used a green and red colouring, as the simplest and most direct message. The city is divided between the green and the red zones, which leave no space for ambiguity. An area is either safe or unsafe, permitted or forbidden. The zoning carefully excludes from the green all informal and rehabilitated informal neighbourhoods. One particularity of the security zoning of Bamako lay in the disconnection of the different parts of the green. Safe areas appear as surrounded and disconnected elements surrounded by some sort of danger.

The rationale in red-colouring informal settlements is to avoid areas correlated with a series of negative characteristics for security officers. The areas are relatively densely populated, inhabitants are poor and the infrastructure does not necessarily include sewers, water and electricity networks. Road layouts are often narrow and irregular, unlike the planned neighbourhoods, which follow an orthogonal grid for the streets and properties. The regularity of the road grid is likely an important argument in deciding the zoning of a neighbourhood, as it affects the possibilities of access and manoeuvrability of cars.

Different types of dwelling are included in the green zones, within a certain number of types of neighbourhoods. Low-density suburban neighbourhoods, almost forming a belt around the city centre, dominates the green areas. Green zoning largely corresponds to villas surrounded by gardens. They include, however, number of apartments in the areas closer to the city centre. The ACI 2000,

Figure 53: Red and green areas of Bamako according to UN Security. This map of risk areas was distributed during security briefings at least until the end of 2013

the Cité du Niger and the Hippodrome areas offer affluent apartments and houses in the north side of Bamako. On the south side, a large belt of "green" areas surrounds, but carefully avoids the dense working-class neighbourhoods.

The generalisation of the green and red zones in Bamako is larger the actual demarcations between wealth and poverty. Working class and informal neighbourhoods are sometimes enclaved within wealthier and "safer" areas marked as "green". In a reverse situation, the private house of the Malian president, lie on an area that is not allowed for dwelling to UN employees. In a number of working-class areas, wealthy houses stand with all amenities and connected to all networks. "Red" areas of the city also include houses that would fully fit the standard for international aid if they were situated in the "green" area. While the scenario of a more subtle look at a particular place is not always excluded, the authoritative nature of the map makes it unlikely. The imperative and the suggestive power of the map prevents security officer to allow dwelling, or even crossing.

Security mapping works as an incremented notch system. It is only possible to increase the extent of forbidden areas and places. Impoverished neighbourhoods within the green areas are never authorised. A map of the UN's actual dwelling in Bamako would likely include only the most affluent parts of the green areas, and totally exclude the red zone. Other organisations with different rules and less bureaucratic power to the security wing might place their offices and allow their employees to live in much more diversity of locations. Nevertheless, within the spectrum of mainstream aid organisations, such as large NGOs, residential choices are similar to the UN zoning.

Residential and Office Areas in Abidjan

The zoning can be based on the location of neighbourhoods in proximity to critical locations, most typically the airport, which facilitates an evacuation of personnel if needed. The city of Abidjan is a good example, although with the lower number of aid organisations and staff, I was not able to find a UN or NGO security map of the city. Despite the invisibility of the zoning of Abidjan, residential choices by neighbourhood are transparent, for representative of the municipalities. Many local laypersons showed that they were fully aware that the zoning Abidjan through perceptions of risk influences residential choices. The spatial distribution of aid, with concentration of agencies and expatriates in certain areas is visible without the map that established the zoning.

The commune of Cocody traditionally hosts foreign embassies. Most of foreign diplomatic offices stand in villas in the area close to the Hotel Ivoire, the showcase five star hotel and the Riviera-Golf neighbourhood. Hosting the presidential palace, the commune of Cocody also hosts multilateral organisations and UN agencies, such as the WFP, Unicef, Save the Children and other major NGOs. More recently, one of the terrains rented by the ONUCI was also located in the commune. In short, concentration of humanitarian agencies followed the proximity of other international institutions.

The commune of Cocody hosts most international agencies, with the exception of the UNDP located on the Plateau, while expatriates tend to live in Marcory. Most presence of international organisations has been located between two of the eight communes of the city. Asked whether the municipality of Marcory had a specific strategy to host the expatriates, Xavier Akoa, Deputy Director of Technical Services explained that the expatriates were attracted by the crossing point location on the lagoon of Abidjan:

> *There are several reasons for the presence of expatriates in Marcory. It's five minutes to the Business District in the Plateau and five minutes to Cocody. It is also five minutes away from the airport. There is the question of rapid evacuation. Marcory also has a possibility to evacuate by the lagoon and the 4th BIMA [French military base] is close. We relish*

this situation. It's an opportunity. International cooperation employees are high-standing residents. It has an impact on real-estate and housing taxes.[31]

Even as the security mapping (or other verbal or written recommendations) is not publicly available, the spatial result of security norms according to zones with possibilities of escape appears visible. The footprint of approaches of security internal to organisations, and the sort of reverse engineering logic in understanding the location of expatriates confirms the power of security zoning. Virtual spaces of aid shapes the real interactions of aid workers with the local environment and its logics are transparent when they translate into physical use.

6.2.2 Through the Lens of Bad News

Projection of fears through the regular exposure of violent events instils a topophobic relation to the panorama. As expatriates rely on regular flow of distressing news, it constructs a fear of the local environment. The serial distribution and regular exposure to security information inform of a relation to space both as specific places and as typologies of locations associated with particular connotations in relation to danger.

The aid industry formalises its use of space through security procedures and the zoning of the urban environment in areas and times that are forbidden or authorised. The use of space is also mediated by organisational hierarchy through the diffusion of information on the security situation, mainly by emails. Most organisations have their own ways, more or less strictly formalised, of diffusing information about security. UN agencies rely largely on the Situation Reports, commonly referred as "SitReps" to inform their employees of the security situation.

These SitReps may contain formal instruction on spatial behaviour to inform employees when and where they are allowed to go or not. They also participate to produce a picture of the place where international employees live. They offer an interesting window of observation of the mindset of the Security wing within international organisations and to the picture that the repetitive effect of the daily diffusion of distressing news has in picturing the outside world as a dangerous place.

These documents are normally limited to the use by UN personnel, as is usually mentioned in every email. They are, however, often being passed to

31 Interview Xavier Akoa, 10 May 2017. Note that the five minutes transit mentioned are a rhetorical exaggeration. It is probably closer to half an hour transit time between these places when traffic is low.

employees that are not in the normal diffusion list. Friends sending these documents informally to NGOs, for example, is a common feature of the discrete interpersonal negotiation that take place within the small circles and networks of friendship and collaboration between aid workers.

SitReps constitute a body of confidential documents. The discussion below on the language of SitReps comprises daily messages for a period of three months in South Sudan. Because of the confidentiality of the documents, names, places dates and times of events are obfuscated, and the presentation will largely rely on quantitative content analysis of serial documents to illustrate the main themes addressed in the messages.

Formally, these documents have senders and receivers. Receivers should normally be from within the organisation. The senders are either security or programme officers with political and security monitoring tasks. This verticality of the diffusion of security news is the first element structuring a representation of risk. The compilation of information contained in the message is part of security units' routine work. Security stories and evaluation are an art built by synthesis of the words of other security officers, political evaluation of newspapers (some of them cited in text), and official reports.

The contents studied for this analysis of SitReps must be taken with its limitation, in time and space and can not be understood to represent the totality of SitReps in all countries. The very particular nature of South Sudan, an especially dangerous place(Stoddard, Harmer, and Czwarmo 2018), makes it prone to contain a large amount of worrying content. However, its structure is congruent to other countries and situations, where I had the occasion to examine or be told of the contents.

The serial and standardised nature of SitReps facilitates the use of quantitative analysis to denote thematic trends. Reinert's hierarchical descending classification(HDC) method (Reinert 1990) creates classifications by calculating the proximity of each word in relation to another. Using this analysis with permits the automatic thematic grouping of the text. Blind to actual meaning of the text, this type of analysis allows the observation of different themes, which might be missed with human reading, because of their marginality or because of blinding ubiquity. As the classification regroups words into categories of proximity, the human interpretation can identify and name the classification into meaningful groups.

A series of clusters of keywords can be gathered and treated as categories of contents. The Reinert classification on the SitReps illustrates a semantic order of five classes grouped in three main clusters: political and military situation, security procedures and security incidents. The clusters and their most significant

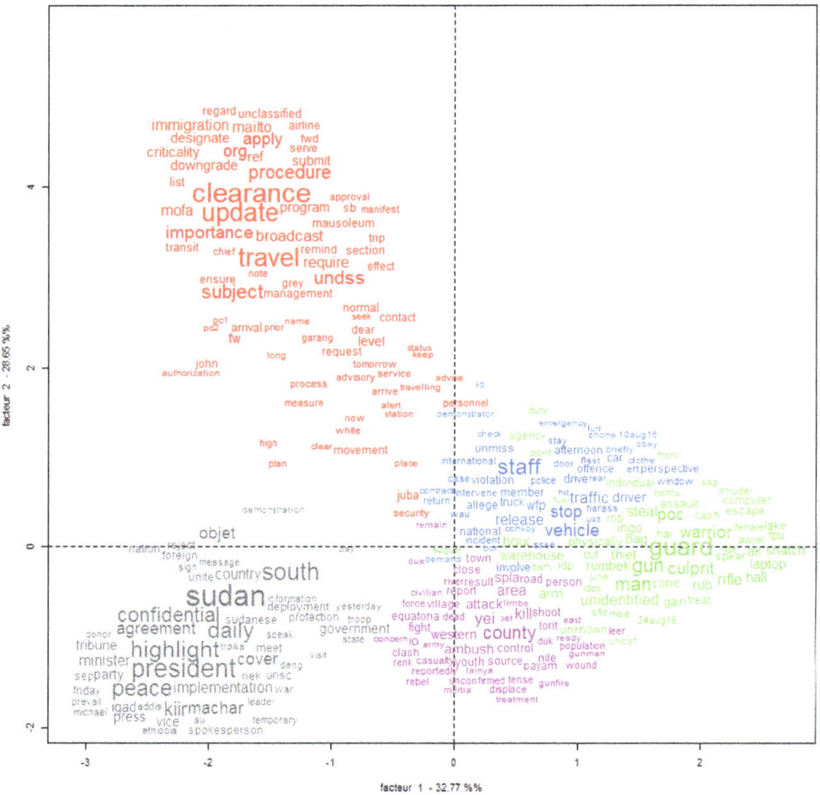

Figure 54: Reinert analysis of SitReps for South Sudan: political and military situation (grey), security procedures (red) and security incidents (blue green and purple). The software assigns the colours of the clusters randomly

words are represented below in a factorial analysis, which illustrates the main thematic (Figure 54).

The classes relating to politics (grey) and procedures (red) represent together around a third of all contents of the daily reports. Part of the SitRep routine is devoted to describe the political situation in the country and the region. The names and roles of the main political-military actors come back as routine of the ongoing conflict. The tone of the political discussion is descriptive and generally attempts to keep a neutral picture of the different actors. On the other hand, instructions relating to procedures mostly concerns in-country travel and regularly indicates changes to obtain the "security clearance" needed before trips in the country.

On the remainder of the security messages, the cluster concerns security incidents. The charting and colouring of the categories of the Reinert classification permits to distinguish broadly three types of incident described in the messages.[32] Within the cluster relating to security incidents, the blue and green classes describe incidents concerning humanitarian personnel and property, while the purple class concerns incidents relating to the local population. This separation in three classes of security incidents illustrates an important distinction in dealing with violent incidents in general and compared to events affecting specifically aid workers.

An examination of the description of incidents affecting the local population reveals a catastrophic picture. The classification of incidents relating to the local population (purple), which includes geographic locations all over the country, describes murderous attacks and the fighting of the civil war. An examination of the most characteristic sentences within this class shows the following results:

> *Insecurity in several areas continued in […] state […] county, […] state and […] county […], where villagers were victims of attacks and looting by armed groups. The […] attack resulted in 13 civilians killed.*

The most characteristic sentence of a cluster of words, which represents 30 % of the contents of all messaging, highlights extreme levels of violence in the country, where a description of the death of numerous civilians is representative of the text. Note that the most characteristic word is the geographic location, more than the violence it describes. The words "state", "county" and "town" are the most used and indicate the dispersion of violent events in the country. The names of exact places, obfuscated here, are locations where the civil war is most intense and appear the most frequently.

The two remaining classes concern incidents involving either staff or property of humanitarian agencies. Interestingly, most incidents involving staff concern the attempts by local police force to racket international staff in their vehicles, and happen on public roads. While official UN discourse on staff security relies on the local authorities for security, the latter are more often identified as a threat than a safety asset (Bertram 1995; Hultman, Kathman, and Shannon 2013). A characteristic segment of the class relating to staff safety notes:

---

32 Colours are assigned randomly to facilitate identification and do not reflect other meaning in the content of the message.

The staff member who was physically assaulted [by the police] and had his driving permit confiscated abandoned his vehicle and run back into the [...] compound for safety. [Response team] successfully negotiated for the unconditional release of the permit and the vehicle.

The last category on attacks on property revolves around fixed locations with valuable items. It regularly involves violence by "unknown gunmen", as a characteristic segment indicates:

[During night-time] unknown armed men gained access into an [NGO] compound, physically assaulted and threatened one staff member. The victim sustained minor injury but managed to alert the security guards.

References to "unknown gunmen", used in SitReps as well as local media has become strongly associated with complicity, or direct responsibility of elements of security forces (Eye Radio Network 2017). The SitReps for South Sudan are representative of the exposure to news of violent events, which have the intended effect to warn staff to beware of characteristic patterns of violence in the country. They indicate patterns of incidents where danger of death and injuries is present everywhere. The messages are presenting, explicitly or implicitly, a discourse on space. This broad discourse instils spatial discipline in line with the general recommendations of security manuals and training.

In the example seen above, the course of the civil war is described at the scale of the country and its administrative levels and status. The description of specific incidents against international staff or property is also related to a specific geographic location. However, the reports also describe the events in the form of a generic relation to categories of places and object, such as the "compounds" and "vehicles" in the examples above.

The generic categories of space permits to understand how the notions of danger and safety are associated or not to types of location. An analysis of similarity charts the relation of lexical proximity between words to highlight the most common associations (Marchand and Ratinaud 2012). In the SitReps, three categories of spaces appear closely associated with the notion of safety: "compound", "office", and "residence" (Figure 55). These three types of spaces are static and belong to the routine spaces of aid workers, either at work or at home. Safety clearly appears correlated with fixed locations and aid organisations who have the capacity to protect the perimeter of compounds. Places names are removed from the graph below as they indicate exact locations of international organisations.

The emphasis of the relative safety of enclosed and protected locations separated from the local social environment set the stage for a usage of the land that restricts movements on the public domain. Roads, on the other hand, are

Figure 55: Analysis of similarity in SitReps. Locations associated with safety are "offices", "compounds" and "residence"

systematically associated with different types of dangers: "attacks", "kill" and "ambush" among others (Figure 55). The stories of the SitReps strongly associates categories of danger to movement, while being static appears as a protection.

The incidents and warnings presented on the SitReps have the stroboscopic effect of the repeated comments on all dangerous events. The case of South Sudan, a country suffering a civil war and the presence of criminal gangs could not really be missed even without the SitReps. However, even in the violent context of South Sudan, the contents of SitReps and other security warnings are often considered exaggerated by UN personnel. However, it is outside humanitarian organisations that the bombarding of bad news is felt as a problem. Diverse social groups affected by the security warnings feel the bad publicity bitterly. For Oliver Smith a hotel manager in Juba, security reports are "business damaging" in the sense that they present a more dramatic picture than the situation really is. The mention of the vicinity of his hotel to a major gun fighting event by a security company was especially bad: "it is only because [the manager

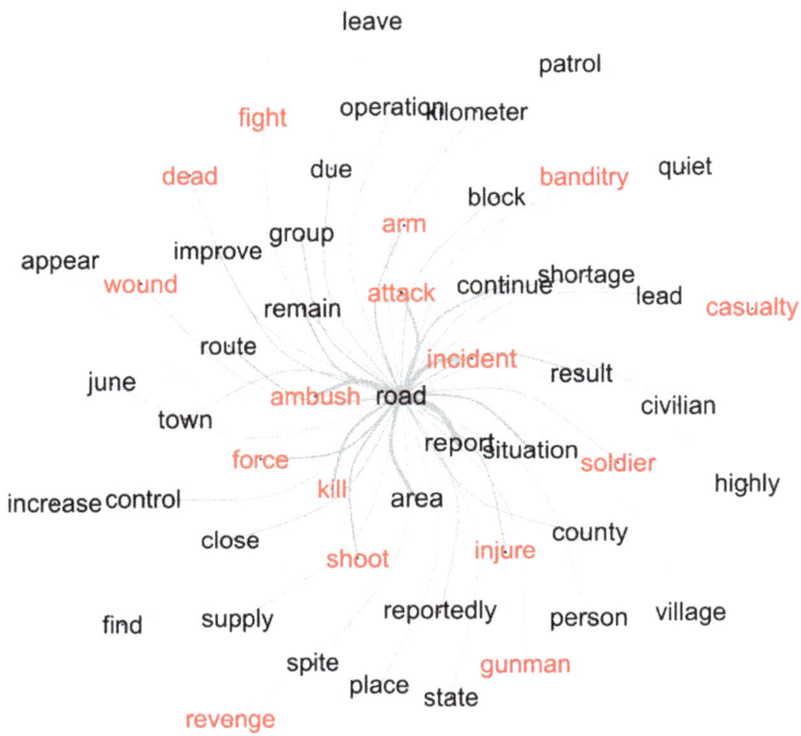

Figure 56: Analysis of similarity. Words and events associated with "road" evoke dangers

of a private security firm] was here at the time that the name of the hotel ends up in the report. But now it looks like the place is located in an especially dangerous place."[33]

SitReps are only one of the different sources of information on violence that are being received by humanitarian workers. That is, of course, especially important in violent contexts. It is impossible to assess how much people do actually read the security information, but the multiplicity of sources gives a good glimpse that people likely follow the events. The repetitive effect does not require attentive reading every day, since there are always alarming informations outside.

33 Observation Notebook, 9 July 2016.

SitReps are shared within the aid community. Nevertheless, these emails are kept secret from outsiders, especially from the local population. As a result, few locals have expressed opinion on how their country and cities are depicted within the aid community during this research. Among the few local citizens aware of the security discourse are the national employees of international organisations, such as Robert* who receives security warnings and SitReps as a UN volunteer in Nairobi.

Aware of the reputation given by security messages Robert* criticises the intimidating language of SitReps and see them as building a distrust and separating aid workers from the local environment. As a local UN volunteer coming from the Mathare slum area in Nairobi, he explains: "I don't read them any more. It just builds fear and provokes alienation from the Kenyans, giving the impression that everything here is dangerous."[34] Indeed, the contents of a standard SitRep for Kenya lists types of events under categories of "Crime, Hazard, Armed Conflict and Terrorism" on a weekly basis. The density of incidents described in the Kenyan SitReps is much lower than in countries in violent conflicts, and the Nairobi section contains incidents of low gravity affecting UN employees.

It also includes incidents of much lesser gravity. Under the Crime headline in Nairobi, the document lists events as distinct in their consequences as home invasion at gunpoint and the theft of unattended items. A SitRep in September 2016 listed the incidents of the preceding week as follows:

> *[…] a staff member and spouse preparing to leave to the airport were robbed in their compound by unknown individuals armed with pistols who managed to rush into the compound as a taxi entered the gate. The assailants threatened the staff and spouse and took away suitcases containing assorted personal items and cash.*
>
> *[…] a staff members' spare tyre was stolen from his car at a parking lot.*
>
> *[…] two UN staff members attending the […] meetings left their respective bags in the conference room for lunch break. Upon return, they discovered that the bags, containing official laptops and IDs as well as personal items, had been stolen. Staff members are reminded to always keep personal items in clear sight and secure valuables – DO NOT leave your belongings unattended.*
>
> *[…] a staff member was attacked by a young man with a stone as she was walking along the road. The motive of the incident is unknown.*[35]

34 Interview Robert*, 31 August 2016.

35 SitRep for Kenya, September 2016. The brackets indicate removal of names, places, date and time of the incident from the citation.

The significance of the events of the week in Kenya is not comparable, although all incidents are listed without apparent order. It tends to conflate violent and non-violent events. The selection and presentation of these events is eloquent in the perception of the link between risks and categories of places. There is no doubt that events described in the SitReps are authentic. However, their selection pointedly addresses many of the key worries and serves as a repetition of the UN Security talking points. The home invasion and the event walking on the road indicate that contacts with the local environment must remain minimal. In addition, the description of petty theft within a UN compound shows that any belonging is at risk, and everywhere.

Regular SitReps participate to representations of space and of the urban environment akin to sensationalist daily newspapers, where fear dominates representations of space. Exposure to repeated news stories of crime tends to cultivate fear in relation to categories of places and people (Chiricos, Eschholz, and Gertz 1997; Chiricos, Padgett, and Gertz 2006). Furthermore, it has the effect of changing behaviour and attitudes, including creating a general anxiety towards the urban (Romer, Jamieson, and Aday 2006). Daily or weekly news of dangerous incidents in the country have a similar effect of the international staff and will affect the pattern of behaviours without needing strict instructions. The careful task of describing the dangers of the local panorama prepares the physical isolation through architectural design and social behaviour.

6.3 The Built Environment and Social Relations

International aid uses the built environment as a resource to work and live. Organisations rent and sometimes constructs buildings and prefabs to install compounds or warehouses supporting humanitarian operations. Aid workers rent houses, apartments and hotel room, directly or through their organisations, to live. The variety of uses of the built environment to sustain the presence differs depending on individuals and organisations. However, an elementary typology of international organisations illustrate the ways aid presence marks its locations in a city. Offices, housing, warehousing all form part for what Smirl coined as the auxiliary space of international aid, a socio-spatial construct that support the presence and mission of international aid (Smirl 2015, p. 89).

The built environment is both a product and a producer (or an organiser) of social relations. To explain this dialectal relation, Hillier and Hanson refer to the notion of buildings as artefacts (Bill Hillier and Hanson 1984; B. Hillier et al. 1987). The purpose of buildings is not the physical object, but the ordering of an "empty" space between its features. The space of possible social interactions is constructed by allowing or cutting circulation with walls and other physical barriers. Once designed the built environment influences social relations and representations.

The section below will examine different types of buildings and spaces used by aid organisations. The built environment is a social ordering through material features that international aid uses it as means to structure a physical and social separation from the local environment. The separation of aid from the local environment is ordered differently depending on the type and function of a building. Despite variations in implementation, aid organisations widely rely on the grammar of defensible space, producing the materiality of a separate layer within the city palimpsest.

6.3.1 Compounds

International organisations' compounds constitute their administrative and logistical centres, and generally refer to either offices or the combination of offices and housing for humanitarians. They may vary in their size and nature depending on the organisation. The security of the premises is political in the sense that the presumed reason for an attack against an agency compound is to hurt the organisation's political role in the country. The notorious 2003 bomb attack in Baghdad, which killed the UN representative in Iraq, led to the wide reform of security procedures within the UN (Dodge 2005).

UN security manuals evoke the notion of "concentric layers" of security and "redundancy" to protect the compound, in a "defence in depth". This policy is reflected in the building of numerous walls and fences around offices, and the limitation and control of entry points:

> *Access control systems, beginning at the perimeter and continuing through each layer of protection within the premises, channel personnel and vehicle access through designated control points for verification of identity, authority to enter and other security checks. (UNDSS 2017, p. 73)*

The practical implementation of installing a number of barriers in and around the compound differ depending on the size of the building and the location. I present here two models of compounds in the cities where the research was conducted. This will not exhaust the number of possibilities of different security designs or cover all visited compounds but present two occurrences of the "defence on depth" of UN premises.

The concentric layers and redundancy in the securing of the compounds involve levels of passage from the public space to the office space. In a simple schema of one UN office, it is possible to distinguish four main different spaces in relation to

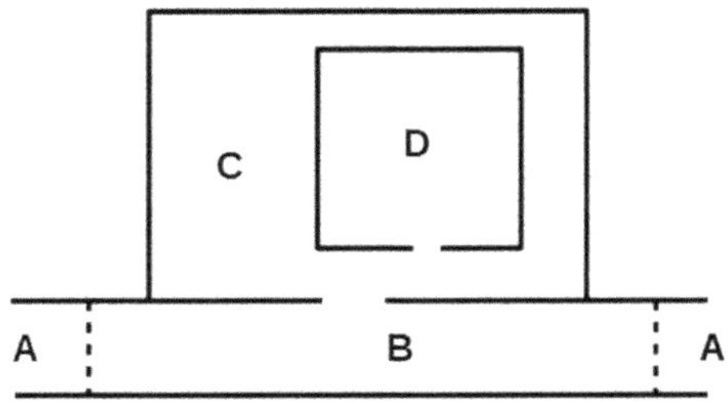

Figure 57: Plan of a UN agency "concentric layers of security", from public space (a) to office space (d)

the city (Figure 57). A passage from A, in the public space, requires the crossing of three levels of control to the office D. The first crossing is actually within the public space between A and B. Agents of a private security company contracted by the UN gaze at pedestrians, and control under the car with a mirror whether an improvised explosive device (IED) might have been hidden. Formally, the space B, in front of the compound is still public land, although the UN and its private contractors operate and control it.

The second passage, from B to C, is the entering of the private domain of the UN, but not yet the offices. In most cases, C is either a garden or a parking space. This passage already requires a legitimising document. This is either the UN identification document for employees of the agency, or a passport that is left to the guards in exchange for a visitor's pass. In some cases, this passage might involve a body check or the crossing of a metal detection portal (Figures 58 and 45).

From inside the compound to inside the office of the agency, another control is required by addressing the reception. Employees simply go to their offices, while another control is operated on visitors to verify whom they want to meet. Accessing individual offices might also require a key to enter personal or shared space.

To examine the "depth" in architecture, Bill Hillier uses graph theory to sketch the numbers of separate rooms needed to access the totality of a building. This method allows charting and understanding space in terms of their topology and measuring how much close or open they are (Bill Hillier and Hanson 1984; Bill Hillier 1996). Nodes represent rooms or other enclosed spaces and vertices schematise the apertures between the spaces. This graphic method allows a count of

Figure 58: Local uniformed guards contracted through a security company operate the control of the double door

levels of depths, which correspond to the "concentric layers" in the language of UN security manuals.

In another case of the UN compound involving a large space of land, blocking direct access to the property may be done with subtracting part of the property to its use to build an interior security buffer (Figure 59). Passage for the public space to the UN compound means the passage of two "concentric layers" before having access to the amenities, which may be housing or offices. Housing and offices have similar levels of depths in relation to the central space of the compound, as both require a key to have access. Depending on the situation, another level of security in the form of a bunker completes the compound. It would be located either as a separate building within the compound, or as a room part of a building.

Borrowing Hillier's technique in using graph theory to identify the levels of depths (UN's "concentric layers") and their structure, it is possible to identify four distinct spaces between the public land and the office/housing (Bill Hillier 1996). The passage between these four levels of depths require different attributes to cross from one space to the other. From the street to the inside of the compound, two levels (from a to b and b to c) require UN identification cards (or invitations for visitors). The graph also illustrates that possibility of movements within the

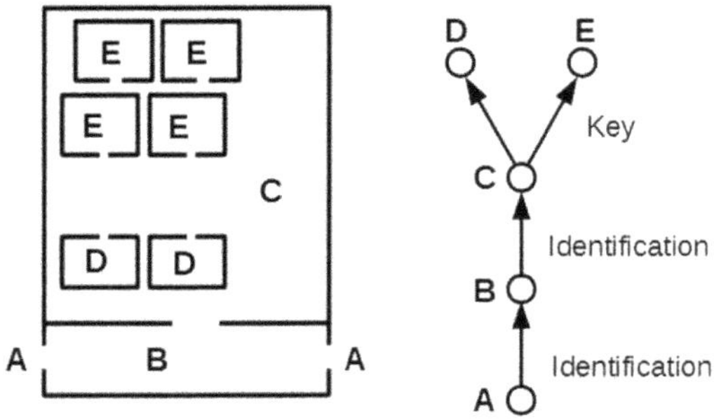

Figure 59: Large compound and the depth from public space to the office

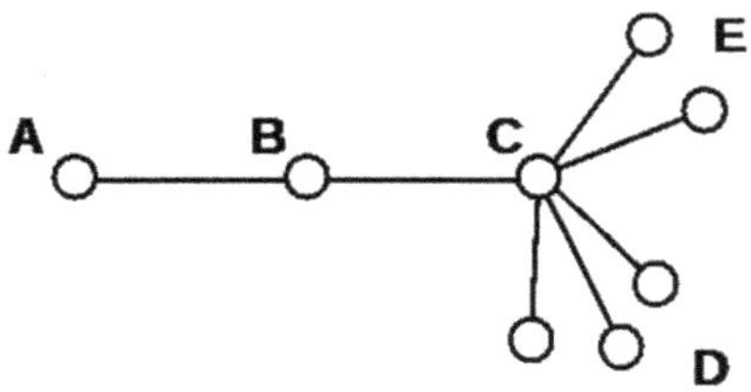

Figure 60: Levels of depth and possibilities of movements

UN compound across the space C, that is an open-air space surrounded by walls, which require two crossing points to access from the outside (Figure 60).

Any passage from the ABC region of the graph requires the check by security guards. Within the UN compound, the region CDE, the security in the use of keys (or badges, in some duty stations) is an individual responsibility. Overall, the redundancy and concentricity of the security features and procedures organises the use and practices of aid workers in their workplace, and sometimes habitat, through the rhythms of security checks.

The organisation of space in large compounds is largely exploded in a variety of separate units. The space of the compound is largely asymmetrical, as opposed to constructions where the distinct units communicate and permit circulation in all directions. None of the "concentric layers" communicate between themselves. This structure is reinforced to installation models meant to be temporary with juxtaposed independent prefabricated units. The asymmetry of the form is doubled by the asymmetry of the procedures, which controls transitions in and out of any of the levels of depths in a compound.

As a result, most essential social interactions take place within an exclusive space where only authorised personnel is present. Within this space, relations of domination reflect the UN categories, where executive come from international contracts and the locals are present, as are classes of subordinates as security, drivers, cleaners and administrative assistants. Relations with the local social environment are still present, but structured in power relations to the advantage of the expatriate employees. Topological relations induced by security structures and design illustrates the practical aspects of building physical depth to control and limit occurrences of socio-spatial interactions, as particular locations in the compounds and their surroundings are assigned specific possible relations.

The takeover of space by security features of the aid industry appears as a striking aspect of the compounds architecture. The material and procedural presence of security occupy large parts of the physical space. More or less willingly, this prominence of a material security shapes humanitarian presence in a country as an external element. These features of UN and major INGOs mark the strongest separation from the local space and territory. Combined together in the cities, networks of offices constitute the backbone of the territoriality of aid as a layer separated from the local environment.

6.3.2 Hotels

The role of hotels is central to the spatiality of the aid industry. It constitutes a mooring place for humanitarians as well as an interface to meet other social actors. The multi-functionality of the hotel makes it more than a place where to sleep. In the perspective of the humanitarians, it is, of course, one of the key places to stay in a new country. Stays at hotels may actually last years depending on the context. The hotel is also an interface between the different worlds of expatriation as well with the local population, or parts of it (Smirl 2015, p. 110). The sight of local elites frequenting hotel bars or restaurants is familiar. Other hotel amenities, such as swimming pools are only present in hotels in a number of cities, and locals use them against an entry ticket.

Hotels offer a form of enclave of a Western-oriented cosmopolitanism. Tastes are reflected in the food served at hotels, which standardises diverse – but predominantly Western – culinary traditions. The "You have these annoying Italians complaining about the food", a US humanitarian expatriate in Juba told me with irritation. "They are like 'How can they call this a pizza?' Man, what do you expect? You're in Juba!"[36] Food in hotels does not imitate the canonical Neapolitan pizza,

36 Observation Notebook, 20 June 2016.

but may refer to an already delocalised transnational food inspired by a faraway original dish. Hotel cosmopolitanism takes inspiration from diverse Western food which may translate in the words "English Breakfast" or "French Fries". It translates culinary traditions into a hotel standard whose main distinction is that it is not as the local food. As such, its imported ingredients make it much more expensive than what locals normally consume.

Illustrative of this distinction between local and cosmopolitan food, the espresso is a beverage only consumed within hotels and other luxury restaurants. The Nespresso brand, with its machine-product package facilitates the spread of yet another originally Italian speciality consumed by humanitarian workers. It is striking that the Nestlé Company, which has popularised a cheap version of coffee with its Nescafé all over African cities also placed itself in the upper part of food and beverage consumption thanks to the cosmopolitan sensibilities of hotel guests in war-torn countries. While Nestlé's cheap products can be found sold in the street all around Africa, Nespresso's different target group, a niche of wealthy cosmopolitans (Matzler et al. 2013), illustrates the social segregation at play through consumption habits.

This segregation between international and local does not mean absence of relation, which is necessary to function. Instead, it structures the verticality of relations with most local employees. Relationships with affluent locals who can afford the prices materialise in conversations and sometimes in small business deals. The multifunctionality of hotels, and their place at the centre of networks for goods and services places them at the centre of the aid industry's use of space. However, the very centrality, and visibility of hotels helped constitute them as targets for attacks by armed groups. The history of violence against hotels is already ancient and famous bombings have repeatedly rocked the industry in the twentieth and twenty-first centuries.

This risk of violence and attacks places hotel at a sensitive point where they constitute in the auxiliary space of aid an important place for the connection of networks of aid professionals (Smirl 2016). The combined use by international aid and the visibility of the hotel has made it a target in numerous instances in Ivory Coast (Bensimon 2016), Mali (Freeman 2015), South Sudan (Anonymous 2016) and Kenya (Gettleman 2017) and numerous other places (Mashal and Faizi 2018). The different attacks were conducted by a diversity of armed groups with different claims and intentions. It does, however, bring the question of security in hotels to the forefront and results in security demands from the part of international organisations.

Hotel Managers and Their Strategies in the Aid Market

Hotels are primarily commercial enterprises, and their managers expect profits. Close to the frontline of conflict areas, the hotel business becomes the particular place of confidence and safety for a public of foreigners. Where tourism hotels might capitalise on seasons and holidays to fill their hotels with guests, managers in conflict areas must address particular demands to attract guests, when the environment is shifting.

Some of the hotels visited were built during the conflicts, while others, in Bamako for example, had been in a quiet and safe area for decades as conflict was far away, and terrorism and crime almost completely absent. In "normal times", some of these hotels would bring luxury goods and international etiquette in a poor country. Prices for a night in a luxury hotel might very easily be more than a monthly local salary. Other hotels commonly welcomed a clientele of backpackers travelling on a smaller budget, although a night stay in a cheaper hotel would remain unaffordable to most Malians.

Hotels develop their approach to market, bringing guests from different geographic and professional origins. In places that have been at war for a long time, the presence of a specific clientele linked to the conflict has oriented hotel owners and managers to adapt their approach to catering. The market and potential clientele are low in conflict areas and the hotel industry is competing to adapt their offer to the demands of the professionals coming to work, and among them, the humanitarian industry, with its specific demands.

The compared research on hotels, conducted in Bamako and Juba, shows different contextual pictures. In Juba, the decade-long conflict and the low economic development means that the hotel industry has always been working from a conflict perspective. Logistics networks have always been very frail and sensitive to bring any product. On the other hand, Bamako witnessed a diverse phenomenon, where the hotel industry was installed for a long time in a city faraway from wars. The conflict in the North had been a remote concern for hotel managers, and kidnapping of foreigners was only a major worry for tour operators (Arieff and Johnson 2013).

Within one city, the hotel industry is not a compact block. It needs to address the needs and demands of guests coming from the different sensibilities of aid. Managers try to find their guests in the amount they are ready to pay and the security measures that may be required from security.

The Juba hotel industry does not include tourism at all. It is completely dependent on working expatriates. However, the expatriation in Juba comprises different sectors of industry, such as banking, communications and oil on top of aid workers and diplomatic personnel. Cosmopolitan crowds operate the hotels. They comprise many nationalities but include very few South Sudanese in the management, although wealthy locals own the land and buildings. Staff comprises some South Sudanese, but many come from neighbouring Kenya and Uganda. The presence of an imported workforce for many of the hotel tasks illustrates the minimal confidence that foreign managers confer to South Sudanese. Nevertheless, security personnel of the hotels is almost exclusively local, as they bear arms and often benefit from contacts with the official security services.[37]

The shapes of Juba hotels are divided between buildings of several storey in the city centre and bungalow villages in the outskirts. In the absence of public services, and running water or electricity, hotels have independent power generators and water tanks. The autonomy of hotels in relation to the local environment is the most striking, as roads are the only network that connects to the city.

In Juba, the decentring of the WFP in the outskirts meant that some hotels were almost completely devoted to housing WFP staff. Rock City, Jebel Lodge and later Acacias Village hotels all attract guests from the WFP because of proximity. Jebel Lodge, owned by a South Sudanese lawyer and managed by an Austro-Ugandan family was shaken, emptied during the July 2016 combats in the city, some of which occurred at the doors of the hotel – including bombardments and tank fights. In conflict with the managers, the hotel owner had one of the managers imprisoned for debts, another one forced to flee, and management itself completely changed two months after the fighting.

The Jebel Lodge is constituted of a small village of forty prefabricated houses over 15'000 square metres surrounded by fences and barbed wire. Amenities include swimming pool and fitness as well as a bar and restaurant. The layout of the hotel resembles a summer holiday resort (Figure 61).

I interviewed Thomas*, the Jebel Lodge manager at the time, of the strategies and difficulties his family had with the hotel.[38] At the WFP, whose employees constitute almost all guests of the hotel, UN finance staff used their position to negotiate with Thomas* to include pricing conditions for rooms. WFP, like most humanitarian organisations cover the housing cost of employees with a voucher system. Organisations have a stake in lowering the prices of rooms to justify the lowering of the vouchers and reduce their administrative costs. This resulted in

37 Observation Notebook, 11 July 2016.

38 Interview Thomas*, 26 june 2016.

Figure 61: Prefabricated bungalows at Jebel Lodge

strong negotiations between the WFP and Jebel Lodge, which eventually brought prices down.

These negotiations between hotel and WFP were part of the financial difficulties of the managers. As many employees pointed out, the managers had to be creative to find solutions and cover their costs. They owed 60'000 US dollars a month to the owner, which was higher than the money they could get from guests. On the other hand, the WFP management, whose employees constitute almost all of the hotel's guests negotiated to force lowering the room price from $95 to $85 a night. WFP management tried to push the prices for rooms down to $75 a night, while lowering the allowance for staff. WFP hierarchy was trying to regroup all staff closer to offices, in a move eyeing at both security and money.[39]

To compensate for the difficulties of the hotel, Thomas* tried to diversify the income with the bar and restaurant. Unable to compensate for the losses of the hotel, the bar and parties brought a curious crowd of contractors and other aid expatriates, as well as some wealthy young South Sudanese. Small groups of escorts and prostitutes watched and surrounded the small crowed. Even if the combats had not occurred, it is likely this economic model would not have

39 Observation Notebook, 4 July 2016.

survived much longer. It seemed more efficient in bringing fights to the hotel than securing the business.

Another hotel I stayed in during my time in Juba was also in a transition period, albeit less chaotic. The Acacias Village Hotel had been designed as the official hotel of the branch of an important East African Bank operating in the country. The hotel comprises twenty brick-made small cottage rooms in a garden, around a swimming pool. Within the same compound, the property of a Kenyan businessman based in Nairobi, a line of villas hosted the long-term humanitarian and business executives. Another building had the HQ of Zain, one of the main mobile phone network operators. When the bank scaled down its operations in the country, the hotel looked closer at potential guests in the aid community.

The changing of clientele required management to lower its prices from $120 a night to prices competitive to the other hotels hosting UN employees. Negotiations between WFP employees and management with Acacias Village brought the prices down to $90 a night. These prices for hotel rooms are in line with other international hotels in Juba (TripAdvisor 2018) although they are unaffordable to most South Sudanese with local salaries and revenues (Trading Economics 2018).

Hotel Industry in Bamako

The configuration of the hotel industry in Bamako is different and built in much calmer times and security conditions than the present conflict and its dangers. The existing hotel industry structures were built at time of peace and was designed for a mix of development NGOs, business travellers and tourists, including many backpackers en route to music festivals or desert trips. The hotel offer includes five star hotels as well as guesthouses to accommodate a diverse clientele. The fall of Mr Gaddafi in Libya in 2012, which affected Mali economically and politically also, had the consequence of stopping the development of luxury hotels on the banks of the Niger. Nevertheless, the consequences for the industry as a whole was felt strongest with the drastic reduction of tourism in the country due to the conflict in the North and kidnapping of foreigners. The renewal of the hotel clientele by the aid industry signified organisational and strategic changes by hotel owners and managers.

In the south bank of the Niger, Badalabougou concentrated many humanitarian workers since 2012 and 2013 when several UN agencies settled in the area. Hotel managers have been trying to place themselves as recipients of the humanitarian housing market. In the area, Hotel Badala and Villa Soudan (and later Casa du Fleuve, which opened in 2015) ranged in an $80 a night, while backpacker hotels Sleeping Camel and Auberge Djamilla targeted the smaller budgets around $15 to $30 a night. When this clientele reduced or stopped their visits to the country in relation to political troubles and kidnappings, the hotel industry felt a painful bite. For hotel managers, the arrival of aid workers was a lifeline that brought new waves of guests which would fit by somewhat corresponding to the peacetime clientele.

In the world of aid in Bamako, the hotels in Badala represent a mid-level of the humanitarians in the city. The most luxurious hotels, all located on the northern bank of the Niger, hosted the highest-ranking officials of the civilian and military missions. The Amitié hotel was taken by the UN mission from mid-2013 and entirely rented to be transformed in an office building. In that sense, the Badala hotels were used by a category of professionals that did not include the highest-ranking VIPs.

The Badala hotel, property of Malian businessman Thiam Mohamed is managed by the seventy-year-old Frenchman Daniel Hougnon. While some backpacker hotels had closed during the crisis, the Badala doubled its surface. In 2015, Thiam Mohamed opened another hotel of a similar category, the Casa du Fleuve, for which he acted both as owner and manager. The public rumour says that Mr Mohamed opened the hotel as a concurrent to Badala to irritate Mr Hougnon with whom he had started having disagreements until their work relationship turned bitter. Whatever the reason, the opening of another hotel in this period of trouble seems to indicate that there is a hotel market open and competitive in Bamako's south shore.

The fifteen rooms and three-storey building of Hotel Badala, with its swimming pool and restaurant doubled its size in the course of 2013. The two parts separated by a small street are famous in town mostly for its French restaurant. When the extension was made to the hotel, it quickly included much stronger security features than before. Right next to the Niger, the hotel now includes barbed wire, metal detectors at the entrance and armed guards on the property.

The apparent prosperity of the Badala does not reassure the manager. He says he might have to close if more terrorist attacks scare off the business travellers. Daniel Hougnon considers his business at risk. According to him, the increase in bed capacity and restaurant tables does not reflect prosperity as much as a low original capacity:

> *We increased from 15 to 32 rooms. Hotel industry is in a very complex situation now. We had many Unicef employees at some point. But since the arrival of [the French military mission] Serval, we don't have business travellers anymore. Even though nothing had happened in Bamako yet.*

Some events did occur. But we are victims and dependent of the media and their presentation. There have been worst attacks in Tunisia with many more victims than here. So in Europe people think that we can not go out. If I wanted to go out, the city has many bars full of white people.[40]

Business also fluctuates under the official travel warnings of Western countries which influence both tourism and business travel. Dependent on the UN and NGOs guests, the hotel has adapted its security policies to stay on the approved "shortlist" of hotels recommended by the UN. The bunkering of the Badala was the strongest after the attacks against the Radisson Hotel in 2015. "I invested a lot and we are completely barricaded. Rooms and restaurant!" explains Mr Hougnon. "I have all I need and armed guards. I have more than tripled the budget for guards and invested a lot in equipment."

Security equipment and guards were also a worry for the concurrent Casa du Fleuve, where Thiam Mohamed told me he was unhappy to be kept out of the shortlist. As Adama*, a national employee of a UN agency pointed out to him "You don't even have barbed wire and the double door is not finished".[41] With few UN personnel among his guests, Mr Mohamed was counting on NGOs to fill the blank. Eager to show that he was not out of step, Mr Mohamed described its clientele as confident in his hotel, even without the approval of the UN security:

My clientele is a melting pot. But the list is very absurd. The UN has its shortlist of hotels. This means I do not house UN personnel as organisations. But some UN personnel come here individually. They feel actually more secure here than in the hotels of the shortlist.[42]

Thiam Mohamed raises here a contradiction in the UN system of certification. Guests may perceive the increased visibility of hotels as more dangerous, in the context of international hotels being targeted precisely because of their visibility. According to this rationale, low-key and discrete safety measures may reduce the risk of terrorist attacks. Nevertheless, this perspective started being coupled with some security measures, even in the original backpacker hotels of the area.

The 2015 Radisson hotel attack was the main trigger for increasing security equipment and staff. Hotel managers enhanced their security in different manners. Mr Mohamed counted on the presence of armed guards already standing on the street to protect an official of the BCAO (West African Central Bank), while Mr Hougnon relied on paying the police to be present with machine guns: "This has a price. I pay cash each month." The strict laws on weapons possession in

40 Interview Daniel Hougnon, 20 April 2016.
41 Observation Notebook, 21 March 2016.
42 Interview Thiam Mohamed, 24 March 2016.

Mali prevent private citizens and security companies to carry arms, which justifies the possibility to hire police officers for private protection.

The backpacker hotel Sleeping Camel maintained the local guards hired directly, but installed double doors and concrete blocks to prevent gunmen to fire through doors into the hotel bar and guests. Matt Christie, the Australian manager, had gone from hosting travellers crossing the country, or the continent, with travel trailers, motorbikes and tents to have UN and NGO personnel, despite being out of the shortlist:

> *In March 2013 we had our first UN guests and from there, it was a change of business when we had people from NGOs and contractors. People started telling me that I should raise prices, but I didn't want to become a UN fortress. So we continued that way for a while.*[43]

The hotel kept its backpacking atmosphere and was frequented by employees who wanted to either save money from their housing allowance, or found the "business traveller" hotel category too impersonal for their taste. Oriented mostly towards an Anglo-Saxon clientele, the hotel offered hamburgers and bacon for food, and introduced quiz nights and dart games. The world travellers had been replaced in large part by the macho-style adventurer-expatriates of the demining and security sectors. As Matt Christie puts it, "[if we could not sell alcohol] it would kill the place. Many of our guests are Brits from [demining and security companies]. They drink!"

The new adventure guests, often working for private security companies, prefer staying out of business-style hotels and seem to prize the dusty and messy appearance of the Sleeping Camel. Mr Christie relied for several years on discretion for safety. However, the panic that the Radisson attack triggered in Bamako also brought transformations to the Sleeping Camel, pushing to him decide that playing low-key was not enough anymore:

> *We needed to be a bit more careful. We made the gates and raised the walls. But didn't paint the outside wall, to let it look shitty. So people passing think "that can't be the hotel".*

Risk management as understood by hotel managers sometimes contradicts the official UN line on their hotel lists, which they deem too strict. However, for many expatriates, other criteria, such as atmosphere and discretion are more important – or important enough – to justify the crossing the line of official security policies to settle in hotels that have not been approved. The philosophy of relying on discretion is most used in the case of former backpacker hotels such as Matt Christie's and the Auberge Djamilla. The Djamilla is a small "hippy" place

43 Interview Matt Christie, 15 April 2016.

nearby in Badalabougou, which brought another crowd, also in the margins of the UN official employee pool. Nevertheless, not being authorised to sell alcohol, it brought a more quiet and discrete clientele, but limited greatly restaurant and bar activities.

This Auberge Djamilla went in different phases since the stormy Malian politics brought people in and out of the country. The hotel with its courtyard carefully cultivate a hippy-but-clean, relax-but-efficient atmosphere where musicians and other artists would often crash in during peacetime and wartime, albeit with reduced presence during the latter.

After the 2012 jihadist advance and a coup in the capital, backpacker hotels had started to close in Bamako. This left the Sleeping Camel along with the Djamilla one of the few of this category of hotels in Badalabougou. For the Swiss manager of the Djamilla, Fanny Mauron, the bunkerisation of her hotel would be difficult and unwelcome. She estimated that since the crisis, three categories of guests had an equal occupation of her hotel. The West African professionals coming for trainings in Bamako had always constituted part of the clientele and did not stop with the crisis. In the specific context of the crisis, the former backpacker hotels started to be used by many freelance journalists, up to a third of the guests of the Djamilla.

The last third of the Djamilla clientele is constituted by NGO and some United Nations personnel. The hotel was, however, never certified in any shortlist, for lack of barbed wire, or double-door system. As Fanny Mauron explains,

> *there was the visit from UN and EU security, to check against their standards and decide to send their people or not. Maybe one or the other advised their staff to come, but they never booked directly. […] When they came, I was a bit stressed not to be in their standards. […] But they never said anything about the absence of barbed wire and other standards, which I don't know about. I don't know if there is a list of security standards. But even if they had asked works to transform the hotel, I wouldn't have done it, except if it could grant a clientele. And people come here because it is low profile. It prevents the place becoming a target. I really want to stay low profile. There is not even a sign saying it is a hotel on the door.*

Stressed from the constant needs to change and adapt to clientele, Ms Mauron says she might want to try something else, finding another work in nearby Senegal. Nevertheless, the persistence of her hotel partly thanks to the presence of aid workers illustrates a diversity in the individual perception of security against the global norms promoted by aid organisations.

Humanitarian workers have mostly replaced business travellers and tourists in the hotels of the capital. The presence of humanitarian workers constitute the new standard client. The adaptation to the requirement of the clientele means that all hotel managers have had to change their security measures compared to peacetime. Even those who have not changed security measures since the conflict have been forced to explicitly think and make choices about potential attacks.

6.3.3 Houses and Apartments

Aside of hotels, aid workers settle in diverse types of houses and apartments. Those might be furnished or not. They might be rented directly by the organisation or by aid workers. The modes of dwelling are still more diverse. Some aid workers live with their families, when it is allowed, in "family duty stations" – and sometimes when it is not allowed, with more or less discretion. While others live alone or with flatmates. Some live with their direct colleagues, either as a choice or because the organisations pay for a large house. The variety of dwelling in houses and apartments could make a long list.

Reasons to live in houses rather than hotels – when it is not an organisation policy – vary. From the discussions and interviews with aid workers the main reason that orient and inform personal residential choices is the will to "feel at home" and save money. This often reflects in wanting to cook. When a mission lasts months or years, aid workers enjoy cooking their own food rather than depending on restaurants for a long period. In climates with high numbers of parasites in food and water, some expatriates consider that cooking themselves is the only way to keep healthy.

More generally, the reason to rent a home highlighted by aid workers is the contrast with the impersonality of hotels. When longing for home in a foreign country, expatriates enjoy their own furniture and other objects. The possibility to enjoy one's own tastes is prized in the context of nostalgic feeling of loss and displacement (Boym 2001). In Juba, the rumour claimed that a UN employee had figured a way to import an aquarium and decorative fishes in the country.[44] The complexity of shipping live animals by plane in a nation at war illustrates a sense of excess as well as the importance of personalising one's private space.

As a result, aid workers settle in a large number of houses and apartments in the cities where they work. While the variety of reasons that brings aid workers into houses and apartments is wide, the main organisational norms that shape dwelling are security and finances. These two criteria appear as the structuring factor in the housing of international aid.

44 Observation Notebook, 10 August 2016.

Security and Luxury Residences

Security standards set the architecture chosen for the aid industry. The form of the buildings invariably involves wall and barriers. In Mali, where crime is very low, security standards of houses imposed by the UN Security are very high, for fear of terrorism and kidnappings. The zoning and the recommendation for the architectural features of the houses imply either the location of apartments or houses with gardens and swimming pool.

This type of house is limited in Bamako to certain areas of the city. The courtyard habitat is widespread, although parts of the upper middle classes increasingly prefer villas. The increasing use by Malian elites of houses surrounded by walls and sometimes swimming pools is still identified with foreigners, as the Commune 5 Chief Urbanist Gouro Landouré explains:

> *Badalabougou is constituted of houses for the 'privileged' as we call them. We used to call it the 'white neighbourhoods' at the time. Everyone there has a closed door.*[45]

Indeed, the houses where UN and NGOs aid workers are located the wealthiest areas of Bamako, often with a garden and swimming pool (Figure 62). Single expatriate sometimes uses two or three-storey houses, although most share houses with colleagues or friends. No families officially settle among NGOs and UN employees, as the official level of risk keeps the city in the "non-family duty station" category. In practice, some aid workers live with their family with just enough discretion to prevent official reprimands or sanctions.

Compared with the standards in Nairobi, however, the security devices marking the separation between the outside and the architectural depths of the buildings are slightly softer. Many of the residences of expatriates are not equipped with barbed wire or electric fences. Most of them still follow the spatial logic of rings of depth from the local environment to the inside of the house and its panic room.

Safety standards differ depending on the type of NGO and places. Large international NGOs tend to have similar housing and security standards than the UN. In contrast, smaller NGOs with reduced budgets tend to have living standards closer to the local population. Working for small technical French NGO specialised in agriculture and climate change, Renaud* is representative of a more modest section of aid workers in Mali. Renaud* rents a house with low walls and no barbed wire. Former regular guest of the Djamilla hotel, this head of a small French NGO started renting the small house of Fanny Mauron, the boss

45 Interview Gouro Landouré, 9 March 2016.

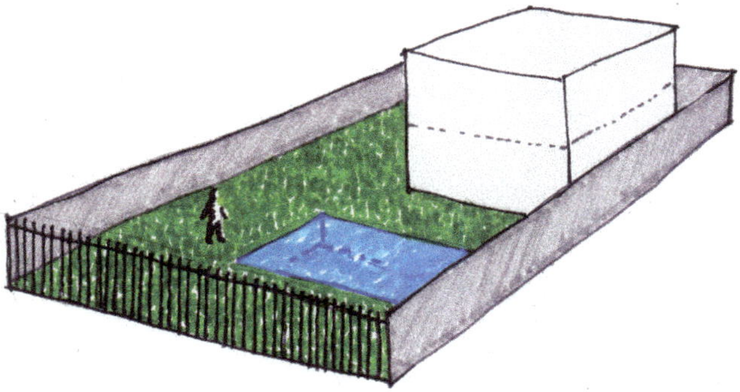

Figure 62: Model of the two-storey house of a UN employee facing the Niger in Badalabougou

of his former favourite hotel, when she left for Senegal. The form of the house would never pass the test of the security visit of any major NGO or the UN. "I do not want, and I could not afford to live in the reserved areas," he explains.[46]

Located in the SEMA part of Badalabougou, the house was part of a housing plan for state employees in the late sixties, in what were the outskirts of Bamako on the South Bank (Figure 63). Inspired by the Malian courtyard housing, the external walls surround a concrete slab. Rooms, kitchen and toilets in cement stand as separate constructions on the slab. Fans or AC systems are added to the rooms to compensate for the accumulated heat in the concrete. The surface is reduced compared to the many villas, more recent and expensive, in other areas of Badalabougou.

Himself the only expatriate – and responsible for security of his small NGO – Renaud* has quite a different outlook on security than most internationals:

> *In Bamako, the main risk is traffic! And mitigation measures are to check that cars are in order. The Bamakoan hazards depend on the non-urbanism of the city, constructed spreading it bit by bit. […] Here I have the problems of the city centre, but I am close to my office.*

The position of Renaud* and his NGO would be squarely rejected by the bigger organisations even before the terrorist attacks in Bamako. No guards, no protection beyond house keys and only counting on his own relative discretion for his safety may well be considered irresponsible and dangerous by security.

46 Interview Renaud*, 12 April 2017.

Figure 63: The entrance of Renaud*'s SEMA-style house in Bamako

Indeed, this limited protection is made possible by the extremely low crime rates in Malian cities, which would not compare in most West African capital cities (Fourchard and Olawale 2003).

Other examples of foreigners living closer to the local population that the extreme examples of gated communities can be found depending on the organisations in most cities. I have not witnessed it in Juba, which might be because I did not stay long enough, but also because the level of both poverty and violence makes it more difficult. Nevertheless, Nairobi, Abidjan and Bamako all had a number of small NGO expatriates living in relatively modest housing similar to Renaud*.

There are also some examples of UN expatriates refusing the instruction of the UN's Minimum Operational Residential Standards (MORSS) and UN Security evaluation visits to enhance the security standards of their houses. Because security standards are bound to contractual obligations and financial allowance, the refusal is not upfront, and might either mean discretion in contravening rules, or through negotiation to obtain MORSS certification or other official approval for NGOs. This was the case of Luisa*, a UN aid worker in charge of the relation with the local community in Mali, whose example was discussed above. The negotiation to avoid installing barbed wire is one among many internal discussions and debates, which shape the use of the built environment. To my knowledge, resistance against security norms rarely took the path of refusing a security device.

However, in relation to a number of security requirements, aid workers negotiate their own perception of reasonable security with their organisations.

Living Allowance and Residential Choices

The living allowance to employees is often a supplement of money for the employee to find a home. Houses can also be directly rented by the organisation for its employees. This case is most likely with compounds combining office and housing functions. It brings the most direct control over the housing of employees and is most often used by NGOs. The living allowance also exerts major control over the choices of employees. This control appeared the most salient in Juba, when the WFP was trying to push employees to regroup mostly in one area close to the main offices of the organisation, located in the outskirts of the city.

For David*, who was living in the city centre of Juba, the move by the WFP hierarchy to push all employees to come closer to the main WFP compound meant he had the choice to relocate or to lose his allowance. "It's a former UN compound. The area is safe, it is more central, and you can walk on the street. But management wants us all to be at the Jebel, or at the WFP compound."[47] The concentration of employees to a limited number of places is an explicit choice that responds to a combination of finance and security concerns.

From the perspective of the management of an organisation, the concentration of staff in a limited number of hotels can serve to negotiate prices from a stronger position with a house owner or a hotel manager. International organisations can actively work to keep housing prices down to prevent having to pay high living allowances. In the context of powerful security sections within humanitarian organisations, managerial decision to stabilise rent prices need the authorisation of the security. The housing policy of an organisation can focus on lowering prices, although it must not contradict security procedures (UNDSS 2017).

Forcing a concentration of staff also responds to a security concern and the internal security of organisations. The concentration of staff is especially useful for international evacuations, when International organisations consider the situation too dangerous to maintain physical presence of expatriates in the country (Macpherson and Pafford 1999; ARC International 2004; IFRC 2011; United Nations 2006). Concentration of staff facilitates convoying employees to the nearest airport grouped together.

---

47 Observation Notebook, 20 June 2016.

Urban Quality

A subjective assessment by aid workers on the urban quality of the neighbourhood where they live constitutes part of the individual choices that orient their spatial distribution. While the notion of urban quality is contingent to variable spatial habitus that inform tastes (McCrea, Shyy, and Stimson 2006), some criteria stand out, such as the feeling of safety and pedestrian access (Talen 2002a). While the importance of these considerations diminishes with the levels of risk, they do not disappear, even in the most dangerous places.

The observation of urban quality, the possibility and practicality of circulating in Juba led several expatriates to voice their willingness to dwell in apartments or houses in the city centre. Most of the NGOs had both houses and offices in the city centre of Juba. As explained to me by the Programme Manager of an Italian NGO, "before the situation got bad, just after independence, you could just walk down the street during daylight. It was not a problem."[48] The urban quality of Juba was not completely lost to all yet in mid-2016, and NGO workers were still talking about walking on the street.

Most of the aid workers still walking on the street, even during the daytime, were African. White aid workers often consider themselves too visible to take the chance of walking on the street when daily SitRep reports announced the story of people robbed in the street, by "unknown gunmen", or be victims of extortion by one or the other security forces. Distinctive signs of pertaining to an international organisation became increasingly perceived as a danger for its visibility, and many expatriates tended to hide their UN pass for even the few metres between the car and shops.[49]

Prices and Standards

Nairobi counts as a place where many aid workers aim to work at some point. The amenities and the possibility to bring one's family are prized and the city usually ranks among the top wanted duty stations. The possibility to live a Western suburban lifestyle compensates the high level of criminality. As Dario*, a Mozambican UN aid worker, told me during the research:

> *When you start building your career in the UN, you have to start in Juba before applying to Nairobi. There is a lot of competition for positions here. You have to go through places you don't like before finding a duty station where you can go out and enjoy nice restaurants.*[50]

48 Observation Notebook, 3 July 2016.
49 Observation Notebook, 5 July 2016.
50 Observation Notebook, 23 July 2016.

The network of cities where humanitarian workers settle is ordered and understood by aid workers in relation to comfort and professional progression. African capitals are weighed against each other in similar patterns for all major duty stations. As sites of intervention, they also constitute vertices within a network of cities understood as a space of professional opportunities and career strategies for aid workers. Local effects of aid presence are conditional to the housing market, to internal security policies, and to the positions of humanitarian workers on their professional and social fields.

Housing patterns of humanitarians in Nairobi mostly follows a suburban model of small houses in the suburbs. The Gigiri UN base in Nairobi is located on the outskirts of the city in the middle of an area of villas. The petty criminality in Nairobi and the numerous mugging incidents encouraged the development of gated communities. Under its "Security" section, Amazing Kenya (Rodriguez Harvey 2016), the welcome booklet to UN employees, warns about the dangers of the city and suggests a way of life circumscribed by security and wary of the environment:

> *In Nairobi, one has to be vigilant when going about daily life. Crime is not uncommon and it ranges from petty theft by domestic staff, to kidnapping and carjacking. In addition, Kenya has been under incessant terrorist threats targeting civilians in public places, particularly in places where members of the international community frequent. Therefore, avoid crowded places.(Rodriguez Harvey 2016, p. 63)*

The case of Nairobi presents a particular picture in the four case studies. As a UN HQ base, work contracts are designed for the long term and designed to accommodate families. As a result, the instructions to staff housing have the greatest emphasis on houses and apartments. Details of all the conditions of finance and security that are allowed to employees are described in much detail in different written documents and orally at security briefings.

The expected locations for housing are listed as gated communities, villas and apartments. All houses must be checked by the UN Department of Safety and Security (UNDSS) to verify if they fit in the security standards. MORSS documentation, which defines residential safety standards for a duty station, and security presentations, advises employees to rent places that were previously rented by UN personnel (Department of Safety and Security 2016). The rationale behind this advice is that if UN staff have already rented a place there is more chance that this place will be already MORSS compliant. At the level of the UN, this means that it simplifies the work of the UNDSS, but also that administratively, this might reduce the cost of security features subsidies. The combined bureaucratic work of the security and management wings of the UN system help channel UN employees in a spatial coherence, as well as temporal continuity of spaces used by the expatriates.

Each protective device whether it is material, like barriers and walls, or human with guards is subject to financial support from the UN. The list of security measures must "ensure that [international] staff members have adequate security features in their dwellings". As the MORSS outlines:

> *Various security allowances are provided to pay for some house enhancements. These allowances cover (up to a certain amount) items and services as security guards, security bars on windows, alarms and the purchase of an electricity generator, to name a few.*

The MORSS describe in detail the location where expatriates can settle and how. The MORSS norms are so explicit that their wording seems to describe international aid workers' use of urban space at every scale. The descriptions concern the general location, as well as the exterior and interior features. Three questions formulate the general checklist to find a dwelling area:

> *Is the property in the Blue Zone? Is the dwelling in a good residential area with low crime rates? Are there a number of alternate routes to and from the dwelling?*

Dwelling in the Blue Zone is not explicitly mandatory, but the "advice" from the UN Security to do so may have financial consequences. As the MORSS documents warns, "if staff members decide to live outside this area, they might not be eligible for security-related allowances covered under the MORSS in Kenya." Within the Blue Zone, the UN effectively subsidises a construction of a city following heavy security norms. A series of physical features are explicitly recommended and paid for when in "stand-alone" residences. The case of shared residency or apartments is slightly different, as the DSS considers the costs of security to be the responsibility of the house owner.

In practice, the security norms are being enforced, and somewhat paced, by the visits of the UNDSS for a mandatory security survey of premises when UN employees arrive in a house. Their recommendations will decide whether the place is safe to dwell and what is needed for securing the premises. The list of the protective features comprises part of the structure of the building, like walls and doors, as well as specifically designed devices for security. As the UN Security summarises it, "In essence, the more security features that come with a property, the better chance that it will be approved by Security."

Protective features as part of the building must block or limit physical access to the building. But also be apart from the view of public access. The outside of the property must bar access, as the checklists points:

> *Is the property well defined with a hedge, fence or wall which is in good condition? Is there an electric fence? Are the gates solid and in good condition? Are there handy access routes (poles, trees, etc.) which may be used to get over the barriers? […]Are balconies, or other apartment windows accessible from another balcony, ledge, roof or window?(Department of Safety and Security 2016)*

The question of physical access is completed during security briefings with examples of trees, which were used by burglars to pass a fence during home invasions. In this perspective, housing places are conceived as stand-alone units that must be autonomous and separated, not only from the outside environment, but also from other similar units.

The segmentation of residential areas includes housing units, but also from the inside of a property. Each door inside a property must have "suitable locks" and a "door viewer or interview grille". Grilles must protect all accessible windows. Series of protective devices must reinforce each level of architectural features. An electric fence secures the link between the property and the outside. Entrances from the garden to the house must be equipped with alarms and an "external alerting device", as well as "transmitter to a central monitor" to warn a security company.

Lastly, the inside of the house must also be compartmented and equipped. "Panic buttons," which dwellers can use to warn their security company of an emergency situation, completing a door alarm system. Inside the house, dwellers are advised to leave a specific room, in case of dangerous home invasion, that can be cut and closed from the rest of the building. This type of room is alternatively called "Panic room" or "Safe Haven" in the MORSS documents. Description of a "Safe Haven" means that space and security features must be allocated to it, as the MORSS checklist goes:

> *Is there adequate space for a family? Does the safe haven have a solid core, metal or metal-clad door? Is there a phone in the safe haven? Are toilet facilities available in the safe haven? Is there an emergency access from the safe haven?(Department of Safety and Security 2016)*

A topological analysis in the form of Bill Hillier's on an MORSS compliant house in Nairobi would show at least three levels of depth (B. Hillier et al. 1987). Each of these levels is meant to block the possibility of an unwanted entrance. Security devices add weight, or cost, to the possibility of crossing through. Combined with the Blue Zone perimeter, and potentially the entrance gates of a gated community, the perfect aid industry house would be separated by five levels of perimeters from the rest of the city as personal protection.

The security practises regarding the night-time procedures reveals the fear of the dark, which leaves space to hide. Checklists regarding lighting mentions that ensuring houses are well lit makes it "worth visiting the residence during hours of darkness". The recommendations for checking whether when the lights are lit are "hiding places near gates, doors, windows and garage or parking areas [must be] illuminated or eliminated." If the architecture of the house have left places for an assailant to hide, electricity will provide 24-hour check of these areas. Similarly, in the case of the electric fence, the UN foots the bill for power, or fuel in the case of a generator.

Complementary to the recommendation and instruction of MORSS documentation and security visits, security briefings present more warnings, and advice for more devices. "Do you think CCTV works?" the security officer asked the thirty new Nairobian employees of the UN during the welcome briefing. While the small crowd seemed to be discussing the matter with some hesitations, she cut it through "Yes! They do work to prevent crime!"[51] The lesson highlights security officers' mindsets: even if not officially recommended, any security device is efficient and it is never too much.

Security guards form part of the package of security measures around housing. UN staff have the responsibility to find guards, whose cost is reimbursed on a monthly basis. The recommendation by the MORSS shows a particular concern with night-time, where the UN agrees to pay for doubling the number of guards during the dark hours. Two twelve-hour shifts of the guards implies the work of three people for one UN employee. The specific MORSS for Nairobi does not recommend more guards for female employees, although the recommendation is common in most duty stations. This might be the case because the extent of security devices in a large capital like Nairobi, combined with relatively fast emergency response services are deemed enough.

The recommendations regarding guards also have a larger sense in terms of security policy, with the publications of recommended companies to provide the guards. The security companies official shortlist comprises eight major transnational companies, such as the British G4S, but also East African or Kenyan companies. These companies are so closely linked with the UN that some have contracting coordinators specifically attached to work with the UN. The G4S, considered the most important private security contractor in Kenya with 13'000 employees (G4S Kenya 2018), is however controversial, as shadowy practices of

51 Observation Notebook, 25 August 2016.

the company created repeated scandals (Chan 2013; Barnard and Hassan 2015; BBC News 2018).

The exotic nature of Nairobi and the tourism amenities such as recreation centres, wildlife reserves and private schools for children participate to create the suburban life in gated communities cut off from the rest of Nairobi. The upper-class life of the expatriates brings them to a higher standard of living than what they might expect in the North with similar salaries. For Robert*, a local volunteer to UN-Habitat who lives in the Mathare slum, the luxury lifestyle that expatriates benefit from the cheap costs of housing and labour makes them arrogant towards the locals:

> *I've been in Europe when I was in an exchange programme in Hamburg. I know that these people do not live like that in their countries. The security procedures and messages separate the UN personnel from the Kenyans, because of the fear. They cannot go to Mathare. And then they fence their houses. But this is also dangerous. It gives the impression that there is something precious inside and it generates envy.*[52]

Robert*'s observation illustrates how the separation through security practises by international aid workers does not only separate the international from the local. It also establishes and constructs a relation of domination mediated through a complex showing and hiding of wealth. Segregation and obfuscation can hide specific items and features. Nevertheless, as a general effect, it reinforces and magnifies the visibility of inequalities and wealth it purports to hide and protect.

At the extreme end in terms of poverty in housing, Nairobi has hosted major slums for decades, and the contrast between the gated communities and the conditions in which many poor Kenyans live is the most striking. Limited contacts tend to take form in mode of "slum tourism" which are often regarded as humiliating by local dwellers drawing comparisons with wildlife tourism (Odede 2010). Other social interactions highlight the domination of expatriates, when, on the other hand, local domestic workers living in the poorest areas of the capital take care of luxury homes (Ondimu 2007).

The life completely cut from the local community is, however, not homogenous across the board, even in a city with high criminality like Nairobi. Emma* and Raphael*, two Europeans living in Nairobi, have been living in places which would be unacceptable according to the standards of large NGOs. Locative housing in Nairobi includes guards at the entrance of the house or the building, which is widely considered a minimal security for foreigners. Working for small NGOs some expatriates can not afford to live in luxury places. Their way to

52 Observation Notebook, 31 August 2016.

reduce the cost of staying is living closer to the standards of the local middle class. The location in affordable areas without large salary or organisation support constitutes a necessity. It is also representative of sections of the expatriate-NGO world, which prizes close contact with the local environment and people as part of the purpose of their aid work.

6.3.4 The Aid Layer and Local Security Practices

Cécile*, a wealthy young Abidjanese woman tells me how security has changed in Abidjan in recent years. Lamenting about her house guards, she comments that "back in the days of 'Houphouët'[53], the guards of my parents' house would rather get killed than let someone hurt their employers. Now, they're just cowards looking for their pay. They would run away at the first sign of trouble."[54] The tale of Cécile* illustrates how local city dwellers have their own understanding of security in relation to social and built environments. It also shows that social classes construct their own understandings of security regarding real and perceived dangers. How do the competing understandings of security of local dwellers and expatriates diverge and converge?

Contrasting the local use of space regarding security and the expatriate modes of dwelling brings the problem of the measure of the comparison. The social position of aid workers in African cities is incomparably higher to most of the local social strata regardless of their professional positions or relative income and wealth. For similar types of tasks, expatriates earn much higher salaries than local workers do, whatever their position in their organisation. Comparing a nurse, a computer expert, an engineer or any other technical or non-technical profession will invariably place expatriates in a much higher social position. Expatriates are able to afford housing in areas that do not correspond to the local standard for their own position.

Housing for expatriate professionals is consistently distinct from their equivalent in the local environment. Aid workers settle in areas with similar housing condition than the wealthiest of the local elites. As security measures between locals and expatriates are not strictly comparable, comparators should extend to other social strata from within the four cities. This is not possible due to lack of comparable data or literature on all case studies. However, using a thematic comparator in three of the cities, this section will contrast local and expatriate

53 Félix Houphuoët-Boigny, first president of Ivory Coast, from Independence in 1960 to his death in 1993.

54 Interview Cécile*, 27 April 2017.

practices of security in relation to crime and terrorism. It will present how informal collective security in Juba aims to protect citizens against urban violence when representatives of the states are themselves perceived as a danger. It will follow with a discussion of the fears of criminality in Nairobi and separate responses of distinct social classes to street crime. Finally, the example of Bamako will illustrate how fears of terrorism travels through mirrors of anxiety between the aid layer and local dwellers.

Armed Violence and Collective Security in Juba

The city of Juba is indirectly affected by the war in its everyday life, as criminal violence and racketeering develop in relation to worsening economic and social conditions caused by the conflict (McMichael 2014). The important presence and the power of the military and paramilitary forces places the chief warlords at the top of chiefdoms. They have largely developed high-end urban areas of Juba – but also in other South Sudanese cities, and abroad – in large luxurious mansions and villas (Adeba 2019).

Locals and expatriates share specific fears of the environment in many regards. The racketeering by "unknown gunmen" in Juba – a code word that generally refers to masked police or military – affects expatriates as well as many locals. The weakness of the state and justice system in Juba has led inhabitants to locally organise street patrols, while conflict resolution is often self-organised by local neighbourhood committees (Kindersley 2019). The methods of dealing with crime by aid organisations and aid workers diverge completely. As expatriates retreat behind walls and avoid the city at night, local committees patrol the street. Moreover, as aid workers rely on the security bodies of organisations, local residents tend to avoid relying on the police, when not openly demonstrating against them (Eye Radio Network 2017).

The collaboration of churches, customary authorities and neighbourhood dwellers to tackle the risks of crime in working-class neighbourhoods shapes local crime prevention. The high militarisation of the society, with significant numbers of citizens with armed background within the population of South Sudan, cultivates a widespread reliance on personal security, bearing arms and allying with other armed actors for security (Kindersley 2019). The construction of walls and other devices is present within local upper-class areas, although it does not follow the organised security as conceptualised by aid agencies, where location, rings of material devices and strict reporting procedures constitute the backbone of aid architecture.

Defensive Designs and Fears of Crime in Nairobi

Crime rates in Nairobi are among the highest in East Africa. The response to theft and attacks by the different social classes diverges in function of the means at their disposition. Everyday security practises of Nairobi includes diverse modes and intends to protect physical integrity and belongings. Behaviour and defensive designs both take part in all social classes' protections against multiple real and perceived danger.

From the use of a padlock on a shack to the 24/7 surveillance by security guards, the means determine the protection to crime, whether it is aimed to protect a weekly salary or expensive luxury goods. Local middle classes tend to rely on a mix of private security and neighbourhood watching. Security, however, is only one problem of numerous middle-class neighbourhoods, often planned and managed without proper water adduction or sewage systems. Local security organising mixes with other urban issues for neighbourhood committees (Bousquet 2008).

The development of gated communities in the capital has been a major feature of high-end urban development. As Glück (2017) notes, upper classes have increasingly designed their security practices as an inward protection of the home and family within secure enclaves, as they project their fears outwards on the city. The fears driving this movement include a representation of safe and danger zones in the city, although less formally coded than the risk mapping of aid agencies.

In the city's most impoverished areas, the slums of Nairobi have themselves developed their own practices of personal security, to protect their belongings and physical integrity. Organised volunteer patrols on the streets, and sometimes mob violence against suspected criminals, replace the police in the local streets. The compensation of efficient crime control by increased levels of violence countering crimes – real and perceived – is by far not limited to mob violence. Section of the police and the army have long been implicated in death squads as response to both crime and terrorism (van Stapele 2016).

Aid workers' housing places them together with the richest Kenyans independently of their own social origins and profession in their home countries. Similarly to the local elites, the main characteristics of aid workers' security practice is its overwhelming reliance on private security, while other social classes often use a combination of collective and private security. This convergence in dwelling habits between the local elite and the layer of aid marks a retreat into privately managed secured island. Similarities between aid and the local elites is the strongest in Nairobi, whereas in other cities, important divergences take place in relation to dwelling and understandings of security, most typically in Bamako where criminality is proverbially low.

Mirror Fears in Bamako

The Malian capital of Bamako is renowned for its low crime levels. Street vigilance – sometimes extremely violent – and solidarity mechanisms are generally credited for maintaining very low crime levels in the city despite regular complains by Bamakoans about increasing insecurity, attributed to various social ills, from laziness to alcohol consumption and individual greed (Sanogo 2014).

In a context of low crime rates, security devices are very limited in the Malian capital. The use of locks, neighbours and the high density of dwellers in family houses are generally the normal combination of human and material security used by most inhabitants. Wealthy areas comprise properties circled by walls. In these areas, guards control the entrance of the property, while material security devices are limited. If some outside walls are covered with broken glass, other defensive designs, such as barbed wire or CCTV, are almost never used by local dwellers. Distinction between local and expatriate security increasingly diverges in Bamako in relation to crime. However, fears of terrorism in the city are modifying the behaviour and protective measures of many local inhabitants.

In March 2016, the Malian press reported that a UN employee in Bamako was arrested by the police for flying an unmanned drone over the house of the main leader of the political opposition, Mr Soumaila Cissé, who suspected a spying operation against him (Sogodogo 2016). Neighbours had called the police worried about a "white man" spying over the wealthy area of Badalabougou. The man flying the drone was an Italian FAO worker playing with a drone on his time off. The FAO worker was arrested by the police and brought to a tribunal before being released. He claimed that his drone was purely recreational and only flew over Mr Cissé's house by accident, as he did not know that his house was there.

This misunderstanding reflects the surprise and fear of local dwellers to see an expatriate using a drone as entertainment in a climate of suspicion, when the use of improvised explosive devices made of bits and bobs extract a deadly toll in parts of the country (Sharland 2015). Such an event also speaks of diverse directions and sources of fears. As expatriates fear the local environment, many locals fear the presence of foreigners, associated either with terror or with the targets of terror attacks.

Local civilians may equally be arrested for taking pictures in front of any foreign agency, as happened at least once in Bamako, in 2013.[55] (It was one of the

55 Observation Notebook, February 2017.

reasons for me not to take pictures of many of the locations mentioned in this book). Fears of expatriates and locals are often shared, even if they do not focus on the similar perceived risks with the same intensity.

This mirroring of fears by local and expatriate actors leads to spatial practices where both consciously avoid each other. A visit at La Terrasse in 2016, a few months after this nightclub was targeted by a jihadist attack presented a place almost completely empty. Expatriates had started going out much less in bars and clubs. On the other hand, many Malians started to fear going to places frequented by expatriates, while others were reassured to see armed foreign militaries eating at the next table.[56]

The installation of barbed wires over walls have largely remained an expatriate phenomenon in Bamako. However, the scare of jihadist cells in the city engulfed other social classes, even if they could not, or did not want to secure their places with renewed security devices. However, fears translate in changes of behaviour. A young civil servant explained to me how in recent years she started exercising, jogging only along the roads with the most traffic. Although the air saturated with dust and CO2 from cars and trucks makes doing sports along these roads difficult, even hard to breathe, she feared kidnappings. "You walk on these dark streets and you end up hostage in the North", she claimed, although no kidnapping of any local or expatriate had taken place in Bamako[57] As the aid industry directs expatriates towards the use of defensive devices, local fears are not constrained by the same framework of security. Individual responses of local dwellers offer a larger spectrum of possible responses within their own representations of dangers, risks and protective measures.

6.3.5 Supermarkets and Malls

Consumption is one major difference between the local population and the expatriates. Malls and supermarkets channel "international" goods more expensive than the standard local does. Emblematic of the separation of modes of consumption between local and international networks, the duty-free shops provide UN employees access to a diversity of goods in all major UN stations. The diplomatic status of UN employees justifies the tax-free access to alcohol, cigarettes, packed food items as well as some electronic equipment and clothes.[58] The limits

56 Observation Notebook, 7 April 2017.
57 Observation Notebook, 15 March 2016.
58 Observation Notebook, 25 June 2016.

of the UN duty-free shops to UN personnel, and the relatively limited number of goods brings the aid community to rely largely on standard commercial shops.

The presence and development of shops with cashing and shelving of packed goods, such as the Nespresso products popular in hotels and offices, relies largely on international private networks of traders and investors. Depending on the size of the shop the private owners may form part of diasporic or local elites. Diaspora networks have often taken an important role in establishing shops of imports in African cities since colonial times (Arsan 2014). Most visible are the Lebanese in former French colonies, such as in Bamako and Abidjan. Greek shops in Juba witness of the ancient presence of the community (Barbarani 2017a). And in Nairobi, it is the important Asian community which is often linked to trade and retail (Kristiansen and Ryen 2002). In the case of the larger supermarkets or malls, international retail companies, such as Carrefour in Abidjan of Nairobi, may be involved.

The use of supermarkets by aid workers as a support for consumption of diverse commodities presents a paradox. As the security instructions recommend avoiding local food, for fear of illnesses, the reliance on malls becomes an essential support to the aid community. However, this reliance on the visible mall, symbol of wealth and the international presence constitute new risks from a security perspective. Front-page news everywhere at the time, the Westgate Mall attack in 2013 in Nairobi saw the murder of dozens of expatriates and tourists along local Kenyans. The choice by the terrorist group to attack a mall was driven by the media visibility guaranteed by attacking Westerners and symbols of "Western culture", wealth and power (Pflanz 2013).

The supermarket becoming a target for terrorist groups does not lead to forbid, or even discourage expatriates to use them. The response from UN security has been to advise employees to prepare for the eventuality, and more generally adapt their behaviour. The UNDSS website offers for example online courses on "active shooter" incidents, which aim to advise how to react when inside a building under attack. "Run, hide and fight" is the order of the response in case of attack. The first reflex, "run" should be to leave the scene as soon and as fast as possible. If there is no possibility of escape, "hide" from the view of the shooter. Finally, as a last resort, one can try to "fight" the shooter with whatever means and object he has at his disposal. Most description of "active shooter" in security briefings and online trainings either include or focus specifically on malls.[59]

59 UNDSS training, "Preparing and Responding to Active Shooter Incidents", 21 March 2018.

Apart of preparing for extreme circumstances, security officers advise reducing the visibility as a member of an international organisation. "I see many of you walking in the mall after work," a severe sounding security officer hauling an attendance of UN employees in Nairobi. "And I see you are so many because you still wear your UN pass on your neck."[60] When the strategy to protect can not be advising avoiding a place, and the bodies cannot be hidden in this place, the tactics must rely on hiding the employee.

The strategy to secure the place by staying in and modifying behaviour is interestingly used only in relation to shops. Other incidents in nightclubs, for example, led humanitarian organisations to advise not going out. This was the case after the Bamako Cotton Club incident (Dembelé 2016), and effectively much less expatriates were frequenting either clubs or restaurants one and two years afterwards. In that regard, the security discourse shows that it can adapt depending on the considered importance of a specific place. Consumer culture appears to be so important to the Western and "westernised" expatriate culture (Bloch, Ridgway, and Dawson 1994; Abaza 2001) that it can not be considered off-limits, even by the all-powerful organisational security.

The social and cultural separation of aid workers from the local environment relies on a spatial habitus and discipline to limit interactions with the local environment in a limited number of places. By designing the physical separation from the local environment, contacts are limited to a number of necessary interactions. It also largely limits the view and direct perception of the social panorama to the official descriptions presented by organisational hierarchy. As much as physical separation requires the instillation of fears of the outside, organised topophobic representation need the bodies of aid workers to be as isolated as possible from the panorama. Despite circular logic of segregation, a number of points of contacts to the local environment are necessary to support the layer of aid. In particular, the built environment constitutes both the object and the location of social relationships with local citizens and institutions.

6.4 The Locals and the Cash Flow

The presence of international organisation brings consequential flows of money into the local economy, or parts of it. The term "peacekeeping economy" has been used in a number of studies to refer to the specific economic impact of UN missions and its effect in creating vulnerabilities on the local population (Higate

60 Observation Notebook, 25 August 2016.

and Henry 2004; Jennings 2015). Taxonomies of the effect of UN missions on the local economy have highlighted three major impacts of peacekeeping presence, comprising salaries of local staff, official procurements and living allowances (Durch 2009). These three forms of cash input influence differently the urban economy. In relation to the built environment, procurements affect the use of official buildings and living allowance is the financial driver of personal housing space.

The layer of international aid rests on the labour of a local workforce to manage the interior of its territory as well as the interstices and interactions with the local environment. This results in directs jobs, for employees working directly under aid agencies. Aside from direct employment, many locals work in the private to accommodate the demands of international aid workers, as indirect jobs or profits. Demands of expatriates agitate a local microcosm of renters and fixers for houses and apartments, and transports. Apart from the local employees of international organisations, the presence of humanitarians creates indirect jobs for numerous professions corresponding to different social classes and cultural capital. According to Adama*, a logistician for the UN mission in Bamako, he interacts with the local contractors or others doing business with the UN.

> *Who makes profit of this mission? Very few people! […] The first were car rental companies, because at the beginning no one had vehicles. The oil companies, transport, and fret businesses. Then house owners and supermarkets. These are the only actual beneficiaries.*[61]

Adama* identified a thin layer of the elite with resources to gain from the presence of expatriates. This analysis seems slightly exaggerated in the sense that some job opportunities in direct and indirect employment present favourable conditions for many local workers (Carnahan, Gilmore, and Durch 2007). It remains true, however, that the biggest part of the share are for a minority of already prosperous individuals, companies and families. The location of large terrains for major logistics compound illustrates who can benefit from the larger dividends. In Bamako, the site of the major UN logistics base in Bougouba belongs to the Bolloré group, whose ramifications extend to a large business web in Africa (Debrie 2001; Debrie and De Guio 2004). Elsewhere, wealthy local families extract regular income from the UN bases.[62]

The Malian intellectual and former Minister of Culture Aminata Traoré also shares this understanding of the limited opportunities that the presence of aid workers represent for the population of Bamako. "Some people in the city benefit,

61 Interview Adama*, 10 April 2016.

62 Interview Mr Ajavon 2 May 2017; interview Fanny Mauron 29 March 2016.

if they have houses to rent, or hotels," she says. Very critical of the French intervention, and later the UN mission, she compares the UN mission in Democratic Republic of Congo to present a grim picture and a link in inefficacy of international aid by both the programme and the presence: "The UN has been in Congo for twenty years. What do people gain from their presence? They gained nothing! You don't develop that way."[63]

Exploitation of the local workforce places Malian employees far below international aid workers in salaries. However, these salaries might be several times higher than the local contracts for the same jobs. Some forms of exploitations normal in the local work relations such as the children house workers, common in most West African rural and urban areas (Jacquemin 2004) do not appear within aid archipelagos. However, exploitation and abuse does not disappear from the layer of aid, but changes its configuration.

The important question of sex abuse and sex work constitute an exception and a contradiction to codes of conducts (Allais 2011). While often tolerated and covered up by international organisations, its large acceptance in practice reduces. The scandalous and somehow structural aspects of sexual exploitation must not hide the fact that it constitute a minority phenomenon, rather than the core of the relations between peacekeeping and the local population.

This new cash inputs in the local economy also provokes indirect effects on the local economy and workers may work in relation to international aid sometimes without direct contact with aid workers. The vulnerability of the local population in the constitution of the layer of aid is structured by their existing relative power. Property owners have more relative power than wage workers do. Moreover, among wage workers, social and cultural capital allows a better positioning and opportunities in the interstices of the aid layer.

6.4.1 Property Owners

The presence of aid workers and their generally higher salaries is seen by house owners as an opportunity to benefit from a higher rent than what they could get from a local tenant. Adama*, a local employee of the UN with family properties in Bamako targets an expatriate clientele to rent and increase the value of his properties. Adama* targets UN staff for his renting and invested to put it on the expatriate market.

63 Interview Aminata Traoré, 15 April 2016.

> *Since my mother left to the US, I rented her house for 300'000 CFA per month. It would not have been possible with a Malian. He is a WFP international employee. I don't even make benefits on it, though. It costed me 2'500'000 in renovating the house. One million just for four new ACs. And the rest in renovating the kitchen, toilets, painting and garden. […] The UN covers the cost of the electricity generators for their staff.*

Adama* used networking connections within the UN system to find a tenant for the house. The tenant was a colleague of his wife, who was also working for the UN as a secretary on a national staff contract. Security approved the renting of the house. UN Security was satisfied even though the house had no barbed wire, because brambles on the exterior wall was considered enough protection against assailants.

As a couple of month rent paid for the renovations, Adama* developed the idea of renting one of the family's houses divided in six to eight "very high standing" apartments to UN expatriates. This would require him to demolish the house and rebuild it completely. The idea of a number of apartments instead of a house is, according to Adama* designed to the UN market: "houses are good for NGOs, they have their compound with the offices at the ground floor and bedrooms upstairs. But the UN have logistics base. Employees need apartments." In 2016, the MINUSMA was still occupying the hotel Amitié, but with the main base moving close to the airport, properties in the area close by would gain value.

The property he had in Faladié would fit well into his plan. When we spoke about his project in 2016, he had already commissioned an architect to draw the blueprint. A Turkish contracting company had proposed a price for a strong and relatively cheap structure. Adama* was most worried about workmanship for the inside finishing. He thought it would be difficult to obtain the luxury apartment standard he wanted for the apartments, a common concern in the Malian construction and tourism sectors (Diahou and Simeu-Kamdem 2018). However, more importantly, his capacity to finance the project is not guaranteed. The hundred thousand euros demanded upfront by the company required a credit he could not obtain from Malian banks with his UN national staff salary as a guarantee.

This difficulty to obtain a credit from banks prevented Adama* to go forward a year later. His example illustrates nevertheless the understanding of international presence as an opportunity for property development by many locals. This capacity of making profits from the presence of aid workers rests on a series of conditions, including the capacity to finance housing projects with little access to credit (Vaa 2016). The connection and knowledge of the expatriates are not always enough to benefit from their presence.

Many land or house owners do not bother investing. Once they can lease the building, they content themselves in using the presence of internationals to raise their rents. Cécile*, a French-Ivorian citizen coming back from the Sofia Antipolis University in Nice, where many African elites study for high school and university was currently unemployed when I came to Abidjan. She spent her time managing the real estate portfolio of her family. Interestingly, the family is renting apartments and houses in different parts of the city. In particular, the family-owned houses in Yopougon and in Marcory, which were at both ends of the social and political spectrum (Steck 2008).

Marcory, and the Zone 4 in particular, is the most favoured area for the housing of expatriates. And Yopougon is strictly forbidden to the UN personnel in Abidjan. Yopougon combines a relatively high density, and higher levels of poverty, as well as being considered politically pro-Gbagbo (Steck 2008). This made the area completely forbidden for UN personnel, long before the UN took sides against Gbagbo during the 2011 combats in Abidjan (Toh and Banégas 2006).

Unaware that Yopougon was actually forbidden to UN expatriates, Cécile* explained that expatriates "don't go to Yopougon because it's all crap". Comparing how she manages the apartments and how much money she can ask for rent to residents in both areas, she adds:

> *When the expatriates come to the Zone 4, we can increase the rents. We can also tell the [local] tenants that we're increasing their rent. And they have no choice. If they don't accept they have to move because we can always rent to the expatriates. In these areas, we can also increase the rent because of the current infrastructure works. Now that they have the asphalt in the street, we don't do any works in the house. And if they're not happy: they move!*

The candour of Cécile* explaining her management of the family's real estate is not so common with house owners. She hints that the poor level of infrastructure combined with the absence of expatriates – the African Development Bank employees are also unlikely to move to Yopougon – prevents her to raise the rent in poor neighbourhoods. This sets the stage for an increase in rents as uneven as spectacular. Her testimony constitutes an interesting example of the perception of expatriates, by wealthy locals, as free to choose their housing, but naturally selecting affluent neighbourhoods.

She does not need strong connections and even direct contact with international aid to benefit from their presence, since their presence in the city is enough to pressure other tenants. These seemingly abusive practices take place in a context of a housing market saturated with frauds and an absence of regulatory power from the state over real estate deals. As an example, one of the common practices in the city is the fake selling of constructible land that does not belong to the sellers. Cécile* herself had been paying a large sum to a seller for a property the seller did not own. When she understood this, she had already paid 45 million CFA she would never get back.[64]

6.4.2 Public Institutions

Increase in housing prices may be perceived as a great benefit for municipalities with contingents of aid workers. This is largely the case with the communes of Cocody and Marcory who have both found an interest in the presence of international organisations and are keen to have and keep them. Mr Ajavon, Director of Technical Services in Cocody explains the strategy of the Municipality:

> *For Cocody the presence of these organisations are prestigious and a question of standing. It has an advantage on the real estate taxes. If the value of the terrains is high, it provokes an increase of the taxes. It represents 90% of the budget of the municipality. […] The value is not the same in the other municipalities. Maybe in Marcory. For example, 100 square metres cost 400 million CFA. […] The land ends up being more expensive than the houses on top.*[65]

For the municipality of Cocody, the presence of most offices of international organisations and embassies is a profitable situation. However, most expatriates live in the commune of Marcory, across Abidjan's most recent Henri Konan Bédié "HKB" toll bridge. Mr Laurent Ebi, head of the public domain directorate (Sous-direction du Domaine Public) explains the installation of expatriates as the best residential choice:

> *We encourage their installation. […] this is the Municipality with the best living environment, which explains the interest of expatriates. You feel at home here. Public ways are open and asphalted. There are green spaces, 'maquis', restaurants and hotels. These places solve the worry of fun and entertainment. It is different from the other municipalities, with the great arteries, shops and gardens.*[66]

For officials of both municipalities, Cocody and Marcory are complementary to each other in providing the space needed for international organisations. The importance of Marcory for housing and Cocody for hosting offices fit with the strategies to increase the value of the land and benefit from the taxes on real estate. Short of statistics and precise information on the fluctuation of land values and taxes, municipalities rely on the word-of-mouth to follow the strategies of

64 Observation Notebook, 27 April 2017.
65 Interview Mr Ajavon, 2 May 2017.
66 Interview Laurent Ebi, 10 May 2017.

investors in their territory. "We simply know that real-estate promoters are interested by the expatriates," considers Xavier Akoa, Deputy Director of Technical Services in Marcory. "From the income they can get renting apartments in the Zone 4, for example."[67]

None of the municipalities can actually measure the impact of the presence of these organisations on the land, because the state perceives the taxes and reverses a percentage to municipalities. "We do not even know if it's true as the municipalities do not participate to the tax collection and we are not informed about what has been collected or not", explains Mr Ajavon. "We do not know if what we get is correct." As a result, the position revenues of the municipality is contingent to the prerogatives of the state. The lack of transparency in the fiscal equalisation between the state and the municipalities of Abidjan is subject to rumours and suspicion from the municipalities. "No one is fooled", concludes Mr Ajavon, "but we can't complain without information."[68]

6.4.3 Transport and Other Services

The market for services to accommodate international aid workers in Juba illustrate the possibility for different types of employees and small entrepreneurs to capture some of the cash that flows with aid workers. The specific situation of Juba as the new capital of South Sudan has brought people from the other regions to the capital, as well as workers from neighbouring countries. Ugandan sellers, for example have staffed large parts of the commerce of fruits and vegetables. The presence of communities of African workers in Juba is widespread and far from limited to international aid.

Supermarkets illustrate the networks brought to Juba to the upper-class locals and expatriates. Greek and Lebanese communities of Juba, present since colonial times, play an important role in trade and some high-end retail supermarkets. Operating these shops, another worldwide labourer diaspora work as cashiers. Filipino workers – Filipinas, as most are women – fill the supermarkets, even though they are not allowed by their own government to travel to South Sudan, due to the civil war (Esmaquel 2013; HDT 2016).

In relation to the economy that supports the presence of international aid, these type of workers could be termed as semi-locals. They are not nationals from the country, but often work on comparable wages. Some of the foreign workers work specifically for a clientele of aid workers. This is the case of Ezra*,

67 Interview Xavier Akoa, 10 May 2017.

68 Interview Mr Ajavon, 2 May 2017.

a Kenyan private taxi driver in Juba. Aid workers usually use the official cars of their organisations for work. Out of work time, the use of official cars to move to the city, for leisure or other non-official matters, is not permitted by all organisations, and many agencies limit the use of cars for official business. This policy has led to the development of private taxi drivers whose clientele is constituted mainly, and sometimes only of aid workers.

The private taxi drivers that aid workers use usually differ from the local standard taxi in the state of the car and that aid workers avoid jumping on a taxi in the street and prefer calling them beforehand. Ezra* came to South Sudan in the days of the country's independence with an old car he brought from Kenya.

> *In Kenya it would be impossible to have a taxi business with such an old car. But here it was easier to start like that. This is why I came here. And it went well! Now I have three brand new cars like this one* [he shows the digital dashboard, AC and sound system] *I work myself in this one and I have two drivers for the other ones.*[69]

Ezra* thought the risk of staying in Juba was worth taking in order to benefit from the economic growth and the possibility to start his business from a small capital.[70] However, Ezra*'s enthusiasm for the opportunities of the new South Sudan did not extend to much sympathy for the locals, who he feared were "spying" on foreigners like him. "I drive only for white people", says Ezra*, "because they pay and they don't make trouble". In fact, by "white people", Ezra* meant NGO and UN people. He had actually many African customers – Including the expatriate who gave me Ezra*'s phone number- in his taxis, although he assimilates expatriates with "Whites".

The reference to "Whites" to identify its expatriate customers relate to a wider trend in the identification of the "transnational whiteness", identified with consumption patterns and lifestyles modelled on the Western middle class, rather than skin colour (Arat-Koc 2012). Aid workers and other expatriates constitute a particular clientele as much as a "culturalisation" of class differences reflecting the gap in living conditions between locals and expatriates. Although Ezra* only works for an elite expatriate community, his own social condition places him midway between the South Sudanese and his "White" passengers.

The efforts of Ezra* to build his taxi business in Juba also meant that he had to save as much money to reinvest it in his own business. This owner of three brand new cars had to live in a small concrete blind room with a corrugated iron roof

69 Interview with Ezra*, 3 July 2016.

70 I did not have the chance to know more of Ezra*'s whereabouts after the fighting in Juba. The deteriorated situation may have changed his opinion.

Figure 64: Sketch of the dimension of Ezra*'s room in Juba. Corrugated iron covers the blind concrete walls

and latrines outside "but clean" to save as much as he could (Figure 64). This standard brought his monthly rent to 30 US dollars, about hundred times less than the living allowance UN employees receive from their agency: "I'm used to living like this and it saves me money."

Opportunities for semi-locals like Ezra* show that many of the workers supporting the presence of international aid exist in relation to the pace of humanitarian interventions. However, the salaries keep most people working for international aid far from the levels international workers get, even for successful small businesses.

6.4.4 Fixers for Houses and Apartments

Many of the arrangements for any of the needs of aid workers are done by mouth to ear. In the case of well-established missions, such as Nairobi, this practice is officially advised, as it guarantees that the house and its security equipment are approved by security. Word to mouth is also common for cleaners (Department of Safety and Security 2013). More than five expatriates between 2013 and 2016 had employed Rokia* as a cleaner and housekeeper. She signed her first contract with UN employees after another housekeeper recommended her. The tacit rule was that she had to give her first month's salary to the cleaning lady who recommended her. Afterwards, she relied on the recommendation of aid workers who advised other expatriates to hire her when they left the country.[71]

71 Observation Notebook, 13 April 2016.

Informal recommendation is the norm for apartments and other types of services, as the local standard. The informality of the enterprise of fixers can extend to the formal sector if the rollover is enough to ensure regular income. The local fixer Mafa Fall and a Belgian friend started working informally as intermediaries in Bamako in 2012, when the first wave of aid workers arrived in the country as part of the humanitarian response to the conflict in the north of the country.

> *Formally, we created the company in September 2013, but we started much earlier, in July of the year before. The crisis created an opportunity with the arrival of many NGOs and expatriates. [..]We had many requests, for houses, equipment, furniture, vehicles and personnel […] It started very well. We used the expat contacts of my friend and an expat website. We saw the needs and we proposed services. That's how we got known in town, and going to expat parties and mouth to ear. Our clients told the next ones that we did the service. We got known by the NGOs' logisticians very fast.*[72]

By the time of the interview, conducted in 2016, the wave of expatriates coming in had slowed down. Requests to Mafa Fall's company, the SOFAF reduced since the peak of 2013 and the arrival of the MINUSMA. The income was good by Malian standard, but not enough for his Belgian friend and colleague, who left the country. In the meantime, Mr Fall and his friend had supported many NGO and UN workers in their installation in the country.

The SOFAF company helped out easing the bureaucratic slowness of Malian formalities, where expatriates found difficulties obtaining what they needed. This was the case when expatriates required the import and registration of cars. "We very quickly sold five cars exclusive of taxes. We did it because it was more complicated for foreigners," Mafa Fall explained. While ethic charters of international organisations forbid all types of gifts and corruption in the host country, bureaucratic complexities and complicated legalities are easy to leave to local fixers to keep a close eye on practices officially strictly forbidden. Being unaware, or uninformed, of the grey zone practises of fixers allows aid workers to get things done without breaching official lines.

Managing the limbo between the official procedures and requirements to aid workers and the complex practices common in the host country are eased and the fixer keeps the balance. "The papers of the car are regular and legal," explains Mr Fall. "But it helps paying something to accelerate the procedure." Interestingly, while the standard NGO language explicitly and strongly prohibits any type of corruption or trade-offs (Carnahan, Gilmore, and Durch 2007; Tavares 2003), fixers are relatively open in their use of under-the-table money to accelerate the

72 Interview Mafa Fall, 22 April 2016.

local bureaucracies for these same NGOs. Wilful ignorance likely facilitates overcoming of contradictions in discourse and practice by NGO employees (Gilson 2011; Zane, Irwin, and Reczek 2016). Fixers solve the issue acting as a protecting screen between idealised practices and social realities that are more complex.

Among the main demands by NGO employees, the description given for houses indicates what standards aid workers expected. "We waited for a description and started looking for houses, not necessarily with prior contact with owners," explained Mafa Fall. The descriptions of the houses NGOs and UN wanted are very similar. "They all wanted a villa with a swimming pool and a big garden in Badalabougou." In addition to finding a house, Mafa Fall and his friend were also asked to coordinate for the construction of security devices required by security departments of aid agencies:

> *They wanted barbed wire. And high walls. If the houses didn't have it already. We took charge to have them installed. Either at the cost of the tenant or the landlord. [...] The organisation takes care of finding the guards. In general, it was two during the day and three at night.*

Individual luxury houses started being developed in Bamako in the 1990s, after reforms in the land laws favouring private property over state concessions (Morin and Séguin 1997; Bertrand 1998). The dominant model remains "courtyard houses" and barbed wire have remained an exception in the city, even in the high-end neighbourhoods. This change did not seem to affect the neighbours so much as they did not complain, according to Mafa Fall: "People knew it was for expatriates. They just noticed and thought, 'Oh! It's a whim of the foreigners'. But they were not really shocked."

The place taken by the SOFAF in organising the Bamakoan life of the expatriates put them in a position of caretakers of whatever is needed against an hourly rate of 2500 CFA – about five US dollars – and administrative costs. "We got a regular clientele very fast, sometimes just to go shopping for them," explains Mr Fall. The hourly rate of local salaries and fees encourages reliance on fixers for a multiplicity of tasks. "Some of them even asked us to manage their houses when they went on holiday. And we just sent them the bills by email."

However, the place taken by the SOFAF started being perturbed by the multiplication of NGO logisticians. In the course of the years, the UN and NGOs directly hired Malian logisticians when the different organisations increased their activities. "Now most business with expats is through them. And they ask for their cut. They want up to 20 % of the price," affirms Mr Fall. The reduction of the number of commands also reduced their working capital, which further limited their capacities to operate. As the activities of the SOFAF reduced, Mr Fall says that now his business is mostly based on "special demands". "Some clients want to change the house, like breaking a wall or something like this."

One of the advantages, which fixers consider in working with expatriates, is how easily money is spent. NGOs and expatriates want things fixed quickly and they are ready to pay the price for it. In an often-repeated claim by local workers, Mafa Fall claims that the factures are paid without discussions when it comes to expatriates:

> *Now I mainly work with Malians. There is less pressure and less crazy demands, but it's much less profitable. When NGOs were asking, there was no problem in footing the bill.*

Fixers, house owners and other employees of the aid community constitute an interface between the world of aid expatriates and the local environment. Their activity is as temporary as the rhythms of the waves of aid workers coming to the country and highly dependent on it. The relatively high profitability of fixer business is contingent to its precariousness. Temporalities in the spatiality of international aid implies that many of the socio-economic relationships created by and for the use of space only exist in a given form for a limited period.

6.4.5 Hotel Employees

Temporary increases of hotel guests during times of crisis and arrivals of aid workers trigger dynamism in the hotel sectors related to its multi-functionality. Hotel guests need beds. Other hotel amenities attract a wider clientele who go to the bars, restaurants and swimming pools. While the strategies of the owners and managers of hotels focus on keeping a clientele corresponding to a situation of scarce tourism, their employees work as wage labour completed with tips.

The arrival or aid organisations present different benefits for local employees depending on their positions. The cost of labour in Africa is so low that salary opportunities witness spectacular variation for similar position depending on the employer. As Matt Christie, manager of the Sleeping Camel guesthouse explained, the conflict in Mali and the subsequent arrival of many NGOs meant changes in employment relations:

> *For us the big change came with an important increase in salaries with the UN coming in. For example, we had a driver for the tours. We paid him 80'000 a month plus 10'000 a day when we were on tour. He was hired by [a UN contractor] that tripled his salary. We cannot compete anymore. But that's better for him.*[73]

---

73 Interview Matt Christie, 15 April 2016.

Tourism provided more jobs at lower salaries. Drivers attached to the tourism sector either saw the reduction of their activities, or increases in salaries. For those able to maintain their position in relation to international aid in a way or another, benefits come uneven. Salaries are variable depending on the employing organisations, which do not work on identical salary grids (Pfeiffer et al. 2008). As direct employment by NGOs can differ substantially, indirect jobs are not monitored by international aid.

One aspect of the workforce in many of the expatriate restaurants, hotels and bars, is the presence of university-educated personnel, working on non-clerical tasks, and in particular waiters and cashiers. "I did not want to apply to be a teacher after studying Humanities", explains a waiter at the Kora restaurant in Bamako. "So I work here and try to write, as my dream is to be a Writer."[74] Waiters' salaries are often comparable to public servants, including teachers, complemented with tips from customers making the job attractive for university-educated Malians. Low salaries in the local public and private sector push many Malian graduates to work directly or indirectly for international aid. The pernicious effects on essential public services of the suction of many graduates by international aid has been criticised elsewhere for depleting the state of its trained professionals (Edwards and Hulme 1996; Pfeiffer 2003). It appears that the suction of trained professionals into the layer of aid has similar effects.

6.4.6 Balance of Salaries and Costs of Living

The wave of expatriates stimulated the restaurant and bar of the Badala hotel, with many aid workers and diplomats keen to enjoy French cuisine. One of the few expatriate restaurants in the expat-crowded area of Badalabougou, it witnessed the mixing of humanitarians, military and some local upper-class Malians. Among the servers hired to cover the increase in clientele was Antoinette*, who worked at the Badala hotel bar during the years 2013 and 2014. At the time, this Cameroonian woman was a medical student at the University of Bamako, and worked part-time as an extra to finance her studies.

Talking about the experience of working at the hotel, Antoinette*, now a medical doctor, presents how she took the opportunity to work five evenings a week and reflects now positively on the experience. "It went well! I saved a lot of money during this period on what my parents sent me. [...] I bought medical equipment, my stethoscope and some books".[75] For her, the past student job at

74 Observation Notebook, 28 March 2017.
75 Interview Antoinette*, 8 April 2017.

the hotel was not her main financial resource, but a useful addition to her normal stipend.

Salaries at the hotel were not fixed by categories of staff. It responded instead to the willingness of the management to hire a particular person. Antoinette* explains the variation of the salaries depending on the looks of the waitresses and their ability to negotiate:

> *At the hotel, the salary depended on your face. And it depended on how you negotiated. Some were paid the same as me working the whole day. I said that I did not want to work for 40'000 [CFA per month]. You can't live like that. [...] My close colleagues made me understand that there is no standard wage.*

Physical appearance combined with cultural and social capital make up for the level of income hotel employees can obtain from the employer. The ability to negotiate and recognise one's assets – physical and social – produces the uneven and unequal wages from the sexist structures in which hotels operate. As a result, the salary for a student job might easily be higher than for full-time employees. Individualisation of pay by arbitrary labour norms prevails thanks to the great poverty and precariat of the local environment.

Supplementing her 60'000 CFA monthly salary, Antoinette* had significant tips from the service, which capped to 120'000 CFA on some months. Compared to Malian standard, the combination of pay and tips makes the salary profitable. However, in the calculation, hotel management are aware that tips completed the salary and use it to lower their already low and profitable labour costs. "Pay was not correct," claims Antoinette*. "We made it round with the tips. That was unfair because management knew it and calculated we would get the tips."

With Malian wages, and costs of living in Bamako, working at an air-conditioned restaurant also provided important savings on everyday consumption. "I went from 13'000 a month in electricity to 1000 by not being at home during the day," Antoinette* explains. She was also able to reduce her costs in food, although the quality was not the same as for the restaurant customers.

> *We really did not eat well. Employees' meals were on the restaurant's leftovers, because normal employees' meals were not good. Sometimes restaurant customers offered us the meals. I ate lots of fish and fries. You never get tired of fries! Strangely, I did not gain weight at the time. All in all, I did not have to cook at home anymore. And that saved me a lot.*

The opportunity to work in catering offers the possibility to save money on basic consumption goods. However, it also brings costs to employees, in particular in relation to transports. Commuting costs are not negligible in Bamako, with a deficient system of public transports. Going out of the main transit roads often implies using taxis, for example to get to relatively isolated places like the

University Hospital in the Point G neighbourhood. Antoinette* went to work hitchhiking during the day and had to find an arrangement with a motorised security guard who lived in the same area to come back at night.

> *I had an average of 3000 to 5000 CFA tips per night. In my arrangement, I gave him 1500 for the ride instead of the 2500–3000 it would cost me on a taxi. It was more secure like that. And I also informed my colleagues of my deal with him.*

Spending up to half of her tips on transport illustrates the costs of living in Bamako in relation to low salaries (Bendech et al. 2000). Working is not just selling labour force. It comes at a relatively high cost. Balance of wages and costs of living only work because of the nature advantages available on the workplace.

6.4.7 Service and Gendered Relationships

The story of Antoinette* emphasises the highly unequal relationships between expatriates and local employees within the places used by the aid community. The selection of waitresses on their appearances likely encouraged sexist reflections from the guests of the hotel. What in other places might not have been accepted becomes normalised in the relationships between expatriates and local waitresses. Antoinette* attributes sexist comments mostly to the military personnel coming as customers at the bar on their free evenings:

> *I had good contact with most customers, a part of some inappropriate remarks. The military guys sometimes made remarks a bit sexual, on the body and shapes. Like 'you have a hot butt!' I said 'thank you' and let go. I had a few weird propositions. He proposes six million to go somewhere abroad with him. […] I was taking it as a joke.*

The atmosphere of normalised sexism in many of the places where international aid operates constitutes one instance where the securing of premises of the aid layer produces other forms of vulnerability. As Antoinette* explains, she never mentioned the comments or sexual demands by hotel guests to the management: "It was just hitting on me with promises and money. I did not take it seriously." While most expatriates do not behave in similar fashion, it remains telling that discrepancies in revenues and status enable some expatriate to behave with local workers in a way that would likely not be permitted in a restaurant in the North.

In their ethnography of the gendered relationships in the American culture constructed in bars, Spradley and Mann (2008) present a variety of diverse behaviours of individuals and groups in relation to female bartenders. Their study highlights and concludes that the tasks of a barmaid include accepting a degree of eroticisation from part of male customers. Construction of gender relations in service highlights that relations of subordination of servers towards customers are repeated in daily rituals. Wide ranges of behaviour may occur, although they often involve a sexualised subtext.

Examples of relations of domination between customers and hotels in the North (MacKinnon 1979; Liladrie 2010) are usually softer than what can be observed in expatriate bars and restaurants. One day, a customer pretends to bite the nipple of a waitress as she brings his drinks. The waitress moves aside with an uncomfortable smile and continues her work. Such a scene is infrequent, but accepted in many restaurants or hotels where this fieldwork took place. In the context of expatriates in missions, such type of behaviour does not break the sacred rule of service highlighted by Hall, where waitresses are expected to "smile, defer and flirt" with customers (Hall 1993). Expected behaviour involves both the projection of the body as implicit relation of seduction, although at a careful distance that would avoid the risk of giving a negative response to overt advances (MacKinnon 1979).

Combinations of racism and financial inequality explain the extreme extent to the behaviour of some customers. The particular context of the French intervention in Mali liberated some of the most racist and sexist remarks and behaviour. Drawing shortly after this period (before starting this research, in 2013) I tried to render the atmosphere of colonial revival of the period. French military presence materialised in the city with many soldiers and officers driving around Bamako. It raised a sense of renewed arrogance among a number of civilian expatriates, who felt comfortable to quietly harass waitresses from their dinner table (Figure 65).

The relations between the bodies of local men working in hotels is less obviously gendered since it does not – or at least not systematically- involve an eroticisation local bodies. Men are also generally less numerous working in bars and restaurants in all the sites of this research, presumably because restaurant and bar managers are counting on the eroticisation of the African women to attract and maintain their clientele. Likely counting on the higher level of tips for women to maintain low salaries, restaurant and hotel managers hire dramatically more women than men for service. Bodies of local men are mostly valorised in the position of security officers. Keeping gates or on the lookout, local security guards are likely to be the first hit in case of an attack.

Lower number of men waiters explains a lower number of interactions and dialogues with expatriates. Interactions are also more limited and discussions are shorter. They involve more often lecturing by customers on "proper" service. From sitting in these bars and restaurants, one can often hear customers and managers shouting at the male employees. The expected body posture of local men centres on running fast service work and silently listen to diverse

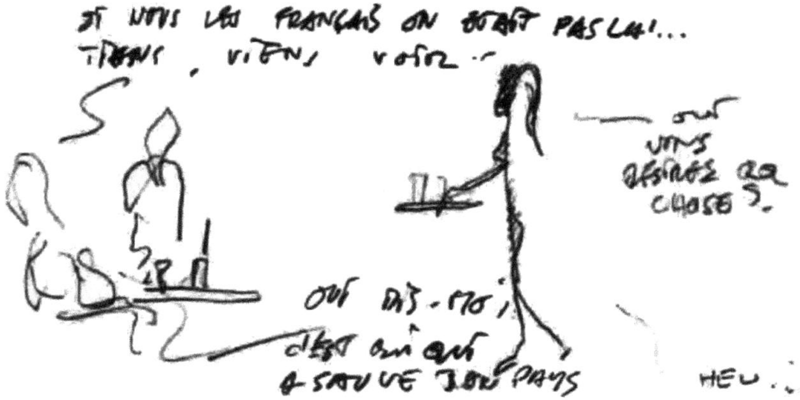

Figure 65: A dialogue between French customers and Malian server in Bamako, in the wake of the 2013 French military intervention

–"If we the French were not here…Hey! Come here!"

–"Do you wish anything?"

–"Yes! Tell me who saved your country?"

– "Erh.."

reprimands. A drawing I did during one of my field visits of a quite common sighting in Bamako cafés represents two male waiters being chided by a customer unsatisfied with their service. The positions of the bodies illustrate expected relation of subordination in the settings of hotel service. Bending the head and hands crossed behind the back, standing silently and listening while the sitting customer talks (Figure 66).

The theme of the relations of the bodies of local workers and the expatriate community is one of the most controversial from within the aid community and in the countries of interventions. The "interplay of masculinities, femininities and security" (Higate and Henry 2004) created by humanitarian presence structures a variety of new insecurities for local women, while ethical codes are used as main barriers to diverse forms of abuse. Scandals related to sex abuse in many countries have led to political shifts and sometimes end of programmes, as was recently the case with Oxfam in Haiti (Reuters and agencies 2018). While all forms of harassment and sexual abuses are formally forbidden, the security environment has limited protection inside the aid layer.

The question of the prostitution in relation to aid workers and military peacekeepers has often been the centre of the discussions on the effects of aid.

Figure 66: Two waiters in a Bamako Hotel wait and listen to complaints from a client

Research on the topic presented critiques of militarism in the production of gendered violence in countries of intervention (Whitworth 2004). The present research includes instead very little on the subject for two main reasons. The first is practical: as a white male doing research, it seemed extremely complicated to construct a convenient and opportune setting in which it would be possible to conduct an inquiry involving, for example, formal interviews. Being so visibly part of the very "market" of expatriates would require a setting, which would likely exclude the other issues from the research for the concentration of efforts needed in this aspect. Encounters with prostitutes in a variety of locations and contexts happened as the ubiquity of local prostitution of the expat market convinced me not to attempt research beyond the simple observation of the coexistence of prostitution and aid workers.

Entering a collective taxi in a Bamako street early one morning, I realised from the loud phone conversation of the other client, a woman sitting on the back seat, that she had just finished her night with an expatriate. "I was with Philippe from the French embassy. He gave me 100 dollars for the night. What about you? How did it go with your guy?" After the short silence in the taxi, when the friend at the other end of the phone finished talking, the woman exclaimed almost shouting: "What!!! He gave you 200 dollars. Oooh! But you're too beautiful darling! You're Shakira!" Once she finished her conversation with her friend on the phone, the young woman asked me for my phone number, "to meet and have fun one of these days".[76] Being a centre of attention of prostitutes looking for their clients assures that I could not miss the ubiquity of prostitution in expatriate circles, as much as it prevents interactions that would not make myself a client.

The other reason to avoid focussing on prostitution relates more to the focus of the inquiry itself. Prostitution is one major question in the gendered relationships between locals and expatriate. However, this question gains its importance for good and bad reasons and risks becoming the tree that hides the forest. Prostitution only constitutes one among many aspects of the gendering of interaction between aid workers and the local environment, as important as it may be. Other relationships constitute the bulk of gendered interactions, themselves profoundly unequal within the "normal" spaces of the aid layer, including hotels, restaurants and other sites of sociability.

Another nuance to the above presentation of modes of gendered relationships in the context of aid presence is needed to clarify the scope of the analysis. A large number of aid workers are women. Depending on positions and agencies, women form an important minority of the aid workforce (Bjerneld 2009). They are likely to influence relationships in all interactions with local actors. I have not focussed on this aspect, which would require a proper investigation in itself. Instead, I choose to reflect on specific modes of domination, which mixes gender, race and social positions. A multiplicity of links and relationships are indeed possible between expatriates and locals, and many if not most are respectful, if not equal. Nevertheless, the possibility left to a predominantly white and male social group to define daily interactions under sexist behaviour presents well the structural domination induced by the presence of the aid industry in African cities.

This discussion on the interactions between the layer of aid and the local environment aimed at highlighting a diverse set of relationships and interactions that occur at the border of the layer of aid. This space of potential interactions is uneven and is mostly understood as services to the humanitarian by the local social environment. The social and economic activities prompted by international aid and made possible by the auxiliary space of aid follows the general characteristics of being highly unequal, with most benefits going to upper ladders of

76 Observation Notebook, 4 April 2016.

the society. Proprietors are the most advantaged with the possibility to gain the full benefit of high rents and often house upgrades. The benefits and advantages of this presence decrease sharply when descending to employees. However, for employees cultural capital and contacts plays a key role in establishing the levels of income that can be expected from direct and indirect work with international aid. University educated employees of aid organisations, self-employed fixers or waiters find their education returning higher incomes in fields sometimes unrelated to their expected professions. In the lowest social classes, the opportunity to work as cleaner or security guards might provide a regular salary higher than local standards. However, it remains often barely enough to cover costs of living in a major African city.

6.4.8 Rebuttals and Frictions

In a Juba hotel, a quarrel between young South Sudanese and NGO workers over the type of music that the barman should put in the Hi-Fi system escalates quickly.[77] A fistfight erupts between the two groups. One of the young South Sudanese shouts, "We fought for this country! We fought for this country!" An NGO worker replies that he has been working in the country for years to support South Sudanese. His claims that his presence in the country since before the independence witnesses his commitment to South Sudan does not help defuse the situation. The tension continues to escalate until one of the South Sudanese brings out his handgun in further show of defiance. Hotel guards come in the middle to separate the crowd. Both sides of the quarrel, expatriates and locals, leave the bar with drunken rage, leaving only a handful of clients behind.

The situation is, of course, not really about music tastes between American rock classics versus East African pop music. As aid workers accuse the ruling classes and warlords of plundering the country, they share the same spaces of socialisation with them. The rich young South Sudanese are not popular among aid workers. An aid workers comments: "There are many South Sudanese starving in the country. But not these guys, far from it. They go clubbing with the money their fathers stole from the country". Another NGO worker summarises her thought even more bluntly: "Rich South Sudanese…They're assholes!" The following day both groups come back to this same bar. Another day they might as well meet again at any other expensive Juba bar or club. Hostility and cold anger echoes the co-dependency between humanitarian aid and the South Sudanese elites (Jansen 2017). Griefs remain, but the same groups share the same space

77 Observation Notebook, 18 June 2016.

again. Connections between customers at leisure places are relatively horizontal and even when they go badly; they are usually settled or forgotten.

These examples of high tensions are coincident with a number of personal connections and friendships that may develop, typically among national and expatriate colleagues, who work during the day and go out together in the evenings. Some limits to these relationships remain for various reasons, among them a significant difference in income coupled with the fact that most local workers already have their social and family circles in the country. Connections of sociability may extend to other straits, as they can support some business agreements by word of mouth, such as renting family houses or access to informal services.

The layer of aid extends its power to different straits of life and at different scales. The standards and disciplines it imposes to the local social fabric is received differently depending on where and how connections are made. When frictions occur between the aid industry and its local workers, the verticality of the relationship tend to either silence local voices or simply lay them off. In Bamako, the head manager of a UN agency spots a Malian janitor driving one of the official white cars of the organisation. The janitor is dismissed on the spot. He does not complain, protest or try to reverse the decision.[78] A janitor is replaceable by many local workers eager to find a regular source of income.

Guards form the bulk of the low-skilled local workforce of aid organisations and are regularly the subject of multiple dissatisfactions from aid workers. The older guard in front of the house of NGO workers slowly falls asleep on his chair. As I walk by on the street, one of the NGO workers leaving the house, gets close to the ear of the sleeping guard, and suddenly screams in the ear of the guard, waking him up in a jolt. Later in the day, other guards in the street comment that this expatriate has been shouting at them and guards of other NGOs in the same street regularly. "He's very mean," one guard tells me. "This guard is an old man", explains another. "This work is hard for him. We work twelve-hour shifts for almost nothing. We're exploited."[79] The multinational security company that employs them pays them the equivalent of 100 dollars per month. While some local work, conditions are worst, this sum remains very little to live in Bamako. The outsourcing of security allows organisations to leave out the question of a fair pay to their workers. The discussion over salaries is not part of any negotiation between aid organisations and employees as long as the security is

78 Observation Notebook, December 2016.

79 Observation Notebook, December 2016.

subcontracted. As a result, the only points discussed between many low-skilled workers and aid organisations is their compliance to the tasks.

Frictions and rebuttals from the least powerful employees are limited by their reduced margins to protest or to make their voices heard. In fact, most of the counteractions to the norms of the aid layer and its corporate support come in forms reminiscent of the dialectic between public and private transcripts. The fact that the guards do not complain openly of their working conditions echoes what Scott call "hidden and public transcripts" (J. C. Scott 1990), where dominated groups tactically keep disagreements with ruling classes silent. While guards and other local employees may formally accept working conditions of low wages and long hours to protect villas and offices of aid workers, they often silently reject them.

Public transcript ensure frictions do not come to the surface and workers tend to avoid open conflicts with aid organisations. Instead, private transcripts indicates how frustrations continuously affect local workers in their relations to aid organisations, and how local workers' hierarchies are set by these organisations. During the end of the mission of an NGO, its expatriate employees decide to give a large TV screen to the housemaid who took care of the house. Other house employees – gardener, guards and drivers – had been working around the house regularly. This expensive gift given to only one of the employees contrasts with what the others received, a small stipend worth some green tea and sugar in recognition for their work during that same period. Although they had preferred not to talk and complain about the difference in the acknowledgement of their work, two of the employees privately say they are disappointed and bitter. They will soon be out of work and consider their work was not recognised. For them, there is not point talking about their frustration to either their lucky colleague or their employers, as the outcome will remain the same in any case. The TV can not be divided; and complaining could turn bad for their work certificates.[80]

In the conditions of a blanket of silence between local workers and aid institutions, rebuttals from guards and other low-paid workers of the layer of aid come in a form reminiscent of the "sabotage without knowing" described by the anarchist Emile Pouget (Pouget 1908). As Pouget considers that exploited workers, who have no possibility to complain or organise when capital-labour relations are too skewed against them, often sabotage their work – consciously or not – and make it as inefficient as possible.

80 Observation Notebook, August 2017.

This "sabotage without knowing it" is widely present in all sites, although they are rarely understood as such by aid agencies. Oftentimes, they are more or less openly attributed to a generic "laziness" that expatriates commonly attach to local workers (Crewe and Fernando 2006; Fechter 2010). In one of the most vocal such example I witnessed, the head of security of a UN agency tours the different private security guards posted in and around a compound. Unhappy with the discipline of the guards – one listening to music on the job and another who left his post – grumps in his thick Afrikaans accent "Arh! These guys! They're gonna bring me back to my racist years!", in reference to his past service in the South African military at the time of Apartheid. Although such crude comments and attitude towards local workers constitute the tip of expatriate arrogance, they reflect a more general tendency to naturalise silent rebuttals from local employees.

The implantation of the layer of aid is far from frictionless. However, its power makes expatriates and organisations likely to be able to get their way, in most cases of their everyday lives. They hold a power unmatched by most local dwellers. Cases in which local actors are able to rebuke the aid layer involves powerful local actors. As will be addressed in more detail in the chapter on Transformations, the layer of aid often collides with local individuals, contractors and institutions. Numerous disagreement such as those relating to work and the sharing of spaces of sociability take place. Other types of frictions can happen when local actors have an advantage in the processes or negotiations at stake. This is especially the case when international aid is in dialogue or competition with proprietors or public institutions.

Transformation of the public space typically creates frictions and tensions between the local authorities and the layer of aid. These tensions may reverberate and involve local and national levels of the state with different responses from an array of actors under different political priorities and different levels and pressure to comply – or not – with aid institutions. As public institutions are pressed to implement urban security features that might clash with the normal use of the public land, the tensions appear and translate in a balance of power where the aid layer generally prevails.

Disagreements with local upper classes, especially house owners and proprietors, most often revolve around prices, but might also affect cultural issues when expatriate and local norms appear too far apart. The example of the proprietor of an expatriate hotel who can benefit from the support of the state to get rid of an unsatisfying manager and his family in Juba illustrates the dependency of aid towards local actors that can end in brutal fashion. Most cases, however, involve disagreements where both sides do not agree on the price. They are usually resolved with an end of contract or changes of contractual conditions. Disputes and agreements are functions of the class relationships that set the frame for physical and social transformations of urban environments.

Chapter 7 Transformations

This chapter focusses on the transformations produced by the presence of international aid in cities. The local fabric of cities is not the same before, during and after a humanitarian mission as the combined forces of crisis and humanitarian presence restructure spatial practices (Büscher 2016). The objective of this chapter is to discuss transformations to the urban environment in the present and its future outcomes. The preceding chapter presented how the layer of international aid uses both the material and human local resources to support its presence. This chapter on transformation aims to discuss changes as perceived by local actors.

Economic and social effects of the presence of international aid on the social fabric of places where it operates is now widely recognised. It is commonly referred to as the "peacekeeping economy", to identify the economic effects that would not have taken place, or at a smaller scale, without the presence of the missions (Jennings 2014). The peacekeeping economy constitutes the major link between aid workers and the local social environment, including "everyone from the white-collar professional to those engaged in the informal, and occasionally illicit, work of providing service, sex, and security to international personnel" (Jennings and Bøås 2015).

The peacekeeping economy is characteristically dual, as foreign direct investments boost some sectors of the economy, albeit precariously, and that the aftermath might reserve additional difficulties for local economies and states (Aning and Edu-Afful 2013). Dual economies' dynamics reflect in urban settings in the social, economic and institutional realms. Transformation in the local environment can be conscious and willingly applied. However, effect that the presence of expatriates create on the local environment is partly uncontrolled. Working on the influences of humanitarian presence on urban governance, Büscher et al. note that "current processes of change that we take as a starting point […] are still very much ongoing, which makes it impossible to fully grasp its outcomes for the future" (Büscher, Komujuni, and Ashaba 2018).

Consequences of aid presence depend on the context itself, the panorama. The overall influence of international organisations are not the same in large and small cities and with large or small aid contingents. The overall size of the urban economy, and its capacity to deliver service provision to international standards before aid presence, defines whether specific urban services will be created for and by expatriates. The function and the purpose of the international presence are also likely to present different outcomes when it is meant to be temporary or permanent. The presence of international agencies in Nairobi is not linked to a particular crisis (with the exception of remote humanitarian management for Somalia, by a number of agencies), while in the other cities international presence is planned for the duration of a specific mission. Whether the mission ends after a number of years, as is the case in Abidjan, or effectively stays for an indefinite period is a matter of political context and the notion of temporary presence remains.

An important issue with the visibility of the transformation in the local environment is that some transformations are, precisely, visible. Physical transformation of the built environment, be they on private or public domain, can be assessed and discussed. However, another category of transformations is more difficult to apprehend. Modifications in the local urban economy are not necessarily either visible or retraceable to their exact origins. As with many social processes, transformations that may occur during the time of a mission are linked to multiplicity of causalities rather than a single origin. In this sense, socio-spatial transformations reflect perceptions and opinions of various actors more than traceable effects.

The notion of unintended effects of the peacekeeping economies recognises that negative influences of aid missions are involuntary (Thakur, Aoi, and De Coning 2007; Jennings 2010; Aning and Edu-Afful 2013; Autesserre 2014). Using a broad definition of the economy and the social, the fact that unintended effects occur on the local settings might indicate that these effects are also somewhat unexpected. However, the repetition of similar unintended consequences in a number of locations indicates instead that although unwanted, many of the effects are predictable. The regular occurrence of similar effects in different sites witnesses the regularity of social and economic transformations across countries (Edu-Afful and Aning 2015).

These transformations, whether one considers them positive or negative, are far-reaching and wide-ranging, although somehow seemingly random. The influence of peacekeepers and humanitarians (gender relations, trade, construction, prostitution) does not locate within a single problematic. The somewhat random and contradictory effects of the aid industry reflect unthought-of urban policies, as consequences are largely involuntary. International presence tends to propose urban policies, without naming them as such, which materialise in an equally disordered fashion. A number of effects on the urban economy and the built environment is expected, and their locations are predictable at some levels, such as the installation of aid workers in certain areas and the securitisation of premises, among others. Nevertheless, the after effect of these practices remain obscure and scattered.

Transformations in the urban environment, the economic and social life are perceived differently depending on the political and cultural context and social position of different urban dwellers. Beyond some visible effects, some transformations, such as institutional relations within a country, may occur in a game of scales and power relations. This case is apparent in the transformations of the public spaces, which is materialised through processes of shifts and balance of powers between and within administrations.

The below discussions on transformations is the analysis and grouping under categories, of a social process of unknown extent and duration. Are these observations the bulk of the phenomenon, or the tip of an iceberg? Only further research and critique of the present work can point whether the main transformations brought by international aid has been addressed or not. They appear here grouped into three broad types: the local urban economy, the transformation of the public space and the effects of defensive aesthetics on the local panorama. Finally, a reflection on the end of the UN mission in Abidjan discusses the shape of a post-humanitarian city. The overall approach of this chapter is double, in trying to understand local perceptions of urban transformations as well as proposing a conjecture of probable outcomes of the humanitarian city in the present and future.

7.1 Shaking Local Urban Economy

The presence of international aid provokes important direct and indirect effects on a variety of aspects of the local urban economy. These effects are grouped here in three categories of influences and transformations. As part of the local urban economy, the issues of employment, public services and modification of the housing market stand out. The first section discusses effects and perceptions of humanitarian presence on employment, both direct and indirect. The second section focusses on how preferences of international agencies for the private counterpart of public services, such as education and health, encourages the development of dual provision to expatriates versus most of the local dwellers. The third section investigates the question of rent hikes, home upgrades and the future of the built environment.

7.1.1 Local Employment

The direct and indirect employment opportunities created by the presence of aid in cities stand out as a major transformation of the local urban economy. Aid organisations rely directly on a local workforce for a variety of tasks, from clerical to manual employees, which largely surpasses the number of expatriates in any given country and city. Indirect employment in relation to aid also constitutes a large component of the workforce mobilised by the presence of aid. The precariousness of employment in relation to humanitarian presence provokes increasing financial difficulties for segments of the local workforce when missions end. The paradoxically negative effect of the end of a crisis provokes worries and tensions just at a time when the overall situation of the country is meant to improve.

The End of Direct Employment

Direct employment by international organisations produces many side effects. The new positions and their impact on the local economy have been described elsewhere and points to a multiplier and problematic effect on the local economy, with local employees investing their salaries in housing or consumption goods (Durch 2009; Beber et al. 2016). The higher salaries provided during missions are welcomed by local employees. However, the relationships between local workers and their organisations produce tensions during reduction of activities.

The reduction of UN activities in Ivory Coast indicates a likely path of direct effects on employment departure may have. Municipal authorities worry openly on the tensions that departure of the ONUCI will produce for the local economy. The Deputy Director of Technical Services in Marcory, Mr Xavier Akoa, notes that his main concern in relation to the departure of the UN mission is employment.

> *The departure of ONUCI will produce changes and affect purchasing power. [There] will be the loss of employment, and collateral damages will be enormous. This is another element of the mission: when they leave, unemployment rises. [...] And solicitations for work at the City Hall will go nonstop.*[81]

When I conducted this research in 2017, the UN mission and other agencies had already started scaling down their activities for a while. A number of former UN employees found themselves looking for new jobs, or going back to former activities.

81 Interview, Xavier Akoa, 10 May 2017.

Among those affected, Mr Jean K*, active as a pastor on Sundays in his community of Port-Bouët, is an organiser for areas social activities. During the week, Mr Jean K* now earns his living as a repairperson in a small residence in the Zone 4 of Marcory. "I worked for Unicef until 2015, but they did not renew my contract," says Mr Jean K*, showing a common distrust for international organisations. "That's because I refused to pay the human resources manager under the table."[82] Accusing local employees of international organisations of corruption is something I frequently heard during my interviews with former local employees or contractors. Whether the accusation is true or not, the insistence on the corruption of local UN employees illustrates well the bitterness created by the shrinking of a series of job opportunities.

In numerous countries of the South, discourses about corruption constitutes an essential representation of the state. Complaints about the state are accompanied by a thorough knowledge of "normal" practices and their comparisons with behaviour and demands of state employees. Distrust of international organisations may represent a sign of its inclusion as a representation of power similar to the state (A. Gupta 1995). The dependence on international agencies for jobs reflects that the departure of a UN mission is not the end of the presence of aid agencies. These have come to be part of the normality in African states and cities.

Mr Jean K*, along with other local UN employees in the sites of study, held a similar distrust with all other agencies in the country. This highlights Gupta's distinctions between the discursive construction of the state and its everyday practices. International organisations tend to view and present their practice of procurement and employment as a positive impact to mitigate corruption in the local markets and administration (Carnahan, Durch, and Gilmore 2006). Regardless of the accuracy in the local perceptions of corruption within these organisations (which I could not verify), bribes and kickbacks form part of the complex and controversial representations of international aid.

In the course of this research, discussions and interviews with current and former employees of the aid industry showed that their situated knowledge is remote from the valorising self-representation of the industry itself. The shrinking opportunities, with the reduction of humanitarian job offers only increases frustration. Direct humanitarian employment, with all its problematic aspects, rely on the "best prevailing local conditions" for employees (Carnahan, Gilmore, and Durch 2007). As these conditions risk depleting the local economy

82 Interview Jean K*, 5 May 2017.

from a number of the most skilled professionals, the closure of a mission poses risks of subsequent unemployment for this locally privileged workforce.

Some of the local clerical employees of aid organisations might find positions abroad, entering the market of international humanitarian staff, with higher salaries than local humanitarians working for the same organisations. Nevertheless, many local employees remain in their countries and cities after the departure of a mission. International staff positions are not necessarily seen as the best options for many, as local Malian UN staffer Adama* told me. "I will go if I can earn a much larger salary than what I am being proposed," he explains. "Otherwise with the combined housing costs I have here anyways with my house and what I will have to pay abroad, it will not make much difference for the effort."[83] Locally, possibilities to find new opportunities in the context of the departure of aid agencies depends on connections and skills as much as what the economic conditions will offer to skilled clerical jobseekers.

The Wide Variety of Indirect Employment and Businesses

The effect of the international presence on consumption and the job market is complex to assess. As Kaly Bagayogo, General Secretary of Koulikoro Town Hall, a provincial capital near Bamako where the European training mission (EUTM 2019) is based, stated: "My answer will be prosaic, non-mathematical, because there has not been any study of impact or scientific literature : We know that they go shopping, they go to entertainment places or bars. But here again, there has not been any assessment"[84]. The three types of places noted by the Mr Bagayogo points to entertainment and consumption. They are also places where the expatriates are visible and their weight in the local economy is easiest to conjecture.

However, a much larger body of local workers supporting the presence of aid forms depends of international missions for their income. The hiring of cleaners, the frequentation of hotels, bars and restaurants, consumption in the local markets or supermarkets by aid workers all reflect increasing activities in the local economy. As it is impossible to figure what might happen to this diverse workforce after the end of a mission, it is possible to conjecture that local employees will have to adapt to new conditions, with probable reduction of income. According to Mafa Fall, a Bamakoan fixer, handy craft activities tend to go back to normal. He explains that during the main surge of aid workers in the

83 Interview Adama*, date 10 April 2017.

84 Interview Kaly Bagayogo, 10 March 2016.

country during the years 2013 and after, the commands of expatriates led some artisans to experiment different materials and tastes.

> *Even for artists and artisans, things changed. There were new types of commands, like furniture in bamboo and rattan. Malians don't like this style much. You never see this type of furniture in Malian houses. We gave work to an artisan for more than six months. [...] It really is a demand targeted on expats. The gentleman says it does not sell any more. He went back to his former craft.*[85]

This suggests that the tastes of expatriates did not influence the Malian population. This particular case might be because adaptations of the local handicraft to expatriate taste does not find its market as it is neither local nor truly "Western", as associated to industrially produced commodities. As Kühn notes in Afghanistan, the production of handicraft for expatriates stimulates specific "orientalised" cultural forms. "In today's few Westernized supermarkets, which are highly protected and sell goods associated with Western demand, some artefacts seem likewise to be bought by Afghans in order to display a Western lifestyle." (Kühn 2016) Instead, in Bamako, the expatriate-oriented African handicraft did not survive the end of the large wave of expatriates.

Indirect employment in the urban economy points to a return to an earlier form of economic activities when possible. The overheating due to influxes of money in the economy might have provided the occasion to make savings or small investments. However, these temporary increases in income might as well have been lost in inflation or everyday consumption. Local needs and demand corresponding to distinct standards might reintegrate a workforce who adapted its skills and expertise to the taste of aid workers. Overall, economic developments in peacetime will determine the reconversion of most indirect activities.

7.1.2 Privatisation of Public Services

An important aspect of the presence of international organisation is the favouring of separate private systems for internationals when the local public services are not able to cope with the standards. These developments are striking in the case of health and, in family duty stations, with schools and education as well. International organisations do not create the duality between private and public institutions in African cities. Reliance in the private is a common occurrence within local elites who largely use it for its higher standards. However, the

85 Interview Mafa Fall, 22 April 2016.

overwhelming reliance on the private tends to favour a boost to the private wing of these services.

Schools in Family Duty Stations

Among the cities visited for this research, it is only in Nairobi that the question of the education of children is relevant for expatriates. Abidjan, Bamako and Juba have not been listed as "family duty stations" for aid workers. The notion of "family duty station" in the UN system refers to places in which employees are allowed to bring their spouses and children (United Nations 2017a). This type of classification of cities and countries is common across most humanitarian organisations, although they may be called differently, such as the "accompanied status" used by the Red Cross movement in similar meaning (IFRC 2019). This notion excludes places considered too dangerous or unstable.

With the possibility to bring children to duty stations, the question of education comes as a major preoccupation for expatriates. With the conditions of public education in African cities, where mentoring standards and resources are low (Materu 2007), internationals use the private sector to school their children. The practice of sending children of expatriates in private schools is not limited to countries of the South. International schools have long been characteristic of transnational elites, representing a high and standardised reference, which allows following a continuous curriculum when the duty station of the parents change.

The recruitment base of the teachers reflects the disconnection with the local schools, as salaries are higher than in the public school to enlarge the recruitment base. Marcy*, a foreign teacher in one of these schools explained how she decided to work in a private school. "It is a privilege bubble to teach there with other foreign teachers. But I could not live in Kenya with a salary of a Kenyan civil servant."[86] Pupils and teachers tend to include mostly expatriates, while in the case of her school, a sizable minority come from wealthy locals. The development of a dual education system in Nairobi goes beyond the expatriates and many of the country upper classes send their children to English-speaking private schools. The reliance of local elites on the private system witnesses how education systems risk a split between high quality education in the private versus an underfunded and understaffed public system.

Education of expatriate children brings the question of the social reproduction of aid workers that goes beyond the ambition of this research. However,

86 Interview Marcy*, 24 August 2016.

as noted in the field of transnational corporate executives, the upbringing of children in transnational, generally English-speaking settings, prepares class reproduction (Lam and Selmer 2004). Growing up in different locations within networks of expatriate schools prepares children to work themselves in highly mobile positions socialised within transnational milieu of networked enclaves of cosmopolitan elites.

Dual Health Services

The discrepancy between public and private health systems is the most striking. International organisations distribute lists of health facilities recommended in the country. In none of the case studies for this research, any of the recommended hospitals and clinics are public institutions. The UN in Nairobi recommends for example a series of facilities. The primary hospital for serious emergencies is the Aga Khan hospital, a non-profit private institution. In cases where the private sector is not considered to be up to the expected level of care and required specialisations, for instance trauma injuries, aid agencies set up their own facilities. This is typically the case in some peacekeeping mission, such as in South Sudan, where field hospitals are set in place by the medical-military components of missions. Recommended places in Juba include private clinics as well as hospitals run by the United Nations, whose access is restricted to internationals.

This use of private clinics encourages the reliance on an existing number of private health providers. The striking differences in the capacity between public and private health sector justifies the reliance on the private as much as it reinforces private clinics. Differences in the level of care is reflected in staffing and the available equipment. Staff working conditions in the two systems are also different, affecting the care in the health systems. In recent years, the salary conditions in both Kenya and Mali have justified long strikes by health workers. For five weeks in 2017, Malian doctors were on strike and only providing vital emergency care (RFI 2017). In Kenya, the same year, nurses took the street for five months over their salaries and general working conditions (Wangui 2017).

The building of the Golden Life hospital appears as an important by-product of the presence of the MINUSMA in Mali. However, the relative importance of the mission and the expatriates is equally difficult to assess, as the construction of the hospital is also entangled in local dynamics and health policies. "The Golden Life hospital is trying to get the injured from the mission in the North", a local employee of the mission considered. "So far, the level of care needed for heavy trauma injuries requires their evacuation to Dakar".[87]

The hospital's public releases do not mention or allude to the UN mission in its public releases. However, the development of a trauma care capacity at the time the injured soldiers of the MINUSMA are sent abroad for sanitary evacuation after first care in field hospitals in the North (Panyue 2016) appears at least as a convergence of interests between the official Malian health strategy and the large numbers of injured Blue Helmets. As public institutions have little capacity for the treatment of heavy trauma, the Minister of health explained to the press, "the quality of the offer could reduce sanitary evacuations. It will also give possibilities of training and internships for the hospital practitioners" (L'Essor 2017).

Treating patients in Mali instead of undertaking sanitary evacuations to other countries is also mentioned by the head of the clinic, Dr Eyüb Ibrahim as the reason for the 15 million dollars investors brought in the Malian capital (Aujourd'hui-Mali 2017). However, while the rumour in expatriate circles in Bamako emphasised that the hospital's first projected clientele would be injured UN personnel from the North, the hospital management only mentioned publicly medical treatment for Malians.[88]

The integration of aid workers within the local private markets of health responds to the limited resource and quality of care in public services. The use of one side of a dual health system reinforces the private sector, which can invest more in a profitable market. Boosting the development of private health system risks having the effect to push further the local elites into private health care. Typically expected result of such dual health system is further defunding of public care (Basu et al. 2012).

A Splintering of Public Services for the Future?

Reliance on the private sector for its better quality in the context of African cities is reminiscent of the other choices of international organisations in relation to the local environment. It is largely autonomous from the local environment and standards. While systematically pushing the standards of living of humanitarian workers up to Northern standards, the presence of aid separates from a local environment, either by material devices, such security devices, or institutional differentiation, relying on the private sector.

---

87 Interview with Adama*, 10 April 2017.

88 Solicited during this research for interview, the management of Golden Life did not respond to my inquiries.

The example of schools and health services functioning in parallel to the public system might seem innocuous since they tend to rely on existing facilities. In areas as sensitive as health and education, it is not surprising that both organisations and people rely on what represents the best available standard. With or without organisational instruction to rely on the private sector in these domains, it is likely that the personal choices of expatriates would orient on similar choices.

Promotion of private initiatives reinforces the bubble effect of populations living under different standards. Particular extensions of private health and education risks reinforcing dual standards for the wealthy and the poor. However, it is also possible to conjecture a different course in the influence of the reinforcement of the quality of care and education. A more contrasted potential effect of the reinforcement of standards in the private could be that the presence of higher-quality services acts as an incentive to reinforce public services. In that scenario the public system would use the highest available care or education as a benchmark for its own development.

It is difficult to conjecture whether the more positive scenario of the implementation of better overall standards will effectively enhance or reduce the local services to the majority. Both scenarios of general improvement and splintering of public services are possible (C. Scott 2002; Brunello and Rocco 2008). However, improvements in the services will largely depend on the capacity of local populations and professionals to be heard and the will of institutions to invest resources in public services. In this regard, the trade union struggles in Mali and Kenya might represent good and bad omen, depending on the perspective. On the one hand, the determination of health care workers to be heard on their work conditions which can ultimately bring better quality of care. On the other hand, the duration of the social movements and the readiness of the state to keep health care facilities closed or understaffed for such a long period indicates a worrying disdain for functioning and functional public services.

7.1.3 The Built Environment in the Local Economy

The following discussion aims to understand the modifications of the built environment at the scale of individual housing units and its social effects. The use of land, houses and apartments by international organisations affects the local housing markets. Documented evidence of the phenomenon relies largely on word-of-mouth from local actors. It is, however, largely recognised among the local populations as a major effect in their own housing possibilities and choices. The section immediately below will provide some context and discussion of the phenomenon of rent increase from the perspective of various actors, including proprietors, tenants and municipalities.

The use of individual apartments and buildings by aid agencies and aid workers translates in upgrades and adaptations of the buildings, either by expatriates themselves, or by proprietors eager to provide a comfort standing adapted to a foreign demand. As the material form and use of houses involves direct modifications, it begs the question whether this type of transformations will be maintained in place in the future, when aid workers' presence decreases. Will new units of different standing form part of the future city or be readapted for the local housing demand?

Fears of Rent Increases

The question of rent hikes where the international aid operates remains unknown, since public or private institutions do not monitor them. However, local inhabitants frequently identify price increases as the principal effect of aid organisation's presence on their lives. However, the perception of the rent hikes, either as burden or as opportunity, is contingent to their social and geographic position. Increases in land prices are not similar to proprietors or tenants. Even among tenants, not all social classes are affected equally by the phenomenon of the rent increase. Middle- and upper-middle classes notice a direct competition with international aid workers on the housing market, while housing for the poor does not fit the standards for expatriates.

The case of PAM Services, a small housing and car rental business in Bamako, exposes the co-occurrence of two separate house rent systems and prices in the same city. Djelika Cissé, an executive in this company consider that the presence of the expatriates did not influence the pricing of the apartments her company rents. Her explanation is justified by the fact that two separate standards of housing already existed in the city. The PAM Services company is present on the house market for the poor and the rich. Furnished apartments are much more expensive than unfurnished ones.

> *The rent for furnished apartments goes up to 900'000 a month for the three rooms and living room. [...] We did not raise the prices with the [UN mission]. And our prices for the locals have not changed in 15 years. It can never be higher than 150'000 a month for a Malian family.*[89]

89 Interview Djelika Cissé, 18 March 2016.

Figure 67: Collected image. Houses rented by PAM services in Bako Djicoroni

The studios and apartments are fully equipped with a washing machine, Wifi, TV, AC and other amenities, stabilised by the presence of an electricity generator (Figure 67). The standard prices for these apartments represent several times the salary of any Malian employee. On the other hand, the prices the company rents to Malian are not in concurrence with the UN mission, as "the MINUSMA is not interested in the houses that the Malians use. They want something more luxurious."

The differences in prices are justified by the amenities and electricity consumption. Djelika Cissé points to the numerous costs distinct from the price of the real estate:

> *Apartments in the city centre are a completely different standing. Here we have a shower, a fridge, a microwave and the AC. And we cover the electricity bills at 5000 per day. Electricity is very expensive in Mali. And the apartments for the Malians have no running water!*

If consumption justifies the existence of two different categories of housing for separate dwellers, the effect of high prices does not affect working-class neighbourhoods, where dwellers can adjust the cost of the rent with their consumption. However, most observers consider that the presence of the expatriates have affected the local middle class.

According to Aminata Traoré, a public intellectual and activist implicated in urban renovation in working class neighbourhoods – and very critical of the UN Mission in Mali –, the presence of the expatriates did have effect on suburban sprawl in Bamako:

The rent of villas increased the prices and pushed the middle classes out of some neighbourhoods. Rent prices increased and are pushing this middle class towards the periphery. Even the secretaries at the UN have higher salaries than the Malians.[90]

This story corresponds to the young family who housed me in Bamako during my field visits. The father of the family, then employee of a small Malian NGO told me how difficult it was finding a house in the city since the arrival of the Mission. The family moved to the outskirts of the city, in the neighbourhood of Sotuba, where they rented the first floor of a small house. Other middle-class families confirmed this push to urban sprawl due to rent increases. It is also congruent with earlier finding in economic geography of aid, whose models "predicts significant intensification of land use along the urban periphery as a result of increased prices for housing" (Alix-Garcia, Bartlett, and Saah 2012). However, the combined and often contradictory effects of humanitarian crises, humanitarian response and humanitarian presence make predicting the influence on market prices complex (Alix-Garcia, Bartlett, and Saah 2013).

Among the difficulties to assess effects is the lack of quantitative data to monitor the phenomenon. Representatives of municipalities and the state were unable to confirm whether the presence of international aid influenced the general rent and real estate prices. No official or quantitative monitoring of rent prices takes place in the cities where I conducted the research. To my knowledge, no monitoring of prices by public institutions exists. Knowledge of the phenomenon is purely based on word to mouth and direct but fractional information. Aboubacar Bougoudogo, the General Secretary of the Commune 4 in Bamako explains why no data or information is collected on the issue:

We know there was a steep rent hike. The prices of buildings increased. As we are in a liberal system, the proprietor is free to decide the rent he wants. There is not yet a law to fix a cap to rents. The state has a project on rent regulation. But there is no uniform price. Even significant variation in the same neighbourhood. […] On our side, we do not monitor it.[91]

The project of rent control has been made into law in 2017. However, there is little chance that it will imply quantitative monitoring of rents, which could give a precise picture of the phenomenon. As Mr Youssouf Sanogo in charge of keeping the planning maps of the Commune 5 and Ms Minte Kouyatu, Head of the Domaines in charge of land properties, monitoring of any aspect of real estate remains limited by the technical resources of the Commune. "We do have some use of the GIS software MapInfo, but we still use paper maps to calculate the

90 Interview Aminata Traoré, 15 April 2016.

91 Interview Aboubacar Bougoudogo, 16 March 2016.

number of square metres in a property," pointed Mr Sanogo.[92] His colleague at the Commune 5, Ms Kouyatu, showed me the Excel files used to keep the names of all property owners, she pointed that the database was "not up to the level we wish it was", despite the importance of the document for house owners as well as the authorities who use the documents as reference for local taxes.[93] Lack of the technical instruments and staff capacity to implement updated registers prevent the implementations of monitoring methods in the near future, even within a legal framework to protect tenants.

Similar responses come from other Bamakoan Communes affected by the presence of international aid workers. As explained by Ousmane Bah, the General Secretary of the Commune 5, rent increases are only known informally, from conversations with inhabitants and businesses. Although the neighbourhood of Badalabougou stands within the limits of the Commune 5's authority, the municipality can only follow the word of mouth for any transformation in the local economy:

> *We do not follow the question of rents directly. But we know that in practice their presence had an effect in increasing rents. It is one part of their contribution to the economy. […] They do shopping, they go to gas stations, and they buy internet and phone credit.*[94]

In some case, as the planning department in Cocody, Abidjan, observers seemed to doubt the effect of the UN mission on prices. Mr Ajavon mainly attributes rent hikes to a general increase in land prices. He considers higher demand in real estate, and subsequent increase in rent in the city as a result of expanding infrastructure and service networks. He recognises the specific role of the UN mission as a very wealthy and generous land tenant:

> *The ONUCI was renting the terrain right here in front. Now that they left, the family will sell the 6'600 square metres at 350'000 per square metre. They will sell. For Sure! Maybe just a little cheaper.* [95]

The stability or increase in housing rents and real estate purchases in Abidjan is indeed supported by economic growth and investments. The Ivorian context of economic recovery after the end of the armed conflict (despite after effects in forms of limited army rebellions) more than compensates the effect of the reduction of direct investment by international organisations. Witnessing numerous

92 Interview Youssouf Sanogo, 9 March 2016.
93 Interview Minte Kouyatu, 9 March 2016.
94 Interview Ousmane Bah, 9 March 2016.
95 Interview Mr Ajavon, 2 May 2017.

land transactions on constructible areas, Mr Ajavon considers that the departure of the mission did not have the effect of reducing land prices. Instead, he notes that his Commune is attractive to all types of land buyers, from lower middle class to the richest in the city:

> *Everything is on the rise. And the boom has no relation with ONUCI. There are embassies, the African Development Bank and private banks. And people want to live in Cocody. The land owners understand it. Increases are spectacular!*

The middle and upper middle class appear as the people most affected and concerned by rent hikes, since they are the ones in concurrence with foreign aid workers. In this particular instance, the prohibition of dwelling in poor areas of a city most likely has a protective effect on the rent hike in the housing market. As Adama*, a local UN employee and house owner in Lafiabougou explains: "I can rent my mother's house in Faladié to an international for a good price when she's away. But in my area, Lafiabougou, there was no change in house prices. It is not in the area permitted to expats."[96] In terms of rent hikes, the zoning of cities may have a protective effect. The inclusion of a neighbourhood in the areas forbidden to internationals protects the inhabitants against the competition of expatriates.

Real estate professionals and private house owners seem quite confident that they can raise prices. While some are reluctant to admit that they raised prices for expatriates, fixers seem to be in a good position to witness. And they are not so cautious to recognise that the prices go up significantly. Mafa Fall, founder of a small company to accommodate expatriates and NGOs when numerous aid organisations arrived in Bamako, claims, "the prices for houses rocketed! Especially at the beginning of 2013. The prices for houses could go up 50 % in one month."[97]

With high demand for houses and large resources of aid workers backed up by their organisations, not much prevents rents skyrocketing. As Mafa Fall recall when helping one WFP expatriate find a house:

> *The house owner decided the price. And no negotiations. Expats actually never complained of the rents. I even had once a client who told himself to the house owner that he could increase the rent from one million to a million and a half. His organisation would pay anyways. I think this is not normal.*

The bubble of skyrocketing rents reduced after the main wave of expatriates arriving in 2013. By 2016, many expatriates who formed part of short-term

96 Interview Adama*, 10 April 2016.
97 Interview Mafa Fall, 22 April 2016.

missions and staff deployment had already left the country for subsequent missions. "Rent went down again. There are numerous empty houses now," according to Mafa Fall. "But it is not yet back at the level of before, three or four years ago." However, the prices will likely not get back to earlier levels, especially if house owners have invested in house upgrades and furniture.

In some cases, the expectation of high returns in renting to international organisation might be so high that they end up crashing deals. The public rumour in relation the land used by the UN mission in Bamako, as reported by hotel manager Fanny Mauron, was that the MINUSMA was eyeing at a large terrain in the north of the city to install offices, barracks and logistics base. To prevent high demands from the proprietors, the UN mission sent an intermediary who cut a deal for a certain monthly amount. "When the proprietor later understood who wanted the terrain, he asked for the triple of the original amount."[98] As a result, the deal broke and the MINUSMA found another location, near the international airport.

Large portions of the housing market seem to be left unaffected by the increase of the prices of rent for the middle class. This includes housing in both the formal and the informal areas. As one house owner in Abidjan cynically told me when discussing how much tenants paid and where she could increase the rents or not. She pointed that she could not increase the rent in the working class municipality of Yopougon. Many working-class areas remain on a separate track of rent increase, related to the development of infrastructure and proximity to services and transport to business districts.[99] As Mr Ajavon, also in Abidjan, noted both as an employee of the Commune of Cocody and as an owner of urban land, the development of new roads massively increased the prices all along the newly asphalted networks.

Increases in land and real estate prices do not only interest proprietors eager to benefit from the housing markets. While municipalities might worry that the dwellers suffer from the burden of high rent, they also see a clear benefit in the phenomenon. Mr Ajavon in Cocody and Mr Akoa in Marcory both pointed that increases in real estate bring higher local tax revenues. Mr Ajavon considers how his Commune collects 90 % of its budget on housing tax. High land price and housing taxes might interest the other municipalities of Abidjan, even if the increases are not located on under their administrative watch. Changes in the

98 Interview with Fanny Mauron, 29 March 2016.
99 Interview Cécile*, 27 April 2017.

division of tax revenues might change in the future, although the main worry of municipal authorities is the transparency of the state tax collection mechanisms:

> *The state says now that it will create a common pot for taxes to equalise, with the Communes disadvantaged by smaller revenues. It is not a bad system, but we must know how the state will collect the taxes.*[100]

In Marcory, town hall administrators were quick to recognise the benefits of UN presence in their part of Abidjan. As Mr Akoa explains, "The impact was the highest when ONUCI officers were staying in the hotels." Housing tax revenue from past, present and future presence of expatriation is welcomed to the municipal budget, and city employees monitor and evaluate the macro effects of multilateral institutions. "The presence of the [African Development Bank] is a good thing for us," explains Mr Akoa. "But they mainly settle in Cocody, where their office is located, and their impact is not comparable to the effect ONUCI had here."[101]

Foreseeable Future for the Uses of a Renewed Built Environment

The building and furnishing of a number of apartment blocks to accommodate many individual tenants for the period of a mission brings the question of the sustainability of these buildings as housing units. As Jennings noted in Monrovia (Jennings 2016), proprietors do not necessarily bother worrying of the aftermath. If a building has been rented at a high price for a certain period, the returns on investment might be already satisfying when aid workers leave the country.

Such housing business model is possible for large investors. The profits in fact are largely dependent on the furnished aspect of the apartment. In any case, AC systems, televisions, and other house furniture can be resold. As studios and small apartments do not fit the local demand, where elites prefer individual houses. However, the opportunity to rent to corporate executives remains a possibility.

At the price of the location of furnished houses, proprietors of multiple apartments can easily afford to keep many of them empty for a long period. At the scale of the city, this might result in keeping large pools of empty apartments and houses for potential clients. Profitability might by reduced compared to periods with large numbers of tenants. However, considering the extremely high rents for an apartment, the investment might remain profitable.

---

100 Interview Mr Ajavon, 2 May 2017.

101 Interview Xavier Akoa, 10 May 2017.

Transformation of an area may occur through undirected process oriented by common norms and practices of a group. The requests for high walls and barbed wires, as well as renovations, if directed on localised areas produce new forms on the territory without formal arrangement between the actors. As Mafa Fall pointed from his work as a fixer, the massive arrival of expatriates created a dynamic changing many areas. "Whole neighbourhoods have been renovated. At the Hippodrome three streets have completely changed", he explains. The list of elements that changed is mostly the response to security concerns: "Walls are higher. Guards! Barbed wire! And new paint. "[102]

Multiple interventions at the scale of a building can transform the outlook of a neighbourhood, by repetition. The security and comfort norms of expatriates, either as a personal initiative informed by spatial habitus or directly ordered by organisational security rules and hierarchy, modify urban aspect.

What the transformations of individual houses express on the long-term effect over individual buildings remain vague. I had witnessed the negotiations of an NGO which was ending its mission in Mali with the owner of the house they had been using for a year to house their staff and office. The NGO had rented the house and invested some material in the house. This included beds, stove and microwave, refrigerator, and more importantly a powerful 20KwH Trident diesel electric generator, which guaranteed continuous power provision for the house during cuts on the city grid. As this agency was leaving the country, logisticians aimed to negotiate with the proprietors to sell him the material before leaving.

The logisticians were keen to point how much all the material used for the house was increasing the overall value of the house, which could be now rented at much higher price with all the upgrades. However, playing on the fact that the NGO was going to leave soon and could not afford to take much time to look for other potential buyers, the proprietor efficiently bargained the prices down and bought all the furniture and generators discounted. Nevertheless, from the perspective of the proprietor the house upgrades were not necessarily meant to stay in place. A few days after the departure of the NGO from Mali, the proprietor came to collect all the material and charged it on a truck, leaving the house in its original state from a year earlier.

I do not know what happened next to all the material. It might have ended in a different house, or simply be sold to another buyer, who could guarantee faster and better return on investment. This episode shows how modification of individual houses by aid workers does not necessarily mean that the changes will

---

102 Interview Mafa Fall, 22 April 2016.

remain on said places. As the future of the modifications and upgrades brought by international aid is complex to predict, this particular example can help imagine not how the built environment will be, but how local entrepreneurs will likely use the transformations. Looking for the highest returns on any of their investments, local property owners search for a diversity of opportunities. Their perception of the best investments will likely affect the future of their properties in all cities.

7.2 Control and Power in the Public Space

Modification of the public space by international organisations constitutes the most apparent of transformations in urban settings. The visibility of such a transformative process strikes when it contrasts with normal uses of space. It involves security devices as well as investment in infrastructure works, as tendering by the largest organisations are regularly published during missions (H. Walker and Harland 2008). The large influx of money on a variety of intervention on the public space marks the presence of international organisations in the local urban panorama.

Transformations in the public domain constitute the primary visible statement of presence by aid institutions. Modifications of the form of public domain constitute the most important statement towards the local population, although the perceptions of the latter might include open opposition, approval or indifference. These transformations reflect silent and invisible processes of negotiations between local actors and the layer of international aid.

Understanding public perceptions of minor or major changes in the public space is a perilous enterprise. Who can tell whether people feel affected by the installation of security devices and other interventions in the public domain? This description of the reactions to changes in the public space instead returns the impressions of a number of specialised observers and actors in the municipalities. It also attempts to echo the impressions of a number of laypeople and other observers of the scene of urban transformations.

7.2.1 Road Blocks and Sand Bastions in the Street

International agencies, embassies, but also hotels and individuals have different emphases on the extent to which they want to increase their security infrastructure, and the visibility of this infrastructure. One of the radical forms of this development of security is when the walls and concertinas not only ornate the houses, but go out on the public space. These transformations were visible in Bamako from the beginning of the year 2013, when roadblocks and Hesco bastions started to be seen in front of important buildings and private barriers be installed in different parts of the city.

The quiet and affluent area of Badalabougou saw the installation of sandbags in the street where the African-led International Support Mission to Mali (AFISMA) installed its HQ, at the beginning of 2013. The AFISMA installed Hesco bastions, a type of sandbags maintained with a wire mesh commonly used by the military for "perimeter protection" (HESCO 2018). These bastions are meant to absorb bullets and limit the destruction caused by explosions. This type of sandbags can also be used to limit traffic and force driving cars to slow down in the area. Soldiers from the African mission operated vehicle checks and surveillance next to the bastions for the following months.

When the UN mission MINUSMA replaced the AFISMA a few months later in July 2013, it resulted in a massive increase in administrative and military personnel. The MINUSMA took its quarters in one of Bamako's largest luxury hotels, l'Amitié. The AFISMA mission left while the sandbags stayed in the area. The Hesco bastions remained in the street and lost their sand quietly to the dusty Bamako streets in the following months and years. Some neighbours, among the remaining modest Malians still living in the area, now use the sandbags to hang their clothes dry after cleaning. The destiny of these sandbags suggests that the traces left of security devices keep being used, albeit in a completely different meaning, after they become obsolete (Figure 68).

This same area of Badalabougou had hosted for years many diplomatic missions. Among those, the German embassy trailed German schools and other institutes, which marked its political and cultural presence in the neighbourhood. Nevertheless, the arrival and installation of UN agencies in the area led to unusual transformations of roads and public space. In the case of three UN agencies (WFP, OCHA and UNMAS) in the area, road barriers were installed to control the passing traffic. The control of the traffic by an actor that does not belong to either the municipality or the state provokes mixed reactions at the different levels of the state.

Local employees of the communes of Bamako explain their difficulties to make the urban laws and regulations be respected. The scarce resource of the different levels of the state in Mali limits its power to have essential safety regulations enforced. A couple of months before my 2016 visit to Bamako, a brand new eight storeys building crumbled in the middle of the night and killed two people driving by in a car (Coulibaly 2015). Gouro Landouré, of the Service of Urban Planning pointed this example to illustrate his difficulties to assess whether construction follows building permits and city standards. The owner and promoter

Figure 68: HESCO sandbags used to hang drying clothes in Badalabougou

of the building had illegally added two storeys from the plan approved by the authorities. Another building belonging to the same property developer had crumbled two years before, in another area of Bamako.

Diverse types of illegal constructions and occupation of the public space are commonplace in Bamako. The persistence of these practices find different explanations when talking to professionals. They illustrate how even in serious cases of public safety, the representatives of the state are not able to make the law be respected. As Urbanist Gouro Landouré pointed in relation to respect of city planning:

> *The problem for us urbanists is we have little resources to verify. We must often be on the field to check constructions. On a Commune like ours, with at least 10 quartiers, we ought to be circling each morning. But we don't even have a car. We're even often out of gas for the moped. Even if we were able to verify everything, we'll have trouble with repeated infringement. If we demand to stop a construction site, the masons will come back as soon as we're gone.*[103]

103 Interview Gouro Landouré, 9 March 2016.

The main base of the MINUSMA in the city of Bamako was not an issue for the city services, as roadblocks and other barriers are all located within the perimeter of the Hotel Amitié, on private land. The major artery Avenue de la Marne, on the front of the hotel was only lightly affected by the presence of the roadblocks and armoured vehicles. Nevertheless, this was not the case for many of the UN offices, where control of the public road form integral part of security measures. The AFISMA had installed sandbags as soon as they arrived in Badalabougou, and at least three UN agencies started to install barriers in several streets during the year 2013 onwards.

Double barriers in the streets at the front entrances of UN agencies are common in Bamako and in other cities. The barriers limit the passing of cars in front of the main office doors. Security guards do not normally check the identification papers of the drivers and passengers before they enter the buildings. Instead, the common practice is that the guards verify if no explosive device is hidden under the car using a small convex mirror. UN employees, visitors, neighbours and other road users are equally screened in the public space.

Barriers in the low traffic neighbourhood streets of Badalabougou did not bother the municipal authorities. As Ousmane Bah, the General Secretary of the Commune 5 describes how the authorisations were signed following reports from the technical services. "They asked if they could install barriers," explains Mr Bah. "We conducted a feasibility assessment to verify if it would not cause too many restrictions for the population and the traffic."[104] Technical assessments are conducted under the authority Mr Amadou Dagno, head of the Urban Environment Protection Brigade (BUPE)[105] for the Commune 5, which approved the barriers.

"The demand for the barriers was submitted to the Mayor's office, who sent the technical services to figure if the barrier would not harm the public and traffic," explains Mr Dagno. "We asked the neighbours if it was a problem for them. As the report came positive, the installation was authorised." In this case, positive responses from the BUPE and other technical services allowed successively all major aid agencies to install their security devices. However, Mr Dagno also points that his services were not asked for some of the new devices. Sandbags in the neighbourhood had been installed without assessments of the town hall's technical services. Installation of these devices were legal, although it did not require the approval of municipal authorities. "We were not involved in

104 Interview Ousmane Bah, 9 March 2016.

105 Brigade Urbaine de Protection de l'Environnement.

the decision", summarises Mr Dagno. "I think it happened at a high level. At the Ministry of Interior, or the Bamako Governorate."[106]

7.2.2 The Radisson Hotel and the Levels of the State

In November 2015, a jihadist commando attacked the hotel Radisson BLU in Bamako. The mass shooting of guests of the hotel left 20 people dead. The strategy of attacking hotels was used in other West African countries, attacking tourist resorts in Burkina Faso and Ivory Coast as well (Bensimon 2016). The attacks against hotels provided in all cases a special visibility, as the news of the incident were front-page news well beyond the region. The publicity provided by assaults against international hotels is in itself the main motive for such attacks by armed groups.

The attack against the nightclub La Terrasse, earlier in 2015 led expatriates to avoid going outside for dinner or drinks. Parties started to be increasingly organised in aid workers' houses. Insistent recommendations by aid agencies not to frequent nightclubs, combined with a genuine fear that similar event might repeat, changed the habits of many who had been used to Bamako nightlife. In parallel, many Malians seemed wary of going out to places frequented by international workers in Bamako. This combined local and expatriate fears led to many previously popular bars and clubs now almost deserted. However, the attack against the Radisson Hotel took another dimension, with consequences for security practices throughout Bamako, because of the unprecedented scale and death toll of the assault.

The Radisson five-star hotel was home to a number of international organisations' representatives and diplomats. Important delegations of high-ranking internationals involved with the political settlement process in the North had been staying there. It was also the regular hotel of the Air France crews during overnight stays in Bamako. The response to the attack from the Radisson BLU was the increase in security measures around the hotel that collided with the public use of space, with the installation of security devices that would completely cut circulation in the street in front of the hotel.

The barriers installed at both ends of the road, completely blocked circulation for vehicles and pedestrians alike. Only guests, employees or visitors of the hotel are now allowed to pass, in an effective privatisation of the road. The complete discussion of the process for the installation of this barrier shows that this breach of the urban regulation mobilised different levels of the state. The municipality,

106 Interview Amadou Dagno, 9 March 2016.

the district of Bamako and the Malian state intervened in the discussion constructing a balance of power resulting in transformation of the public space.

The politics of scale in the case of Bamako suggests the intervention of interconnected economic, social and political processes results in the transformation of a locality. As Swyngedouw and Heynen explain, "there is no longer an outside or limit to the city, and the urban process harbours social [...] processes that are embedded in dense and multi-layered networks of local, regional, national and global connections." (Swyngedouw and Heynen 2004). The barrier on the road is the physical and social result of the cross-scalar relations of power resulting in the transgression of official spatial norms and regulation.

Located in the ACI 2000 quartier, an urban development project on the site of the former military airport, the Radisson stands on the Commune 4, whose Mayor is former Prime Minister Moussa Mara. The General Secretary of the Commune 4, Aboubacar Bougoudogo, explained that the Mayor office accepted "all" demands for new road barriers in the Commune. "The partner is the King," explains Mr Bougoudogo.[107] He justifies his position by the numerous programmes held by international cooperation in the goals of the social, cultural and economic development for Mali.

The General Secretary of the Commune sums the position of the Mayor office as coordinating development programmes with an array of different local and international actors, which includes embassies and multilateral organisations, as well as the private.

> *After the attack against the Radisson, we reduced traffic around the hotel. There is a reduction of mobility. It is not the only example. The Spanish embassy also asked us to install barriers to reduce traffic.*

However, while the municipality, as the local level of the state, accepted all demands from its international partners, others have been more reluctant to subordinate the planning laws to the demands. The Environment Brigade (BUPE)[108], in charge of environment and the public road domains for the whole District of Bamako, with offices in the different municipalities was opposed to the barriers. In her evaluation of the demand for closing the road, Ms Fatima Sidiba, claims that demands to block completely the road were anterior to the shooting. At the time, BUPE only authorised concrete roadblocks and a barrier to reduce traffic.

107 Interview Aboubacar Bougoudogo, 16 March 2016.

108 Brigade Urbaine de Protection de l'Environnement.

Private guards operated the manned barriers, lifting them after control, but the road was not completely blocked to cars and pedestrians.[109]

The severity of the attack against the Radisson hotel changed the compromise between the services of the districts and the Mayor. Mr Bakary Fané, head of the BUPE for the Commune 4 was still opposed to the barriers completely blocking the road after the attack. Nevertheless, major works and upgrade of the barrier were authorised by a change in the scale of the assault.

The political repercussions and the publicity around the attack had been overwhelming for the municipality. For Mr Fané, urban security features had been eventually installed because the assault against the hotel Radisson "is a particular case. It became a national issue, even international with all the foreigners involved. City Hall authorised the barrier, because the Mayor was overwhelmed."[110] According to Mr Fané, the Commune 4 accepted a transformation bypassing the authority of the District of Bamako that he represents, because political and economic actors of a higher scale pressured on the issue.

The Radisson BLU private company and the Malian state were powerful enough to convince municipal authorities to authorise the barrier. However, some representatives of the Malian state were not keen to allow the transformation either. The urban planning services (Services de l'Urbanisme), directly respondent to the Ministry of Urbanism had opposed the transformation. "Here in the Commune 4, we did not accept anything, but the Mayor signed the authorisation nevertheless," claimed Mr Dramane Dembelé, head of urban planning at the Commune 4. His authority as representative to the municipalities of the Ministry of Urbanism was not enough to stop the project of the barrier.

> *This hotel is a private property. It cannot keep the public domain as hostage. It was the same in the ACI 2000, where a barrier blocks the road in front of a hotel where the French military took quarters.[…] The road is now completely blocked. It prevents free movements on the public roads. And it generates traffic now that people are forced to circumvent the street. [..] The Radisson should have thought this through and planned their security from the outset, similar to fire alarms and exits […] when they submitted the building authorisation.*

Use and control of the public domain by a private actor is problematic for Mr Dembelé, who considers that the foreign presence in the hotel explains this exception to the local rules of urbanism. "The Radisson became a target when the Westerners came there," he considers. "Other hotels do not have such barriers.

---

109 Interview Fatima Sidiba, 16 March 2016.

110 Interview Bakary Fané, 16 March 2016.

It only happens when MINUSMA and [the French military mission] Serval are there." Many of his colleagues in Bamako share his frustration with the power of foreign organisations.

As an Urbanist, Mr Dembelé is certain of his role in protecting the application of the national law regarding territorial and urban regulations. "All cases of barriers which have been submitted, the Services of urban planning refused them. The law does not accept people blocking the public domain"[111] According to Mr Dembelé, other urbanists representing the state as advisors to the six Mayors of the district of Bamako support his position. Despite representing the power of the state, local authorities were not listened to.

> *We have our regional briefings. All Urbanists are against [the barriers]. Blocking a road is not efficient for security. There are thousand ways to arrive in an area. [...]I am not a security specialist, but we can install smaller barriers. Cameras and so on. We are in the 21st century. This can not be accepted like that. Blocking the street completely is unfair for the public. And by the way, a zero danger situation does not exist.*

Mr Dembelé suggests his expertise was sidelined by more political consideration by the state and his technical expertise on planning overruled by considerations of security design. The exposition of the case and the acceptance by the Mayor to transform the public domain has put him in contradiction with representative of higher levels of the state. Nevertheless, under the scrutiny of Malian political authorities and a major private company, the Mayor bypassed the higher authority of district and national laws to grant a private actor the authority to block a public road with security devices.

The works to repair the Radisson and build the security devices took six weeks (BBC News 2015). When I visited the hotel, a couple of months later, it was reportedly at only 15 % full. The reduced number of guests was visible from the almost empty restaurant and terrace. Visiting the hotel in 2016, I sat at the outside bar and talked with the young employees serving drinks to the rare customers. Replying to my question whether they, or their families, were worried about working there, one employee told me, "on the contrary, the place had become the most secure in the city since the attack".[112] However, the reassurance of the staff did not extend to all, especially among customers. Another employee told me the anecdote of the hotel fitness users who hid themselves in panic, because a cleaner was listening Coran recitations on his MP3.

---

111 Interview Dramane Dembelé, 16 March 2016.

112 Observation Notebook, 15 April 2016.

Other actors and businesses continue having diverging understandings of risk and protection from danger. The frequentation of the hotel remained low. An institution like Air France was not keen to send its staff to rest at the Radisson, even with the new security measures, repairs and upgrade. A Radisson staff who wishes to remain anonymous told me almost two years later that, Air France staff had not come back to the hotel, and changed their reference hotel in Bamako, as they asked tougher security measures before agreeing to come back as guests. Reportedly, the attackers wished to specifically target Air France staff as retaliation against the French military intervention in Mali (Freeman 2015).

The example of the Radisson Hotel illustrates the complex net of power relations set in a controversy on the public space. Different levels of the state at different scalar responsibilities contradicted themselves. Individual reactions to the event and security policies were also variable. Private and public, local and international actors understood risk and protection differently, resulting on a compromise as a blocking device and increased surveillance.

Beyond the surroundings of the hotel, the event triggered a chain reaction to many other actors in the aid industry sector in modifying their approach of security. Expatriates were visibly less present in many bars and restaurants in Bamako. Hotel managers all across the city started to review their security policy in light of the event. Protection measures by increasing security staff or adding material devices intend to prevent the risk of renewed attacks. Some bars located on main roads installed bulletproof glass between their terrace and the public space.[113]

The shockwave of a particular violent event spread in a moral panic and widespread changes of attitude towards security. The Radisson attack presents a case in point where an extreme event transforms the normality of some modes of social life. The repetition of armed attacks against foreigners within Mali and beyond, in Burkina Faso and Ivory Coast for instance, has indeed marked the deepening of security policies beyond Bamako and Mali itself. The attack against a hotel in Grand-Bassam, a seaside resort on the outskirts of Abidjan, by Malian jihadists reduced tourist frequentation and transformed security measures around hotels. Hotels on the beachfront have hired armed guards, screening passers-by and guests with hunting rifles in their hands.

Transformations and the installation of barriers may be well accepted by municipalities. In Abidjan the urban planners of Cocody and Marcory often welcome the presence of international organisations as guests. Heads of the Urban

113 Observation Notebook, 7 April 2017.

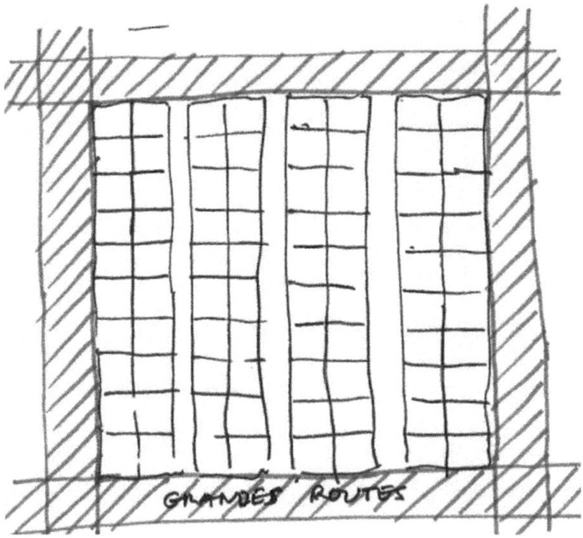

Figure 69: Sketch of a residential neighbourhood in Cocody. Four main roads close the neighbourhood. Barriers on each side of a residential street effectively close the traffic, with control delegated to private guards

Planning in Cocody and Abidjan are keen to show their willingness to accommodate international organisations to incite them to settle in their areas.

Demands from international organisations to install urban barriers on the public domains are frequent, according to Mr Ajavon, at the Urban Planning of Cocody. Many of the residential areas of Cocody are structured as a rectangular neighbourhood of parallel streets and the houses facing each other on parcels of equal size (Figure 69). When Unicef took one of the houses, they asked the permission to build barriers at each end of the street. Paid for and operated by Unicef guards, the closing of the public domain is not normally accepted in Abidjan's urbanism regulations.

The demand for barriers by Unicef was accepted along demands from other organisations and embassies, as Mr Ajavon explains:

> *Unicef installed a barrier for security reasons. We accepted although it was on the communal way. We have to give them good conditions, because they come to help. We derogate to the rule. [...] We might refuse in some cases if it is too bothersome. But people are*

reasonable and the modifications are not too problematic. With Unicef, people can still circulate. They were not arrogant in their demand.[114]

The Cocody municipality is keen to derogate to various demands related or not to security. As Mr Ajavon explains, the Chinese embassy "privatised" the public domain with a parking lot and the French cooperation agency installed speed bumps in front of their offices. "We tell them the procedure and they pay for the works."

Marcory is equally open to override urban regulations to please international organisations. "These [security] devices cause some inconveniences," explains Mr Akoa. "They obstruct the roads." While Mr Akoa admits some of their citizens had "gnashing teeth" over the most visible security installations, he summarises the position of the Municipality: "We just bow to all caprices of the UN Mission and the internationals." The municipality of Marcory not only accepted to let organisations using the public domain for security. It also supported the installation of the security devices by slashing the normal taxes for occupying public space.[115]

The conditions to install sandbags and barbed wire on the public domain would normally be billed to the institution as a monthly tax per square metre.[116] In the case of ONUCI, the use of public land is free. "It is up to the municipality," explains Mr Akoa. "The Council decided to give it for free to the ONUCI, as they come here to help." This symbolic gesture illustrates the willingness of Marcory to support the implementation of the UN mission on its territory, where local authorities consider UN control of the public space benevolently.

The marks of the presence of the UN Mission are still present in Marcory. Now as the Mission has left, sandbags and barbed wire are left behind on the street. "We are not aware of their movements," says Mr Akoa, explaining the absence of coordination regarding the material abandoned on the public domain. The description of the technical and administrative void in clearing the area by Roger Gnably, for the Sub-direction of the Environment, illustrate how past missions can leave behind traces on the public space:

They just abandoned the roadblocks when they left. We can't remove the barriers and sandbags because of the barbed wire. […] We did not ask ONUCI to remove it when they left. We have a company contracted to remove it. They asked me to join the Ministry of

---

114 Interview Mr Ajavon, 2 May 2017.

115 Interview Xavier Akoa, 10 May 2017.

116 500 CFA for permanent and 1000 for temporary installations. Interview Xavier Akoa, 10 May 2017.

> *Defence to remove first the barbed wires. We do not have their answer yet, so we wait to remove them.*

As for the costs of removing the barrier, the municipality pays, in another facilitation for the international organisations. As with the services of the municipality, most cases of transformation of the built form went through without an official authorisation, as a standard practice for both local and international dwellers. The laws of urbanism would normally require permission for any modification of a building; including elevating a wall or installing barbed wire on top. As Mr Akoa explains:

> *In relation to walls, they never made a demand. […] We only really look at it if the structure of the building is modified, or if it affects the public domain. Taxpayers don't worry about it.*

In this context, even the proverbially procedural international institutions are not worried by local regulations on the use of the public domain. The International Criminal Court started installing a parking lot on public land without asking permission. The municipality was understanding as Mr Gnably explains:

> *The ICC started their parking before the authorisation. We asked them to stop and asked some corrections. It was just about the form. When people are not informed, they don't know how to proceed. Every modification requires permission. […] They're always very procedural, but here they just didn't know.*

Practices of private use of public roads are not limited to security reasons. In the context of municipalities keen to boast the presence of international organisations, planning regulations can be flexible. The abandonment of material on the street, or the construction without authorisation witness the power of international organisations as much as the willingness of municipalities to accommodate them. It also reflects the limited power and resources of local authorities.

Acceptance and tolerance for contravening the rules of urban planning reflect the acceptance of degrees of informality and flexibility from the law. Contravention to normal urban rules are easier when supported by wealth and influence, the possibility to ask for tailored and flexible regulation is almost guaranteed to large foreign organisations. Integrated within the extra margins of tolerance provided to the wealthy, international organisations receive an open ear by most services of urbanism across different cities.

7.2.3 Fragmented Upgrades in the Public Domain

A number of local civil servants note positive changes from the presence of UN missions for urban development. Ousmane Bah, the General Secretary of Bamako's Commune 5, is pleased to be supported in some urban programmes by aid agencies. He also remarks that the presence of offices or employees of the Mission in an area might bring infrastructure improvements. In a city where guarantees of basic services are not provided by the state, "their installation participates to the development of neighbourhoods," considers Mr Bah. "When they come, they also bring water and power with them. That is an advantage for the population."[117] With the exception of fully planned private neighbourhood development, provision of water and electricity is the responsibility of local dwellers. In normal times, and in most of Bamako, services like water and electricity are brought to a street by the first dweller with enough resources to invest for the hardware. The other inhabitants then connect to the networks and pay a fee to the person who installed the networks. Regular service fees are paid to the electricity and water companies.

The disconnection and territorial disparities in terms of access to electricity and water in Bamako is largely due to the cheap value of land as Malian urbanists explain. The cost of land and property taxes is not enough to install water and electricity networks. Land properties sold by the municipality only cover for roads and parcellation into concessions or properties.[118] The issue of the low cost of land in African cities stems for decades of housing policy after the African independences (Vauthrin 1989). The emphasis and priority of the state to provide housing encouraged local authorities to provide land at the lowest possible cost. The result is that the municipalities do not collect enough money to ensure urban services.

The scaling in time of urban services depending on the local private capacity to install infrastructure reflects how the presence of aid workers and their foreign salary can fasten processes. This presence and capacity in local investment does come at a price for local inhabitants. Access to networks and functioning infrastructure tend to increase the prices of rent and land ownership in a neighbourhood.

There is a set of spatial limits to the expatriate-financed urban upgrades. The location of upgrades is limited to areas where aid workers are authorised to live. As these areas are located in affluent areas, which are usually already equipped

117 Interview Ousmane Bah, 9 March 2016.

118 Interview Gouro Landouré, 9 March 2016.

with viable networks, investments by expatriates in electricity and water beyond the houses themselves are relatively rare.

7.2.4 Scales of Intervention

Disconnection between development projects implemented by the various types of entities involved, states, multilateral organisations, large and small NGOs, is a common feature in Global South countries. In the city of Juba, the three-year-old, yet already extinct, project for public lighting in the main arteries illustrates the issue well. At the independence of South Sudan, the Chinese cooperation offered to Juba a complete system of public lampposts for kilometres of main streets. In the absence of electricity networks, each lamppost came with a solar panel and battery to charge electricity during the day, and diffuse it at night. Few years later, almost all of the lampposts were already broken or non-functional. The city of Juba did not have either trained personnel to do the repairs, nor the budget to manage it.

The short term lifetime of many development projects, often combined with spatial discontinuity partly stems from modes of design and implementations through "project management" (Krause 2014). The coined expression "projectorate", a play of words combining the project, the central mode of management in contemporary capitalism, with the protectorate, the subjection of local authorities to foreign supervision, describes the unequal powers between foreign agencies and local institutions and population (Carmona 2008). In urban contexts, the overwhelming financial power of aid agencies tends to produce discontinuous and fragmented cities where the power of municipalities is consistently reduced in defining planning priorities (Lombart, Pierrat, and Redon 2014).

Spatial and temporal discontinuities even increase when aid agencies operate projects to sustain their own presence. Sustaining the large logistics traffic of major aid agencies requires interventions and upgrades of localised sections of the public domain in the form of small-scale infrastructure projects. With their meagre resources, local municipalities welcome intervention in road asphalting, even if the sustainability of the project is not guaranteed, or is very localised. UN agencies have often large logistical bases that need road infrastructure to simply support the operations. In Bamako, the Minusma has issued for example several requests for expressions of interest to civil engineering companies to asphalt the inside of their premises, but also the immediate surroundings.

The United Nations Multidimensional Integrated Stabilisation Mission in Mali (MINUSMA) seeks Expressions of Interest (EOI) from duly registered and licensed

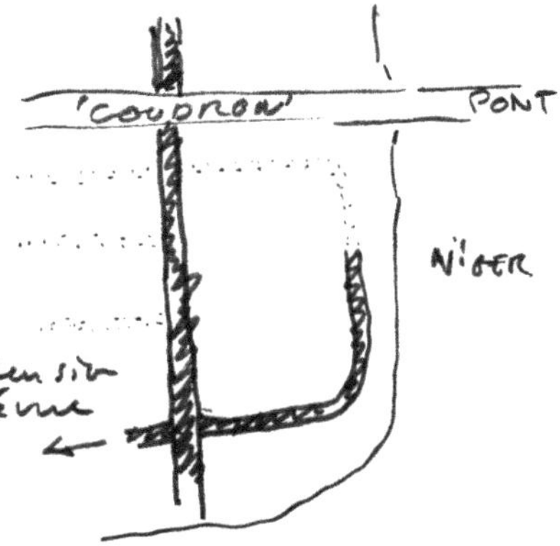

Figure 70: Sketch of the asphalting work conducted by the UN in Badalabougou. From the main asphalt road in the continuity with the Pont des Martyrs to give access only the areas directly useful to the agency, located in the bend of the road by the Niger River

> *companies for the provision of asphalting works of the Mission Operational Base service entrance lateritic road.('MINUSMA' 2017)*

This document dating from the end of 2017 reflects a standard practice of arranging immediate vicinity of UN bases. An earlier demand in Badalabougou was in the phase of completion during one of my visits in Bamako. The sketches of the work completion and planning of this road project illustrate the limitation of the infrastructure works to parts of an urban area directly used by an aid agency (Figure 70). The agency located on the bend of the road has an asphalted access to their premises. It is financing the works even slightly beyond the immediate vicinity of its premises. However, many small roads of the same areas remain as dirt or laterite access.

The costs of these works alone mounted to hundred thousand euros to the aid agency. The local authorities, struggling to finance any type of work for new infrastructure, or even maintenance of existing ones, welcome funding for infrastructure. However, they are problematic in the uneven territories it produces. Unrelated to existing priority planning in relation to the public realm, they mostly reflect the capacity of foreign actors to accommodate their own presence through their funding capacities.

Interventions on infrastructures by international organisations mark physically a regime of multiple sovereignties. The possibility by the local population to benefit from infrastructure investments with limited spatial extent is congruent with the unequal relations they keep with powerful foreign actors. Locals might use a road at the cost of losing part of their own control over the public domain. The capacity of a private company to invest in infrastructures also differentiates a public space of general interest and public space built to its own interests (Ferguson 2005).

Infrastructure projects of international organisation in relation to their logistics needs does not come as the only alternative to the state. Normal functions of the state have integrated the presence of other actors of cooperation, who assist with the financing and engineering of road infrastructures. Chinese presence, for instance, is notable both as financing of projects as well as direct intervention in large-scale projects (Sautman and Hairong 2009). Massive Chinese infrastructure project appear as the most thorough and integrated in recent years, although its technical quality is often questioned (Corkin and Burke 2006).

The spatial discontinuities echo the temporal discontinuities in the practice of urban renovations in relation to international events. In Abidjan, the Francophonie games led to the construction of an Olympic village by the lagoon in Marcory. Road works and other infrastructure are being upgraded for the occasion, in parallel to the destruction of informal shops and bars on the side of the road. Large sporting events in Southern cities constitute a classic of urban renewal. Olympic games and Football World Cups have been used in most cities to renew infrastructure and intent projecting a modernist and polished image of the city (Essex and Chalkley 1998; Hiller 2000). It often results in clearing urban areas from the poor living in the city. Demolitions or street regulations can implement these changes at events of less importance and visibility, such as continental sporting, cultural or political events or other multilateral summits.

Similar dynamics have touched Bamako in preparation of the France-Africa summit, in 2017; infrastructure works and upgrading were visible along with the demolition of a number of informal shops. Workers were cleaning or installing large new canalisations in the main axes of the city. Changes in the urban space as discontinuous spatially and temporally illustrate models of development where intervention of the state is unequal. As result of diverse interventions, cities witness transformations of different scales and scopes. Large private actors, or international organisations, shape the temporal and spatial continuities and discontinuities of the public domain.

The relation of the cities with intervention by foreign actors on the public domain is diverse, and correlated to the resources of the state. In the "emergent markets", such as Ivory Coast and Kenya, the general planning of infrastructure is more related to the strategic planning within the country than in Juba and Bamako, where the resources for an autonomous infrastructure policy is much more limited. In Nairobi, the direct intervention of international organisations is rare beyond their premises. The presence of international cooperation projects is generally limited to the upgrading of the poorest areas of the city (Rodriguez-Torres and Charton-Bigot 2010). Installation of sanitation in a slum comes from a variety of actors of cooperation with projects aiming at the poorest areas and inhabitants, the marginalised populations of the metropolis.

The discontinuity of infrastructure projects reflects the self-serving nature of direct investments by large international organisations. Institutional support for the municipalities centres equally on security, even when the overall impact is beyond the vicinity of their premises. "MINUSMA also helped us with urban management," explains Ousmane Bah, the General Secretary of the Commune 5. "They supported us to build and establish a police station and a local centre for the civil registry."[119] Support to local security and control mechanisms echoes wider political support for reinforcement of the Malian state's capacity in security and control. Enhancing the civil registry form integral part of the EU financial support for "controlling, transmitting, centralising and analysing data, which is essential in development policies" (Le Guilloux 2019). Development of police and control technologies at the level of the municipalities reflect a localised aspect of a large development of technologies of control for the Malian state, visible at the airports and other border in the form of biometric instruments (Andersson 2016).

7.3 Aesthetics of Defensive Design

Defensive architecture and design for international organisations present an aggressive aesthetics whose reception is not controlled. The language of security features surrounding compounds is the contradictory subject of a "transaction", where the intended message is perceived diversely depending on the receivers. Fortress architecture may be intended as a show of force in the ability to secure premises from various threats. Conversely, the reception of the message sent by the image of a barricaded building may have the unintended result of presenting a vulnerability that can only be mitigated by security features (Coaffee, O'Hare, and Hawkesworth 2009). Security design show fear of the outside when it intends to display force.

The continuum in the logics of security aesthetics between the fortress architecture and the stealthy security features presents a wide variety of aesthetics. The choices of international organisations varies depending on the organisation

119 Interview Ousmane Bah, 9 March 2016.

of the location. However, the dominating trend is the outside visibility of security features, in international agencies premises, as well as in the other private spaces used by aid workers. Walls, barbed wires and electric fences must be seen and understood. The UN security manual describes the devices that must surround UN compounds:

> *Wall constructed as per UN guidelines. […]*
>
> *Additional temporary barriers for example, barbed/razor wire, sandbags, jersey barriers and other filled barriers are to be available within one day of being required.*
>
> *Anti-Ram barriers/gates at vehicle entrance as per UN guidelines.(United Nations 2006)*

These guidelines are implemented with varying degree depending on context. They present the outside face of UN organisations to the local population as a series of small fortresses inaccessible without proper permission. As Duffield notes in his observation of numerous UN field offices in South Sudan, UN compounds are "exclusionary and disempowering in their workings and appearance" (Duffield 2010b). In the ambiguous transaction process of security aesthetics and its reception, it is not clear whether the compounds show strength, or the precariousness of the UN political influence.

The UN security policy manual specifies that the visibility of premises must be limited from the outside. UN agencies must have "the ability to oppose or negate the effects of an action against the premises, including denying access to information on the layout and contents of the premises." (UNDSS 2017, p. 72). Part of the defensive architecture of international aid consists in hiding from the eye of the public and the local populations. The protection from the vision of the outside is two-fold. It hides the inside of a compound or a house to prevent attacks. It may also serve to hiding the organisation of space and sociability of the inside to the outsiders' eyes.

A cross section of a hotel in Juba distinguishes the outside public space, where the scarce resources of the state allows only the most minimal urban infrastructure, while the inside is propped up to sustain luxury and housing and leisure, in the form of a swimming pool. Security features block, or rather limit, the vision that the local communities may gather from the inside. While the cross section was drawn in Juba, it could resemble many hotels or houses for international aid in other African cities (Figure 71).

The protection from the outside view may in fact exacerbate the representation of debauchery associated with international aid workers, raised many times during the research. For Ousmane Bah, the General Secretary of the Commune

Figure 71: Security devices as frontiers for the eye. Cross section of a hotel in Juba

5 in Bamako, the arrival of internationals in a neighbourhood is worrying for the local morals:

> *Some of them do not have the same traditions as we do. And now young women might be tempted. There is a form of depravation of morals. Also in relation to alcohol. We drink as well, but not as much as they do.*[120]

A small hotel in Badalabougou experienced the consequences of the image of expatriate debauchery behind the closed doors of the international archipelago. Fanny Mauron had sold alcohol for years in her hotel's small restaurant to her relatively discreet clientele without trouble. The combination of closed doors and expatriate cars parked in front of her guesthouse signalled increased presence and drew suspicions:

> *We sold and drank alcohol discreetly for a long time, but the cars parked in the street made it more visible. It became a problem when the neighbours complained. It scared the landlord for his reputation as he is from a religious family. And he imposed this [prohibition] on alcohol in the hotel.*[121]

7.3.1 Spikes of All Sizes

The language of security design towards the local environment is difficult to interpret, but the presentation of spikes directed towards the outside often offers the vision of a fortress surrounded by multifaceted enemies. Defensive architecture starts with strong walls or another separation from the city. The next step is the installation of material devices, which intend not only to block or make passage more difficult, but also to hurt the person who might try to pass. Security devices used to protect the perimeter of building typically involve barbed wire,

120 Interview Ousmane Bah, 9 mars 2016.
121 Interview Fanny Mauron, 29 March 2016.

and alternatively other types of objects that can sting or cut the skin of people trying to trespass. Broken bottle glass cemented on top of a wall stands as a common alternative.

The aggressive aesthetics of barbed wire acts as a signal to potential intruders, which may be interpreted as a general signal of fear and segregation. Spiky vegetation on the outside wall stands as a softer and less aggressive feature for houses in some cases. This alternative witnesses an awareness of the problematic nature of the message (Razac 2000). The use of semi decorative security devices limits the trespassing while limiting the message of hostility towards the outside. This softer messaging remains limited to places where house maintenance is practicable. Moreover, it is generally considered as a complement to other sharp barriers rather than replacement.[122]

The spikes are used at different sizes. The spike of a barbed wire may be one centimetre long while the spear topping a fence may be ten times longer. Anti-ram iron beams facing outwards are much larger than glass or iron wire designed to hurt the skin and may be one metre long or more (Figure 72). Inside the wealthy suburbs of Nairobi, some NGO and UN compounds protect their gates from cars or truck attacks with a large bevelled steel beam in the middle of the garden gates. Different mechanical devices allow the heavy steel beams to be lifted down or removed to allow passage.

At every size, the outwards aggressiveness of sharp devices maintains the closure of expatriate space from the outside. This separation is supported by the aesthetics of devices, which cease to be purely mechanical to embed a discourse of intended defiance and an unintended message of fear (Coaffee, O'Hare, and Hawkesworth 2009). Spikes and spears are a message as much as a physical obstacle.

Security devices are often hidden from the inside of a compound or a hotel, preventing the aggressive aesthetics to be reached from the inside, while being visible from the outside. One Bamako hotel hid a double concertina barbed wire from the direct view of its guests installing the devices underneath the terrace of the restaurant. The view on the Niger River is only slightly obfuscated by a simple wall and grille starting at the height of the tables. When seated at the tables of the restaurant, the barbed wire does not appear in the field of vision sparing the panoramic view on the Niger (Figure 73).

The architectural balance of the installation of the two devices illustrates the unequal access to the landscape between the powerful investors and the local

122 Observation Notebook, 25 August 2016.

Figure 72: Nairobi, a bevelled steel beam protects the gates of a compound

population. The two metres wide passage on the shores of the Niger is frequented by the local fishermen installed in the remaining pockets of poor dwellers of this affluent neighbourhood. Incidentally, the Malian law prohibits construction in a 10-metre distance from the river. While already illegal in its current dimension, the hotel figured to reduce even more the walkable access to the shore of the river.

As a complement to the effect of the device and the message transmitted to the local population, the hotel manager regularly orders the few locals walking or sitting in front of the hotel terrace to move away.[123] The specific design of this security device has completed three tasks of preventing intrusions in the hotel, presenting a scenery undamaged by the visual message of barbed wire, but also sending a message to the local fishermen that they are not welcome here.

In the context of both the security requirements and power of the aid community and the limited resources of the different levels of the state compared to a number of priorities in the governance of cities, local urbanists have rarely voiced aesthetical concerns in relation to security features. Local urbanists in Bamako and Abidjan have seemed relatively indifferent towards the aesthetics of security. Safety issues with the relatively high-rise buildings, or the blocking of public roads, appears more problematic for most of those interviewed. As the

123 Observation Notebook, 21 March 2016.

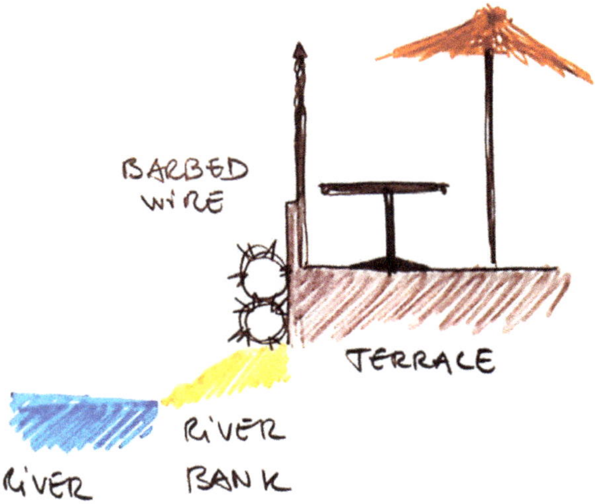

Figure 73: Cross-section of a hotel in Bamako. The view of the barbed wires is hidden from the guests but explicit to the outside

head of the Services Techniques explains in relation to Cocody, respect for planning regulations depend on the area:

> *The heights of Cocody are already the "presidential neighbourhood". Even if you own the parcel, it is very difficult to build. It is highly regulated. Including for the height of barriers. They should never surpass 3.5 to 4 metres. [...] The local town plan is well respected. But elsewhere is not the case. Where I live for example, you can build a multi-storey building on top of my house and I lose my intimacy.*[124]

Among the complex tasks of an urbanist, the aesthetics of security features are not mentioned as a disturbance. Associated with wealth, the security features are likely to produce increases in land value. In turn, the modification of land values increases the relative power of proprietors while the capacity of tenants reduces. Proprietors see revenues increasing while tenants are forced to devote larger proportions of their income to housing. Security aesthetics symbolises as much as it materialises shifts of power relations in favour of the wealthiest sections of the local populations within the local urban environment.

124 Interview Mr Ajavon, 2 May 2017.

7.3.2 Cars as Symbols

The highly publicised image of the white SUVs has become one of the main symbols of international aid presence and missions (Smirl 2015). UN, Red Cross and most major NGOs along with their organisation flags or logos have adopted the white car. This practice of self-identification of humanitarian aid originates in the confidence that the identification of humanitarians as humanitarians will guarantee safe passage and respect of their missions by the parties in conflict. In some contexts, international organisations have stopped using recognisable cars to avoid being targeted by their foes, opposed to either the humanitarian or the political mission, as was the case in Iraq after attacks by forces resisting US occupation and UN altogether (Egeland, Harmer, and Stoddard 2011).

The debate within the aid community over extreme cases of vehicles attacked by armed forces may obfuscate a silent but more general feeling of distrust by the local community towards international aid. The white car and its visibility illustrate the contradictions in the aesthetic transaction between international aid and the local population. International organisations' white cars intend to convey both security and respect for the mission. Local populations may receive diversely, and associate it to different types of griefs.

Many Malians resent the armed soldiers passing in their armoured cars in Bamako as a humiliation. This presence is a reminder of the defeats of the Malian army and state as much as the arrogance of the French army and the West more generally. The Malian conflict as a side effect of the war against the Libyan head of state Muammar Gaddafi only seemed to increase the pace of foreign interventions in Africa (Bergamaschi 2013). In this context, non-armed white car of the humanitarians may well be associated with its UN political-military counterpart.

"The UN mission only brings white cars," says the outspoken writer Aminata Traoré, pointing to the mobile symbol of the international response visible on the streets of Bamako, before explaining her grief:

> *It's a problem of national sovereignty when people see foreign militaries in Mali. It comes with the salaries and the armies of international experts. But what prevents us to think our country ourselves? This system is just self-entailing.*[125]

The use of the white-painted coachwork originally intended as an evocation of the peaceful intentions of the humanitarian aid ends up blended in a category of foreigners whose power concurrences the state.

125 Interview Aminata Traoré, 15 April 2016.

International organisations mobility is not limited to the white car. In some contexts, organisations use unmarked vehicles tactically. Nevertheless, individual expatriates also use unmarked cars, which they buy or rent in their everyday life. The "PAM services" company in Bamako have a large range of their activities in the rent-a-car business. Djélika Cissé describes the car her company rents as "seven SUVs and three sedans". The expatriate community, humanitarians and others, prize the robust cars with functioning seatbelts and AC to drive on Bamako's uneven roads: "we had renting contracts with the French army, and other international clients including embassies and corporations."[126]

Looking at parking lots of international organisations reveals a range of different cars from small three-doors to the tacky Hummers, while standard SUVs constitute the bulk of expatriates' personal vehicles. The SUV stands in the middle of two important developments in contemporary African cities: fear of crime and the development of a mass car culture and road infrastructure.

The rise of the SUV correlates with a growing fear of crime in cities since its early success in the USA. This "luxury car in disguise" has attracted the "upscale, active lifestyle-oriented, college-educated couples, aged 25–49, some with children, who don't drive vehicles off-road" (Lauer 2005). The picture corresponds to many expatriate workers, especially in family duty stations, where the car constitutes the mobility model to support the suburban lifestyle and commuting between house, work, leisure and consumption.

The development of the SUV echoes dynamics of the spread of a car culture reflected in investment in road infrastructure in many developing countries. Kenya and Nairobi represent an eloquent example of this tendency. Road investment follows a tendency centred to the use of the personal car, as other modes of transportation remain underfunded. In contrast, public transport receives limited attention and investments. Pedestrians do not receive much more investment as sidewalks are often just the non-constructed sides of the drivable road (Kawachi and Wamala 2006), or private property (Figure 74). In addition, popularity of the SUV in African cities rests on the often-unfinished character of road works, where the four-wheel drive allows easier passage.

The social prestige reflected in the SUV influences well beyond the expatriate and African elites. As Robert* – a Kenyan UN volunteer in Nairobi- explains, the car constitutes the major symbol conveyed to the local population by international aid. He simply summarises: "Everybody wants to work for the UN,

126 Interview Djélika Cissé, 18 mars 2016.

Figure 74: "Keep off the grass" signs signals the interdiction to step on sidewalks in Gigiri, Nairobi. 14 August 2016

because they have big cars."[127] International aid projects social status and wealth through security aesthetics.

Encouraging the use of cars is fitting with more generalised transport policies centred on the car. Nairobi is renowned for its lack of integration of transports and disregard for pedestrians (Figure 74), even though car owners are a small minority in the capital (Khayesi 1997). In this regard, UN policies on mobility in the capital is in symbiosis with urban policies. It is striking that the UN's main HQ for environment (UNEP) performs so openly a practice of mobility in contradiction with a current mainstream of mobility policies, which emphasises the importance of public transport and soft mobility (Rocca 2009).

7.4 Outcomes in Abidjan

Among the four case studies, the city of Abidjan is the only one that has a clear sight of scaling down and ending UN mission. It was scheduled to end in July of 2017. This did not mean the departure of all UN agencies, and much less so NGOs. It was, however, the occasion to witness the effect of a massive scaling down of operations in a country. In fact, when I arrived in Abidjan in March

127 Interview Robert*, 31 August 2016.

2017, the contingent of peacekeepers was already reduced to a few dozens, while the number of aid workers also decreased dramatically when the conflict consumed after the fall of Laurent Gbagbo, in 2011.

The departure of the UN mission went organised while other organisations returned in Abidjan after the years of trouble. While Abidjan has never been completely abandoned by either private companies or multilateral organisations, the city witnessed a decrease of activities and presence of personnel. Balancing movements of war and peace cast expatriate presence in continuities and discontinuities. The phenomenon encompasses a variety of fears, hopes, opportunities and frustrations depending on the position of the viewers.

Peacetime multilateral organisations return to the city. The African Development Bank (AfDB) having displaced its activities to Tunis during the civil war, from 2003 to 2014, is returning its seat and staff to Abidjan (Sanogo 2014). Opportunities to continue renting houses to expatriates switches to other customers, as a property owner told me. "It is the AfDB that will replace the mission as the major tenants."[128] Moreover, the trend of new employees coming to Abidjan is not ending. Aid employment websites show constant advertisements for positions in Ivory Coast, but this time shifting from the humanitarian to development sector.

The AfDB is indeed the first single international job provider for the month of April 2018, recorded on UN Jobs website. Other international aid positions offers in Abidjan concern typically health, especially AIDS, as well as poverty reduction and agriculture (UN Jobs 2018). As the flow of expatriates diminishes, proprietors try to find new institutional clients with similar living standards. "Now that the UN are leaving, we struggle to find new guests," explains Ms Kady K*, the owner of a single furnished apartment that was rented to UN mission employees at the height of the mission. "Other institutions and companies are coming now."[129]

The social composition of the Zone 4 neighbourhood, which was identified as the main area for internationals, becomes more corporate than aid-related. Nevertheless, the main outline remains similar. The rent price is adapted to expatriates and unaffordable to most locals. The effect of the departure of the UN mission in Ivory Coast had already started to be felt in Abidjan since aid organisations scaled down their operations and presence after the 2011 arrest of Laurent Gbagbo. Although some difficulties in the adaptation to the departure

---

128 Observation Notebook, 9 April 2017.

129 Interview Kady K*, 4 May 2017.

of expatriates and the loss of some relatively well paid local jobs were mentioned, the difference in the social composition and the effects on the city had been presented as relatively benign in the overall economic picture.

The inclusion in 2017 of Ivory Coast in the list of "emerging markets" reflects the relatively important economic resources and infrastructures of the country, especially the port of Abidjan (Barnenstein 2017). The country's economy has long stood out in the West African region. The ancient presence of multilateral organisations, such as the International Cocoa Organisation and African Development Bank might also explain the confidence of local actors for the future. As economic prospects had bettered since the end of the civil war, the effects of general economic trends in the city largely surpass the effect of the presence of aid workers.

This should not be generalised to other countries and cities, especially with scarcer resources. What can be generalised, however, is precisely that the most important effects of both the presence and the departure of large UN missions is largely dependent on the local environment. The size of the city compared to the size of a mission plays a role as well as the weight of the local economy. The panorama, largely determines its own capacity to absorb international presence and its forms of extraterritoriality.

Capital cities regularly show their capacity to absorb forms of autonomy and extraterritoriality. Embassies, for instance, constitute regular occurrences in cities well beyond the time of a mission. Effects of an extraterritorial physical and political presence can more easily be dealt with when the local economy is strong. More precisely, the discrepancy between the power of international versus local actors affects territories the most when their relative power are most contrasted.

Effects of the presence and departure of aid organisations are different depending on their relative weight in the local context, as they might be dramatic or marginal. However, the wider issue with the presence and the departure of aid lies in their influence on institutional and class relations. International aid participates to legitimise and reinforce contraventions to local regimes of sovereignty by consistently derogating with urban regulations, weighting in financially and politically. Within the private realm, the changes in power relations in favour of wealthy locals appears as a worrying prefiguration of increasing socio-spatial inequalities.

Perceptions of international aid by local citizens can be positive or negative for different reasons, generating enthusiasm or frustration. From the outset, local dwellers might have a good or bad opinion of the goals of the mission. In their everyday life, the presence of aid might benefit them as much as it can hinder their livelihood. Contradictory reactions to aid presence and departure illustrate the conflictual conditions brought by transformations to the urban environment directed from the outside.

Chapter 8 Synthesis

This work highlights the specific ways in which international aid produces cities. It shows that within a general canvas for the installation of aid workers and their territoriality, particular declinations create a variety of uses of the cities. The implantation of international organisations in Bamako, Juba, Nairobi and Abidjan constitutes a process of power constructing and transforming urban environments. The presentation of these case studies means to show the links at numerous scales between the security norms of the aid industry, and the creation of a transnational space of aid workers. The definition and description of international aid as a social field allows understanding the spatialisation of a diversity of humanitarian aid practices not just as organisational policies but as a structured and structuring component in the making of many contemporary African capitals. What does this research show concerning the four cities that constituted the case studies of this research?

The extent and depth of this research is not identical in the four case studies. I spent more time studying the presence of aid in Bamako than in any of the three other cities. Conditions of access were different, although the combination of visits allowed me to build a picture of each city individually and in relation to the influence of aid. Overall, the research shows that the presence of aid in separate contexts influences the urban environment at different levels.

The research showed how international aid presence participates in the territorial development of African cities. Although problematic, this presence and the overwhelming influence on the local environment integrate in a game of spatial power relations visible in the urban materiality as well as in social life. Each city has important specificities, although a summary of observations of some of the major effects of aid can highlight the main patterns and processes of transformations.

In Nairobi, the presence of international organisations presents the most integrated influence, in the sense that aggressive security policies seem to be widely shared, by the public and private sectors. The inclusion of aid organisations within the development of dual local systems of social and spatial inequalities has, at the very least, the effect of legitimising socio-spatial inequalities. The urban isolationism of major aid organisations and aid workers in the city fits in well with the splintering path taken by urban development in the East African metropolis.

The effects of the presence of aid in Abidjan has shown to produce sets of relations entangled within the local urban conditions. Spatially limited in an already splintering model of urbanism, international organisations have integrated parts of the city. The departure of the UN mission from the country and its local perceptions seem to indicate that the city will follow its own path of social and material development. The legacy of the aid presence might have been the maintenance of housing and commodity markets during the period of conflict in which the regional economic and social influence had slowed down.

In Bamako, the recent massive presence of international organisations illustrates the rapidity in which new norms in the public and private spaces can be adopted. Multiple and radical transformations of urban form took place at a fast pace producing a panorama of fragmented upgrades of the built environment at the same time as a normalisation of security devices and procedures in concurrence with local sovereignties. The combined use of existing social and material structures of the city results in rapid urban changes, although the depth of these changes can not be known given the unforeseeable future of Malian political situation.

Juba presents the sharpest contrast between the conditions of local populations and expatriates. The scarcity of public services provides an ideal setting for a nearly total fragmentation of urban space and living conditions depending on social classes. An extremely violent context completes the dramatic process in increasing the closure and autonomy of exclusive spaces. In this regard, the conditions in Juba come closest to the dystopic predictability of the complete autonomy of humanitarian presence in relation to a city. A catastrophically fragmented and violent capital city for the future of South Sudan seems the most credible prediction, although different approaches and improvement of local conditions could still reverse the dangerous current developments.

The general rule that seems to emerge from the logic of the territoriality of aid is that the influence of a particular set of institutions and social bodies is contingent upon their political and financial power. In contrast, the relative power of influence of aid over cities depends on the strength of local economies and institutions. This indicates how predictable, the effects of the presence of aid are, even if unintended.

This presence has current effect on a number of cities, in Africa and other sites of massive humanitarian interventions. As change in ecological conditions might signal some even deeper crises looming in the future, humanitarian presence might well expand to more sites of interventions in the future. As the West African region and the Sahel currently seem to navigate towards a widening of the geographic scope of armed conflicts, some of the direct neighbouring capital cities of Mali and Ivory Coast could also be confronted with the unthought-of security urbanism of international aid.

The dialectic between the aid industry and the local environment illustrates highly unequal relationships. Given all the negative consequences of the presence of international agencies, this work also aims, nevertheless, to nuance a catastrophic representation. With all the possible and justified criticism of aid presence, and the modalities of presence, the territorial dynamics created are contextual to historical moments in the life of cities. Major risks for an increase in urban fragmentation stem from how aid presence supports the reinforcement of class power relations to benefit the wealthiest sections of the urban population. Future urban development can integrate – or disintegrate – modifications of the urban space in different ways and the actions and power of local actors will determine the cities' fates.

The overall structure of this book into four main chapters follows the theoretical framework of the research and intends to describe driving processes and influence of aid organisations in African cities. It highlights an unequal dynamic where powerful political actors and a wealthy body of expatriates can transform urban environments. This work intended to present a working theory to discuss the presence of international aid in African cities.

The concept of the landscape of aid explains how international organisations produce and implement security norms translated into the management of the built environment in the form of increased segregation. This research highlights the double effects of social norms and institutional regulations to invest and transform physical and social spaces. The social field, which constitutes the aid industry, observes a panorama of existing urban conditions. Its settlement process, distinct to, albeit associated with local social forces forms a distinct layer of organisations and individuals. This newly formed local social body in turns participates in the transformation of the local urban fabric.

The notion of the landscape to support the understanding of territorial processes permits the integration of a dynamic and iterative definition of urban change. The development of the argument characterises the implementation of global power relations, security policies and their effects at all scales on specific locations into the everyday life of aid workers and African city dwellers. As an analytical device, the theoretical framework of the landscape of aid can help conjecture likely outcomes of similar enterprises in other urban settings, in Africa and elsewhere.

The central notion of the layer permits modelling socio-spatial relations in both their materiality and their representations. As the chorème of the layer (Figure 45) allowed to depict virtual spaces and the use of the built environment, it highlights the spatiality of power relations between the global-local and the local-local (Figure 3), translated into instances of territorialisation. The conceptualisation of the layer of aid as an unthought-of mode of urbanism illustrates how similar territorialities are found in a multiplicity of cities across the African continent and beyond. The layer explains both the local territorialities of aid in cities and the construction of a single wider networked space of aid across many capitals.

One limit to the application of this approach through the dynamic creation of a landscape lays in highlighting a single social layer. Multiple social layers share any given space. The emphasis on the layer of aid brings the risk of depicting other social groups as a single homogenous entity. While this work did not develop on the different layers that may constitute the social panorama of African cities, it did denote that cities are complex and contradictory entities. Further development of a dynamic approach of the landscape may find it resourceful to integrate a variety of communicating or separate socio-spatial layers to the analysis.

The restriction of the research on the presence of aid to the focus on a social field left aside the goals and missions of agencies. Could the urban influence of international aid be an echo or a reflection of their programmes? The massive funding devoted to saving lives in humanitarian operations stems from a variety of social, cultural and political reasons. Refugee policies seem to prevent migration to the North as much as supporting populations (Agier 2013). Humanitarian aid can be used to pressure government or favour one side in a conflict (Autesserre 2002). Particular problematic cases in the construction of humanitarian aid reflect the propensity of aid agencies to work in the South from the North, socially and politically. In this regard, the potential association between programmatic components of policy and practical aspects of presence remains subject to further investigation and questioning.

Chapter 9 Conclusion

This research has emphasised an association between four African cities. They are all part of a wider network of capitals where the presence of aid influences urban outcomes. While some connections existed between these cities, including flows of people, goods and capital, humanitarian aid links these places through an immediate and far-reaching set of policies and practices. I have presented these cities as units of a single global space. This approach considers that the presence of aid produces a new and distinct set of relations between these African capitals, and beyond. This transnational urban space is connected by humanitarian policies and practices that reshape city metabolisms.

Most research on aid presence and programming in urban environments either explicitly states or hints at the arguments presented in this book. The sociology of aid workers illustrates the influence of social habitus on the insularity of aid and its effects on social changes in the neoliberal era (Mosse 2011; Dandoy 2014). The study of peacekeeping economies demonstrates how the combination of intended and unintended consequences of peacekeeping operations transforms social relations in predictable fashion. It attributes transformations of economic structures (Jennings and Bøås 2015), of institutional governance (Roach and Hudson 2018), and of class and gender relations (Aning and Edu-Afful 2013; Jennings 2014; Henry 2015) to the influence of international organisations in sites of humanitarian crisis.

The concept of humanitarian urbanism proposes a dynamic framework to describe and analyse the specific effects of aid on urban environments. The notion proposes that the multiplicity of political, social and spatial processes produced by humanitarian aid serves as an operational concept to evaluate and analyse urban transformations (Büscher, Komujuni, and Ashaba 2018). Humanitarian urbanism proposes that sets of policies, norms and practices shape urban outcomes. The fluidity of the framework of humanitarian urbanism allows an assemblage of critical approaches of policies and practices around both programmes and presence of aid workers. It accounts for the spatial translation of the neoliberal hegemony that shapes humanitarian governance (Potvin 2013).

The focus of this work, the sole presence of aid in African capitals, is thematically more limited than most studies of humanitarian urbanism. The landscape of aid complements other approaches to study the effect of the presence of humanitarian workers in cities. Circumscribed to a landscape of aid workers in African cities, this book excludes a landscape of beneficiaries from the analysis.

In doing so, this work addresses one side of the phenomenon. By reducing the thematic focus, this research attempted to simplify a complex multiscale mode of territoriality.

This simplification offers the possibility to propose a theory for an iterative process of urban change and for the interactions between scales, social fields and individuals. It presents a cycle of urban transformation focussed on practices, from the global structures of the aid industry to everyday lives in African cities. Originating from personal experience and from a growing literature on the effects of aid, it aims to propose a consolidated analytical framework of aid presence.

Empirical research across four cities permitted identifying trends in the production of urban spaces by international aid. This analysis structured around the landscape and the layer of aid permits presenting the constants in the territoriality of aid. Patterns of interactions between aid industry and cities illustrate connections of collaboration and competition. This work also highlights the importance of the local settings, in terms of social and institutional power.

The use of the relatively rigid concept of landscape enables identifying agents of urban change within a complex assemblage of institutions, individuals, social groups, representations, physical features, networks and scales. The aid industry appears as a set of practices of power spatialised within a global network of cities. The urban panorama is a palimpsest and contradictory space where the form reflects and structures social tensions and inequalities. The layer appears as the combination of spaces of representation and lived space. Urban transformations are as significant as they are precarious and contingent to a degree of acceptance of aid presence.

This approach of the layer in the palimpsest brings forward the presence of aid as a historical moment in urban histories. It also permits considering the settlement of aid workers in relation to the history of the built form and the territoriality of aid as a product of African urban history. This historical account, with its complex data gathering, places African capitals as agents of the territoriality of aid, where past urban policies influence the settlement of aid. This, in turn, prepares urban futures in a multiplicity of ways. Outcomes of previous urbanisation, urban form, relative density, the presence or absence of infrastructure, and architecture all influence the territoriality of aid.

This historicising of the built form and social structures places cities not only as socio-spatial entities shaped by the presence of aid, but also as parts of the global construction of the aid industry. As interactions between two pairs of localness, the dialogue between local declination of aid in a city and the city itself illustrates a co-construction. Capital cities, in all their contradictions, produce, orient and transform the social field of aid and its habitus. As the aid industry takes its part in urban history, the past and present of African cities shape humanitarian history, as much as it reveals its contradictory nature.

This theme of the co-construction of the presence of humanitarian aid brings to the broader question of the African structures of the aid industry. As capital cities host and shape international organisation's installation, a predominantly African labour force provides aid to beneficiaries. It has already been noted that local workers form the bulk of deliveries and support to beneficiaries (Vannier 2013). African urban societies, in turn, support the presence of the administrative and decisional arms of the aid industry in the form of labour, housing, institutional support, including at the municipal level, thus defining the current shapes of a global industry.

African cities do not shape the nature of their relationship with the aid industry, which presents its own urban norms and practices through various power mechanisms. However, they are agents in the local applications of these norms and practices, as their own dynamics of violence, gender and class relations, urban norms and land use support or confront the aid industry. Recognising the role of African cities in the global networks of aid also emphasises that the layer of aid and its urban consequences is contingent to a modified assemblage of material environments, representations, scales, institutions and individuals.

The use of a variety of methods allowed working across scales and places to investigate the relation between the spatial norms of international aid from the North-South relations of power in a global workforce to its implication in everyday relationships with local social panoramas. A multiplicity of techniques combined to a multiplicity of sources permitted the investigation of the different scales of a transformative phenomenon, as well as the articulations between policies and practices. This work is largely indebted to other examples of combining investigative methods, in particular those used by US geographer William Bunge who navigated between qualitative and quantitative approaches to highlight the multiple scales of power and domination (Bunge 1971, 1979, 1988).

The incorporation of a number of techniques of research proves conclusive in grasping the different scales of the problematic. It also proves complex in its articulation. This work constitutes a test on the use of mixed methods. Most geographers, and social scientists more generally tend to develop a limited number of techniques and to exploit fully their potential. From this perspective, one limit of the methodology of this research is that the level of mastering and control I had on data of all types is not as strong as it would have been if I had focused on a single technique.

The use of mixed techniques proves to be a complex exercise. It brings into question the status of each type of data. The collection or creation of data and the subsequent analysis mean assigning to each type an exploratory value, or a value of proof. All methods require a degree of confidence on the part of the researcher in both his ability to use specific techniques as well as relying on his honesty in the treatment and analysis of the data (Taussig 2011). I summarise below some examples of original observation permitted by the different techniques of research.

The quantitative analysis of staff data is, to my knowledge, a first experiment within the study of humanitarian practices and the geography of aid. It has allowed me to describe three important aspects of the geography of aid. At the global scale, it describes various aspects of the North-South polarity in sites of intervention and the origins of humanitarian personnel. At the continental scale, it illustrates the relative importance of humanitarian presence in different countries. At the scale of the countries, it emphasises the predominantly urban nature of the presence of aid, concentrated in the country capitals. This demonstration vindicates the importance of studying the urban impacts of the presence of aid capital cities.

Participant observation from within international aid permits the description of security design and discourses. It allowed familiarising with a culture of fear built through training, exposure to violent news and the physical position from within humanitarian defensive architecture. By sharing the physical and social viewpoint of aid workers, the immersion within the social field of aid allows one to be fully integrated in the territorial landscaping processes. The violent events I witnessed during this study illustrate best the tensions between a critical outlook at security procedures and the inclusion in the same social group that relies in this security apparatus.

The use of a continuum of visual techniques, from hand-drawn sketches to cartography and topological models and photographs provides a renewed description of the typologies of security devices and the organisation of space. Visual methods support description and analysis of the structures of aid at the scales comprised between the city and the body. By positioning and constraining the production of visual representations, the drawing process highlights the tensions between the researcher's body and a broader space, revealing inherent strain in the fragmentation of the landscape.

Long interviews permits extending the understanding of the territoriality of aid into the perception of the presence of aid by the local population. This attempt to reach different social and professional groups confronted with the presence of aid allows the illustration of different local perceptions. The coexistence of various local voices and positions are guided by their social position within the social and spatial palimpsest of African cities.

The potential of this methodology using a number of diverse sources and datasets brings an important complexity of treatment and certain as well as promising potential. In particular, it presents the possibility of navigating across scales. Socio-spatial phenomenon of global scales present complex challenges to researchers in grasping their implication and dynamics from their overall resources and policies to the everyday life that they create. Despite the limitations in the depth in the investigation of each scale of a social process, this combination of research techniques gives access to an overview of multiscale processes.

The approach to the landscape of aid through multiple scales highlights specificities of the territoriality of humanitarian organisations. It was assumed at the beginning of this research that Africa – as a continent of multiple humanitarian intervention – and city capitals – as localised centres of humanitarian operations – constitute a central ground for urban transformations in relation to the presence of aid. The humanitarian landscape appears in a variety of ways as a distinctively urban and African territorial system.

The number of humanitarian interventions in Africa and the literature on the presence and programmes of aid nourished this assumption. The development of the discussion on the aid industry aimed to observe how African cities receive aid and how this presence could modify them. The available data on aid workers presence confirms this quantitative importance of the urban and African centrality in the landscapes of aid, as mapping the distribution of aid workers worldwide illustrates. Moreover, there is a quality in the quantity, which helps understand the urban nature of humanitarian interventions.

The numbers of aid workers in urban environments at a global scale not only dominate quantitatively those in smaller towns and rural areas. They respond to a signature of the aid presence in the form of a Pareto chart, where capitals concentrate up to 90 % of the total of foreign aid workers. This means not only that expatriate aid workers are numerous in African cities, but also that their spatial logic corresponds to a model of interventions that places cities as sites of humanitarian management presence. Capital cities are the link between the global networks of aid and direct field interventions. This function of the capital as an instrument of humanitarian intervention structures the presence of aid as a concentrated body of executive workers in African capitals.

The African context presents a stronger contrast between the field of international aid workers and the local population than in most other humanitarian interventions. Social and economic conditions, infrastructure development and levels of services places most African cities in heterogeneous settings where the formal and the informal intermingle in the provision of services. As wealth and power largely determines the possibility to act upon built and social environments, the landscape of aid concentrates the application of social and security norms over cities. The predominantly white bodies of expatriate aid workers only make social and economic discrepancies more visible. This contrast in visibility between the local and international spheres might be self-reinforcing in the creation of a layer of aid cumulating the contrasts of physical appearance and wealth inequalities.

The centrality of the urban environment in the world of aid also highlights a relationship to the outside environment mediated by political and contractual agreements where the urban norms and social conditions make possible the installation of large number of aid workers. These conditions allow an urban surplus – labour and various modalities of capital – to play its part in the presence and functioning of aid presence. The labour surplus allows the employment of numerous local dwellers with varying cultural capital to sustain aid presence, from cleaners and guards to university-trained clerical workers.

All forms of capital surplus play their part in the global space of aid in cities. Humanitarian aid relies on local cultural capital, with the employment of local workers trained in the national universities based in the main city. However, economic capital, in particular in the form of real estate, plays a major part in providing the built space needed to sustain aid presence in its current form. A foreign management supervises humanitarian programming from a central city while a local workforce distributed across the country commits to implement it.

Cities and capitals constitute a spatial base for the functions of humanitarian aid. They produce the resources needed to sustain the newly settled social field as well as a combination of urban dangers. As producers of social norms and specific risks, cities concentrate perceived hazards, mixing threats of conflict violence with petty criminality and accidents. Urban density justifies a security response based on the closure of immediate space and restrictions of movements.

As this work focussed on a segregation process between expatriate norms and local environments it highlighted a paradox of humanitarian presence, as aid organisations use the resources of the city to seclude itself from the urban fabric. This practice is only an appearance of contradiction that highlights an opportunistic use of local environments. Territorial processes of segregation are in fact only possible thanks to modes of exchange between the inside and the outside of segregated spaces. The layer of aid constitutes a partially segregated space, which require the urban – as a site of networks, exchanges and circulation – to produce its own anti-urban norms of access controls and social insularity.

This research describes and analyses problematic aspects of the implementation of security procedures and the presence of aid workers in African cities. The analysis of this process has brought particular attention to the potential outcomes producing fragmented cities. Urban fragmentation and segregation in the production of new spatial power relations highlight problematic aspects of humanitarian interventions from different perspectives, including spatial, economic and gender inequalities. The results of this research hint at possible alternatives.

The most important aspect might not be in the recommendation of specific measures. Rather this book sheds light on the processes at stake in the production of the layer of aid. The visibility of unthought-of processes and their unsought results might be the most important contribution. The failure of the aid industry to think of itself within the city as an urban actor, whose acts have consequences for the urban environment because of a unique commitment to security, may be resolved when the industry fully considers its role as a builder and transformer of cities and landscapes.

Some aid agencies take a critical look at the projected effects of elite lifestyles that might negatively influence the purpose of their mission. Measures such as updating security policies to mitigate influence, or applying organisational ethics more strictly might bring about some positive results. Supporting a less invasive presence and preventing the most offensive way that aid organisations use to settle in a city could mitigate fragmenting effects. However, the structural disequilibrium between the power of international organisations and the scarce resources of the local environment leave little space for real effects on current policies and practices. The commitment to principles weigh little in comparison to actual practices and behaviour when the differences in power and wealth are so flagrant.

For African urban dwellers and municipalities, the description of the processes of socio-spatial fragmentation induced by aid presence could, in fact, be the most useful and effective. The early recognition of a problematic process of urban transformations by local authorities and anticipation of the impacts of aid presence might provide them with powerful instruments to limit damages to socio-spatial cohesion. Such hope might prove delicate to count on. Contradictions in the social fabric of cities and diverging local interests combined with limited resources are likely to impede mitigation or corrective measures from the parts of local authorities. Urban history is not written in advance and possible futures remain to be known, as the new African urban panoramas might reserve unexpected new social relations.

List of Figures

Bibliography

Abaza, Mona. 2001. 'Shopping Malls, Consumer Culture and the Reshaping of Public Space in Egypt'. *Theory, Culture & Society* 18 (5): 97–122. https://doi.org/10.1177/02632760122051986.

AbouAssi, Khaldoun. 2013. 'Hands in the Pockets of Mercurial Donors: NGO Response to Shifting Funding Priorities'. *Nonprofit and Voluntary Sector Quarterly* 42 (3): 584–602. https://doi.org/10.1177/0899764012439629.

Abu Sa'Da, Caroline, and Xavier Crombé. 2015. 'Volunteers and Responsibility for Risk-Taking: Changing Interpretations of the Charter of Médecins Sans Frontières'. *International Review of the Red Cross* 97 (897–898): 133–55. https://doi.org/10.1017/S1816383115000740.

Abu-Lughod, Janet. 1997. 'The Specificity of the Chicago Ghetto: Comment on Wacquant's "Three Pernicious Premises"'. *International Journal of Urban and Regional Research* 21 (2): 357–62. https://doi.org/10.1111/1468-2427.00078.

Abu-Lughod, Janet. 2007. 'The Challenge of Comparative Case Studies'. *City* 11 (3): 399–404. https://doi.org/10.1080/13604810701669140.

Adar, Korwa G. 2000. 'The Internal and External Contexts of Human Rights Practice in Kenya: Daniel Arap Moi's Operational Code'. *African Sociological Review/Revue Africaine de Sociologie* 4 (1): 74–96.

Adar, Korwa G., and Isaac M. Munyae. 2001. 'Human Rights Abuse in Kenya Under Daniel Arap Moi, 1978'. *African Studies Quarterly* 5 (1).

Adeba, Brian. 2019. 'A Hijacked State: Violent Kleptocracy in South Sudan'. Enough. https://enoughproject.org/wp-content/uploads/AHijackedState_Enough_February2019-web.pdf.

Adekanye, J. 'Bayo. 1995. 'Structural Adjustment, Democratization and Rising Ethnic Tensions in Africa'. *Development and Change* 26 (2): 355–74. https://doi.org/10.1111/j.1467-7660.1995.tb00556.x.

Adly, Hossam. 2013. 'Fonctionnaires Internationaux à Genève: Le Poids Du Privilège'. *Espaces et Sociétés*, no. 3: 71–85.

Aebischer Perone, S, H Van Beerendonk, L Loutan, and J Avril. 2009. 'Prevention of Non Infectious Health Problems in Expatriates and Humanitarian Workers'. *Revue Medicale Suisse* 5 (May): 1012–14.

Agier, Michel. 2013. 'Espaces et temps du gouvernement humanitaire'. *Pouvoirs* 144 (1): 113–23. https://doi.org/10.3917/pouv.144.0113.

AIP. 2019. 'Côte d'Ivoire/Trois Présumés Coupeurs de Route Abattus à Yamoussoukro'. Abidjan.Net. 17 February 2019. https://news.abidjan.net/h/652782.html.

Alexander, Jennifer. 2000. 'Adaptive Strategies of Nonprofit Human Service Organizations in an Era of Devolution and New Public Management'. *Nonprofit Management and Leadership* 10 (3): 287–303. https://doi.org/10.1002/nml.10305.

Alix-Garcia, Jennifer, Anne Bartlett, and David Saah. 2012. 'Displaced Populations, Humanitarian Assistance and Hosts: A Framework for Analyzing Impacts on Semi-Urban Households'. *World Development* 40 (2): 373–86. https://doi.org/10.1016/j.worlddev.2011.06.002.

———. 2013. 'The Landscape of Conflict: IDPs, Aid and Land-Use Change in Darfur'. *Journal of Economic Geography* 13 (4): 589–617. https://doi.org/10.1093/jeg/lbs044.

Allais, Carol. 2011. 'Sexual Exploitation and Abuse by UN Peacekeepers : The Psychosocial Context of Behaviour Change'. *Scientia Militaria : South African Journal of Military Studies* 39 (1): 1–15.

Amutabi, Maurice N. 2005. 'Captured and Steeped in Colonial Dynamics and Legacy: The Case of Isolo Town in Kenya'. *African Urban Spaces in Historical Perspective* 213.

Anand, Nikhil. 2015. 'Leaky States: Water Audits, Ignorance, and the Politics of Infrastructure'. *Public Culture* 27 (2 (76)): 305–30. https://doi.org/10.1215/08992363-2841880.

———. 2017. *Hydraulic City: Water and the Infrastructures of Citizenship in Mumbai*. Duke University Press.

Anderson, David M., and Jacob McKnight. 2015. 'Understanding Al-Shabaab: Clan, Islam and Insurgency in Kenya'. *Journal of Eastern African Studies* 9 (3): 536–57. https://doi.org/10.1080/17531055.2015.1082254.

Anderson, Mary B. 1999. *Do No Harm: How Aid Can Support Peace--or War*. Lynne Rienner Publishers.

Andersson, Ruben. 2016. 'Here Be Dragons: Mapping an Ethnography of Global Danger'. *Current Anthropology* 57 (6): 707–31. https://doi.org/10.1086/689211.

Andersson, Ruben, and Florian Weigand. 2015. 'Intervention at Risk: The Vicious Cycle of Distance and Danger in Mali and Afghanistan'. *Journal of Intervention and Statebuilding* 9 (4): 519–41. https://doi.org/10.1080/17502977.2015.1054655.

Aning, Kwesi, and Fiifi Edu-Afful. 2013. 'Unintended Impacts and the Gendered Consequences of Peacekeeping Economies in Liberia'. *International Peacekeeping* 20 (1): 17–32. https://doi.org/10.1080/13533312.2013.761828.

Anonymous. 2016. 'An Eye for an Eye Is the Wrong Response to Attacks on Humanitarians'. *The Guardian*, 15 September 2016, sec. Global Development Professionals Network. https://www.theguardian.com/global-development-professionals-network/2016/sep/15/attack-terrain-south-sudan-to-attacks-on-humanitarians?CMP=share_btn_tw.

Appadurai, Arjun. 1996. *Modernity Al Large: Cultural Dimensions of Globalization*. U of Minnesota Press.

Arat-Koc, Sedef. 2012. 'A Transnational Whiteness? New Middle Classes, Globalism and Non-European "Whiteness"'. *On Whiteness*, 59.

ARC International. 2004. *ARC International Safety & Security Guidelines June 01, 2004.*

Arieff, Alexis, and Kelly Johnson. 2013. 'Crisis in Mali'. In . Congressional Research Service, Library of Congress.

Arsan, Andrew. 2014. *Interlopers of Empire: The Lebanese Diaspora in Colonial French West Africa*. Oxford University Press.

Ashworth, John. 1987. 'The Relationship between Capitalism and Humanitarianism'. *The American Historical Review* 92 (4): 813–28. https://doi.org/10.2307/1863948.

Ati, Hassan Abdel, Sara Pavanello, Susanne Jaspars, Ellen Martin, and Irina Mosel. 2011. 'City Limits : Urbanisation and Vulnerability in Sudan Juba Case Study'. *Humanitarian Policy Group*, no. January.

Atkinson, Rowland, and John Flint. 2001. 'Accessing Hidden and Hard-to-Reach Populations: Snowball Research Strategies'. *Social Research Update* 33 (1): 1–4.

Aujourd'hui-Mali. 2017. 'Maliweb.Net - "Golden Life" : Un Hôpital Ultramoderne Implanté à Bamako'. *Maliweb.Net* (blog). 2 July 2017. http://www.maliweb.net/sante/golden-life-hopital-ultramoderne-implante-a-bamako-2360592.html.

Autesserre, Séverine. 2002. 'United States "Humanitarian Diplomacy" in South Sudan'. https://doi.org/10.7916/D81N7Z78.

———. 2014. *Peaceland: Conflict Resolution and the Everyday Politics of International Intervention*. Cambridge University Press.

———. 2017. 'International Peacebuilding and Local Success: Assumptions and Effectiveness'. *International Studies Review* 19 (1): 114–32. https://doi.org/10.1093/isr/viw054.

Baas, Jorn. 2017. 'The International NGO Safety Organisation - INSO'. The International NGO Safety Organisation - INSO. 2017. http://ngosafety.org/.

Badiey, Naseem. 2013. 'The Strategic Instrumentalization of Land Tenure in'State-Building': The Case of Juba, South Sudan'. *Africa: The Journal of the International African Institute* 83 (1): 57–77.

Badiey, Naseem, and Christian Doll. 2018. 'Planning amidst Precarity: Utopian Imaginings in South Sudan'. *Journal of Eastern African Studies* 12 (2): 367–85. https://doi.org/10.1080/17531055.2018.1408305.

Barbarani, Sofia. 2017a. 'Juba in the Spotlight: Ongoing Turmoil in the World's Youngest Capital'. *The Guardian*, 8 May 2017, sec. Cities. https://www.theguardian.com/cities/2017/may/08/juba-spotlight-turmoil-world-youngest-capital-south-sudan.

———. 2017b. 'A Day in the Life of Juba's Bicycle Water Vendors'. Aljazeera. 18 May 2017. https://www.aljazeera.com/indepth/features/2017/05/day-life-juba-bicycle-water-vendors-170503113204777.html.

Bardelli, Nora. 2019. 'When the Refugee Status Becomes an Economic Asset: How Malians in a Burkinabé City Negotiate the "Refugee" Category'. *Ethnic and Racial Studies* 0 (0): 1–18. https://doi.org/10.1080/01419870.2019.1583351.

Barkan, Joel D. 1993. 'Kenya: Lessons From a Flawed Election'. *Journal of Democracy* 4 (3): 85–99. https://doi.org/10.1353/jod.1993.0045.

Barnard, Ryvka, and Riya Hassan. 2015. 'Why Does UN Hire G4S, Accomplice to Israeli Torture? | The Electronic Intifada'. 2 July 2015. https://electronicintifada.net/content/why-does-un-hire-g4s-accomplice-israeli-torture/14661.

Barnenstein, Ben. 2017. 'Hot Spots in Emerging Markets This Week: Turkey, Ivory Coast', 14 May 2017. https://www.bloomberg.com/news/articles/2017-05-14/hot-spots-in-emerging-markets-this-week-turkey-ivory-coast.

Basu, Sanjay, Jason Andrews, Sandeep Kishore, Rajesh Panjabi, and David Stuckler. 2012. 'Comparative Performance of Private and Public Healthcare Systems in Low- and Middle-Income Countries: A Systematic Review'. *PLOS Medicine* 9 (6): e1001244. https://doi.org/10.1371/journal.pmed.1001244.

Baumgart, Prof Dr-Ing Sabine, and Prof Dr Volker Kreibich. 2011. 'Informal Urbanization—Historical and Geographical Perspectives'. *DisP - The Planning Review* 47 (187): 12–23. https://doi.org/10.1080/02513625.2011.10654015.

Bazin, Laurent. 1997. 'Anthropologie Politique Dans Une Entreprise En Côte d'Ivoire : Domination et Logique d'accusation'. Thesis, Paris, EHESS. http://www.theses.fr/1997EHES0053.

BBC News. 2015. 'Hotel Reopens after Mali Attack', 15 December 2015, sec. Africa. https://www.bbc.com/news/world-africa-35101130.

BBC News. ———. 2018. 'Birmingham Prison: Government Takes over from G4S', 19 August 2018, sec. Birmingham & Black Country. https://www.bbc.com/news/uk-england-birmingham-45240742.

Beber, Bernd, Michael Gilligan, Jenny Guardado, and Sabrina Karim. 2016. 'Challenges and Pitfalls of Peacekeeping Economies'.

Beerli, Monique. 2017. 'Legitimating Organizational Change through the Power of Quantification: Intra-Organizational Struggles and Data Deviations'. *International Peacekeeping* 24 (5): 780–802. https://doi.org/10.1080/13533312.2017.1383565.

———. 2018. 'Saving the saviors: Security practices and professional struggles in the humanitarian space'. *International Political Sociology* 12 (1): 70–87.

Bellamy, Alex J., and Paul D. Williams. 2013. *Providing Peacekeepers: The Politics, Challenges, and Future of United Nations Peacekeeping Contributions.* OUP Oxford.

Bendech, M. Ag, M. Chauliac, P. Gerbouin Rérolle, N. Kante, and D. J. M. Malvy. 2000. 'Les Enjeux de La Consommation Alimentaire En Milieu Urbain à Bamako'. *Santé Publique* 12 (1 Suppl): 45Á.

Bendix, Regina. 2002. 'Capitalizing on Memories Past, Present, and Future: Observations on the Intertwining of Tourism and Narration'. *Anthropological Theory* 2 (4): 469–87. https://doi.org/10.1177/14634990260620567.

Bensimon, Cyril. 2016. 'Côte d'Ivoire : « Sous la pression militaire française, les djihadistes privilégient une politique de contournement »'. *Le Monde.fr*, 15 March 2016. http://www.lemonde.fr/afrique/article/2016/03/15/cote-d-ivoire-sous-la-pression-militaire-francaise-les-djihadistes-privilegient-une-politique-de-contournement_4882921_3212.html.

Bergamaschi, Isaline. 2013. 'French Military Intervention in Mali: Inevitable, Consensual yet Insufficient'. *Stability: International Journal of Security and Development* 2 (2). https://doi.org/10.5334/sta.bb.

Berry, Craig, and Clive Gabay. 2009. 'Transnational Political Action and "Global Civil Society" in Practice: The Case of Oxfam'. *Global Networks* 9 (3): 339–58. https://doi.org/10.1111/j.1471-0374.2009.00257.x.

Berthiaume, Lee. 2019. 'Canada Won't Extend Peacekeeping Mission in Mali: Freeland | National Post', 29 March 2019. https://nationalpost.com/pmn/news-pmn/canada-news-pmn/canada-wont-extend-peacekeeping-mission-in-mali-freeland.

Bertin, Jacques. 1973. 'Sémiologie Graphique'. *Flammarion, Paris.*

———. 1977. *La Graphique et Le Traitement Graphique de l'information.* 91 (084.21) BER.

Bertram, Eva. 1995. 'Reinventing Governments: The Promise and Perils of United Nations Peace Building'. *Journal of Conflict Resolution* 39 (3): 387–418. https://doi.org/10.1177/0022002795039003001.

Bertrand, Monique. 1998. 'Marchés Fonciers En Transition : Le Cas de Bamako (Mali)'. *Annales de Géographie* 107 (602): 381–409.

Besse, Jean-Marc. 2004. 'Quatre notes conjointes sur l'introduction de l'hodologie dans la pensée contemporaine'. *Les Carnets du paysage*, no. 11: 26–33.

———. 2006. 'Cartographie et pensée visuelle: réflexions sur la schématisation graphique'. https://halshs.archives-ouvertes.fr/halshs-00256710/document.

Bjerneld, Magdalena. 2009. 'Images, Motives, and Challenges for Western Health Workers in Humanitarian Aid'. http://urn.kb.se/resolve?urn=urn:nbn:se:uu:diva-100891.

Blaikie, Piers, Terry Cannon, Ian Davis, and Ben Wisner. 2014. *At Risk: Natural Hazards, People's Vulnerability and Disasters*. Routledge.

Blakely, Edward James, and Mary Gail Snyder. 1997. *Fortress America: Gated Communities in the United States*. Washington D.C. [etc.]: Brookings Institution Press.

Bloch, Peter H., Nancy M. Ridgway, and Scott A. Dawson. 1994. 'The Shopping Mall as Consumer Habitat'. *Journal of Retailing* 70 (1): 23–42. https://doi.org/10.1016/0022-4359(94)90026-4.

Blue Zone Properties. 2018. 'Estate Agency Profile for Blue Zone Properties'. 2018. https://www.property24.co.ke/estate-agency/blue-zone-properties/25986.

Bøås, Morten, and Liv E Torheim. 2013. 'The International Intervention in Mali: "Desert Blues" or a New Beginning?' *International Journal* 68 (3): 417–23. https://doi.org/10.1177/0020702013505430.

Boeing, Geoff. 2017. 'OSMnx: New Methods for Acquiring, Constructing, Analyzing, and Visualizing Complex Street Networks'. *Computers, Environment and Urban Systems* 65 (September): 126–39. https://doi.org/10.1016/j.compenvurbsys.2017.05.004.

———. 2018. 'Measuring the Complexity of Urban Form and Design'. *URBAN DESIGN International* 23 (4): 281–92. https://doi.org/10.1057/s41289-018-0072-1.

Boje, David M. 1991. 'The Storytelling Organization: A Study of Story Performance in an Office- Supply Firm'. *Administrative Science Quarterly* 36 (1): 106–26. https://doi.org/10.2307/2393432.

———. 2008. *Storytelling Organizations*. SAGE.

Boltanski, Luc, and Eve Chiapello. 2011. *Le Nouvel Esprit Du Capitalisme*. Tel 380. Paris: Gallimard.

Bouju, Jacky. 2000. 'Clientélisme, Corruption et Gouvernance Locale à Mopti (Mali)'. *AUTREPART-BONDY PARIS-*, no. 14: 143–164.

Bouquet, Christian, and Irène Kassi-Djodjo. 2014. '«Déguerpir» Pour Reconquérir l'espace Public à Abidjan.' *L'Espace Politique. Revue En Ligne de Géographie Politique et de Géopolitique*, no. 22.

Bourdieu, Pierre. 1980. *Le sens pratique*. Le sens commun. Paris: Ed. de minuit. http://data.rero.ch/01-0268806/html?view=GE_V1.

———. 1986. 'Habitus, code et codification'. *Actes de la Recherche en Sciences Sociales* 64 (1): 40–44. https://doi.org/10.3406/arss.1986.2335.

———. 2004. *L'habitus en sociologie entre objectivisme et subjectivisme.*

Bourdieu, Pierre, and Luc Boltanski. 1976. 'La production de l'idéologie dominante'. *Actes de la Recherche en Sciences Sociales* 2 (2): 3–73. https://doi.org/10.3406/arss.1976.3443.

Bourdieu, Pierre, Loïc J. D. Wacquant, and Etienne Ollion. 2014. *Invitation à La Sociologie Réflexive*. Liber. Paris: Seuil.

Bousquet, Anne. 2008. 'Développement urbain au Kenya : une sécession territoriale sous couvert de développement durable ?' *Afrique contemporaine* n° 226 (2): 269–90.

Boutellis, Arthur. 2015. 'Can the UN Stabilize Mali? Towards a UN Stabilization Doctrine?' *Stability: International Journal of Security and Development* 4 (1): Art. 33. https://doi.org/10.5334/sta.fz.

Boym, Svetlana. 2001. *The Future of Nostalgia*. New York: Basic Books.

Brabant, Koenraad Van, and Overseas Development Institute. 2010. 'Operational Security Management in Violent Environments: A Field Manual for Aid Agencies'. *HPN Good Practice Review* 8 (June): 194.

Britt, Thomas W., and Amy B. Adler. 1999. 'Stress and Health During Medical Humanitarian Assistance Missions'. http://www.dtic.mil/docs/citations/ADA365364.

Bronfenbrenner, Urie. 1977. 'Lewinian Space and Ecological Substance'. *Journal of Social Issues* 33 (4): 199–212. https://doi.org/10.1111/j.1540-4560.1977.tb02533.x.

Brown, Stephen. 2001. 'Authoritarian Leaders and Multiparty Elections in Africa: How Foreign Donors Help to Keep Kenya's Daniel Arap Moi in Power'. *Third World Quarterly* 22 (5): 725–39. https://doi.org/10.1080/01436590120084575.

Brown, Stephen, and Chandra Lekha Sriram. 2012. 'The Big Fish Won't Fry Themselves: Criminal Accountability for Post-Election Violence in Kenya'. *African Affairs* 111 (443): 244–60. https://doi.org/10.1093/afraf/ads018.

Brugger, Patrick. 2009. 'ICRC Operational Security: Staff Safety in Armed Conflict and Internal Violence'. *International Review of the Red Cross* 91 (874): 431. https://doi.org/10.1017/S1816383109990075.

Brunello, Giorgio, and Lorenzo Rocco. 2008. 'Educational Standards in Private and Public Schools'. *The Economic Journal* 118 (533): 1866–87. https://doi.org/10.1111/j.1468-0297.2008.02194.x.

Brunet, Roger. 1986. 'La Carte-Modèle et Les Chorèmes'. *Mappemonde* 86 (4): 2–6.

Bunge, William. 1971. *Fitzgerald: Geography of a Revolution*. Cambridge Mass. ; London England: Schenkman Publ.

———. 1979. 'Perspective on Theoretical Geography'. *Annals of the Association of American Geographers* 69 (1): 169–74. https://doi.org/10.1111/j.1467-8306.1979.tb01248.x.

———. 1988. *Nuclear War Atlas*. Oxford: B. Blackwell.

Burawoy, Michael. 1998. 'The Extended Case Method'. *Sociological Theory* 16 (1): 4–33. https://doi.org/10.1111/0735-2751.00040.

Burgess, Ernest W. 2008. 'The Growth of the City: An Introduction to a Research Project'. In *Urban Ecology*, 71–78. Springer.

Burke, Jason. 2016. 'South Sudan's Situation "dire and Deteriorating" as Fighting in Juba Rages'. *The Guardian*, 12 July 2016, sec. World news. https://www.theguardian.com/world/2016/jul/11/south-sudan-dire-deteriorating-fighting-juba-humanitarian-crisis.

Büscher, Karen. 2016. 'Reading Urban Landscapes of War and Peace: The Case of Goma, DRC'. In *Spatializing Peace and Conflict*, 79–97. Rethinking Peace and Conflict Studies. Palgrave Macmillan, London. https://doi.org/10.1057/9781137550484_5.

Büscher, Karen, Sophie Komujuni, and Ivan Ashaba. 2018. 'Humanitarian Urbanism in a Post-Conflict Aid Town: Aid Agencies and Urbanization in Gulu, Northern Uganda'. *Journal of Eastern African Studies* 12 (2): 348–66. https://doi.org/10.1080/17531055.2018.1456034.

Büscher, Karen, and Koen Vlassenroot. 2010. 'Humanitarian Presence and Urban Development: New Opportunities and Contrasts in Goma, DRC'. *Disasters* 34 (April): S256–73. https://doi.org/10.1111/j.1467-7717.2010.01157.x.

Calderón, César, and Luis Servén. 2010. 'Infrastructure and Economic Development in Sub-Saharan Africa'. *Journal of African Economies* 19 (suppl_1): i13–i87.

Carmona, Antonio Rodríguez. 2008. *El proyectorado: Bolivia tras 20 años de ayuda externa*. Intermón Oxfam Editorial.

Carnahan, Michael, William J. Durch, and Scott Gilmore. 2006. *Economic Impact of Peacekeeping*. United Nations, Peacekeeping Best Practices Unit.

Carnahan, Michael, Scott Gilmore, and and William Durch. 2007. 'New Data on the Economic Impact of UN Peacekeeping'. *International Peacekeeping* 14 (3): 384–402. https://doi.org/10.1080/13533310701422943.

CCAPS. 2019. 'CCAPS Social Conflict Analysis Database'. The Strauss Center. 2019. https://www.strausscenter.org/scad.html.

Chan, Szu Ping. 2013. 'Timeline: How G4S's Bungled Olympics Security Contract Unfolded', 21 May 2013, sec. Finance. https://www.telegraph.co.uk/finance/newsbysector/supportservices/10070425/Timeline-how-G4Ss-bungled-Olympics-security-contract-unfolded.html.

Chandler, Allison, and Benno Zogg. 2017. 'Mali's Fragile Peace'. *CSS Analyses in Security Policy* 215.

Chandler, David. 2007. 'The Security–Development Nexus and the Rise of "Anti-Foreign Policy"'. *Journal of International Relations and Development* 10 (4): 362–86. https://doi.org/10.1057/palgrave.jird.1800135.

Chandrasekaran, Rajiv. 2010. *Imperial Life in the Emerald City: Inside Iraq's Green Zone*. Vintage.

Chege, Peninah W., and Andanje Mwisukha. 2013. 'Benefits of Slum Tourism in Kibera Slum in Nairobi, Kenya'. *International Journal of Arts and Commerce* 2 (4): 94–102.

Chenal, Jérôme. 2009. 'Abidjan, La Métropole'. Les éditions du Lasur.

Chiricos, Ted, Sarah Eschholz, and Marc Gertz. 1997. 'Crime, News and Fear of Crime: Toward an Identification of Audience Effects'. *Social Problems* 44 (3): 342–57. https://doi.org/10.2307/3097181.

Chiricos, Ted, Kathy Padgett, and Marc Gertz. 2006. 'Fear, Tv News, and the Reality of Crime*'. *Criminology* 38 (3): 755–86. https://doi.org/10.1111/j.1745-9125.2000.tb00905.x.

Choplin, Armelle. 2018. *La mondialisation des pauvres : loin de Wall Street et de Davos*. La république des idées. Paris: Seuil. http://data.rero.ch/01-R008765493/html?view=GE_V1.

'Christie & Co'. 2018. 2018. http://christieand.co/.

Christopher, Anthony J. 2011. 'Secession and South Sudan: An African Precedent for the Future?' *South African Geographical Journal* 93 (2): 125–32. https://doi.org/10.1080/03736245.2011.619322.

CIVIC. 2016. 'Under Fire: The July 2016 Violence in Juba and UN Response'. Centre for Civilians in Conflict.

Coaffee, Jon. 2016. *Terrorism, Risk and the Global City: Towards Urban Resilience*. Routledge.

Coaffee, Jon, Paul O'Hare, and Marian Hawkesworth. 2009. 'The Visibility of (In)Security: The Aesthetics of Planning Urban Defences Against Terrorism'. *Security Dialogue* 40 (4–5): 489–511. https://doi.org/10.1177/0967010609343299.

Collinson, Sarah, Mark Duffield, Carol Berger, Diana Felix Da Costa, and Karl Sandstrom. 2013. 'Paradoxes of Presence: Risk Management and Aid Culture in Challenging Environments'.

Combaz, Emilie. 2013. 'The Impact of Integrated Missions on Humanitarian Operations'. GSDRC Working Paper. Birmingham: GSDRC, University of Birmingham.

Corboz, André. 1983. 'Le Territoire Comme Palimpseste'. *Diogène*, no. 121: 14.

Corkin, Lucy, and Christopher Burke. 2006. 'China's Interest and Activity in Africa's Construction and Infrastructure Sectors'. *Report Prepared for DFID China. Stellenbosch, South Africa: Centre for Chinese Studies*, 37–39.

Cottey, Andrew. 2008. 'Beyond Humanitarian Intervention: The New Politics of Peacekeeping and Intervention'. *Contemporary Politics* 14 (4): 429–46. https://doi.org/10.1080/13569770802519342.

Coulibaly, Diango. 2015. 'Mali : Hamdallaye ACI 2000 : Un Immeuble de 8 Étages s'effondre'. *Le Reporter*, 21 September 2015. http://maliactu.net/mali-hamdallaye-aci-2000-un-immeuble-de-8-etages-seffondre/.

Cox, Louis. 2008. 'What's Wrong with Risk Matrices?' *Risk Analysis* 28 (2): 497–512. https://doi.org/10.1111/j.1539-6924.2008.01030.x.

Crampton, Jeremy W. 2013. 'Space, Territory, Geography'. In *A Companion to Foucault*, 384–99. John Wiley & Sons, Ltd. https://doi.org/10.1002/9781118324905.ch19.

Crang, M. 1996. 'Envisioning Urban Histories: Bristol as Palimpsest, Postcards, and Snapshots'. *Environment and Planning A: Economy and Space* 28 (3): 429–52. https://doi.org/10.1068/a280429.

Creative Associates International. 2005. 'Juba Assessment : Town Planning and Administration'. http://www.southsudanmaps.org/resources/juba%20assessment%20report.pdf.

Crewe, Emma, and Priyanthi Fernando. 2006. 'The Elephant in the Room: Racism in Representations, Relationships and Rituals'. *Progress in Development Studies* 6 (1): 40–54. https://doi.org/10.1191/1464993406ps126oa.

Cullen, Poppy. 2016. 'Funeral Planning: British Involvement in the Funeral of President Jomo Kenyatta'. *The Journal of Imperial and Commonwealth History* 44 (3): 513–32. https://doi.org/10.1080/03086534.2016.1175737.

Custer, Samantha, Tanya Sethi, Carmen Cañas, Jose Sierra, David Castillo, Taryn Davis, Dina Abdel-fattah, et al. 2017. *Avoiding Data Graveyards : Insights from Data Producers & Users in Three Countries.*

Dandoy, Arnaud. 2013. 'Insécurité et Aide Humanitaire En Haïti: L'impossible Dialogue?'

———. 2014. 'Towards a Bourdieusian Frame of Moral Panic Analysis: The History of a Moral Panic inside the Field of Humanitarian Aid'. *Theoretical Criminology*, November, 1362480614553522. https://doi.org/10.1177/1362480614553522.

Dandoy, Arnaud, and Marc-Antoine Pérouse de Montclos. 2013. 'Humanitarian Workers in Peril? Deconstructing the Myth of the New and Growing Threat to Humanitarian Workers'. *Global Crime* 14 (4): 341–58. https://doi.org/10.1080/17440572.2013.831345.

Darcy, J., and C. Hofmann. 2003. 'According to Need?: Needs Assessment and Decision-Making in the Humanitarian Sector'. http://agris.fao.org/agris-search/search.do?recordID=GB2013203835.

Daughtry, J. Martin. 2015. *Listening to War: Sound, Music, Trauma, and Survival in Wartime Iraq*. Oxford University Press.

Davis, Mike. 1991. *City of Quartz: Excavating the Future in Los Angeles*. Third impression. London: New York : Verso.

———. 2006. *Planet of Slums*. London: Verso.

Debrie, Jean. 2001. 'Transport et Espaces d'entreprise: Les Stratégies Africaines Du Groupe Bolloré'. *Les Cahiers Scientifiques Du Transport* 39: 43–54.

Debrie, Jean, and Sandrine De Guio. 2004. 'Interfaces Portuaires et Compositions Spatiales: Instabilités Africaines'. *Autrepart*, no. 4: 21–36.

Dembelé, David. 2015. 'A Bamako, la direction du Radisson Blu sort de son silence'. *Le Monde.fr*, 25 November 2015. http://www.lemonde.fr/afrique/article/2015/11/25/a-bamako-la-direction-du-radisson-blu-sort-de-son-silence_4817169_3212.html.

———. 2016. 'Mali : fin de cavale pour Fawaz Ould Almeida, chef du groupe terroriste Al-Mourabitoune'. *Le Monde.fr*, 22 April 2016. https://www.lemonde.fr/afrique/article/2016/04/22/mali-fin-de-cavale-pour-fawaz-ould-almeida-chef-du-groupe-terroriste-al-mourabitoune_4907217_3212.html.

Denoiseux, Delphine. 2010. 'L'exportation de déchets dangereux vers l'Afrique : le cas du Probo Koala'. *Courrier hebdomadaire du CRISP* n° 2071 (26): 5–47.

Department of Safety and Security. 2013. 'Kenya Security Advisory'.

———. 2016. 'Minimum Operating Residential Security Standards (MORSS) - Kenya'.

Diahou, Alphonse Yapi, and Michel Simeu-Kamdem. 2018. 'Les «Finishing Touches» Ou Le Maillon Faible de l'hôtellerie de Luxe En Afrique Subsaharienne'. *Les Politiques de La Ville En Question: A La Recherche d'une Meilleure Gouvernance Urbaine En Afrique Subsaharienne*, 111.

Dobson, Jerome E., Stephen L. Egbert, Matthew D. Dunbar, and John C. Kostelnick. 2010. 'Geographers Tackle Landmines'. *Focus on Geography* 53 (3): 92–102. https://doi.org/10.1111/j.1949-8535.2010.00012.x.

Dodge, Toby. 2005. 'Iraqi Transitions: From Regime Change to State Collapse'. *Third World Quarterly* 26 (4–5): 705–21. https://doi.org/10.1080/0143659050 0127982.

Doevenspeck, Martin. 2012. '10 An Impossible Site?' *The Spatial Dimension of Risk: How Geography Shapes the Emergence of Riskscapes* 27: 137.

Dogra, Nandita. 2012. *Representations of Global Poverty: Aid, Development and International NGOs*. I.B.Tauris.

Donini, Antonio. 2007. 'Local Perceptions of Assistance to Afghanistan'. *International Peacekeeping* 14 (1): 158–72. https://doi.org/10.1080/135333 10601114376.

Duffield, Mark. 1994. 'Complex Emergencies and the Crisis of Developmentalism'. *IDS Bulletin* 25 (4): 37–45. https://doi.org/10.1111/j.1759-5436.1994.mp2 5004006.x.

———. 2007. *Development, Security and Unending War: Governing the World of Peoples*. Polity.

———. 2010a. 'The Liberal Way of Development and the Development—Security Impasse: Exploring the Global Life-Chance Divide'. *Security Dialogue* 41 (1): 53–76. https://doi.org/10.1177/0967010609357042.

———. 2010b. 'Risk-Management and the Fortified Aid Compound: Everyday Life in Post-Interventionary Society'. *Journal of Intervention and Statebuilding* 4 (4): 453–74. https://doi.org/10.1080/17502971003700993.

———. 2012a. 'Risk Management and the Bunkering of the Aid Industry'. *Development Dialogue* 58: 21–37.

———. 2012b. 'Challenging Environments: Danger, Resilience and the Aid Industry'. *Security Dialogue* 43 (5): 475–92. https://doi.org/10.1177/09670 10612457975.

———. 2014. 'From Immersion to Simulation: Remote Methodologies and the Decline of Area Studies'. *Review of African Political Economy* 41 (sup1): S75–S94.

Durch, William. 2009. 'The Economic Impact of Peacekeeping: An Update'. *Washington, DC, Center on International.*

ECHO. 2006. *Security Handbook for Humanitarian Organisations*. Edited by ECHO.

Edkins, Jenny. 2003. *Trauma and the Memory of Politics*. Cambridge University Press.

Edu-Afful, Fiifi, and Kwesi Aning. 2015. 'Peacekeeping Economies in a Sub-Regional Context: The Paradigmatic Cases of Liberia, Sierra Leone and Côte d'Ivoire'. *Journal of Intervention and Statebuilding* 9 (3): 391–407. https://doi.org/10.1080/17502977.2015.1070020.

Edwards, Michael. 1999. 'International Development NGOS: Agents of Foreign Aid or Vehicles for International Cooperation?' *Nonprofit and Voluntary Sector Quarterly* 28 (1_suppl): 25–37. https://doi.org/10.1177/08997649977 3746410.

Edwards, Michael, and Hulme. 1996. 'Too Close for Comfort? The Impact of Official Aid on Nongovernmental Organizations'. *World Development* 24 (6): 961–73. https://doi.org/10.1016/0305-750X(96)00019-8.

Egeland, Jan, Adele Harmer, and Abby Stoddard. 2011. 'To Stay and Deliver: Good Practice for Humanitarians in Complex Security Environments'.

Ehrenreich, John H., and Teri L. Elliott. 2004. 'Managing Stress in Humanitarian Aid Workers: A Survey of Humanitarian Aid Agencies' Psychosocial Training and Support of Staff'. *Peace and Conflict: Journal of Peace Psychology* 10 (1): 53–66. https://doi.org/10.1207/s15327949pac1001_4.

Elkins, Caroline. 2005. 'Imperial Reckoning: The Untold Story of Britain's Gulag in Kenya'.

Ellin, Nan. 1997. *Architecture of Fear*. Princeton Architectural Press.

ENS Mali. 1993. *Bamako*. Presses Univ de Bordeaux.

Esmaquel, Paterno. 2013. 'PH Tells Filipinos to Leave South Sudan'. Rappler. 23 December 2013. http://www.rappler.com//nation/46502-philippines-volunt ary-repatriation-south-sudan.

Essex, Stephen, and Brian Chalkley. 1998. 'Olympic Games: Catalyst of Urban Change'. *Leisure Studies* 17 (3): 187–206. https://doi.org/10.1080/02614369 8375123.

Euronews. 2017. 'Italy's Code of Conduct for NGOs Involved in Migrant Rescue: Text'. Euronews. 3 August 2017. http://www.euronews.com/2017/08/03/text-of-italys-code-of-conduct-for-ngos-involved-in-migrant-rescue.

EUTM. 2019. 'Home - EUTM Mali'. 2019. http://eutmmali.eu/.

Evans-Pritchard, E. E. (Edward Evan). 1940. *The Nuer : A Description of the Modes of Livelihood and Political Institutions of a Nilotic People*. Oxford : Clarendon Press.

Eye Radio Network. 2017. 'Peaceful Demonstration Interrupted'. *Eye Radio Network* (blog). 11 December 2017. http://www.eyeradio.org/peaceful-demonstration-interrupted/.

Fast, Larissa. 2007. 'Characteristics, Context and Risk: NGO Insecurity in Conflict Zones'. *Disasters* 31 (2): 130–54. https://doi.org/10.1111/j.1467-7717.2007.01001.x.

———. 2014. *Aid in Danger: The Perils and Promise of Humanitarianism*. University of Pennsylvania Press.

Featherstone, Mike. 1995. *Undoing Culture: Globalization, Postmodernism and Identity*. SAGE.

Fechter, Anne-Meike. 2010. 'Gender, Empire, Global Capitalism: Colonial and Corporate Expatriate Wives'. *Journal of Ethnic and Migration Studies* 36 (8): 1279–97. https://doi.org/10.1080/13691831003687717.

Fechter, Anne-Meike, and Heather Hindman, eds. 2011. *Inside the Everyday Lives of Development Workers: The Challenges and Futures of Aidland*. Sterling, VA: Kumarian Press.

Felix Da Costa, Diana. 2013. 'Working in Challenging Environments: Risk Management and Aid Culture in South Sudan–Field Report'.

Ferguson, James. 2005. 'Seeing like an Oil Company: Space, Security, and Global Capital in Neoliberal Africa'. *American Anthropologist* 107 (3): 377–382.

———. 2015. *Give a Man a Fish: Reflections on the New Politics of Distribution*. The Lewis Henry Morgan Lectures. Durham: Duke University Press.

FlightGlobal. 2013. 'Fire Closes Nairobi's Jomo Kenyatta Airport'. 7 August 2013. https://www.flightglobal.com/news/articles/fire-closes-nairobis-jomo-kenyatta-airport-389229/.

Foucault, Michel. 1975. *Surveiller et punir : naissance de la prison*. Bibliothèque des histoires. Paris: Gallimard. http://data.rero.ch/01-0060628/html?view=GE_V1.

———. 2004. *Sécurité, territoire, population : cours au Collège de France (1977–1978)*. Hautes études. Paris: Gallimard : Seuil. http://data.rero.ch/01-R003731879/html?view=GE_V1.

Fourchard, Laurent, and Isaac Olawale. 2003. *Security, Crime and Segregation in West African Cities since the 19th Century*. KARTHALA Editions.

'Fragile States Index | The Fund for Peace'. 2019. 2019. https://fragilestatesindex.org/.

Frampton, Kenneth. 1985. *Modern Architecture*. Thames and Hudson.

Freeman, Colin. 2015. 'Mali Gunmen Were Hunting for Air France Staff at Radisson Hotel', 22 November 2015, sec. World.

https://www.telegraph.co.uk/news/worldnews/africaandindianocean/mali/12010682/Mali-gunmen-were-hunting-for-Air-France-staff-at-Radisson-Hotel.html.

Frenzel, Fabian. 2012. 'Beyond "Othering": The Political Roots of Slum Tourism'. In *Slum Tourism*, 67–83. Routledge.

'G4S Kenya'. 2018. 2018. https://www.top-employers.com/en/companyprofiles/ke/g4s-kenya/.

Garland, Elizabeth. 2008. 'The Elephant in the Room: Confronting the Colonial Character of Wildlife Conservation in Africa'. *African Studies Review* 51 (3): 51–74. https://doi.org/10.1353/arw.0.0095.

Gaulme, François. 2001. 'L'« ivoirité », recette de guerre civile'. *Etudes* Tome 394 (3): 292–304.

Gettleman, Jeffrey. 2017. 'Militants Bomb Kenya Hotel, Killing 12; Shabab Claim Responsibility'. *The New York Times*, 21 December 2017, sec. World. https://www.nytimes.com/2016/10/26/world/africa/kenya-shabab-attack.html.

GICHD, and Stockholm International Institute. 2018. 'Global Mapping and Analysis of Anti-Vehicle Mine Incidents in 2017'. *Global CWD Repository*, May. http://commons.lib.jmu.edu/cisr-globalcwd/132.

Gillem, Mark L. 2007. *America Town: Building the Outposts of Empire*. University of Minnesota Press. https://muse.jhu.edu/book/31490.

Gilson, Erinn. 2011. 'Vulnerability, Ignorance, and Oppression'. *Hypatia* 26 (2): 308–32. https://doi.org/10.1111/j.1527-2001.2010.01158.x.

Glück, Zoltán. 2017. 'Security Urbanism and the Counterterror State in Kenya'. *Anthropological Theory* 17 (3): 297–321. https://doi.org/10.1177/1463499617729295.

Graham, Mark. 2013. 'The Virtual Dimension'. In *Global City Challenges*, 117–39. Palgrave Macmillan, London. https://doi.org/10.1007/978-1-137-28687-1_8.

Graham, Stephen, ed. 2007. *Cities, War, and Terrorism: Towards an Urban Geopolitics*. Transferred to digital print. Studies in Urban and Social Change. Malden: Blackwell Publ.

———. 2010. *Cities under Siege: The New Military Urbanism*. London: Verso.

Graham, Stephen, and Simon Marvin. 2001. *Splintering Urbanism: Networked Infrastructures, Technological Mobilities and the Urban Condition*. London [etc.]: Routledge.

Groth, Hans. 2017. *Africa's Population: In Search of a Demographic Dividend*. New York, NY: Springer Berlin Heidelberg.

GTC Global. 2018. 'CTG | Committed to Good | International Humanitarian Support'. CTG - Humanitarian Enablers. 2018. http://ctg.org/.

Guerin-Pace, France. 1998. 'Textual Statistics. An Exploratory Tool for the Social Sciences'. *Population: An English Selection* 10 (1): 73–95.

Guillot, Philippe. 1994. 'France, Peacekeeping and Humanitarian Intervention'. *International Peacekeeping* 1 (1): 30–43. https://doi.org/10.1080/13533319408413490.

Gupta, Akhil. 1995. 'Blurred Boundaries: The Discourse of Corruption, the Culture of Politics, and the Imagined State'. *American Ethnologist* 22 (2): 375–402. https://doi.org/10.1525/ae.1995.22.2.02a00090.

Gupta, Sumeet, B. S. Sahay, and Parikshit Charan. 2016. 'Relief Network Model for Efficient Disaster Management and Disaster Recovery'. In *Managing Humanitarian Logistics*, edited by B.S. Sahay, Sumeet Gupta, and Vinod Chandra Menon, 85–104. Springer Proceedings in Business and Economics. New Delhi: Springer India. https://doi.org/10.1007/978-81-322-2416-7_6.

Guterres, Antonio. 2019. 'Déclaration attribuable au porte-parole du Secrétaire général sur le Mali'. MINUSMA. 20 April 2019. https://minusma.unmissions.org/d%C3%A9claration-attribuable-au-porte-parole-du-secr%C3%A9taire-g%C3%A9n%C3%A9ral-sur-le-mali-14.

Haeringer, Philippe. 1985. 'Vingt Cinq Ans de Politique Urbaine à Abidjan, Ou La Tentation de l'urbanisme Intégral'. *Politique Africaine* 17: 20–40.

Haksöz, Çağrı, Sridhar Seshadri, and Ananth V. Iyer. 2011. *Managing Supply Chains on the Silk Road: Strategy, Performance, and Risk*. CRC Press.

Hall, Elaine. 1993. 'Smiling, Deferring, and Flirting: Doing Gender by Giving "Good Service"'. *Work and Occupations* 20 (4): 452–71. https://doi.org/10.1177/0730888493020004003.

Hamman, Philippe, Virginie Anquetin, and Céline Monicolle. 2017. 'Contemporary Meanings of the "Sustainable City": A Comparative Review of the French- and English-Language Literature'. *Sustainable Development* 25 (4): 336–55. https://doi.org/10.1002/sd.1660.

Hannam, Kevin, Mimi Sheller, and John Urry. 2006. 'Editorial: Mobilities, Immobilities and Moorings'. *Mobilities* 1 (1): 1–22. https://doi.org/10.1080/17450100500489189.

Hannerz, Ulf. 2003. 'Being There…and There…and There! Reflections on Multi-Site Ethnography'. *Ethnography* 4 (2): 201–16. https://doi.org/10.1177/14661381030042003.

Harley, John Brian. 2006. 'Deconstructing the Map'. *Cartographica: The International Journal for Geographic Information and Geovisualization*, October. https://doi.org/10.3138/E635-7827-1757-9T53.

Harmer, Adele. 2008. 'Integrated Missions: A Threat to Humanitarian Security?' *International Peacekeeping* 15 (4): 528–39. https://doi.org/10.1080/13533310802239824.

Harrison, Elizabeth. 2013. 'Beyond the Looking Glass? "Aidland" Reconsidered'. *Critique of Anthropology* 33 (3): 263–79. https://doi.org/10.1177/0308275X13490308.

Hartford, Kassandra. 2017. 'Listening to the Din of the First World War'. *Sound Studies* 3 (2): 98–114. https://doi.org/10.1080/20551940.2017.1392227.

Harvey, David. 1989. 'From Managerialism to Entrepreneurialism: The Transformation in Urban Governance in Late Capitalism'. *Geografiska Annaler. Series B, Human Geography*, 3–17. https://doi.org/10.2307/490503.

———. 2005. *A Brief History of Neoliberalism*. Oxford etc.: Oxford University Press. http://data.rero.ch/01-R003935742/html?view=GE_V1.

Haskell, Thomas L. 1985a. 'Capitalism and the Origins of the Humanitarian Sensibility, Part 1'. *The American Historical Review* 90 (2): 339–61. https://doi.org/10.2307/1852669.

———. 1985b. 'Capitalism and the Origins of the Humanitarian Sensibility, Part 2'. *The American Historical Review* 90 (3): 547–66. https://doi.org/10.2307/1860956.

HDT. 2016. 'POEA Allows Deployment of OFWs to South Sudan'. Sunstar Philippines. 24 January 2016. http://www.sunstar.com.ph/article/54347/.

Hearn, Julie. 2007. 'African NGOs: The New Compradors?' *Development and Change* 38 (6): 1095–1110. https://doi.org/10.1111/j.1467-7660.2007.00447.x.

Hendrickson, Dylan. 1998. 'Humanitarian Action in Protracted Crisis: An Overview of the Debates and Dilemmas'. *Disasters* 22 (4): 283–87. https://doi.org/10.1111/1467-7717.00092.

Henry, Marsha. 2015. 'Parades, Parties and Pests: Contradictions of Everyday Life in Peacekeeping Economies'. *Journal of Intervention and Statebuilding* 9 (3): 372–90. https://doi.org/10.1080/17502977.2015.1070021.

Henry, Marsha, and Paul Higate. 2013. *Insecure Spaces: Peacekeeping, Power and Performance in Haiti, Kosovo and Liberia*. Zed Books Ltd.

Henshaw, Victoria. 2013. *Urban Smellscapes : Understanding and Designing City Smell Environments*. Routledge. https://doi.org/10.4324/9780203072776.

Hervieu, Sébastien. 2017. 'Côte d'Ivoire : des rebelles « démobilisés » grognent aussi à Bouaké', 12 May 2017. https://www.lemonde.fr/afrique/article/2017/05/12/cote-d-ivoire-les-rebelles-demobilises-grognent-aussi-a-bouake_5126780_3212.html.

HESCO. 2018. 'MIL UNITS'. Hesco. 2018. https://www.hesco.com/products/mil-units/.

Higate, Paul, and Marsha Henry. 2004. 'Engendering (In)Security in Peace Support Operations'. *Security Dialogue* 35 (4): 481–98. https://doi.org/10.1177/0967010604049529.

Hiller, Harry H. 2000. 'Mega-Events, Urban Boosterism and Growth Strategies: An Analysis of the Objectives and Legitimations of the Cape Town 2004 Olympic Bid'. *International Journal of Urban and Regional Research* 24 (2): 449–58. https://doi.org/10.1111/1468-2427.00256.

Hillier, B., R. Burdett, J. Peponis, and A. Penn. 1987. 'Creating Life: Or, Does Architecture Determine Anything?' *Architecture et Comportement/Architecture and Behaviour* 3 (3): 233–50.

Hillier, B., A. Leaman, P. Stansall, and M. Bedford. 1976. 'Space Syntax'. *Environment and Planning B: Planning and Design* 3 (2): 147–85. https://doi.org/10.1068/b030147.

Hillier, Bill. 1996. *Space Is the Machine: A Configurational Theory of Architecture*. Cambridge: Cambridge University Press.

Hillier, Bill, and Julienne Hanson. 1984. *The Social Logic of Space*. Cambridge ; London [etc.]: Cambridge Univ. Press.

Hillier, Jean, and Emma Rooksby. 2005. *Habitus: A Sense of Place*. Ashgate.

Hoelscher, Kristian, Jason Miklian, and Håvard Mokleiv Nygård. 2017. 'Conflict, Peacekeeping, and Humanitarian Security: Understanding Violent Attacks Against Aid Workers'. *International Peacekeeping* 24 (4): 538–65. https://doi.org/10.1080/13533312.2017.1321958.

Hofnung, Thomas. 2011. *La crise ivoirienne: De Félix Houphouët-Boigny à la chute de Laurent Gbagbo*. La Découverte.

Hood, Christopher. 1995. 'The "New Public Management" in the 1980s: Variations on a Theme'. *Accounting, Organizations and Society* 20 (2): 93–109. https://doi.org/10.1016/0361-3682(93)E0001-W.

Hudson, Alan. 2001. 'NGOs' Transnational Advocacy Networks: From "Legitimacy" to "Political Responsibility"?' *Global Networks* 1 (4): 331–52. https://doi.org/10.1111/1471-0374.00019.

Hugman, Richard, Eileen Pittaway, and Linda Bartolomei. 2011. 'When "Do No Harm" Is Not Enough: The Ethics of Research with Refugees and Other

Vulnerable Groups'. *The British Journal of Social Work* 41 (7): 1271–87. https://doi.org/10.1093/bjsw/bcr013.

Hultman, Lisa, Jacob Kathman, and Megan Shannon. 2013. 'United Nations Peacekeeping and Civilian Protection in Civil War'. *American Journal of Political Science* 57 (4): 875–91. https://doi.org/10.1111/ajps.12036.

'Humanitarian Outcomes'. 2019. Humanitarian Outcomes. 2019. https://www.humanitarianoutcomes.org/.

Humphrey, Michael, and Estela Valverde. 2017. 'A Tale of Dual Cities: The Urban Miracle and Humanitarian Crisis Maps of Medellín (2002–2015)'. *Journal of Iberian and Latin American Research* 23 (2): 159–77. https://doi.org/10.1080/13260219.2017.1365927.

Hwang, Sohin, and Pablo De Roulet. 2017. 'Cover – Bibliography(Chorème)='. *O A R*, 2017. http://www.oarplatform.com/cover-bibliographychoreme/.

Hyndman, Jennifer. 2000. 'Gender and Geography at Work: The Perils of Perfect Pluralism at the United Nations High Commissioner for Refugees'. *Canadian Woman Studies* 19 (4): 48.

Ibrahim, F. N. 1991. 'The Southern Sudanese Migration to Khartoum and the Resultant Conflicts'. *GeoJournal* 25 (1): 13–18. https://doi.org/10.1007/BF00179762.

ICC Press Release. 2019. 'ICC Trial Chamber I Acquits Laurent Gbagbo and Charles Blé Goudé from All Charges'. ICC. 15 January 2019. https://www.icc-cpi.int/Pages/item.aspx?name=pr1427.

IFRC, ed. 1994. *Code of Conduct for The International Red Cross and Red Crescent Movement and Non-Governmental Organization (NGOs) in Disaster Relief.* Geneva: Disaster Policy Department International Federation of Red Cross and Red Crescent Societies.

———. 2011. *Stay Safe : The International Federation's Guide for Security Managers*. Edited by IFRC. Geneva.

———. 2019. 'Frequently Asked Questions - IFRC'. 2019. https://www.ifrc.org/en/who-we-are/working-with-us/frequently-asked-questions1/.

IGN France. 1980. 'Bamako et ses environs'. Bamako: Institut Géographique National.

Inglis, David. 2016. 'Sewers and Sensibilities: The Bourgeois Faecal Experience in the Nineteenth-Century City'. *The City and the Senses: Urban Culture Since 1500* 1: 105.

IRIN. 2013. 'What Future for Private Sector Involvement in Humanitarianism?' IRIN. 26 August 2013. http://www.irinnews.org/analysis/2013/08/26/what-future-private-sector-involvement-humanitarianism.

———. 2016. 'The Humanitarian Economy'. IRIN. 2016. http://newirin.irinnews.org/the-humanitarian-economy/.

Ivanova, Maria. 2007. 'Designing the United Nations Environment Programme: A Story of Compromise and Confrontation'. *International Environmental Agreements: Politics, Law and Economics* 7 (4): 337–61. https://doi.org/10.1007/s10784-007-9052-4.

Jackson, Ashley, and Steven A Zyck. 2017. 'Presence & Proximity: To Stay and Deliver, Five Years On'.

Jackson, John Brinckerhoff. 1994. *A Sense of Place, a Sense of Time*. Yale University Press.

Jacobs, Allan B. 1993. *Great Streets*. Cambridge Mass. ; London: MIT Press.

Jacquemin, Mélanie Y. 2004. 'Children's Domestic Work in Abidjan, Côte D'ivoire: The Petites Bonnes Have the Floor'. *Childhood* 11 (3): 383–97. https://doi.org/10.1177/0907568204044889.

Jaglin, Sylvy. 2004. 'Être branché ou pas'. *Flux* n° 56–57 (2): 4–12.

Jansen, Bram J. 2017. 'The Humanitarian Protectorate of South Sudan? Understanding Insecurity for Humanitarians in a Political Economy of Aid'. *The Journal of Modern African Studies* 55 (3): 349–70. https://doi.org/10.1017/S0022278X17000271.

———. 2018. *Kakuma Refugee Camp: Humanitarian Urbanism in Kenya's Accidental City*. Zed Books Ltd.

Jenkins, P. 2013. *Urbanization, Urbanism, and Urbanity in an African City: Home Spaces and House Cultures*. Springer.

Jenkins, Richard. 1984. 'Bringing It All Back Home: An Anthropologist in Belfast'. *Social Researching: Politics, Problems, Practice*, 147–164.

Jennings, Kathleen M. 2010. 'Unintended Consequences of Intimacy: Political Economies of Peacekeeping and Sex Tourism'. *International Peacekeeping* 17 (2): 229–43. https://doi.org/10.1080/13533311003625126.

———. 2014. 'Service, Sex, and Security: Gendered Peacekeeping Economies in Liberia and the Democratic Republic of the Congo'. *Security Dialogue* 45 (4): 313–30. https://doi.org/10.1177/0967010614537330.

———. 2015. 'Life in a "Peace-Kept" City: Encounters with the Peacekeeping Economy'. *Journal of Intervention and Statebuilding* 9 (3): 296–315. https://doi.org/10.1080/17502977.2015.1054659.

———. 2016. 'Blue Helmet Havens: Peacekeeping as Bypassing in Liberia and the Democratic Republic of the Congo'. *International Peacekeeping* 23 (2): 302–25. https://doi.org/10.1080/13533312.2016.1141055.

Jennings, Kathleen M., and Morten Bøås. 2015. 'Transactions and Interactions: Everyday Life in the Peacekeeping Economy'. *Journal of Intervention and Statebuilding* 9 (3): 281–95. https://doi.org/10.1080/17502977.2015.1070022.

Jeune Afrique - AFP. 2018. 'Mali : arrestation d'un commando qui « planifiait des attaques » à Bamako'. *JeuneAfrique.com* (blog). 11 August 2018. https://www.jeuneafrique.com/614731/politique/mali-arrestation-dun-commando-qui-planifiait-des-attaques-a-bamako/.

'Juba in the Making'. 2019. Juba in the Making. 2019. http://jubainthemaking.com/.

Kabran, Estelle, and Irit Eguavoen. 2019. 'Ferry Transportation in Abidjan: Establishment, Operation and Sustainability of a Paratransit System'. In . Center for Development Research, University of Bonn.

Kaika, Maria, and Erik Swyngedouw. 2000. 'Fetishizing the Modern City: The Phantasmagoria of Urban Technological Networks'. *International Journal of Urban and Regional Research* 24 (1): 120–38. https://doi.org/10.1111/1468-2427.00239.

Kamusoko, Courage. 2017. 'Bamako Metropolitan Area'. In *Urban Development in Asia and Africa: Geospatial Analysis of Metropolises*, edited by Yuji Murayama, Courage Kamusoko, Akio Yamashita, and Ronald C. Estoque, 275–91. The Urban Book Series. Singapore: Springer. https://doi.org/10.1007/978-981-10-3241-7_14.

Karlsrud, John. 2015. 'The UN at War: Examining the Consequences of Peace-Enforcement Mandates for the UN Peacekeeping Operations in the CAR, the DRC and Mali'. *Third World Quarterly* 36 (1): 40–54. https://doi.org/10.1080/01436597.2015.976016.

Katumanga, Musambayi. 2005. 'A City under Siege: Banditry & Modes of Accumulation in Nairobi, 1991–2004'. *Review of African Political Economy* 32 (106): 505–20. https://doi.org/10.1080/03056240500466981.

Kawachi, Ichiro, and Sarah Wamala. 2006. *Globalization and Health*. Oxford University Press.

Keen, David. 2008. *Complex Emergencies*. Polity.

Kemoni, Henry, and Patrick Ngulube. 2008. 'Relationship between Records Management, Public Service Delivery and the Attainment of the United Nations Millennium Development Goals in Kenya'. *Information Development* 24 (4): 296–306. https://doi.org/10.1177/0266666908098074.

Khayesi, Meleckidzedeck. 1997. 'Livable Streets for Pedestrians in Nairobi: The Challenge of Road Traffic Accidents'. *World Transport Policy and Practice* 3: 4–7.

Khayesi, Meleckidzedeck, Heiner Monheim, and Johannes Michael Nebe. 2010. 'Negotiating "Streets for All" in Urban Transport Planning: The Case for Pedestrians, Cyclists and Street Vendors in Nairobi, Kenya'. *Antipode* 42 (1): 103–126.

Kindersley, Nicki. 2019. 'Rule of Whose Law? The Geography of Authority in Juba, South Sudan'. *The Journal of Modern African Studies* 57 (1): 61–83. https://doi.org/10.1017/S0022278X18000629.

Knudsen, Tonny Brems. 1996. 'Humanitarian Intervention Revisited: Post-cold War Responses to Classical Problems'. *International Peacekeeping* 3 (4): 146–65. https://doi.org/10.1080/13533319608413644.

Korff, Valeska. 2012. *Between Cause and Control Management in a Humanitarian Organization*. s.n. https://www.rug.nl/research/portal/en/publications/between-cause-and-control-management-in-a-humanitarian-organization(ae3c1ecf-2921-4784-b6f4-c0ad24ecb179).html.

Korff, Valeska, Nicoletta Balbo, Melinda Mills, Liesbet Heyse, and Rafael Wittek. 2015. 'The Impact of Humanitarian Context Conditions and Individual Characteristics on Aid Worker Retention'. *Disasters* 39 (3): 522–45. https://doi.org/10.1111/disa.12119.

Kostelnick, John C., Dave McDermott, Rex J. Rowley, and Nathaniel Bunnyfield. 2013. 'A Cartographic Framework for Visualizing Risk'. *Cartographica: The International Journal for Geographic Information and Geovisualization* 48 (3): 200–224. https://doi.org/10.3138/carto.48.3.1531.

Kovats-Bernat, J. Christopher. 2002. 'Negotiating Dangerous Fields: Pragmatic Strategies for Fieldwork amid Violence and Terror'. *American Anthropologist* 104 (1): 208–22. https://doi.org/10.1525/aa.2002.104.1.208.

Krause, Monika. 2014. *The Good Project: Humanitarian Relief NGOs and the Fragmentation of Reason*. University of Chicago Press.

Krings, Thomas. 1995. 'Marginalisation and Revolt among the Tuareg in Mali and Niger'. *GeoJournal* 36 (1): 57–63. https://doi.org/10.1007/BF00812527.

Kristiansen, Stein, and Anne Ryen. 2002. 'Enacting Their Business Environments: Asian Entrepreneurs in East Africa'. *African and Asian Studies* 1 (3): 165–86. https://doi.org/10.1163/156921002X00040.

Kühn, Florian P. 2016. 'The Ambiguity of Things: Souvenirs from Afghanistan'. *Journal of Intervention and Statebuilding* 10 (1): 97–115. https://doi.org/10.1080/17502977.2015.1137397.

Lam, Hon, and Jan Selmer. 2004. 'Are Former "Third-culture Kids" the Ideal Business Expatriates?' *Career Development International* 9 (2): 109–22. https://doi.org/10.1108/13620430410526166.

Larkin, Brian. 2013. 'The Politics and Poetics of Infrastructure'. *Annual Review of Anthropology* 42 (1): 327–43. https://doi.org/10.1146/annurev-anthro-092412-155522.

Lascoumes, Pierre, ed. 2011. *Gouverner Par Les Instruments*. Gouvernances. Paris: Presses de Sciences Po.

Lauer, Josh. 2005. 'Driven to Extremes: Fear of Crime and the Rise of the Sport Utility Vehicle in the United States'. *Crime, Media, Culture* 1 (2): 149–68. https://doi.org/10.1177/1741659005054024.

Lavergne, Marc. 1997. 'La violence d'Etat comme mode de régulation de la croissance urbaine: le cas de Khartoum (Soudan)'. *Espace Populations Sociétés* 15 (1): 49–64. https://doi.org/10.3406/espos.1997.1789.

Lawhon, Mary, David Nilsson, Jonathan Silver, Henrik Ernstson, and Shuaib Lwasa. 2018. 'Thinking through Heterogeneous Infrastructure Configurations'. *Urban Studies* 55 (4): 720–32. https://doi.org/10.1177/0042098017720149.

Le Guilloux, Marion. 2019. 'Etat Civil Au Mali : Une Stratégie Nationale de Formation Pour Les Acteurs de l'état Civil En Préparation'. Text. EU Emergency Trust Fund for Africa - European Commission. 7 January 2019. https://ec.europa.eu/trustfundforafrica/all-news-and-stories/etat-civil-au-mali-une-strategie-nationale-de-formation-pour-les-acteurs-de_en.

Lefebvre, Henri. 1974. *La Production de l'espace*. Paris: Ed. Anthropos.

———. 1978. *La pensée marxiste et la ville (3 éd.) / par Henri Lefebvre*. Casterman (Tournai). http://ark.bnf.fr/ark:/12148/bpt6k4805166c.

Lemanski, Charlotte. 2006. 'Spaces of Exclusivity or Connection? Linkages between a Gated Community and Its Poorer Neighbour in a Cape Town Master Plan Development'. *Urban Studies* 43 (2): 397–420. https://doi.org/10.1080/00420980500495937.

Lemay-Hébert, Nicolas. 2018. 'Living in the Yellow Zone: The Political Geography of Intervention in Haiti'. *Political Geography* 67 (November): 88–99. https://doi.org/10.1016/j.polgeo.2018.08.018.

L'Essor. 2017. 'Golden life hospital : du haut de gamme!', 2017. http://www.essor.ml/golden-life-hospital-du-haut-de-gamme/.

Lewin, Kurt, and Jonathan Blower. 2009. 'The Landscape of War'. *Art in Translation* 1 (2): 199–209.

Lewis, David, and David Mosse. 2006. *Development Brokers and Translators: The Ethnography of Aid and Agencies*. Kumarian Press.

Liebschutz, Sarh F. 1992. 'Coping by Nonprofit Organizations during the Reagan Years'. *Nonprofit Management and Leadership* 2 (4): 363–80. https://doi.org/10.1002/nml.4130020405.

Liladrie, Sirena. 2010. '"Do Not Disturb/Please Clean Room": Hotel Housekeepers in Greater Toronto'. *Race & Class* 52 (1): 57–69. https://doi.org/10.1177/0306396809354177.

Lind, J., P. Mutahi, and M. Oosterom. 2015. 'Tangled Ties: Al-Shabaab and Political Volatility in Kenya'. IDS Evidence Report IDS Evidence Report;130. IDS. https://opendocs.ids.ac.uk/opendocs/handle/123456789/6018.

Loada, Augustin. 2006. 'L'émigration burkinabè face à la crise de « l'ivoirité »'. *Outre-Terre* no 17 (4): 343–56.

Loeffler, Jane C. 2005. 'Embassy Design: Security vs. Openness'. *Foreign Service Journal* 82: 44–50.

Logistics Cluster. 2016. 'South Sudan - NGO Offices in Juba, Aug 2016 | Logistics Cluster'. World Food Programme. https://logcluster.org/map/south-sudan-ngo-offices-juba-august-2016.

Lombart, Marie, Kevin Pierrat, and Marie Redon. 2014. 'Port-au-Prince : un « projectorat » haïtien ou l'urbanisme de projets humanitaires en question'. *Cahiers des Amériques latines* 2014/1 (75): 97–124.

Low, Setha. 2001. 'The Edge and the Center: Gated Communities and the Discourse of Urban Fear'. *American Anthropologist* 103 (1): 45–58. https://doi.org/10.1525/aa.2001.103.1.45.

———. 2004. *Behind the Gates: Life, Security, and the Pursuit of Happiness in Fortress America*. Routledge.

Lund, Christian. 2011. 'Property and Citizenship: Conceptually Connecting Land Rights and Belonging in Africa'. *Africa Spectrum* 46 (3): 71–75. https://doi.org/10.1177/000203971104600304.

MacKinnon, Catharine A. 1979. *Sexual Harassment of Working Women: A Case of Sex Discrimination*. A Yale Fastback 19. New Haven: Yale University.

Macpherson, Robert, and Bennett Pafford. 1999. *CARE International Safety and Security Handbook*. Edited by CARE International.

Magassa, Kaourou. 2019. 'Mali : après le massacre il faut des "soldats éthiques" pour mettre fin à "l'épuration ethnique"'. TV5MONDE. 24 March 2019. https://information.tv5monde.com/video/mali-apres-le-massacre-il-faut-des-soldats-ethiques-pour-mettre-fin-l-epuration-ethnique.

Maier, Florentine, Michael Meyer, and Martin Steinbereithner. 2016. 'Nonprofit Organizations Becoming Business-Like: A Systematic Review'. *Nonprofit and*

Voluntary Sector Quarterly 45 (1): 64–86. https://doi.org/10.1177/0899764014561796.

Mamdani, Mahmood. 2016. 'Who's to Blame in South Sudan?,'. *Boston Review* 28.

———. 2018. 'Opinion | The Trouble With South Sudan's New Peace Deal'. *The New York Times*, 28 September 2018, sec. Opinion. https://www.nytimes.com/2018/09/24/opinion/south-sudan-peace-agreement.html.

Manji, Firoze, and Carl O'Coill. 2002. 'The Missionary Position: NGOs and Development in Africa'. *International Affairs* 78 (3): 567–84. https://doi.org/10.1111/1468-2346.00267.

Manzi, Tony, and Bill Smith-Bowers. 2005. 'Gated Communities as Club Goods: Segregation or Social Cohesion?' *Housing Studies* 20 (2): 345–59. https://doi.org/10.1080/0267303042000331817.

Marchand, Pascal, and Pierre Ratinaud. 2012. 'L'analyse de Similitude Appliquée Aux Corpus Textuels: Les Primaires Socialistes Pour l'élection Présidentielle Française (Septembre-Octobre 2011)'. *Actes Des 11eme Journées Internationales d'Analyse Statistique Des Données Textuelles. JADT* 2012: 687–699.

Marcus, George E. 1995. 'Ethnography in/of the World System: The Emergence of Multi-Sited Ethnography'. *Annual Review of Anthropology* 24 (1): 95–117. https://doi.org/10.1146/annurev.an.24.100195.000523.

Mashal, Mujib, and Fatima Faizi. 2018. 'Siege at Kabul Hotel Caps a Violent 24 Hours in Afghanistan'. *The New York Times*, 22 January 2018, sec. World. https://www.nytimes.com/2018/01/21/world/asia/afghanistan-hotel-attack.html.

Materu, Peter Nicolas. 2007. *Higher Education Quality Assurance in Sub-Saharan Africa*. World Bank Working Papers. The World Bank. https://doi.org/10.1596/978-0-8213-7272-2.

Matzler, Kurt, Franz Bailom, Stephan Friedrich von den Eichen, and Thomas Kohler. 2013. 'Business Model Innovation: Coffee Triumphs for Nespresso'. *Journal of Business Strategy* 34 (2): 30–37.

Mbembe, Achille. 2008. 'Necropolitics'. In *Foucault in an Age of Terror: Essays on Biopolitics and the Defence of Society*, edited by Stephen Morton and Stephen Bygrave, 152–82. London: Palgrave Macmillan UK. https://doi.org/10.1057/9780230584334_9.

McCrea, Rod, Tung-Kai Shyy, and Robert Stimson. 2006. 'What Is the Strength of the Link between Objective and Subjective Indicators of Urban Quality of Life?' *Applied Research in Quality of Life* 1 (1): 79–96.

McMichael, Gabriella. 2014. 'Rethinking Access to Land and Violence in Post-War Cities: Reflections from Juba, Southern Sudan'. *Environment and Urbanization* 26 (2): 389–400. https://doi.org/10.1177/0956247814539431.

———. 2016. 'Land Conflict and Informal Settlements in Juba, South Sudan'. *Urban Studies* 53 (13): 2721–37. https://doi.org/10.1177/0042098015612960.

McMichael, Gabriella, and Asa Massleberg. 2010. 'Landmines and Land Rights in Southern Sudan'. *Geneva: Geneva International Center for Humanitarian Demining.*

Mednick, Sam. 2018. 'South Sudan Plans to Build New Capital in Former Game Park'. AP NEWS. 15 November 2018. https://apnews.com/db001b30af8b4412a193ce335162a980.

Methiaux, Florence. 2018. 'A Juba, des archivistes au chevet de l'histoire du Soudan du Sud', 3 April 2018. https://www.lemonde.fr/afrique/article/2018/04/03/a-juba-des-archivistes-au-chevet-de-l-histoire-du-soudan-du-sud_5280135_3212.html.

Miettaux, Florence. 2019. 'Reaching the Unreachable'. *Juba in the Making* (blog). 14 January 2019. http://jubainthemaking.com/reaching-the-unreachable/.

Miliband, David. 2014. 'It's Time to Reassess the Goals of Humanitarian Aid'. *The Guardian*, 28 February 2014, sec. Global development. https://www.theguardian.com/global-development/poverty-matters/2014/feb/28/humanitarian-aid-goals-david-miliband.

Miliband, David, and Ravi Gurumurthy. 2015. 'Improving Humanitarian Aid'. *Foreign Affairs*, 16 June 2015. https://www.foreignaffairs.com/articles/2015-06-16/improving-humanitarian-aid.

Mills, L. R. 1985. 'The Growth of Juba in Southern Sudan.' http://www.popline.org/node/422178.

'MINUSMA'. 2017. MINUSMA. 2017. https://minusma.unmissions.org/.

Mitchell, Don. 2001. 'The Lure of the Local: Landscape Studies at the End of a Troubled Century'. *Progress in Human Geography* 25 (2): 269–281.

Monmonier, Mark Stephen. 1995. *Drawing the Line: Tales of Maps and Cartocontroversy*. New York: H. Holt.

Morbe, Thomas Tombe. 2018. 'Local Government Administration and Potable Water Supply in Juba Payam, South Sudan'. Thesis, Kampala International University. http://ir.kiu.ac.ug/xmlui/handle/20.500.12306/1406.

Moretti, Franco. 2005. *Graphs, Maps, Trees: Abstract Models for a Literary History*. Verso.

Moretti, Franco, and Dominique Pestre. 2015. 'Bankspeak'. *New Left Review*, II,, no. 92: 75–99.

Morgan, Hiba. 2018. 'South Sudan Archivists Fear Loss of Historical Texts'. 3 January 2018. http://www.aljazeera.com/news/2018/01/south-sudan-archivists-fear-loss-legacy-texts-180102110555354.html.

Morin, Richard, and Anne-Marie Séguin. 1997. 'La Banque Mondiale et Les Politiques Urbaines: Le Cas de Bamako, Mali'. *Canadian Journal of Development Studies / Revue Canadienne d'études Du Développement* 18 (1): 23–47. https://doi.org/10.1080/02255189.1997.9669693.

Mosse, David. 2005. *Cultivating Development : An Ethnography of Aid Policy and Practice (Anthropology, Culture and Society Series)*. {Pluto Press}. http://www.amazon.ca/exec/obidos/redirect?tag=citeulike09-20&path=ASIN/0745317987.

———. 2011. *Adventures in Aidland: The Anthropology of Professionals in International Development*. Vol. 6. Berghahn Books.

Mosse, David, and David Lewis. 2005. 'The Aid Effect'. *Giving and Governing in International Development. London: Pluto.*

Mueller, Susanne D. 2008. 'The Political Economy of Kenya's Crisis'. *Journal of Eastern African Studies* 2 (2): 185–210. https://doi.org/10.1080/17531050802058302.

Muggah, Robert. 2013. *Stabilization Operations, Security and Development: States of Fragility*. Routledge.

Müller-Mahn, Detlef. 2012. *The Spatial Dimension of Risk: How Geography Shapes the Emergence of Riskscapes*. Routledge.

Mwaruvie, John, and Peter Kirui. 2012. 'The Dilemma of Hosting Refugees: A Focus on the Insecurity in North-Eastern Kenya', April. https://karuspace.karu.ac.ke/handle/20.500.12092/1689.

Myers, Garth. 2011. *African Cities: Alternative Visions of Urban Theory and Practice*. Zed Books Ltd.

Nader, Laura. 1972. 'Up the Anthropologist: Perspectives Gained From Studying Up'. https://eric.ed.gov/?id=ED065375.

Natsios, Andrew S. 1995. 'NGOs and the UN System in Complex Humanitarian Emergencies: Conflict or Cooperation?' *Third World Quarterly* 16 (3): 405–420.

Ndlovu-Gatsheni, Sabelo J. 2013. *Coloniality of Power in Postcolonial Africa*. African Books Collective.

Newman, Oscar. 1972. *Defensible Space: Crime Prevention through Urban Design*. New York N.Y: Macmillan.

———. 1973. *Defensible Space: People and Design in the Violent City*. London: Architectural Press.

Nossiter, Adam. 2011. 'Hundreds Killed in Ivory Coast Town as Conflict Intensifies'. *The New York Times*, 2 April 2011, sec. Africa. https://www.nytimes.com/2011/04/03/world/africa/03ivory.html.

Noy, Chaim. 2008. 'Sampling Knowledge: The Hermeneutics of Snowball Sampling in Qualitative Research'. *International Journal of Social Research Methodology* 11 (4): 327–344.

OCHA. 2017. 'Financial Tracking Service'. 2017. https://fts.unocha.org/.

Odede, Kennedy. 2010. 'Slumdog Tourism'. *The New York Times*, 2010.

Olson, Lara. 2006. 'Fighting for Humanitarian Space: NGOs in Afghanistan'. *Journal of Military and Strategic Studies* 9 (1). https://jmss.org/jmss/index.php/jmss/article/view/121.

Ondimu, Kennedy Nyabuti. 2007. 'Workplace Violence among Domestic Workers in Urban Households in Kenya: A Case of Nairobi City'. *Eastern Africa Social Science Research Review* 23 (1): 37–61. https://doi.org/10.1353/eas.2007.0005.

Palen, Leysia, Robert Soden, T. Jennings Anderson, and Mario Barrenechea. 2015. 'Success & Scale in a Data-Producing Organization: The Socio-Technical Evolution of OpenStreetMap in Response to Humanitarian Events'. In *Proceedings of the 33rd Annual ACM Conference on Human Factors in Computing Systems*, 4113–4122. CHI '15. New York, NY, USA: ACM. https://doi.org/10.1145/2702123.2702294.

Panyue, Huang. 2016. 'UN Medical Officer Visits Chinese Peacekeeping Hospital in Mali - China Military'. 8 November 2016. http://eng.chinamil.com.cn/view/2016-11/08/content_7348970.htm.

Parenteau, René, and François Charbonneau. 1992. 'Abidjan: Une Politique de l'habitat Au Service Du Plan Urbain'. *Cahiers de Géographie Du Québec* 36 (99): 415–437.

Park, Robert E., and Ernest W. Burgess. 2012. *The City*. University of Chicago Press.

Parker, Ken W. 2002. 'Making Connections : Travel, Technology and Global Air Networks'. In, edited by B. E. Hanna, E. J. Woodley, J. A. Summerville, and E. L. Buys. QUT, Brisbane: Queensland University of Technology. https://eprints.qut.edu.au/699/.

Patterson, M. 2009. *Privatising Peace: A Corporate Adjunct to United Nations Peacekeeping and Humanitarian Operations*. Springer.

Peck, Jamie, and Nik Theodore. 2012. 'Follow the Policy: A Distended Case Approach'. *Environment and Planning A* 44 (1): 21–30. https://doi.org/10.1068/a44179.

Pennington-Gray, Lori, Yvette Reisinger, Jung Eun Kim, and Brijesh Thapa. 2005. 'Do US Tour Operators' Brochures Educate the Tourist on Culturally Responsible Behaviours? A Case Study for Kenya'. *Journal of Vacation Marketing* 11 (3): 265–84. https://doi.org/10.1177/1356766705055719.

Persky, Joseph, and Wim Wiewel. 1994. 'The Growing Localness of the Global City'. *Economic Geography* 70 (2): 129–43. https://doi.org/10.2307/143651.

Pfeiffer, James. 2003. 'International NGOs and Primary Health Care in Mozambique: The Need for a New Model of Collaboration'. *Social Science & Medicine* 56 (4): 725–38. https://doi.org/10.1016/S0277-9536(02)00068-0.

Pfeiffer, James, Wendy Johnson, Meredith Fort, Aaron Shakow, Amy Hagopian, Steve Gloyd, and Kenneth Gimbel-Sherr. 2008. 'Strengthening Health Systems in Poor Countries: A Code of Conduct for Nongovernmental Organizations'. *American Journal of Public Health* 98 (12): 2134–40. https://doi.org/10.2105/AJPH.2007.125989.

Pflanz, Mike. 2013. 'Nairobi Shopping Mall Attacks: Britons among Those Caught up in Terrorist Assault', 21 September 2013, sec. World. https://www.telegraph.co.uk/news/worldnews/africaandindianocean/kenya/10325536/Nairobi-shopping-mall-attacks-Britons-among-those-caught-up-in-terrorist-assault.html.

Piétri, M. 1881. 'Mission Gallieni, 1880–1881: Itinéraire de Dio à Bammako'. Mission Gallieni, 1880–1881.

Piveteau, Jean-Luc. 1996. 'Notre Territorialité n'est-Elle Pas Essentiellement Masculine?' *Géographie et Cultures* 20: 69–80.

Plett, Barbara. 2011. 'Did UN Forces Take Sides in Ivory Coast?', 7 April 2011, sec. Africa. https://www.bbc.com/news/world-africa-13004462.

Potvin, Marianne. 2013. 'Humanitarian Urbanism under a Neoliberal Regime'. In *Cities*, 29:31. Berlin.

Pouget, Emile. 1908. *Le sabotage*. Bibliothèque du mouvement prolétarien. Paris: M. Rivière. http://data.rero.ch/01-R004254604/html?view=GE_V1.

Pozo Marín, Alejandro. 2017. 'Perilous Terrain - Humanitarian Action at Risk in Mali'. MSF.

PRIO. 2019. 'Peace Research Institute Oslo (PRIO)'. 2019. https://www.prio.org.

Rader, Emilee, Rick Wash, and Brandon Brooks. 2012. 'Stories As Informal Lessons About Security'. In *Proceedings of the Eighth Symposium on Usable Privacy and Security*, 6:1–6:17. SOUPS '12. New York, NY, USA: ACM. https://doi.org/10.1145/2335356.2335364.

Raffestin, Claude. 1983. 'Les Grandes Villes Sont Frappées de Cancer Galopant'. *Le Temps Stratégique*, 75–82.

Rajak, Dinah, and Jock Stirrat. 2013. 'Parochial Cosmopolitanism and the Power of Nostalgia'. In *Adventures In Aidland: The Anthropology of Professionals in International Development*. Berghahn Books.

Raleigh, Clionadh, Andrew Linke, Håvard Hegre, and Joakim Karlsen. 2010. 'Introducing ACLED: An Armed Conflict Location and Event Dataset: Special Data Feature'. *Journal of Peace Research* 47 (5): 651–60. https://doi.org/10.1177/0022343310378914.

Razac, Olivier. 2000. *Histoire Politique Du Barbelé: La Prairie, La Tranchée, Le Camp*. La Fabrique éditions.

Reinert, Max. 1990. 'Alceste Une Méthodologie d'analyse Des Données Textuelles et Une Application: Aurelia De Gerard De Nerval'. *Bulletin of Sociological Methodology/Bulletin de Méthodologie Sociologique* 26 (1): 24–54. https://doi.org/10.1177/075910639002600103.

Renouf, Jean S. 2011. 'Understanding How the Identity of International Aid Agencies and Their Approaches to Security Are Mutually Shaped'. Phd, The London School of Economics and Political Science (LSE). http://etheses.lse.ac.uk/171/.

Reporters. 1986. 'International Court Settles West African Land Dispute'. *Chicago Sun-Times*, 24 December 1986. https://www.highbeam.com/doc/1P2-3802162.html.

———. 2018. 'Oxfam Faces Further Allegations of Harassment Cover-Up'. *The Telegraph*, 17 March 2018. https://www.telegraph.co.uk/news/2018/03/17/oxfam-faces-allegations-harassment-cover-up/.

Reuters. 2017. 'Heavy Gunfire in Ivory Coast as Military Tries to End Mutiny'. *The Guardian*, 15 May 2017, sec. World news. http://www.theguardian.com/world/2017/may/15/heavy-gunfire-ivory-coast-military-tries-end-mutiny.

Reuters, and agencies. 2018. 'Haiti Shuts down Oxfam GB over Prostitution Scandal'. *The Guardian*, 14 June 2018, sec. World news. http://www.theguardian.com/world/2018/jun/14/haiti-shuts-down-oxfam-gb-over-prostitution-scandal.

RFI. 2017. 'Mali: fin de la grève des travailleurs de la santé'. RFI Afrique. 16 April 2017. http://www.rfi.fr/afrique/20170416-mali-fin-greve-travailleurs-sante-publique-medecine-hopital.

Roach, Steven C., and Derrick K. Hudson. 2018. *The Challenge of Governance in South Sudan: Corruption, Peacebuilding, and Foreign Intervention*. Routledge.

Robinson, Anthony C., Robert E. Roth, and Alan M. MacEachren. 2011. 'Understanding User Needs for Map Symbol Standards in Emergency Management'. *Journal of Homeland Security and Emergency Management* 8 (1).

Robinson, Jennifer. 2011. 'Comparisons: Colonial or Cosmopolitan?' *Singapore Journal of Tropical Geography* 32 (2): 125–40. https://doi.org/10.1111/j.1467-9493.2011.00423.x.

———. 2016. 'Thinking Cities through Elsewhere: Comparative Tactics for a More Global Urban Studies'. *Progress in Human Geography* 40 (1): 3–29. https://doi.org/10.1177/0309132515598025.

Rocca, Rosa Anna La. 2009. 'Soft Mobility and Urban Transformation'. *Tema. Journal of Land Use, Mobility and Environment* 2. https://doi.org/10.6092/1970-9870/125.

Rodriguez Harvey, Karla. 2016. 'AMAZING KENYA - WELCOME BOOKLET Relocation Guide for United Nations Secretariat Staff & Families', no. May 2016: 74.

Rodriguez-Torres, Deyssi, and Hélène Charton-Bigot, eds. 2010. *Nairobi Today: The Paradox of a Fragmented City*. Dar es Salam, Tanzania: Mkuki na Nyota.

Roger, Benjamin. 2015. 'Il y a trente ans éclatait la « guerre de Noël » entre le Mali et le Burkina Faso'. *JeuneAfrique.com* (blog). 25 December 2015. http://www.jeuneafrique.com/288381/politique/il-y-a-quarante-ans-eclatait-la-guerre-de-noel-entre-le-mali-et-le-burkina/.

Rogers, Charles, and Brian Sytsma. 1999. *WorldVision Security Manual: Safety Awareness for Aid Workers*. Edited by WorldVision. Geneva.

Rolandsen, Øystein H. 2015. 'Small and Far Between: Peacekeeping Economies in South Sudan'. *Journal of Intervention and Statebuilding* 9 (3): 353–71. https://doi.org/10.1080/17502977.2015.1070024.

Romer, Daniel, Kathleen Hall Jamieson, and Sean Aday. 2006. 'Television News and the Cultivation of Fear of Crime'. *Journal of Communication* 53 (1): 88–104. https://doi.org/10.1111/j.1460-2466.2003.tb03007.x.

Roy, Ananya. 2005. 'Urban Informality: Toward an Epistemology of Planning'. *Journal of the American Planning Association* 71 (2): 147–58. https://doi.org/10.1080/01944360508976689.

———. 2011. 'Slumdog Cities: Rethinking Subaltern Urbanism'. *International Journal of Urban and Regional Research* 35 (2): 223–238.

Ryfman, Philippe. 2016. *Une histoire de l'humanitaire*. La Découverte.

Salmon, Christian. 2013. *Storytelling: La machine à fabriquer des histoires et à formater les esprits*. La Découverte.

Sanogo, Bakary. 2014. 'Flag-Raising Ceremony Marks AfDB's Return to Its Official Headquarters in Côte d'Ivoire'. African Development Bank. 8 September 2014. https://www.afdb.org/en/news-and-events/flag-raising-ceremony-marks-afdbs-return-to-its-official-headquarters-in-cote-divoire-13474/.

Saraceno, Francesco. 2015. 'Reflections on Azawad Crisis and Malian Democracy: The Statehood, Its Deficiencies and Inclusion Failure'. *Journal of Asian and African Studies* 50 (3): 343–58. https://doi.org/10.1177/002190961 4529265.

Sassen, Saskia. 2013. *The Global City: New York, London, Tokyo*. Princeton University Press.

Sautman, Barry, and Yan Hairong. 2009. 'African Perspectives on China–Africa Links'. *The China Quarterly* 199 (September): 728–59. https://doi.org/10.1017/S030574100999018X.

Says, Magda. 2016. 'Lisa Smirl, "Spaces of Aid"'. *Development Book Review* (blog). 8 June 2016. https://developmentbookreview.com/2016/06/08/lisa-smirl-spaces-of-aid/.

Schindler, Seth. 2017. 'Towards a Paradigm of Southern Urbanism'. *City* 21 (1): 47–64. https://doi.org/10.1080/13604813.2016.1263494.

Schouten, Peer. 2011. '3. Political Topographies Of Private Security In Sub-Saharan Africa'. *African Engagements*, January, 56–83.

Scott, Colin. 2002. 'Private Regulation of the Public Sector: A Neglected Facet of Contemporary Governance'. *Journal of Law and Society* 29 (1): 56–76. https://doi.org/10.1111/1467-6478.00211.

Scott, James C. 1990. *Domination and the Arts of Resistance: Hidden Transcripts*. New Haven ; London: Yale Univ. Press.

———. 1998. *Seeing like a State: How Certain Schemes to Improve the Human Condition Have Failed*. Yale Agrarian Studies. New Haven: Yale University Press.

Sexton, Alexandra E., Allison Hayes-Conroy, Elizabeth L. Sweet, Mara Miele, and James Ash. 2017. 'Better than Text? Critical Reflections on the Practices of Visceral Methodologies in Human Geography'. *Geoforum* 82 (June): 200–201. https://doi.org/10.1016/j.geoforum.2017.03.014.

Shankleman, Jill. 2011. 'Oil and State Building in South Sudan'. *United States Institute of Peace. Special Report* 282.

Sharland, Lisa. 2015. 'Counter-IED Technology in UN Peacekeeping: Expanding Capability and Mitigating Risks'. *International Peacekeeping* 22 (5): 587–602. https://doi.org/10.1080/13533312.2015.1096368.

Sheppard, Eric, Helga Leitner, and Anant Maringanti. 2013. 'Provincializing Global Urbanism: A Manifesto'. *Urban Geography* 34 (7): 893–900. https://doi.org/10.1080/02723638.2013.807977.

Silver, Jonathan. 2014. 'Incremental Infrastructures: Material Improvisation and Social Collaboration across Post-Colonial Accra'. *Urban Geography* 35 (6): 788–804. https://doi.org/10.1080/02723638.2014.933605.

———. 2015. 'Disrupted Infrastructures: An Urban Political Ecology of Interrupted Electricity in Accra'. *International Journal of Urban and Regional Research* 39 (5): 984–1003. https://doi.org/10.1111/1468-2427.12317.

Simondon, Gilbert. 2012. *Du Mode d'existence Des Objets Techniques*. Nouv. éd. rev. et corr. Philosophie. Paris: Aubier.

Simplr.co.za. 2018. 'The Misperception of the "Third Party Contractor"'. CTG - Humanitarian Enablers. 12 February 2018. http://ctg.org/ctg-we-are-humanitarians/.

Sleeping in Airports. 2017. 'Worst Airports for Overall Experience 2017'. Sleeping in Airports. 15 October 2017. https://www.sleepinginairports.net/2017/worst-airports.htm.

Sluka, Jeffrey. 1990. 'Participant Observation in Violent Social Contexts'. *Human Organization* 49 (2): 114–26. https://doi.org/10.17730/humo.49.2.h033174683462676.

Smirl, Lisa. 2008. 'Building the Other, Constructing Ourselves: Spatial Dimensions of International Humanitarian Response'. *International Political Sociology* 2 (3): 236–53. https://doi.org/10.1111/j.1749-5687.2008.00047.x.

———. 2009. 'Plain Tales of the Reconstruction Site: Spatial Continuities in Contemporary Humanitarian Practice'. In *Empire, Development & Colonialism: The Past in the Present*, edited by Mark Duffield and V. Hewitt. James Currey. http://sro.sussex.ac.uk/12741/.

———. 2015. *Spaces of Aid: How Cars, Compounds and Hotels Shape Humanitarianism*. London: Zed Books.

———. 2016. '"Not Welcome at the Holiday Inn": How a Sarajevan Hotel Influenced Geo-Politics'. *Journal of Intervention and Statebuilding* 10 (1): 32–55. https://doi.org/10.1080/17502977.2015.1137398.

Smit, Warren. 2018. 'Urban Governance in Africa: An Overview'. *International Development Policy | Revue Internationale de Politique de Développement* 10 | 2018 (10): 55–77. https://doi.org/10.4000/poldev.2637.

Snyder, William M., and Etienne Wenger. 2010. 'Our World as a Learning System: A Communities-of-Practice Approach'. In *Social Learning Systems and Communities of Practice*, 107–24. Springer, London. https://doi.org/10.1007/978-1-84996-133-2_7.

Söderström, Ola. 2006. 'Studying Cosmopolitan Landscapes'. *Progress in Human Geography* 30 (5): 553–558.

Sogodogo, Aguibou. 2016. 'Pour Avoir Filmé Le Domicile de l'honorable Soumaïla Cissé: Un Expatrié Arrêté Par La Police Du 4ème Arrondissement'. *Le Républicain*, 15 March 2016. http://news.aBamako.com/h/123530.html.

Soo, Kwok Tong. 2005. 'Zipf's Law for Cities: A Cross-Country Investigation'. *Regional Science and Urban Economics* 35 (3): 239–63. https://doi.org/10.1016/j.regsciurbeco.2004.04.004.

Sorkin, Michael. 2008. *Indefensible Space: The Architecture of the National Insecurity State*. Routledge.

Soviet Army General Staff. 1979. 'Dzhuba'. Juba: Military Topographic Directorate of the Soviet Army.

Spearin, Christopher. 2007. *Humanitarian Non-Governmental Organizations and International Private Security Companies: The" Humanitarian" Challenges of Moulding a Marketplace*. DCAF.

———. 2008. 'Private, Armed and Humanitarian? States, NGOs, International Private Security Companies and Shifting Humanitarianism'. *Security Dialogue* 39 (4): 363–82. https://doi.org/10.1177/0967010608094034.

Specia, Megan. 2018. '383,000: Estimated Death Toll in South Sudan's War'. *The New York Times*, 1 November 2018, sec. World. https://www.nytimes.com/2018/09/26/world/africa/south-sudan-civil-war-deaths.html.

Spradley, James P. 2016. *The Ethnographic Interview*. Waveland Press.

Spradley, James P., and Brenda E. Mann. 2008. *The Cocktail Waitress: Woman's Work in a Man's World*. Waveland Press.

Stapele, Naomi van. 2016. '"We Are Not Kenyans": Extra-Judicial Killings, Manhood and Citizenship in Mathare, a Nairobi Ghetto'. *Conflict, Security & Development* 16 (4): 301–25. https://doi.org/10.1080/14678802.2016.1200313.

Steck, Jean-Fabien. 2005. 'Abidjan et Le Plateau: Quels Modèles Urbains Pour La Vitrine Du «miracle» Ivoirien?' *Géocarrefour* 80 (3): 215–226.

———. 2008. 'Yopougon, Yop city, Poy…périphérie et modèle urbain ivoirien'. *Autrepart*, no. 47: 227–44. https://doi.org/10.3917/autr.047.0227.

Stepputat, Finn. 2012. 'Knowledge Production in the Security–Development Nexus: An Ethnographic Reflection'. *Security Dialogue* 43 (5): 439–55. https://doi.org/10.1177/0967010612457973.

Stern, Maria, and Joakim Öjendal. 2010. 'Mapping the Security—Development Nexus: Conflict, Complexity, Cacophony, Convergence?' *Security Dialogue* 41 (1): 5–29. https://doi.org/10.1177/0967010609357041.

———. 2011. 'Mapping Security–Development, A Question of Methodology?' *Security Dialogue* 42 (1): 105–10. https://doi.org/10.1177/0967010610393776.

Stoddard, Abby, Adele Harmer, and Monica Czwarmo. 2018. 'Aid Worker Security Report 2018 : Figures at a Glance'. Humanitarian Outcomes.

Stoddard, Abby, Adele Harmer, and Katherine Haver. 2006a. 'Briefing Paper 24 Providing Aid in Insecure Environments : Trends in Policy and Operations'. Humanitarian Policy Group.

———. 2006b. 'Providing Aid in Insecure Environments : Trends in Policy and Operations'. *Humanitarian Policy Group*, no. September.

Stoddard, Abby; Harmer, Adele; Haver, Katherine. 2011. 'Aid Worker Security Report Spotlight on Security for National Aid Workers : Issues and Perspectives Key Findings'.

Stoddard, Abby, and Shoaib Jillani. 2016. 'The Effects of Insecurity on Humanitarian Coverage'. SAVE.

Stoddard, Abby, Shoaib Jillani, John Caccavale, Peyton Cooke, David Guillemois, and Vassily Klimentov. 2017. 'Out of Reach: How Insecurity Prevents Humanitarian Aid from Accessing the Neediest'. *Stability: International Journal of Security and Development* 6 (1). https://doi.org/10.5334/sta.506.

Subbaraman, Ramnath, Jennifer O'brien, Tejal Shitole, Shrutika Shitole, Kiran Sawant, David E Bloom, and Anita Patil-Deshmukh. 2012. 'Off the Map: The Health and Social Implications of Being a Non-Notified Slum in India'. *Environment and Urbanization* 24 (2): 643–63. https://doi.org/10.1177/0956247812456356.

Swyngedouw, Erik, and Nikolas C. Heynen. 2004. 'Urban Political Ecology, Justice and the Politics of Scale'. *Antipode* 35 (5): 898–918. https://doi.org/10.1111/j.1467-8330.2003.00364.x.

Talen, Emily. 2002a. 'Pedestrian Access as a Measure of Urban Quality'. *Planning Practice and Research* 17 (3): 257–278.

———. 2002b. 'Help for Urban Planning: The Transect Strategy'. *Journal of Urban Design* 7 (3): 293–312. https://doi.org/10.1080/1357480022000039349.

Tanabe, Mihoko, Kristen Schaus, Sonia Rastogi, Sandra K. Krause, and Preeti Patel. 2015. 'Tracking Humanitarian Funding for Reproductive Health: A Systematic Analysis of Health and Protection Proposals from 2002–2013'. *Conflict and Health* 9 (1): S2. https://doi.org/10.1186/1752-1505-9-S1-S2.

Taussig, Michael T. 2011. *I Swear I Saw This : Drawings in Fieldwork Notebooks, Namely My Own*. Chicago ; London: The University of Chicago Press. http://data.rero.ch/01-R006380369/html?view=GE_V1.

Tavares, José. 2003. 'Does Foreign Aid Corrupt?' *Economics Letters* 79 (1): 99–106. https://doi.org/10.1016/S0165-1765(02)00293-8.

Thakur, Ramesh Chandra, Chiyuki Aoi, and Cedric De Coning. 2007. *Unintended Consequences of Peacekeeping Operations*. United Nations University Press Tokyo, Japan.

The Economist. 2018. 'A Chilling Story from Kenya', 8 March 2018. https://www.economist.com/international/2018/03/08/a-chilling-story-from-kenya.

Toh, Alain, and Richard Banégas. 2006. 'La France et l'Onu devant le « parlement » de Yopougon, France and the United Nations at the « parliament » of Yopougon'. *Politique africaine*, no. 104: 141–58. https://doi.org/10.3917/polaf.104.0141.

Townsend, Janet G., Gina Porter, and Emma Mawdsley. 2004. 'Creating Spaces of Resistance: Development NGOs and Their Clients in Ghana, India and Mexico'. *Antipode* 36 (5): 871–89. https://doi.org/10.1111/j.1467-8330.2004.00459.x.

Trading Economics. 2018. 'South Sudan GDP per Capita PPP | 2008–2018 | Data | Chart | Calendar'. 2018. https://tradingeconomics.com/south-sudan/gdp-per-capita-ppp.

Tratnjek, Bénédicte. 2010. 'Carte postale d'un habitat sur cour (Abidjan)', June, http://www.cafe-geo.net/article.php3?id_article=1949.

TripAdvisor. 2018. 'THE BEST Hotels in Juba, South Sudan for 2018 - TripAdvisor'. 2018. https://www.tripadvisor.com/Hotels-g776943-Juba_Central_Equatoria_State-Hotels.html.

UCDP. 2019. 'UCDP - Uppsala Conflict Data Program'. 2019. https://www.ucdp.uu.se/.

UN Board. 2017a. 'Definition of HR Terms | United Nations System Chief Executives Board for Coordination'. 2017. http://www.unsceb.org/content/definition-hr-terms.

———. 2017b. 'Definition of Staff Categories | United Nations System Chief Executives Board for Coordination'. 2017. http://www.unsceb.org/content/definition-staff-categories.

'UN DGACM'. 2017. 2017. https://www.un.org/depts/DGACM/RegionalGroups.shtml.

UN Jobs. 2018. 'Vacancies with UN and Other International Organizations | UNjobs'. 2018. https://unjobs.org/.

UNDP. 2013. 'UN Supplier Code of Conduct', no. January: 1–4.

UNDSS. 2017. *UNSMS Security Policy Manual.*

UN-Habitat. 2019. 'Explore Urban Open Data'. 2019. http://urbandata.unhabitat.org/.

United Nations. 2006. 'United Nations Field Security Handbook: System-Wide Arrangements for the Protection of United Nations Personnel and Property in the Field'.

———. 2016. 'Executive Summary of the Independent Special Investigation into the Violence in Juba in 2016 and the Response by the United Nations Mission in South Sudan'. UN Security Council. https://reliefweb.int/sites/reliefweb.int/files/resources/N1635591.pdf.

———. 2017a. 'UN Conditions of Service-Non-Family Duty Stations'. United Nations Salraies, Allowances, Benefits and Job Classifications. 2017. http://www.un.org/Depts/OHRM/salaries_allowances/allowances/nonfam.htm.

———. 2017b. 'Rapport Final Du Secrétaire Général Sur l'Opération Des Nations Unies En Côte d'Ivoire'. S/2017/89. United Nations Security Council. https://onuci.unmissions.org/sites/default/files/rapport_sg_final_sur_la_ci.pdf.

Unwin, Simon. 2007. 'Analysing Architecture through Drawing'. *Building Research & Information* 35 (1): 101–10. https://doi.org/10.1080/09613210600879881.

'Urbanisme : revue française'. 1969, no. 111. http://data.rero.ch/01-0721889/html?view=GE_V1.

Vaa, Mariken. 2016. 'Housing Policy after Political Transition: The Case of Bamako': *Environment and Urbanization*, June. https://doi.org/10.1177/095624780001200103.

Van Brabant, Koenraad. 2010a. 'Managing Aid Agency Security in an Evolving World: The Larger Challenge'. In *European Interagency Security Forum.*

———. 2010b. 'Operational Security Management in Violent Environments: A Field Manual for Aid Agencies'. *Humanitarian Practice Network Good Practice Review* 8 (June): 194.

Vannier, Christian Neil. 2013. 'Indigenous Professional Development Workers in Haiti'. *Michigan Academician* 41 (3): 332–54. https://doi.org/10.7245/0026-2005-41.3.332.

Vauthrin, Jak. 1989. *Villes Africaines: Anarchie et Raison d'une Architecture*. Paris: L'Harmattan.

Vaux, Toni, Chris Seiple, Greg Nakano, and Koenraad Van Brabant. 2002. 'Humanitarian Action and Private Security Companies'. *London: International Alert.*

Verquin, Béatrice. 2000. 'Du "Modèle Migratoire Colonial" à La Circulation Mondiale Des Élites Professionnelles : Le Cas Des Français à l'étranger'. Thesis, Poitiers. http://www.theses.fr/2000POIT5015.

Vlassenroot, Koen, and Karen Büscher. 2009. 'The City as Frontier: Urban Development and Identity Processes in Goma', November. http://www.crisisstates.com/Publications/publications.htm.

———. 2013. 'Borderlands, Identity and Urban Development: The Case of Goma (Democratic Republic of the Congo)'. *Urban Studies* 50 (15): 3168–84. https://doi.org/10.1177/0042098013487772.

Volvey, Anne. 2016. 'Sur le terrain de l'émotion : déconstruire la question émotionnelle en géographie pour reconstruire son horizon épistémologique'. *Carnets de géographes*, no. 9 (August). https://doi.org/10.4000/cdg.541.

Von Moltke, Konrad. 1996. 'Why UNEP Matters'. *Green Globe Yearbook*, 55–64.

Wadham, Helen, and Richard Warren. 2013. 'Inspiring Action, Building Understanding: How Cross-Sector Partnership Engages Business in Addressing Global Challenges'. *Business Ethics: A European Review* 22 (1): 47–63. https://doi.org/10.1111/beer.12006.

Walker, Helen, and Christine Harland. 2008. 'E-Procurement in the United Nations: Influences, Issues and Impact'. *International Journal of Operations & Production Management* 28 (9): 831–857.

Walker, Peter. 2005. 'Cracking the Code: The Genesis, Use and Future of the Code of Conduct'. *Disasters* 29 (4): 323–36. https://doi.org/10.1111/j.0361-3666.2005.00295.x.

Wallace, Tina. 2004. 'NGO Dilemmas: Trojan Horses for Global Neoliberalism?' *Socialist Register* 40 (40).

Wang, Jian-Ye. 2007. *What Drives China's Growing Role in Africa?* International Monetary Fund.

Wangui, Joseph. 2017. 'Nurses End Their 5-Month Strike'. *Daily Nation*, 2 November 2017. https://www.nation.co.ke/news/Kenyan-nurses-end-4-month-strike-after-deal-with-State/1056-4166940-mo35skz/index.html.

Weiss, Thomas G. 2018. *Humanitarian Challenges and Intervention*. Routledge.

Weizman, Eyal. 2007. *Hollow Land: Israel's Architecture of Occupation*. London: Verso.

———. 2011. *The Least of All Possible Evils: Humanitarian Violence from Arendt to Gaza*. Verso Books.

Westrope, Clay, Robert Banick, and Mitch Levine. 2014. 'Groundtruthing OpenStreetMap Building Damage Assessment'. *Procedia Engineering*, Humanitarian Technology: Science, Systems and Global Impact 2014, HumTech2014, 78 (January): 29–39. https://doi.org/10.1016/j.proeng.2014.07.035.

Whittall, Jonathan. 2014. 'Why David Miliband Is Wrong about Humanitarian Goals'. *The Guardian*, 10 March 2014, sec. Global Development Professionals Network. https://www.theguardian.com/global-development-professionals-network/2014/mar/10/david-miliband-humanitarian-goals-mdgs.

Whitworth, Sandra. 2004. *Men, Militarism, and UN Peacekeeping: A Gendered Analysis*. Lynne Rienner Publishers.

Wille, Christina, and Larissa Fast. 2013. 'Operating in Insecurity Shifting Patterns of Violence against Humanitarian Aid Providers and Their'. *Insecurity Insight Report*, Report 13-1.

World Bank. 2011. 'Republic of South Sudan: Issues in Urban Development Phase 1 – An Overview of the Urban Landscape in South Sudan', no. 63786: 1–65.

Yala, Amina. 2006. 'Les paradigmes coloniaux de l'action humanitaire'. In *Culture post-coloniale 1961–2006*, 203–13. Mémoires/Histoire. Paris: Autrement. https://www.cairn.info/culture-post-coloniale-1961-2006--9782746708952-p-203.htm.

Yi-Chong, Xu, and Patrick Weller. 2008. '"To Be, but Not to Be Seen": Exploring the Impact of International Civil Servants'. *Public Administration* 86 (1): 35–51. https://doi.org/10.1111/j.1467-9299.2007.00706.x.

Zane, Daniel M., Julie R. Irwin, and Rebecca Walker Reczek. 2016. 'Do Less Ethical Consumers Denigrate More Ethical Consumers? The Effect of Willful Ignorance on Judgments of Others'. *Journal of Consumer Psychology* 26 (3): 337–49. https://doi.org/10.1016/j.jcps.2015.10.002.

Zhang, Dongsong, Lina Zhou, and Jay F. Nunamaker Jr. 2002. 'A Knowledge Management Framework for the Support of Decision Making in Humanitarian Assistance/Disaster Relief'. *Knowledge and Information Systems* 4 (3): 370–85. https://doi.org/10.1007/s101150200012.

Zounmenou, David. 2013. 'The National Movement for the Liberation of Azawad Factor in the Mali Crisis'. *African Security Review* 22 (3): 167–74. https://doi.org/10.1080/10246029.2013.823794.

Zwi, Anthony B, Ruairi Brugha, and Elizabeth Smith. 2001. 'Private Health Care in Developing Countries'. *BMJ : British Medical Journal* 323 (7311): 463–64.

www.ingramcontent.com/pod-product-compliance
Ingram Content Group UK Ltd.
Pitfield, Milton Keynes, MK11 3LW, UK
UKHW021921120926
8556IPUK00042BA/1089

9 783034 344128